W9-CGV-162

FOURTH EDITION

ADVANCED BUSINESS COMMUNICATION

JOHN M. PENROSE
San Diego State University

ROBERT W. RASBERRY
Southern Methodist University

ROBERT J. MYERS
Baruch College, City University of New York

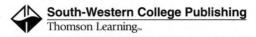
South-Western College Publishing
Thomson Learning™

Australia • Canada • Denmark • Japan • Mexico • New Zealand • Phillipines
Puerto Rico • Singapore • South Africa • Spain • United Kingdom • United States

Advanced Business Communication, Fourth Edition, by Penrose, Rasberry, Myers

Team Director: Dave Shaut
Acquisitions Editor: Pamela M. Person
Product Sponsor: Taney Wilkins
Marketing Manager: Rob Bloom
Production Editor: Tamborah E. Moore
Media Production Editor: Robin Browning
Manufacturing Coordinator: Sandee Milewski
Cover Design: Michael H. Stratton
Production House: Trejo Production
Printer: RR Donnelley & Sons Company,
      Crawfordsville Manufacturing Division

For more information contact South-Western College Publishing,
5101 Madison Road, Cincinnati, Ohio, 45227 or find us on the Internet at
http://www.swcollege.com
For permission to use material from this text or product, contact us by
• telephone: 1-800-730-2214
• fax: 1-800-730-2215
• web: http://www.thomsonrights.com

Library of Congress Cataloging-in-Publication Data
Penrose, John M.
  Advanced business communication / John M. Penrose, Robert W. Rasberry,
    Robert J. Myers.—4th ed.
    p. cm.
  Includes bibliographical references and index.
  ISBN 0-324-03739-2 (alk. paper)
  1. Business communication. I. Rasberry, Robert W. II. Myers, Robert J., 1946–   III. Title.
HF5718.P43 2000
  658.4'5—dc21

                      00-036998

This book is printed on acid-free paper.

About the Authors

JOHN M. PENROSE is Professor of Business Communication and Chair of the Information and Decision Systems Department at San Diego State University. At SDSU he teaches undergraduate, MBA, and Executive MBA courses. He taught at the University of Texas Graduate School of Business for 16 years; courses included public relations for mangers, nonverbal communication, and writing computer software documentation. He was active in the Ph.D. in Business Communication program. He has served as president of the Association for Business Communication and won its major awards. He has served on a variety of editorial boards, as a referee to associations for papers and publications, is an active researcher, and is a consultant to business.

ROBERT W. RASBERRY, Ph.D. (University of Kansas) has been teaching in the Cox School of Business at Southern Methodist University in Dallas, Texas, since 1974. He is a professor in the Organizational Behavior and Business Policy Division. His major areas of research and teaching include: ethics, leadership, communication skills, and life planning. He has authored numerous journal and magazine articles and is the author and coauthor of several books, one of which is a South-Western book, *Effective Managerial Communication*. He has extensive training and consulting experience. Among his clients are: The United States Chamber of Commerce, Mobil Exploration, and the United States Tennis Association.

ROBERT J. MYERS is Chair of the Department of Communication Studies and director of the master of arts program in corporate communications at Baruch College, City University of New York. He has coauthored two textbooks on business communication, published articles in the *Journal of Business Communication* and the *ABC Bulletin*, and has presented numerous papers at professional conferences. Since 1979 he has offered training sessions on management-level writing, oral presentation skills, and interviewing to over a thousand executives in business, industry, and the public sector. He is also the Executive Director of the Association for Business Communication, an international professional society whose mission is to foster excellence in business communication research, pedagogy, and practice.

Preface to the Fourth Edition

As a business communication student or professional, you are aware of how dramatically the worlds of business and communication have changed since 1989 when the first edition of *Advanced Business Communication* appeared. The same might be said if we looked back to the second edition's appearance in 1993. However, the changes in society, communication, and business from the 1997's third edition to today are the most dramatic.

In 1997, the Internet was just emerging as a communication and research tool, many people were still purposefully avoiding electronic mail as a messaging system, and we were still in awe of Wal-Mart's ability to see the need to keep inventory at almost a zero level and expect suppliers—ones electronically and figuratively wired to the company—to meet overnight demands.

In the years since 1997, we have seen CD-ROM players become a standard item on computers, and CD writers an important accessory, along with an eight-gigabyte hard drive. We bid farewell to the five-and-a-quarter-inch floppy drive and hello to the Zip drive. Laptop computers, cell phones, pagers, and personal electronic assistants are so prevalent there is starting to be a backlash against the usage of some of them in public places. Today's students have relatively few choices in word processing software, but feel comfortable with the prime product's extensive power. Similarly, they are likely to embed audio or video clips in their PowerPoint presentation, have animation of slide parts, and include a picture of a new product picked from a Web site of a company that is the subject of their presentation.

Few instructors need to have the number of Web sites in a current bibliography pointed out to them, or need to be reminded by their advanced students that "we don't write many letters anymore; we send e-mail."

With this fourth edition, we have tried to reflect these dramatic changes with parallel changes in content. Our effort has not been to just use examples of these changes, but rather to capture the importance of the changes for the advanced business student. As but one example of this effort, you will find a new and extensive discussion of how to conduct electronic research using the Internet. This discussion includes time-proven research techniques that are now applied to electronic systems of awesome power.

Other significant additions, expansions, or updates to this edition include the topics of critical reading skills, business ethics, communication apprehension, PowerPoint presentation development and delivery, audience analysis, e-mail usage, electronic etiquette, and new proposal and business case examples.

Just as society and its technology change, so too must teachers change. Upon the shoulders of instructors—increasingly—is the need to stay ahead of their students while still coaching them through the infinitely complex world of advanced business communication.

As teaching faculty ourselves, we have relied upon our own students and many colleagues in the profession to guide us in the development of this edition, and we thank them all.

There are a number of individuals we wish to thank specifically, as well. Graduate assistants who run down research citations, find relevant examples, or act as an extra set of eyes to look over a rough draft, are an invaluable asset. Included in this group is Ernie Climenson at San Diego State University. Among the students who have assisted in various ways is Sue Curtis at San Diego State University. Marcella Stark, Head Librarian at Fondren Library, Southern Methodist University, also helped tremendously in the preparation of the technology of the Report chapter.

Through the various editions of this text, we have been blessed with wonderful reviewers. They have guided the editions and kept us focused. These comments are certainly true for the reviewers for this edition, and we extend our appreciation to them. They are Dana Loewy, California State University; John Waltman, Eastern Michigan University; Paul Sawyer, Southeastern Louisiana University; Virginia Hromulak, Concordia University; and Mary Tucker, Ohio University.

We have been especially pleased to work on this edition with the professionals at South-Western College Publishing. Their advice has been sound and their support readily available. Our gratitude goes to Pamela Person, Taney Wilkins, Tamborah Moore, and many others.

Contents

3

Advanced Visual Support 38

PART TWO

WRITTEN COMMUNICATION

4

A Process for Advanced Writing 82

5

Writing Direct Messages 114

6

Writing Indirect Messages 130

7

Writing Situational Messages 147

8

The Planning and Writing of Persuasive Proposals 173

9

Report Writing: From Formal Documents to Short Summaries 202

PART THREE

Oral Communication

10

The Business Presentation 239

11

Meeting Management 258

12
Crisis Management 273

13
Media Management 299

PART FOUR
Reporting Case Analyses

14
Analyzing a Case and Writing a Case Report 330

15

Discussing and Presenting a Case Study 352

PART FIVE

JOB SEARCH STRATEGIES

16

Résumés and Employment Letters 370

17

The Job Interview 408

APPENDICES

Appendix A
A Formal Case 431

Appendix B
A Written Analysis of a Formal Case 435

Introduction to Advanced Business Communication

Advanced Business Communication

Welcome to the fast-paced world of advanced business communication, and to a paradox: for all the lip service given to the importance of communication, little is done to improve it. This paradox is especially noticeable in the business world, which focuses on bottom-line profits and performance. Managers proclaim the need for improved communication skills but hesitate to invest in training their employees in communication skills. Managers see that those who are effective in communication are promoted and rewarded financially, but seldom do they themselves have access to formal programs that are designed to improve these crucial skills.

Educational institutions—aware of the demand for communication skills—try to supply graduates with some degree of competence in communication. However, many demands compete for the students' attention; new topics work their way into the curriculum and new teaching methods are explored. One result is that for several decades the verbal skills of high school graduates have been slipping. Concern also exists about the skills of college graduates. A recent report from the Carnegie Foundation for the Advancement of Teaching[1] takes a clear stand on communication: "The foundation for a successful undergraduate experience is proficiency in the written and spoken word." As the report examines the undergraduate experience, it clearly attacks the amount of instruction and the approaches used in the teaching of communication in the United States.

College programs that prepare students for business feel pressures on their curricula, too. For example, in the last 15 years the study and use of computers has grown, typically, from one undergraduate course to inclusion in almost every business course. To allow examination of new topics, such as computer applications, colleges often sacrifice basic skills, such as writing and speaking. All too often, one business communication course and several English courses are expected to turn around 20 years of laxity in communication training and to produce a graduate possessing the written and oral communication skills demanded by business.

Unfortunately, graduate business programs often widen this gap between what is wanted and what is delivered. The graduating MBA or MS with solid writing and speaking skills, as well as an appreciation for when and how to use them, is the exception. Those with this background usually have acquired it informally, over many years, from a maturity of vision few hold. Those who both work and concurrently seek a graduate business degree may be better able than others to see the importance of effective communication in business and its lack of attention in the graduate curriculum.

Communication skills can be taught relatively quickly and are not particularly difficult to acquire, especially when a person has a solid foundation with the basics. When the students are bright and motivated, and the skills being taught are tailored to them, the improvement can be dramatic.

Consider yourself lucky to be exposed to advanced business communication. The skills you acquire will assist you in studying, in acquiring a better job or more responsibility on your present job, and in doing that job more effectively than those who lack the skills. For a "fast-tracker"—the person with a mission, a plan for how to achieve it, and the skills and knowledge that will be required—extraordinary communication skills are a necessity.

This book is written for use in an advanced business communication course, such as management, organizational communication, or business communication. The text is especially appropriate for advanced undergraduate studies and for graduate-level studies when these students have some knowledge of and experience in business. The text works well in business training seminars for the same reasons.

The goal of this chapter is to examine the crucial place and function of communication in business. To accomplish this goal, we look at the views of business leaders and scholarly literature as they relate to the importance of communication skills, to communication in business, to communication and management, to the special topics of ethics and cross-cultural messages, and to fears about communication. Finally, this chapter identifies how top businesspeople differ in their communication from others in business.

THE IMPORTANCE OF COMMUNICATION SKILLS

Communication does not exist in a vacuum; it is not something you do in the absence of other information. While you may *practice* accounting or finance in a mutually exclusive fashion, when you communicate, it is usually about something other than communication. Communication is a process that oils the gears that turn the machinery of business. Supporting this process are the skills of communication—skills that occupy as much as 90 percent of a top executive's working day.[2]

Research supports the view that communication skills are important in business. For example, in a study of 139 Texas business executives, knowledge of business communication was rated *very important* by 85 percent (far ahead of knowledge of principles of management, at 20 percent). The skills that require attention, according to 100 randomly selected Fortune 500 executives, are oral presentations, memo writing, basic grammar, informational report writing, and analytical report writing. Another study of executives in Fortune 500 companies supports these findings but extends the important communication skills to include external communication and technical applications.[3]

Visual Skills

About 85 percent of our learning comes from visual stimuli; when spoken and visual stimuli are combined, enhanced learning can occur. Additional studies of comprehension endorse the value of visual support. For example, when participants only listened to a message, they remembered 70 percent of the message after three hours and only 10 percent after three days. Using only a visual message, recall was 72 percent after three hours and 35 percent after three days. These figures jumped dramatically, however, to 85 percent and 65 percent, respectively, when both spoken and visual communication were used. Other studies substantiate these results.[4]

Even though businesspeople have long been aware of the visual element of communication, they have been negligent in paying it much respect. Perhaps this lack of respect occurs because visual communication exists in a more artistic realm (as opposed to more central business issues, such as finance or management). However, numerous studies of the value of visual matter (particularly in supporting written and spoken communication) and of new technologies for preparing and sharing such visuals have increased the attention given to visual support.

The rationale for recall of pictures versus words lies in the speed advantage of learning from pictures. This speed is due at least partially to the ability of pictures to evoke mental images. Therefore, presentations—written or spoken—benefit from visual support. Seeing words improves recall; seeing pictures provides even more benefits.

Balchin and Coleman extend the distinction between forms of visual communication to four basic intellectual skills: literacy, numeracy, articulacy, and graphicacy.[5] **Literacy** includes the basic skills of reading and writing. **Numeracy** expresses communication in numbers and mathematical notation. **Articulacy** brings in the art of spoken communication. **Graphicacy** connotes the visual communication of relationships not found in the other three skills. Integration of these four skills, the authors believe, leads to truly effective communication. As we move into the twenty-first century, an additional literacy is emerging: technical literacy, which is the ability to appropriately use technological tools in an information society. Such tools include the Internet, e-mail, Web sites, and computers in general.[6] Certainly technical literacy is rapidly changing. Typing has given way to keyboarding; soon we will be relying on computer input by voice rather than through the fingers.[7] In many ways technical literacy will determine one's ability to communicate through the other four literacies.

The need to teach graphics (as well as speaking and writing) is supported by the research of Pollock and others. Their study of 150 executives listed in *Who's Who in Finance and Industry* recommends teaching graphic analysis to better prepare the advanced student.[8]

Chapter 3 of this text is devoted to understanding the role of visual support of written and spoken business communication. That chapter also explores various methods of preparing visual support.

Written Skills

Most studies—particularly the older ones—indicate that people see written communication as a neglected skill. Indeed, 79 percent of 218 executives in one study identified the ability to write as one of the most neglected business skills.[9] Within that same group, 44 percent said *writing more clearly, in a better organized way*, was a major goal. Approximately the same percentage felt that better writing skills increased their productivity and was of high importance in their own career advancement.

When *Fortune* magazine reporters talked to successful corporate executives about business training, executive after executive said, in frustration, "Teach them to write better." The plea was not for the ability to do fancy writing but, rather, fundamental writing, "with clarity, precision, brevity, and force of logic." Hoyt Hudson, vice president of information systems at InterAccess, adds this: "One of the most surprising features of the information revolution is that the momentum has turned back to the written word. Someone who can come up with precise communication has a real advantage in today's environment."[10] Companies appear to be increasing their emphasis on internal written communication skills and are therefore offering more training in this area. In some studies, the recommendation for areas needing improvement is quite specific; for example, one such study identifies long and short reports, progress reports, and analytical reports.[11]

Leaders in the accounting profession, including both practicing CPAs and educators, have indicated how important they believe written communication to be. In 1994 the CPA exam began to evaluate candidates' writing skills.[12] Another exam, the Graduate Management Admission Test (GMAT), has also added a writing component to this entrance examination.[13]

Spoken Skills

Not all the experts or surveys point to written communication as the most important skill area. Many suggest that spoken communication, which may take up more of an executive's time than written communication, is more important and demands more training.[14] A study of business and engineering graduates, for example, found that oral skills are used more frequently than written skills at the beginning corporate levels.[15]

Educators and employers, however, do not always agree on the relative importance of the specific areas of business communication. In a survey of business communication educators and employers, employers placed much heavier emphasis on oral communication, interpersonal skills, and listening. Educators, on the other hand, advocated written communication and theoretical aspects of communication.[16]

Sometimes the effects of spoken communication in the workplace are subtle. Tannen,[17] among others, chronicles differences in spoken communication in men versus women. She believes lessons learned in childhood carry over to the workplace. Boys learn to play in larger groups, follow a leader's directives, and use language to call attention to themselves. Girls learn to play with a best friend, establish consensus, and ostracize those who seek to stand out. These behaviors that most follow but few recognize may translate into females being disadvantaged in a male-dominated business world or even having problems with other females when they "break the rules." For suggestions on how to communicate across genders, see Table 1.1.

Table 1.1	Strategies for Cross-Gender Oral Communication

Some strategies for women dealing with men in business include the following.
1. Speak up! Don't allow yourself to be interrupted.
2. Avoid tag endings that may make you sound unsure of yourself, such as "isn't it?" "don't you think?" or "is that OK?"
3. Don't take male comments too personally. Remember that most men are direct and like to get straight to the point.
4. Focus on being logical and avoid giving unnecessary details (storytelling).
5. Avoid personal items. Stick to job-related issues and current affairs.

Some strategies for men dealing with women in business include the following.
1. Focus on being polite by using words such as "please" and "thank you."
2. Avoid monopolizing conversations, speaking for the woman, or interrupting her.
3. Don't call a woman names such as "honey," "dear," or "sweetheart."
4. Avoid barking commands to women. They prefer and respond much better to polite requests.
5. Pay attention when women speak. Use good eye contact, nod, and use "I'm listening" sounds such as "uh-huh."

Source: Adapted from C. Tymson, "Business Communication—Bridging the Gender Gap," retrieved November 11, 1999, at http://www.tymson.com.au/article1.html.

With speaking comes its equally important counterpart, listening. Some estimates suggest we spend up to 60 percent of each workday listening, yet most research indicates we do not listen well. One problem is that we listen passively rather than actively. Active listeners become involved with the message, anticipate what is coming next, periodically summarize, and listen "between the lines" for additional meaning.[18]

While many surveys underscore the importance of either written or spoken (and listening) communication, others encourage a balance between the two. This combination of topics is strongly endorsed in the development of an MBA business communication course syllabus. Academic experts, managers, and MBA recipients agree on the essential nature of both written and spoken communication. Both, they feel, need to be addressed in an MBA-level business communication course.[19]

Reading Skills

Certainly not everyone reads in the same fashion, but since businesspeople spend so much time reading e-mail, reports, memos, or letters, some suggestions for improving your critical reading ability are in order.

1. Think about the title of the manuscript if it has one; what does it suggest regarding the content? Is it a comprehensive article ("A Thorough Discussion of . . ."), a historical or documentary review ("A Review of . . ."), an organization of existing information ("A Taxonomy of . . ."), a position statement ("The School Board's Failing Marks"), or persuasion to action ("A Proposal to . . .")?
2. Get a feel for the whole package. This might come from a table of contents, which should be scrutinized for major sections and amount of space devoted

to each of them. If there is an abstract or executive summary, certainly read it and reread it. However, be aware that it may not fairly represent the article. Keep an open and critical mind.

If there is no table of contents or abstract, page through the article and pay attention to sections, headings, and subheadings. Note also the relative space given to the sections.

3. Now—finally—read the text. You might read once quickly for an overall feel for the content. If so, then you will need to reread for deeper understanding of the content. Others prefer their first reading to be careful, slow, and methodical. With either technique, consider highlighting (to capture your reactions) or annotating (which combines underlining or highlighting but adds margin notes that interpret or react to the keyed phrases).

Annotation is the more valuable approach if you need a thorough analysis of a complex message. You might want to generate your own system of highlighter colors or penciled circles, underlines, brackets, or arrows to represent places of confusion, disagreement, importance, or summary.

4. Examine tables, graphs, or other illustrations and think about how they complement or supplement the text. You might also challenge them to see if they misrepresent data, as discussed in Chapter 3.

5. Compare the message to other known information and challenge its assumptions and arguments. One approach for testing arguments is the "ABC Test" that asks: Is the information *a*ppropriate, is the support *b*elievable, and is the support *c*onsistent and *c*omplete?[20]

Following these steps should help you to read more critically and with greater understanding and comprehension. It may be more memorable as well.

COMMUNICATION IN BUSINESS

While the results of research presented so far suggest that communication is important in business, the focus has been more on the importance of communication itself and less on its business application. This section presents the importance of communication in three main business dimensions: obtaining a job, doing a job, and maintaining and improving a career. Additional support is found in Chapters 16 and 17.

Communication and Obtaining a Job

Communication skills can help you acquire a first job or a better job. Surveys of business recruiters emphasize the esteem they hold for communication skills. One hundred forty recruiters picked written and oral communication skills as the most important ability for applicants—over computer sciences, accounting, management, and six other business areas. Studies of personnel managers, upper-level managers, business managers, and businesspeople drew the same conclusion. Another study concluded, "The most common skill sought by MBA hiring organizations was communication (verbal and nonverbal), with 85 percent of respondents including this characteristic on the candidate-evaluation form."[21] A study of 500 managers determined oral communication was the highest-ranked competency in hiring decisions.[22] Additional testimonials from individual recruiters and in the popular press abound.[23]

Communication on the Job

On the job, poor communication skills can be harmful. A study of 443 companies asked whether they were happy with worker skills. Eighty percent said employees need improvement in their written communication skills.[24] A survey of business school deans and personnel directors of Fortune 500 companies clearly identified poor writing skills as the most common weakness of young executives. On the other hand, the survey identified the most successful executives as those who can communicate their own ideas to others. Not only are business practitioners more successful when they possess effective communication skills, but superior-subordinate communication also is considered the single most important factor in enhancing job satisfaction and group cohesiveness.[25]

Communication Related to Promotions

Just as communication skills are important in getting and doing a job, they also continue to support businesspeople throughout their business careers. Larry McConnell, deputy register for information services at the Massachusetts Registry of Motor Vehicles, says that unless you can communicate, your career will level off.[26] Other executives attest that ability to communicate facilitates promotions, upward mobility, and *success*.

In a study that examined 5,299 newly promoted executives, the authors found that these executives cited communication as playing the most significant role in their promotions.[27] Both oral and written communication were cited by nearly 80 percent of the executives as the single most important factor in the career preparation of a young person. Finance and accounting ranked second and third, respectively. Bennett and Olney's study of vice presidents at Fortune 500 companies determined that 97.7 percent of them believe communication skills had boosted their advancement to a top executive position.[28]

COMMUNICATION AND MANAGEMENT

Although some writers separate communication from management, the two are tightly interwoven. The importance of communication in management has a tradition of endorsements even longer than in the business communication discipline.

Most of the major writers on management philosophy stress the central role of communication in successful management. The trend of identifying this central role continues today. Table 1.2 presents a chronology of management views of communication from early in this century.[29]

Also stressing the important joint role of communication and management,

TABLE 1.2   **Management's View of Communication**

Year	Person	Observation
1916	Fayol	Managerial work is a set of composite functions that includes communication.
1930s	Gulick	Management has seven functional areas, including directing and reporting (which include communication).
1938	Barnard	The first executive function is providing a system of communication.
1957	Simon	The administrative process cannot influence the decisions of the individual without communication.
1966	Katz & Kahn	The exchange of information and transmission of meaning are the very essence of an organization.
1973	Mintzberg	Managerial jobs have ten working roles; communication and interpersonal relations are found in three of the roles.
1974	Drucker	Communication is one of five basic management functions.
1982	Peters and Waterman	Open, informal communication is one of eight characteristics of the best-run American companies.
1983	Kanter	The most common roadblock for managers to overcome is poor communication.
1991	Blanchard	Communication is a basic skill for the effective one-minute manager.
1995	Gates	Communication is the new revolution; the information superhighway is part of it.

former *Harvard Business Review* editor David Ewing says, "Management communication is the number one problem in business today. While the technology [that supports management communication] has advanced in leaps and bounds, managers' and academics' understanding of the substance of the process has not."[30]

COMMUNICATION OF ETHICS AND CROSS-CULTURAL MESSAGES

Recently two new topics have received substantial endorsement as critical knowledge areas for today's effective businesspeople: ethics and cross-cultural situations.

Business Ethics

Today's advanced business communicator is faced with a number of ethical considerations; technology seems to be increasing this number.

In these days that carry increasing accounts of improprieties at brokerage houses, inappropriate political influence, and devious business dealings, many are calling for a greater focus on ethics, as well as continuing attention to legal implications. See Figure 1.1 and determine whether your actions would be legal or ethical. While examination of ethical issues is not the primary domain of communication studies, certainly the communication of messages in an ethical fashion is germane to the study of advanced business communication. Therefore, appearing throughout this text are comments and suggestions regarding the need for ethical behavior.

Figure 1.1   **Legal or Ethical—How Do You Score?**

Assume you work for one of the major brokerage houses as an analyst. Would the following behaviors be legal? Ethical?

1. You become aware that one of your clients has a new process that could lead to sizeable profits from a new product. The news is not public. Would it be legal to buy stock in the company? Ethical?
2. Based on #1 above, you chat with a friend about the situation and are overheard by a person nearby. Can that person buy stock before the public announcement? Would it be ethical?
3. Your boss offers to let you in on some insider trading that you both know is illegal as a favor for something you did for her. Ethical?
4. A broker friend at another firm recommends buying stock in an unknown organization and appears to have inside information. You don't ask any questions. Can you buy stock in the company?

Answers. Legal? 1, 3, and 4 are illegal. Ethical? As is so often the case, it depends on whom you ask and your own values and principles.

Source: Modified from Thor Valdmanis and Tom Lowry in "Wall Street's New Breed Revives Inside Trading," *USA Today,* November 4, 1999, p. B-1.

To give you the flavor of how questions of ethics work their way into communication, consider how easily we can digitally modify photographs. Here are some incidents:

- When actor Dustin Hoffman was digitally given high heels and an evening gown in a *Los Angeles Magazine* story, he was awarded $3 million in a lawsuit over the image.
- *Time* was criticized for altering a cover picture of O. J. Simpson to make him look more sinister.
- *Newsweek* upset the Society of Professional Journalists for touching up the teeth of Bobbi McCaughey, the woman who gave birth to seven children.[31]
- A newspaper acquires a photograph of a prominent person who is visiting the city. The problem is that the person has a cigarette much in evidence. Since the newspaper does not want to promote cigarette smoking, an electronic darkroom is used to remove the offending cigarette.[32]

Technology has brought about new concerns about ethics and communication. Photographs, drawings, and commercial designs can now be easily and quickly scanned with high resolution into a computer, modified slightly (to avoid copyright infringement), and issued as one's own work. Software is available with hundreds of images, but an inexpensive scanner can duplicate images from magazines or newspapers at no cost. Laws are relatively clear about taking someone else's copyrighted work, but the issue of how much electronic modification may legally occur is still being decided.

Another ethical, as well as legal, consideration that is emerging but not yet resolved relates to the ownership of another person's text or graphic image. The ease with which one can scan text from a publication; capture a graphic image, a digital music file, or source code from a Web page on the Internet; or locate and copy original text via electronic information databases ensures that this issue will continue to receive attention.

Figure 1.2	**A Question of Ethics**

A survey of 250 meeting planners and industry suppliers asked 12 questions and compared answers to an ethics experts panel's feelings. Selected results appear below.

| | Percent saying "yes" | | |
Question	Meeting Planners	Suppliers	Ethics Rating*
Have you ever "borrowed" company office supplies for personal use?	64%	**	2.5
Have you ever "stretched the truth" on a résumé to make yourself look more appealing?	49%	**	9.5
Have you ever spent a good portion of a work day on personal business?	36%	**	7.5
Have you or has anyone in your organization ever accepted a personal vacation or similar "perk" from a supplier as a thank you for booking business?	33%	63%	7.5
Have you ever padded an expense report?	37%	49%	6.5

* "1" is minor infraction, "10" major violation
** not reported

Source: Melinda Ligos, "True Confessions—Begging, Borrowing, and . . . Stealing?" *Successful Meetings*, November 1999, pp. 34–40.

Cross-Cultural Communication

Cross-cultural communications support international business, and international business is the business of the 1990s and beyond. In the 1980s and 1990s the Pacific Rim countries acquired attention for the strength of their economies, their management styles, their productivity, and their innovativeness. Perhaps the early twenty-first century will be the years of Europe because of the emergence of the European Community and the dramatic changes in Europe's formerly communist countries. Or will China or India use their huge populations to increase their influence? As important as these countries and regions are in their influence on American business, equally important will be the ability of Americans to conduct business across cultures. Unfortunately, few Americans are prepared for such cross-cultural activity.

Many major American companies misjudge foreign business partners or distant markets. All too often, Americans seem to rush insensitively into unknown cultures only to make major business and social mistakes. An understanding of some of the dimensions of cross-cultural communication may better prepare Americans with the skills needed to conduct international business.

All communication is either verbal or nonverbal. Verbal communication consists of sharing thoughts through the meanings of words, while nonverbal communication shares thoughts through all other means. Some nonverbal communication is associated with the delivery of words and some is not (see Figure 1.3). While the understanding of verbal and nonverbal communication, and the interplay between them, is essential among businesspeople who share the culture of the United States, it is even

FIGURE 1.3   **Senses Appealed to by Nonverbal Communication**

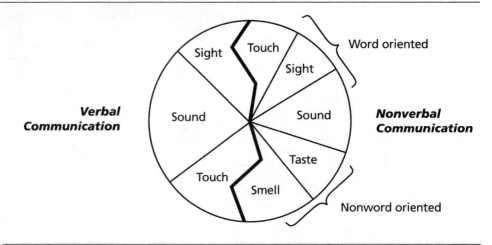

more important with cross-cultural communications because of the influences of religion, etiquette, customs, and politics. These four influences mediate communication far beyond mere language differences. Few topics can bring about such heated discussions as can religion; alienation can occur if the rules of etiquette are not observed; every person defends his or her own customs against all others; and disagreements over politics can start wars. These four influences surround and dictate the international business setting (see Figure 1.4).

While the extensive review of different countries' religions, etiquettes, customs, and politics is outside the purview of this text, examples of how they affect some of the major verbal and nonverbal communication activities illuminates how much preparation is required before entering into an international business transaction.

Verbal Communication Within verbal communication, four areas deserve attention: *jargon and slang, acronyms, humor,* and *vocabulary and grammar.*[33] English is rich with colorful but American-based cultural phrases, such as "in the ballpark," "raining cats and dogs," and "put in your two cents worth." Jargon has more of a business orientation, but still has phrases unique to American culture, such as "the bottom line" or delivering a "dog and pony show." Even though the words may translate directly into another language, the meanings often do not. Avoid jargon and slang.

Acronyms—the initial letters of a series of words—also should be avoided. People from other counties may be unfamiliar even with such common American acronyms as CEO, R&D, or VP. Use the full version the first time, and perhaps each time.

A third area of verbal difficulty is humor. Clearly, what is defined as humor varies dramatically across cultures. Americans often stereotype British humor as understated and dry or perceive Asians as sharing little humor. Conversely, many non-Americans

FIGURE 1.4   **The Relationships of International Business Communication and Verbal and Nonverbal Communication**

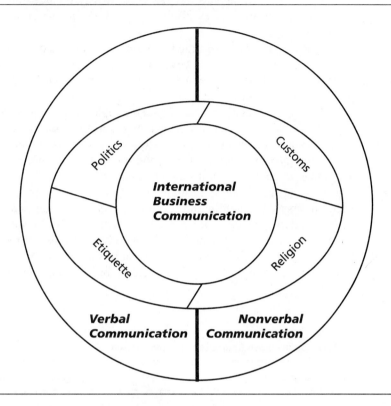

view American humor as coarse and heavy-handed. Because of the serious threat of damaging an otherwise potentially viable business setting with inappropriate humor, the American businessperson is advised to avoid initiating humor.

Help your reader or listener by using your best grammar and by writing with accepted punctuation. English is often the language of business, but not all foreign businesspeople are adequately prepared to handle faulty communication. Since written punctuation carries rules for how to speak, you should speak your punctuation. Hesitate at commas, and speak in sentences. Select a tone that is not condescending, but rather appropriately businesslike.

Nonverbal Communication While some important elements of nonverbal communication—such as subtle voice intonations, slight facial expression changes, or flamboyant clothing—have relatively clear meanings to us, the meaning may be missed or misinterpreted in other countries. Some of the areas of nonverbal communication that can be misused are *color, time, distance, voice, body movements,* and *clothing.*

Many assume that the impression or image associated with certain colors crosses cultural boundaries. Actually, the interpretation of colors varies extensively. For example, while red means danger to us, it may be associated with festive occasions in China; mourning is symbolized by black in our culture but by yellow in the Philippines.

The American use of time is not universal either. We tend to set and respect deadlines and appointments. However, Latin Americans, for example, do not feel as compelled to stick to time schedules. Efforts to impose our standards of time on others can elicit opposition or anger.

The spatial relationships between people in the United States are approximately in the middle of a spectrum of behavior for other countries. For example, our speaking distance in business settings is typically about two feet; this distance would generally be too close for the British and too distant for those from the Middle East.

The voice—even as it delivers English that is to be translated into another language—carries meaning. From the viewpoint of those from many cultures, Americans tend to speak too loudly and too much. They often do not give adequate time for a reply and fill uncomfortable silences with words. In some cultures, such as the Japanese, silence is not negative, but rather may be a time for introspection. (See Table 1.3.) In some countries, the custom may allow men to speak loudly and in a gruff voice, and women—if they speak in business settings at all—are to sound quiet,

TABLE 1.3   U.S. Versus Japanese Approaches to Negotiation

U.S. Negotiating Style	Japanese Negotiating Style
Speaks directly	Speaks indirectly
Is assertive	Is nonassertive
Speaks to the point	Uses ambiguity
Uses hard sell	Uses soft sell
Focuses on short term	Focuses on long term
Is argumentative	Is nonargumentative
Acts in a confrontational way	Acts in a conciliatory way
Favors verbal	Favors nonverbal
Is verbose	Is suspicious of words
Avoids silence	Uses silences and pauses amply
Values eloquence	Values humility
Makes direct eye contact	Avoids direct eye contact
Uses expansive gestures	Uses small gestures
Employs relatively informal style	Employs relatively formal style
Uses dramatic, animated style	Uses restricted, quiet style
Projects speaking voice	Restrains voice
Challenges other negotiators	Seeks to save face of all involved
Favors decision by majority vote	Wants complete consensus

Sources: Roger E. Axtell, ed. *Do's and Taboos Around the World,* John Wiley & Sons, New York, 1985; Philip R. Harris and Robert T. Moran, *Managing Cultural Differences,* Gulf Publishing Company, Houston, 1987, pp. 388–401; Robert T. Moran and William G. Stripp, *Successful International Business Negotiations,* Gulf Publishing Company, Houston, 1991, pp. 105–115.

reserved, and perhaps childlike. Indeed, attitudes toward women in business across cultures, for vocal and other reasons, can vary dramatically.[34]

The various body movements that are comfortable to us may be inappropriate in other settings. Normal social gestures in the United States, such as the way we cross our legs, may be offensive elsewhere. We tend to look a speaker in the eyes, perceiving the action to be one of openness and honesty. In another country, such conduct may be interpreted as far too aggressive.

American business attire is widely defined even in the United States, where we stereotype the appearance of such professionals as bankers, advertisers, accountants, or artists. And even those stereotypes may be hazardous when we encounter a "Casual Friday." When we wear our usual clothing in another country, we may find the colors too flamboyant, the weight uncomfortable for local conditions, or the length of the skirt noticeably incorrect.

Given these pitfalls of cross-cultural communication, how can you prepare for international business? The answer lies in these steps:

- Undertake thorough and unhurried research and preparation.
- Maintain a nonjudgmental mind open to new ideas.
- Cultivate a desire to achieve maximum understanding and complete communication.
- Avoid assuming that the U.S. culture is the only correct one.

Associated with cross-cultural communication is the rapidly emerging role of cultural diversity awareness in the workplace. Estimates are that in 2000, white males became a minority in the U.S. workplace; the customer base is changing dramatically too.[35] Rather than encouraging the cultural melting pot of just a few generations ago in which workers tried to lose their accents, Americanized their names, or dressed like other Americans, today pride of background, language, and culture is respected. We are learning that differences are strengths. Extensive effort is under way researching and documenting ways to enhance the perception of cultural diversity, and developing training programs that promote it.[36] Figure 1.5 illustrates the dimensions of diversity.

COMMUNICATION APPREHENSION

Many of us fear communicating and communication media. For example, some of us merely dislike or tolerate the task of writing; others hate or fear it. As the fear of communicating exceeds the perceived gain, individuals avoid communicating. Further, research suggests that those high in apprehension of communication are likely to avoid jobs calling for high communication interaction or will be unhappy if forced into such jobs. Those with such fears appear to select communication channels perceived to be the least threatening.[37]

Public speaking can produce high anxiety. As the size of the audience grows, the fear may increase. Speaking in front of a group is our greatest fear, according to one survey, even outranking fears of height, insects, financial problems, and deep water.[38] As might be guessed, communication apprehension can adversely affect organizational efficiency and attainment of personal goals.

FIGURE 1.5   **Dimensions of Diversity**

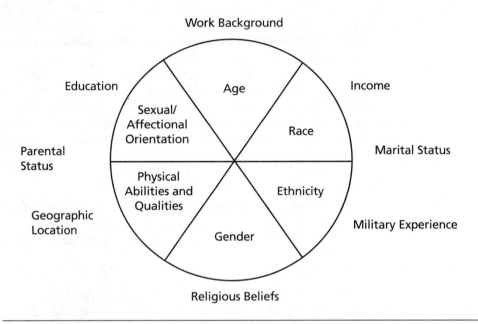

Source: Berkshire Associates, Inc. http://www.berkshire/app.com/diversity.html (1995).

An area related to apprehension is electronically mediated communication. On encountering some of the complex, challenging communication technologies, such as computers or two-way video teleconferencing, some of us modify the message or our delivery or we seek alternative media. We may avoid new technologies because we are unfamiliar with them or because we are afraid of embarrassment over incorrect use. Indeed, some of us avoid such commonplace business media as telephones and answering machines. Others cringe at the idea of delivering a computerized slide show rich with builds, transitions, and audio and video clips.

Training and experience can help overcome the fear of speaking. Chapter 3 demonstrates the ease with which one can prepare computerized slide shows. Chapter 13 discusses ways of overcoming the fears that arise in various business situations, such as being your company's spokesperson to the press.

ADVANCED COMMUNICATION

Thus far, you have seen evidence of the importance of communication in business. The research, for the most part, has focused on the advanced businessperson rather than the entry-level person. Going to work for a business organization with your advanced education, you may start as a mid-level manager. Your aspirations, no doubt, will be for advancement through the hierarchy. What communication skills will you need immediately and what skills will be needed later in your career? Figure 1.6 presents some answers to these two questions.

Hierarchical business communication has five stages. At the entry level, minimal skills beyond accepted grammar and punctuation are needed or expected; literacy is assumed. Communication is generally directed toward peers and upward, toward immediate supervisors. Messages may be complex and detailed but the audience, both immediate and ultimate, is small. In formal communications, the audience may be limited to a single supervisor.

The second level is the supervisory level, which requires entry-level skills plus the ability to organize sentences, paragraphs, and messages for coherence. Spoken

FIGURE 1.6   **The Five Stages of Executive Communication**

Stages	Characteristics	Importance of Language Rules	Message Complexity	Audience Size	Exposure to Subordinates	Breadth of Topics
5. Top Management	Communication at top levels with other executives; comfortable with large groups and media; compelling writer and speaker.					
4. Upper Management	Effective with outside exposure (i.e., luncheon talks, reports, company spokesperson) and internally (i.e., newsletters, union negotiations).					
3. Middle Management	Effective with common business media (i.e., letters, memos, staff meetings).					
2. Supervisors	Can organize sentences, paragraphs, and messages for coherence.					
1. Entry Level	Has basic spelling, grammar, and pronunciation skills.					

communication, which may be relied upon heavily, is usually one-to-one or one-to-a-few. A substantial portion of the supervisor's formal communication is directed downward and is on relatively few topics.

Middle managers build on the communication skills that exist at the lower levels. For these middle managers, written communication may increase in importance, be of a routine nature, and flow both upward and downward. Middle managers may experience more of a balance between what is sent and what is received than personnel at lower levels of the organization. Those at lower levels tend to receive more information than they initiate. Communication is important for middle managers because they must be quite adaptable. They must be capable of transmitting clear directions to supervisors, perhaps with a motivational or authoritarian tone, and also of responding concisely to messages from the upper levels. Yet another set of skills may be called on for communication with peers, with whom they share ideas, work, and social occasions. The audiences of middle managers range from a variety of superiors to peers and supervisors; these audiences receive a diversity of messages from middle managers.

For the upper manager, audience size increases. The upper manager is called on to represent the organization as a speaker at community group meetings and may be a leader in church or civic groups, such as the Rotary Club. Internally, the upper manager has control over the final appearance of many written documents, such as reports or newsletters, which often are largely prepared by subordinates. This manager edits weak communication and appreciates clear communication. Writing prepared at lower levels may feel the heavy pencil of the upper manager. Clarity and precision often characterize this manager's communication style. The upper manager may prepare communications for top management, such as written speeches or reports to a board of directors. Top management will assess the quality of the upper manager's communication abilities as it determines future assignments.

Top managers spend much of their time communicating with their peers. They often present terse, clear, goal-oriented messages to large audiences at one time, such as in annual reports, commencement addresses, or media interviews. Usually, the message is less complex than communications at lower levels in order to make the information more easily understood by many levels of the organization and by the public. Topics are broad and are often a synthesis of information that has moved up the organization or from outside. Communicators at this level tend to be more cautious about what they say because the message often affects many people. Top managers also will communicate to a substantial degree with subordinates, usually at a level or two below. The top manager's communication may be directive or persuasive. This manager often has extraordinary leadership skills, is charismatic, and engenders intense loyalty. See Figure 1.7 for a breakdown of how one study found chief executive officers (CEOs) spent their contact time.

The effective executive communicator (at middle, upper, or top management) is the product not only of business knowledge and skills, but also of communication knowledge and skills. These knowledge and skill areas work in concert for the truly effective communicator. Figure 1.8 outlines some of the more important knowledge and skill areas and illustrates the important interactions between general and specific business and communication abilities.

FIGURE 1.7   **How American CEOs Spend Their Time**

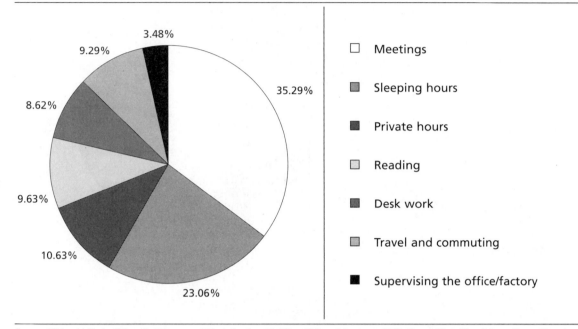

Source: Hideyuki Kudo, Takeo Tachikawa, and Noriniko Suzuki, "How U.S. and Japanese CEOs Spend Their Time," *Long Range Planning,*
Vol. 21, November 6, 1988, pp.72–82.

FIGURE 1.8   Knowledge and Skill Areas

THE EFFECTIVE
EXECUTIVE
COMMUNICATOR

BUSINESS KNOWLEDGE AND SKILLS

General
   Accounting
   Economics
   Finance
   Information Systems
   Marketing
   Computer science
   Management
      Decision sciences
      Organizational behavior
      Business policy
   Electronic commerce
Specific
   Knowledge and skills specific to the
      executive's industry and
      company
   Technical knowledge
      Trade practices
      Competitors and company personnel
   Corporate culture
   Decision-making skills
      Information-processing skills
      Insight
      Judgment
      Knowledge of external publics and
         environmental factors
   Leadership skills
      Organizing
      Planning
      Controlling
      Directing
      Leading
   International business skills
      Language fluency
      Cross-cultural training
      Diversity appreciation

COMMUNICATION KNOWLEDGE AND
SKILLS

General
   Listening
   Writing
   Reading
   Editing
   Speaking
   Nonverbal communication
   Technology skills
      Phone etiquette
      Word processing
      Spreadsheets
      Computerized slide presentations
      E-mail procedures
   Communication theory and processes
Specific
   Progress reporting
   Meeting coordination and leadership
   Industrial relations
   Supervisory relations
   Arbitration and negotiation
   Interviewing
   Persuasion
   Public speaking
   Media relations
   Social relations (as a company representative)
   Multidirectional communication skills
      Internal vs. external
      Personal vs. mass communication
      Peer vs. superior vs. subordinate
   Organizational communications
      Newsletters
      Mass meetings
      Management conferences
      Training sessions
   Company communications policies
      Formats
      Media choice
      Crisis management policy
      Corporate identity

SUMMARY

Just as middle, peer, and top managers use communication skills that are different from those of supervisors and entry-level employees, advanced students have different communication needs than lower-level students.

Effective communication is crucial in business. Those who are effective communicators rise quickly in their organizations. Those without such abilities—even if they are functional experts—often are held back. Numerous studies support conclusions that communication—written, spoken, and visual—should be an integral part of the college curriculum, can get you a job or a better job or a promotion, and can make you a better manager.

Many people are unprepared to communicate at the international level or fear some form of communication, such as public speaking or being televised. Because audience size and topic importance are likely to grow as a manager rises in the organizational hierarchy, overcoming communication apprehension while improving skills is important.

The chapters that follow are directed toward helping you sharpen the communication skills you use as a manager. Included in these skills are the understanding of the importance of visual support, effective writing of various business messages, polished speaking skills in a diversity of settings, and the ability to select from media options to best accomplish your goals. Whatever your situation now—student or manager—these chapters will help you be an advanced communicator.

DISCUSSION QUESTIONS

1. Why do you think so much importance is placed on communication in business, but the subject is often overlooked in college business programs?
2. What college courses have been most valuable to you and why? How does your answer compare to what (a) business experts and (b) surveys of academicians report?
3. Which is most important in business: writing, speaking, or visual skills? Why?
4. What communication skills are you likely to use in a job interview? Which will be most important to the recruiter?
5. Which of your skills will be most important as you are assessed for promotion?
6. What is the relationship of communication to management?
7. What is communication apprehension, and how is it overcome?
8. How do employees communicate at various levels in the hierarchy? What variables come into play?
9. Which is more important in cross-cultural communication: verbal or nonverbal communication? Why?
10. Discuss some ways in which differing perceptions of time can hinder cross-cultural communication.

Applications

1. Interview three people in relatively low-level positions in an organization regarding their views on the importance of communication. Then interview three top managerial-level people within the same organization for their views. Is there a difference between the two sets of views? If so, why? What could be done to bring the two views together?

2. Select a different culture that you might visit, preferably in a business setting. Research that culture and generate a list of guidelines that, when followed, would enhance your chance of business success.

3. Exchange the list you generated in Application 2 with someone who selected a different culture. What are your reactions to that list? How much overlap exists?

4. Learn the correct pronunciation of appropriate forms of business greetings, use of business titles, and departure phrases for a culture with which you are unfamiliar.

5. From fellow students or work colleagues who are fluent in another language, generate identical counterparts for these words: hot, slow, angry, tall, small, nervous, quick, expensive, dead, and fun. Select languages that are substantially different from English, such as Swahili or Thai. In column 1 list the ten English words, in column 2 the same words in a random order in the second language, and then a third column with words in a random order in a third language. Distribute the lists to classmates and have the native speak the words in her or his language in the order on the handout. Have classmates see if they can guess which words mean the same as the English words. Repeat with the other languages. Check results. Often many unfamiliar words from another language can be guessed correctly for their English counterparts.

6. Rate the following on a 1-to-5 scale from ethical to unethical. Compare your results to those of classmates.

   - Cheating on an exam
   - Not returning excessive and incorrect change from a purchase
   - Exaggerating on a résumé
   - Purchasing a report from the Internet for a class
   - Not citing information from a Web site and including it in a report as your own
   - Submitting an excessive or unsubstantiated report to an insurance company so as to get reimbursement beyond that justified
   - Lying on your income tax forms

NOTES

1. Ernest L. Boyer, *College: The Undergraduate Experience in America*, Harper & Row, New York, 1987, pp. 59–85.
2. Jack E. Hulbert, "Facilitating Intelligent Business Dialogue," *Business Education Forum* 33, no. 8, May 1979, pp. 10–15.
3. Robert J. Olney, "Executives' Perceptions of Business Communication," paper presented at Southwest Conference of the Association for Business Communication, San Antonio, Texas, March 2, 1984; and Dan H. Swenson, "Relative Importance of Business Communication Skills for the Next Ten Years," *Journal of Business Communication* 17, no. 2, Winter 1980, pp. 41–49.
4. Stephen S. Pride, *Business Ideas: How to Create and Present Them*, Harper & Row, New York, 1967, p. 172; Conwell Carlson, "Best Memories by Eye and the Ear," *Kansas City Times*, April 19, 1967, sec. A, p. 13; Paul R. Timm, *Functional Business Presentations: Getting Across*, Prentice-Hall, Englewood Cliffs, New Jersey, 1981, pp. 130–150; B. Berelson and G. Steiner, *Human Behavior: An Inventory of Scientific Findings*, 2nd ed., Harcourt, Brace & World, New York, 1978; and Jerry W. Koehler and John Sisco, *Public Communication in Business and the Professions*, West, St. Paul, Minnesota, 1981; E. Raudsepp, "Present Your Ideas Effectively," *IEEE Transactions on Professional Communication* 22, 1979, pp. 204–210.
5. W. G. V. Balchin and Alice M. Coleman, "Graphicacy Should Be the Fourth Ace in the Pack," *The Cartographer* 3, 1966, pp. 23–28.
6. R. Evans, "Serving Modern Students in a Modern Society at the Community College: Incorporating Basic Technological Literary," *T.H.E. Journal*, October 1999, pp. 102–108.
7. A. Bork as quoted in S. Charp, "Technical Literacy—Where Are We?" *T.H.E. Journal*, October 1999, pp. 6–8.
8. Terry L. Childers and Michael J. Houston, "Imagery Paradigms for Consumer Research: Alternative Perspectives from Cognitive Psychology," *Advances in Consumer Research* 10, Association for Consumer Research, 1983, pp. 59–64; W. G. V. Balchin and Alice M. Coleman, "Graphicacy Should Be the Fourth Ace in the Pack;" W. G. V. Balchin, "Graphicacy," *Geography* 57, 1972, pp. 185–195; Calvin F. Schmid, *Statistical Graphics: Design Principles and Practices*, John Wiley & Sons, New York, 1983, pp. 11–12; and John A. Pollock et al., "Executives' Perceptions of Future MBA Programs," *Collegiate News and Views*, Spring 1983, pp. 23–25.
9. "U.S. Execs Rate Business Writing," *Training and Development Journal*, December 1984.
10. H. Hudson as quoted in P. Jacobs, "Strong Writing Skills Essential for Success, Even in IT," *Infoworld*, July 6, 1998, p. 86.
11. Kenneth Roman and Joel Raphaelson, *Writing That Works*, Harper & Row, New York, 1981, p. 1; Rollin H. Simonds, "Skills Businessmen Use Most," *Nation's Business*, November 1960, p. 88; Homer Cox, "Opinions of Selected Business Managers about Some Aspects of Communication on the Job," *Journal of Business Communication* 6, no. 1, Fall 1968, pp. 3–12; M. Glassman and E. Farley, "AACSB Accredited Schools' Approach to Business Communication Courses," *Journal of Business Communication* 16, no. 3, 1979, pp. 41–48; Marie Flatley, "A Comparative Analysis of the Written Communication of Managers at Various Organizational Levels in the Private Business Sector," *Journal of Business Communication* 19, no. 2, 1982, p. 48; James M. Lahiff and John D. Hartfield, "The Winds of Change and Managerial Communication Practices," *Journal of Business Communication* 15, no. 4, 1978, pp. 19–28; and Menkus Belden, "Effective Systems Reports," *Journal of Systems Management* 23, no. 9, September 1976, pp. 18–20.
12. "Writing Skills: What They're Looking For," *Journal of Accountancy*, October 1991, p. 39.
13. 1999 Graduate Management Admission Test GMAT Bulletin and Registration Form, Graduate Management Admission Council, 1995, Princeton, New Jersey, pp. 28–29; and James D. Blum and Cosmo F. Ferrara, "Writing Skills: Another Hurdle for CPA Candidates," *New Accountant*, September 1994, pp. 16–17.
14. M. Rader and Alan Wunsch, "A Survey of Communication Practices of Business School Graduates by Job Category and Undergraduate Major," *Journal of Business Communication* 17, no. 4, 1980, pp. 33–41.
15. Jon M. Huegli and Harvey D. Tschirgi,

"Communication Skills at the Entry Job Level," *Journal of Business Communication* 12, no. 1, Fall 1974, pp. 24–29.

16. Timothy W. Clipson and Marlin C. Young, "A Comparative Study of Business Employers and Educators Concerning Most Significant Business Communication Topics," Proceedings, Association for Business Communication, Southwest, New Orleans, March 7–9, 1985, pp. 55–65.

17. Deborah Tannen, "The Power of Talk: Who Gets Heard and Why," *Harvard Business Review*, September–October 1995, pp. 138–148.

18. "The Art of Listening," *Royal Bank of Canada Monthly Letters* 60, no. 1, January 1979; and Lyman K. Steil, Larry L. Baker, and Kittie W. Watson, *Effective Listening: Key to Your Success*, Addison-Wesley, Reading, Massachusetts, 1983, pp. 1–33.

19. "How Undergraduate Business Communication Programs Can Meet the Communication Needs of Business: Report of the Undergraduate Studies Committee," *ABCA Bulletin* 36, no. 2, June 1973, pp. 5–7; John M. Penrose, "A Survey of the Perceived Importance of Business Communication and Other Business-Related Fields," *Journal of Business Communication* 13, no. 2, Winter 1976, pp. 17–25; Rader and Wunsch, "A Survey," pp. 33–41; and Steven Golen et al., "Empirically Tested Cognitive Communication Skills for the MBA, with Implications for the AACSB," *The Organizational Behavior Teaching Review* 13, no. 3, 1988–1989, pp. 45–58.

20. Rise B. Axelrod and Charles R. Cooper, *The St. Martin's Guide to Writing*, 5th ed., New York, St. Martin's Press, 1997, p. 459.

21. Karen O. Dowd and Jeanne Liedtka, "What Corporations Seek in MBA Hires: A Survey," *Selections—The Magazine of the Graduate Management Admission Council*, Winter 1994, pp. 34–39.

22. Jeanne D. Maes, Teresa G. Weldy, and Marjorie L. Icenogle, "A Managerial Perspective: Oral Communication Competency Is Most Important for Business Students in the Workplace," *The Journal of Business Communication* 34, no. 1, January 1997, pp. 67–80.

23. David J. Hyslop and Kay Faris, "Integrate Communication Skills into All Business Classes," *Business Education Forum*, April/May 1984, pp. 51–57; John M. Penrose, " A Discrepancy Analysis of the Job-Getting Process and a Study of Resume Techniques," *Journal of Business Communication* 21, no. 3, Summer 1984, pp. 5–15; A. Edge and R. Greenwood, "How Mangers Rank Knowledge, Skills, and Attributes Possessed by Business Administration Graduates," *AACSB Bulletin* 11, October 1974, pp. 30–34; Simonds, "Skills Businessmen Use Most," p. 88; Cox, "Opinions of Selected Business Managers," pp. 3–12; and "Jobs of the Future," *Getting Jobs* 1, no. 1, November–December 1986, p. 1.

24. L. Marilyn Stinson, "Communication in the Workplace: Implications for Business Teachers," *Business Education Forum*, October 1995, pp. 28–30.

25. Henry H. Beax, "Good Writing: An Under-rated Executive Skill," *Human Resource Management*, Spring 1981, p. 2; D. Stine and D. Sharzenski, "Priorities for the Business Communication Classroom: A Survey of Business and Academe," *Journal of Business Communication* 16, no. 3, 1979, pp. 15–30; and John E. Baird and Patricia H. Bradley, "Communication Correlates of Employee Morale," *Journal of Business Communication* 15, no. 3, 1978, pp. 47–55.

26. Larry McConnell, as quoted in Paula Jacobs, "Strong Writing Skills Essential for Success, Even in IT," *Infoworld*, July 6, 1998, p. 86.

27. F. A. Bond, H. W. Hildebrandt, and E. L. Miller, *The Newly Promoted Executive: A Study in Corporate Leadership*, University of Michigan Graduate School of Business Administration, Ann Arbor, Michigan, 1981, pp. 1–23.

28. James C. Bennett and Robert J. Olney, "Executive Priorities for Effective Communication in an Information Society," *Journal of Business Communication* 23, no. 2, 1986, p. 14.

29. Henri Fayol, *General and Industrial Management*, translated from the original French, 1916, reprint, Pittman & Sons, London, 1949; C. S. George, Jr., *The History of Management Thought*, Prentice-Hall, Englewood Cliffs, New Jersey, 1972; Chester I. Barnard, *The Functions of the Executive*, Harvard University Press, Cambridge, Massachusetts, 1938; Herbert A. Simon, *The Models of Man*, John Wiley & Sons, New York, 1957; D. Katz and R. L. Kahn, *The Social Psychology of Organizations*, John Wiley & Sons, New York, 1966; H. Mintzberg, *The Nature of Managerial Work*, Harper & Row, New York, 1973; Peter Drucker, *Management: Tasks, Responsibilities, Practices*, Harper & Row, New

York, 1974; Thomas J. Peters and Robert H. Waterman, *In Search of Excellence*, Harper & Row, New York, 1982; and R. M. Kanter, *The Change Masters*, Simon & Schuster, New York, 1983; Bill Gates, *The Road Ahead*, Viking, 1995 as excerpted by *Newsweek*, November 1995, p. 60.

30. David Ewing, in brochure announcing introduction of *Management Communication Quarterly*, Sage Publications, 1987.

31. Kathryn Ballint, "Photo Magic," *ComputerLink* magazine of the *San Diego Union-Tribune*, October 26, 1999, pp. 6–7.

32. Jane Hundertmark, "When Enhancement Is Deception," *Publish*, October 1991, pp. 51–55.

33. Roger E. Axtell, ed., *Do's and Taboos Around the World*, John Wiley & Sons, New York, 1985, pp. 140–159.

34. Lillian H. Chaney and Jeannette S. Martin, *International Business Communication*, 2nd ed., Prentice Hall: Upper Saddle River, New Jersey, 2000, pp. 47–49.

35. Lawrence M. Baytos, *Designing and Implementing Successful Diversity Programs*, Prentice-Hall, Englewood Cliffs, New Jersey, 1995, p. xxiv.

36. A five-person panel examined "Challenges to Communicating Multicultural Values: A Workplace Assessment," at Association for Business Communication International Convention, Orlando, Florida, November 1–4, 1995.

37. "U.S. Execs Rate Business Writing," *Training and Development Journal*, December 1984; J. C. McCroskey, "Measures of Communication-Bound Anxiety," *Speech Monographs* 37, 1970, pp. 269–277; F. I. Falcone, J. A. Daly, and J. C. McCroskey, "Job Satisfaction as a Function of Employees' Communication Apprehension, Self-Esteem, and Perceptions of Their Immediate Supervisor," *Communication Yearbook*, 4th ed. B. D. Ruben, *International Communication Association*, New Brunswick, New Jersey, 1977, pp. 263–276; and N. L. Reinsch, Jr. and Phillip V. Lewis, "Communication Apprehension as a Determinant of Channel Preferences," *Journal of Business Communication* 21, no. 3, Summer 1984, pp. 53–61.

38. David Wallechinsky and Irving Wallace, *The Book of Lists*, William Morrow, New York, 1977.

'2'

Information
and Persuasion

The goal of this chapter is to lightly touch on themes that will be developed more fully in later chapters. First, some general principles for presenting information effectively will be outlined. Second, some of the basic issues related to the process of persuasion will be considered.

PRESENTING INFORMATION EFFECTIVELY

In the first edition of *Advanced Business Communication* we observed: "We are drowning in a sea of letters, memos, reports, printouts, and faxes." We stand corrected: We are now drowning in a sea of e-mail, voice mail, cell phone calls, *and* letters, memos, reports, printouts, and faxes.

Consider the results of a survey reported in 1997 by the Institute of the Future and the Gallop Organization. They found that the average number of messages sent and received by employees of Fortune 1000 companies was about 178 *a day*.[1] The *Wall Street Journal*, reporting on the survey, wrote of "message mania" and a "communications barrage."[2] And in the several years since the survey, the number of messages, especially e-mail messages, has increased in most organizations.

But the quantity of information is not the only problem faced by executives. In fact, what makes this "information overload" all the more vexing is that so many of the messages present information ineffectively, and by doing so waste time and create confusion. Consider how often we find ourselves muttering: "What is the point of this memo or e-mail?" "What does this letter mean?" "Couldn't he say this in fewer words?" "Why is this report organized like this?" and so forth. The problem of too much information, therefore, is coupled with the problem of information that is presented ineffectively. Although ambiguity is sometimes intentional in business communication (see the discussion of "Strategic Ambiguity" below), more often writers and speakers intend their readers or listeners to understand and retain information. To these two ends, understanding and retention, these six general principles of presenting information apply: directness, conciseness, organization, clarity, redundancy, and multisensory messages. And it's our conviction that the application of these principles will help your readers and listeners to manage the "message mania" in their professional lives.

Directness

Put simply, the strategy here is to get to the point. Routine memos and letters, as well as positive or good news messages, can be organized according to the direct plan. As Chapter 5 will explain and illustrate, the **direct plan** takes its name from the placement of the main point of the message, usually in the first sentence.

A wise approach to presenting information is to think of the direct plan as the rule and any departure from the direct plan as an exception. Most executives should be able to employ the direct plan in 75 percent of their writing and, in doing so, make their writing easier to understand and retain.

What are the exceptions to presenting information by the direct plan? The two major categories are negative or bad news messages and persuasive messages. These two types of messages usually require an indirect plan. Chapter 6 will explain and illustrate indirect plan messages in depth. At this point, let it suffice to say that in the **indirect plan**, the beginning of a message is the position of most emphasis, the end is the position of the second most emphasis, and the middle is the position of least emphasis. In routine and positive messages the main point should be given the position of most emphasis: the beginning. In a persuasive message, the main point should be delayed because resistance from the reader is expected. The main point is accorded the position of second most emphasis and preceded by a series of steps designed to motivate or induce the reader to accept the writer's point of view (more on persuasion later in this chapter). In negative messages, the main point should usually be de-emphasized by placing it in the middle of the message and preceding it by an explanation preparing the reader for the bad news.

In short, while situations will occur in which you will want to de-emphasize the point, employing the direct plan to get to the point will be appropriate in most of your writing. In doing so you will create a more efficient document—that is, less effort (input) will be required by your readers to understand your memos or letters (the output).

Conciseness

Conciseness may be expressed in two ways: use as many words as you need or use as few words as necessary. In either case, conciseness will improve the presentation of information.

Chapter 4 will offer some specific suggestions for making your writing more concise. The purpose in this chapter is to make an important distinction between conciseness and brevity, and in doing so to clarify the notion of conciseness.

Conciseness does not mean brevity. **Brevity** simply means using few words. We would all agree that a memo consisting of a two-sentence paragraph is brief. But it is not necessarily concise. Conciseness requires that the message contain an adequate number of words to achieve the writer's purpose. If, for example, the two-sentence memo leaves the reader puzzled, it has sacrificed both conciseness and the reader's understanding for the sake of brevity.

Some organizations have missed this important distinction with their insistence on one-page memos and other such requirements. If, after eliminating any unnecessary words and phrases (see Chapter 4 for examples), a writer still requires a page and a half to make a point clearly, explain a problem adequately, or offer a few recommendations, then it makes sense to use the extra space. Use as many words as you need to adequately convey information to your readers. Be concise.

Organization

The understanding and retention of information is enhanced when the appropriate mode of organization for a message is employed. Here are nine basic patterns of organization to consider while planning messages. They may be employed singly to organize an entire message or in combination to organize sections within a message or even paragraphs within sections. The nine basic patterns are direct, indirect, order of importance, chronology, problem–solution, causal, spatial, structure/function, and topical.

1. **Direct Plan.** As noted above, this is the pattern of choice when planning the organization of an entire message, particularly messages that are routine, neutral, and pleasant. The basic outline for the direct plan is

   Main point

   Support for, or explanation of, main point

   Restatement of the main point (optional)

   The paragraphs in support for or explanation of the main point may be organized according to the patterns described below. (See Chapter 5 for illustrations of messages organized according to the direct plan.)

2. **Indirect Plan.** The second major pattern to consider when planning an entire message is the indirect plan. Again, the indirect plan of organization is most appropriate for messages that the reader may find unpleasant and that may meet resistance from the reader. The basic outline for a negative message is

   Buffer (delayed opening)

   Reasons for negative message

   Negative message

   Positive ending

Persuasive messages, organized according to the indirect plan, often have their steps labeled differently by different writers. We outline the steps of a persuasive message as

Attention

Interest

Desire

Conviction

Action

(See Chapter 6 for illustrations of messages organized according to the indirect plan for negative or persuasive messages.)

3. **Order of Importance.** Suppose you have outlined a direct plan memo with the main point being a recommendation to promote an employee to a supervisory position. You have three reasons to support your recommendation. A sensible way to organize the presentation of the reasons is by decreasing order of importance—that is, state the most important reason first, then follow with the next most important and the least important reasons. Here is an example of how an actual outline of such a memo might look.

Recommend Denise Brown for supervisor (main point)

She has great interpersonal skills (most important reason)

She possesses excellent technical knowledge (next most important reason)

She has the most seniority among staff (least important reason)

This is an effective and efficient way to organize a message.

4. **Chronology.** The organizing criterion in this case is time. A clear example of this type of organization is seen on the typical résumé. The chronological résumé format, in fact, is so named because the work experience section of the résumé is organized in reverse chronological order.

Chronology is a useful organizing principle for other types of messages as well. For instance, accident reports are usually written using the chronological approach. Also, sections of memos or longer reports that provide background on a problem under study are often organized chronologically. Here is an outline illustrating how a section of a report might be organized chronologically.

1999   Roberts-Stevens was acquired by The Gibson Group

2000   The Gibson Group was acquired by Dee Communications

2001   Dee Communications was acquired by The FSB Media Group

Another important use of the chronological pattern of organization is the writing of instructions and directions. The steps or stages are explained and presented in chronological order. Here is a partial outline of instructions prepared for a customer service representative answering a telephone.

    Greet caller

    Identify yourself

    Ask for customer's account number

    Ask how you may assist the customer

This is a natural and useful way to organize information for readers.

5. **Problem–Solution.** Readers and listeners are very comfortable with this pattern of organization because it is used so frequently. In short messages, the first part of a message describes a problem, and the second part proposes a solution. Here is an example of a problem–solution outline.

    Employees accepting gifts from contractors (problem)

        Christmas gifts

        Other gifts

    Communicate corporate policy prohibiting gifts (solution)

        Memo to employees

        Letter to contractors

Such a familiar pattern as this facilitates a reader's understanding and retention.

6. **Causal.** You have two options here: moving from cause to effect and from effect to cause. With the cause-to-effect pattern, you begin by identifying a present cause and then describe a probable effect—you reason forward in time. With effect to cause, you begin by describing an observed effect and then propose to explain the probable causes—that is, you reason backward in time. Both are common ways to organize messages or parts of messages. Here are examples of both patterns.

Cause to Effect

    The high school population in the city has declined by 20 percent (cause).

    Therefore, companies face a shortage of clerical help (effect).

Effect to Cause

    The high school population has declined by 20 percent (effect).

    The declining middle-class birth rate is the likely cause (cause).

7. **Spatial.** Also called the **geographic pattern**, this is another common pattern of organization. The basis for this pattern is spatial relationship, or geography. Where physical objects or their locations are described, this pattern may be appropriate. An example of a spatial pattern of organization is

    Sales forecast by region (2001):

        Northeast region

        Southeast region

        Midwest region

Northwest region

Western region

For such a topic, the spatial pattern seems most appropriate.

8. **Structure/Function.** Typically, this is a two-part pattern: the first part describes the structure of something; the second part describes the functions of the structural parts. Another variation of this theme is to describe the structure and function of each part in turn. An illustration of the latter version is

Employee Relations Division

Affirmative Action (structure and function)

Compensation and Benefits (structure and function)

Personnel Operations (structure and function)

Labor Relations (structure and function)

Training and Development (structure and function)

9. **Topical.** Sometimes called the **categorical pattern** of organization, this is often used to organize messages, particularly when the patterns described above seem inappropriate. With this pattern, topics or subjects are broken down into subtopics or categories. Here is an illustration of the topical pattern.

Employee behavior subject to disciplinary action

Unsatisfactory work performance

Insubordination

Violation of safety rules

Falsification of company records

Destruction of company property

Absence from work

Theft

Use of controlled or intoxicating substance

These nine ways to organize messages, used alone or in combination, present information in a way that enhances reader understanding and retention of information.

Clarity

Ensuring that information is clear to readers and listeners requires careful consideration of your audience and the application of these four techniques: define or eliminate unclear words; compare or contrast unfamiliar information with information that is familiar; exemplify; and quantify meaningfully.

1. **Define or Eliminate Unclear Words.** If you believe that your reader or listener might not understand a word, either define it or substitute another word

more likely to be understood. This is particularly important when making oral presentations. Although a reader can reach for a dictionary, the listener is condemned to sit there puzzled or confused.

Be especially careful about professional jargon when writing or speaking to people outside the profession. Many words and expressions you use daily may be baffling to an audience unschooled in the lingo of your profession. Even when writing to someone within the same organization, be careful to avoid this barrier to clarity—for example, a data processing specialist writing to a marketing manager, or a benefits manager speaking to a group of management interns, must tailor the speech to the audience.

2. **Compare or Contrast the Unfamiliar with the Familiar.** One of the best known techniques for ensuring that information is clear to an audience is to compare or contrast information that may be unfamiliar with information that is known to the reader or listener. A consultant hired to train a group of secretaries to use a new word-processing program may compare and contrast the functions, commands, and features of the old (familiar) program with those of the new (unfamiliar) program—for example, "Although WORDMASTER requires many menu selections and options choices, LOGOEASE requires a single mouse click to select a template for a standard page format."

3. **Exemplify.** Information is usually clarified when a writer or speaker offers an example, real or hypothetical, brief or extended. A benefits manager explains how a major medical insurance policy supplements the basic plan by offering a hypothetical example of an employee filing a claim after a hospital stay. A sales manager, writing a directive for the sales force, offers examples of correct and incorrect uses of an expense account.

4. **Quantify Meaningfully.** Business writing and speaking usually contains numbers or statistics that often require a context to be meaningful. For example, "We are proposing a modest budget increase of 6 percent" is not as meaningful as "We are proposing to increase the budget $7,800,000, or 6 percent, over last year's budget of $130,000,000." Compare "Net income for common stock in 2000 was $4.26 per share on an average of 123 million shares outstanding" with "Net income for common stock in 2000 was $4.26 per share on an average of 123 million shares outstanding. This is down from last year's record of $4.48 per share on an average of 130 million shares outstanding, but better than 1998 when we earned $4.16 per share on an average of 129 million shares outstanding." The comparison of financial results over three years places the 2000 results in a more meaningful context.

An interesting exception to such strategies employed by business communicators to ensure *clarity* is the practice of *strategic ambiguity*.

As Eric Eisenberg explains, some communicators achieve their goals by creating messages that are *deliberately and strategically unclear.* The strategy works because of the inherent ambiguity of language, which allows people to assign different meanings to the same message. Examples are a strategically ambiguous corporate mission statement that allows members of the same company to assign different meanings yet subscribe to the same statement, or a strategically ambiguous statement to the public by a corporate spokesperson during a time of crisis which later allows for more specificity, or even deniability, as more information on the crisis becomes available to the corporation.

Redundancy

Writers and speakers enhance the understanding and retention of information when they design their messages to include a degree of redundancy. This is especially important for oral messages because listeners, unlike readers, do not have the message in front of them to consult or reread.

Repetition and Restatement Repetition (repeating the same words) and restatement (expressing the same message in different words) ensure that writers and speakers emphasize key points and ideas. For example, in criticizing a newspaper article about her firm, a speaker, over the course of her presentation, could refer to it as "inaccurate," "incorrect," "faulty," "fallacious," "unreliable," "imprecise," "inexact," "wide of the mark," "mistaken," and "off target." Get the impression that she didn't care much for the article? Her audience could hardly miss her point. Note, too, that as a matter of style, it can be more effective to restate and rephrase the same point ten times than to simply repeat the word "inaccurate" ten times.

Internal Summaries Long written or oral messages benefit greatly from internal summaries. Such summaries permit a writer or speaker to remind the reader or listener of what main points have been made before moving on to the next. For example,

> So far, I have offered two reasons as to why we should move the firm to New Jersey: a 30 percent reduction in the cost of utilities, and substantially lower state and local taxes. Add to these two reasons a third: quality of life considerations.

If this were the last reason, the summary at the end of the message could recapitulate all three reasons.

Multisensory Messages

One more technique to consider as an aid to understanding and retaining information is the use of multisensory messages—that is, the combination of oral, visual, written, and graphic messages. As we noted in Chapter 1, research suggests that oral and visual messages together increase recall over just oral or visual messages alone. We devote an entire chapter, Chapter 3, to visual support.

In sum, the effective communication of information can be enhanced by attention to these six principles: directness, conciseness, organization, clarity, redundancy, and multisensory messages.

THE PERSUASIVE PROCESS

Sometimes, even when information is presented according to these six principles, the message still will be ineffective. Usually, these cases involve writers or speakers asking readers or listeners to do something that they do not want to do—that is, the readers or listeners resist the purpose of the message.

As noted earlier in this chapter, the likelihood of resistance on the part of readers or listeners is one rationale for employing the indirect plan of organization. With this plan of organization, the request or call for action is delayed until the end of the message. By doing so, the beginning of the message is used to secure the attention of the reader or listener, and the middle of the message is used to motivate the reader or listener to accept the purpose. Because resistance is expected, we do not risk a reader rejecting the request at the beginning of a memo and reading no further; we do not risk an audience tuning out from our oral presentation at the very beginning. As we employ the term, persuasion is a process by which we motivate readers and listeners to (1) change existing attitudes and behavior or (2) adopt new attitudes and behavior or (3) do both.

Changing Existing Attitudes and Behavior

Often our persuasive goal is to change attitudes and behavior that already exist. For instance, your company might discover that employees view pilferage (taking home pens, pencils, pads of paper, and so forth) as a kind of fringe benefit. You are asked to write a memo that will persuade them that it is more like petty theft, and they should desist. Or a survey by the Human Resource Department might find that most employees view the forthcoming merger of your organization with another larger firm as something very negative. You must draft a letter from the president of the firm, to be sent to the home of every employee, that seeks to persuade them that the merger will be beneficial and positive.

In both cases, the assumption underlying the decision to employ persuasion is that simply requesting employees to stop pilfering company supplies, or telling them that the merger is a good thing, will not work. They know that the company does not approve of pilferage; yet they still do it. They have been told that the merger will benefit them; they do not believe it. Persuasion is needed.

Adopting New Attitudes and Behavior

At other times, the persuasive purpose is to motivate readers or listeners to adopt new attitudes or behavior. For instance, you might write a proposal to persuade management to adopt a centralized word-processing system for your company. Or a department store might decide to persuade customers who use American Express and VISA cards to accept and use the store's own charge card. For this, the persuasive letter is designed.

As was the case with the examples of changing existing attitudes and behavior, both of these examples assume resistance by readers and listeners. For instance, simply proposing and describing a central word-processing system to a group of senior executives is unlikely to motivate them to approve the expenditure. They need to be persuaded. Similarly, writing to customers who use VISA or American Express and offering the department store's charge card is likely to be ignored or rejected. Why should they bother? They need to be persuaded, too.

Changing and Adopting Attitudes and Behavior

At times, you may need to pursue both of the goals simultaneously. That is, you need to change attitudes or behavior and induce the adoption of new attitudes or behavior. The design of your message will reflect this more complex purpose.

The most obvious case of such a dual purpose is the task often faced by salespersons: they must change the attitude of a potential customer toward the product that they are using and motivate the customer to buy a new product or service. In another example, to motivate an executive to replace his firm's photocopying equipment with a competitor's brand may require persuading him that (1) the equipment in use is not as good as he thought, and (2) he should choose the competitor's particular brand of new equipment. Failure to achieve the first purpose may make the second purpose superfluous. The executive may respond, "Yes, your photocopier is impressive, but our present equipment seems just as good. Why should I change?"

SUMMARY

Effective managers present information that can be understood and retained. To this end, we have considered the principles of directness, conciseness, organization, clarity, redundancy, and multisensory messages.

Effective managers also design persuasive messages to change existing attitudes and behavior and to motivate others to adopt new attitudes and behavior.

The themes presented in this chapter about the communication of information and the process of persuasion will be developed more fully and illustrated with concrete examples of business communication in the chapters that follow.

Applications

1. Take a random sample of memos and letters received over the course of a week at work and determine which of the nine patterns of organization apply.

2. Consider an unclear message, written or oral, that you have received recently. Which of the four techniques listed as aids to clarity would have helped you to understand the message?

3. Read Eric Eisenberg's article on strategic ambiguity (see note 3) and apply the concept to communication at work.

DISCUSSION QUESTIONS

1. What is the distinction between brevity and conciseness? How might an emphasis on brevity reduce the effectiveness of business communication?
2. Identify the pattern of organization employed in a variety of business communications—e.g., direct-mail sales letters received at home, routine memos at work, or commercial messages on radio and TV.

Why do you think that these plans or organization were chosen? Do you agree with the choice?
3. Think of a time when you failed to be persuasive at work. Why do you think you failed?
4. Think of a time when you succeeded at being persuasive at work. Why do you think you succeeded?

NOTES

1. "Managing Corporate Communications in the Information Age" (Executive Summary). Institute for the Future, April 1997.
2. "Memo 4/9/97, FYI: Messages Inundate Offices," *Wall Street Journal,* April 8, 1997, p. B1.

3. Eric M. Eisenberg. "Ambiguity as Strategy in Organizational Communication," *Communication Monographs* 51, 1984, pp. 227–242.

3

Advanced Visual Support

In many ways, the visual support that accompanies your written or spoken words has the most powerful impact because it clarifies, entices, and emphasizes the message content. Research indicates that visual data are usually retained longer and more accurately than text or oral presentations alone. This is especially true when the information is complex, difficult, or new. Further, the way you deliver your visual support can have a direct influence on your professional image, particularly during corporate presentations. According to Walter Kiechel III, formerly of *Fortune*'s board of editors,

> Let us in no way minimize the opportunity, or the danger, involved. The thirty minutes an executive spends on his feet formally presenting his latest project to corporate superiors are simply and absolutely the most important thirty minutes of that or any other managerial season.[1]

This chapter discusses how to extend the impact of written and oral communication through visual support, which can enhance such business media as reports, presentations, and training sessions. Five main topics are presented: principles of graphic excellence; types of visuals; when to use visual support; media selection, preparation, and usage; and planning and execution hints.

PRINCIPLES OF GRAPHIC EXCELLENCE

Many, perhaps most, of the visual aids that businesspeople use are poorly thought out, incorrectly prepared, and misleading. Unfortunately, many are also either drab and lifeless or so cluttered that they are incomprehensible. Others demonstrate high-quality presentation yet fail to present the data in a comprehensible manner. All of these visuals fall outside the principles of graphic excellence.

Successful visuals integrate substance, statistics, and design to achieve four principles: clarity, precision, efficiency, and integrity.[2] The best visuals give the viewer the greatest number of ideas as quickly as possible in the least amount of space. Clarity, precision, and efficiency come with effort and reflect understanding of some general design concepts: emphasis, unity, balance, space, scale, shade and color, texture, and pattern.[3] Let us look at each of these design concepts in detail.

Emphasis makes an item stand out from others through special treatment, such as typeface or pattern. Overuse of emphasis, such as too much of a bright color, just causes confusion.

Unity is the relationship among parts that makes them function as one. Figure 3.1 shows, in the top example, a lack of unity—there appear to be eight separate bars. In the unified revision below it, one sees four pairs of bars.

Balance refers to the placement of elements in pleasing ways. One type, formal balance, has shapes arranged symmetrically. The other type, informal balance, can combine multiple smaller objects on one side against a sole larger object on the other. An example of informal balance would be a large photograph balanced by two small graphs.

Space is either positive or negative. An image such as a bar is positive and is surrounded by empty, negative space. Place positive elements in negative space so that the bars or other images seem to be resting upon the negative space. One way to accomplish the desired effect is to make sure that for bar graphs, the bars are wider than the space between them.

Applying **scale** involves presenting data so that it is not disproportionate; for instance, a small x-axis compared to a much larger y-axis is a scale problem. Figure 3.2 illustrates a scale problem with the y-axis on a graph. By varying the scale, the same data

FIGURE 3.1   Lack of Unity Versus Use of Unity

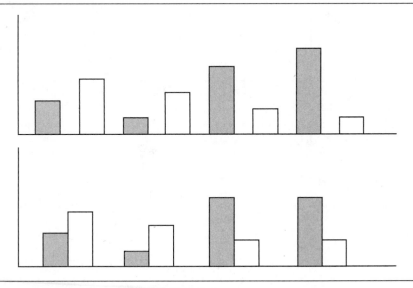

give a much different impression. To avoid giving a biased presentation, most statisticians follow the convention that the height of the y-axis should be about three-fourths the length of the x-axis and then make the appropriate adjustment to the scale increments.

Shades and colors should be planned as well. Light and bright colors jump forward and should be used for emphasis, while darker and more muted colors recede. In cases where multiple colors are not trying to emphasize specific elements, arrange the colors from dark to light. Many colors carry specific connotations—some of which are positive (green signals growth) and some of which are negative (red shows danger). Additional comments about color appear near the end of this chapter.

In using **texture and pattern**, avoid visual distortion by not putting patterns that interact visually, such as diagonal lines in opposite directions, next to each other. Bear in mind that vertical lines make items appear taller whereas horizontal lines make them look shorter.

The goal is to represent data accurately; that is, to achieve graphic integrity. To measure graphical integrity, Tufte uses his lie factor.[4]

$$\text{Lie factor} = \frac{\text{Size of effect shown in graphic}}{\text{Size of effect in data}}$$

For example, if a graph is drawn to exaggerate a bank's financial resources by 50 percent more than the data support (by using a bar that is too large, or a three-

FIGURE 3.2   **Variation in Impact Because of Scale Change**

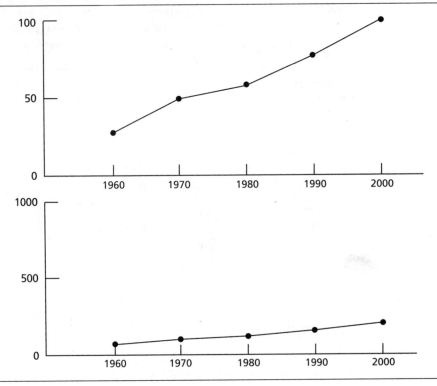

dimensional object rather than a two-dimensional object), the lie factor is 1.5. A 1.0 factor reflects accurate representation.

The debate between the artistic delivery of data regardless of the cost in accuracy versus avoiding a high lie factor at all costs brings out interesting philosophical and artistic questions and arguments.[5] Being aware of these potential pitfalls in both directions is a partial safeguard against major blunders in either direction.

Careful observation of graphics in many prominent newspapers, magazines, and television advertisements will identify lie factors well above 1.0. Sometimes the designer of the graphic did not intentionally mislead but was overwhelmed by the data or became too involved in its presentation.

Keep these four principles—clarity, precision, efficiency, and integrity—in mind as you read the balance of this chapter and as you prepare your illustrations.

TYPES OF VISUALS

Most business visuals fall into one or more of the following categories: tables; graphs; charts, drawings, and diagrams; maps; photographs; and text. This section describes these visuals and suggests how they should be designed.

Tables

Tables present data in words, numbers, or both, usually in columns and rows. While tables are often the least enticing technique visually, they can be the most accurate method. As with most visuals, there are rules or standardized approaches to preparing tables, not all of which are always followed, but of which you should be aware.

- Keep tables as simple as possible. As a table becomes too complicated, consider breaking it into two or more tables.
- If you wish to follow common practice for printed or typed tables, enumerate tables by inserting Arabic numerals above each one.
- Place a descriptive phrase after the table number, such as *Relationship of Income to Expenditures, 2001 to Present.* For a table that accompanies an oral presentation, you may wish to simplify the phrase.
- Place units of time (if included) in a row rather than a column.
- Try to present the data in logical fashion (increasing years, alphabetically, and so on) where the logic is immediately apparent.
- Employ good design techniques, such as ample white space, judicious use of boldface, and appropriate use of shading when designing tables.
- Use the word *Source* and follow it with a bibliographical citation if the data in the table come from a source other than your own primary research. In an oral presentation, you can speak your citation.

See Table 3.1 for a sample table, which shows the standard table format and identifies the parts of a table.

With the widespread use of computerized spreadsheets and printers capable of a variety of visual treatments, many of the long-standing rules for tables prepared with typewriters are fading. Tables now often incorporate different weights of lines (called rules), shading, italic and boldface type, and different sizes of type. Table 3.2 duplicates the data in Table 3.1 to show some of these treatments.

Graphs

Graphs, probably the most widely used visual support, come in many forms. Among the most popular are the line, bar, pictograph, geographic, pie, 3-D, high–low–close, Gantt, and scatter graphs.

TABLE 3.1   **Sample Table**

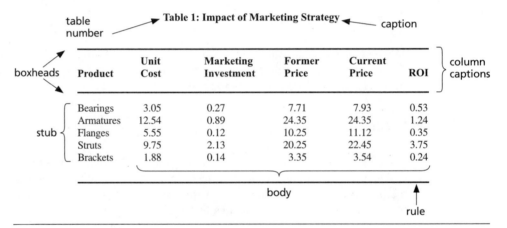

Source: Enter a bibliographic citation or a note explaining the origin of the table if it is not your original work.

TABLE 3.2   **A Table Prepared with a Computerized Spreadsheet**

Table 1: Impact of Marketing Strategy					
Product	*Unit Cost*	*Marketing Investment*	*Former Price*	*Current Price*	*ROI*
Bearings	3.05	0.27	7.71	7.93	0.53
Armatures	12.54	0.89	24.35	24.35	1.24
Flanges	5.55	0.12	10.25	11.12	0.35
Struts	9.75	2.13	20.25	22.45	3.75
Brackets	1.88	0.14	3.35	3.54	0.24

Line Graphs Line graphs plot data on a two-dimensional axis. When a single line is plotted, a trend is shown. Most trends are plotted over time. When more than one line is plotted, comparisons of the trends can be made. Use line graphs to reflect frequencies, percentages, and distributions, and to compare multiple trends.

In designing line (and many other) graphs, keep these thoughts in mind:

- Differentiate between multiple lines by using different techniques, such as solid, dashed, or dotted lines. Use solid lines for the primary data and dashes for secondary data, projections, or extensions. If no obvious primary (or first or most recent) line emerges, make the lowest line the heaviest or the solid line.
- Be wary of having more than four lines; readers become confused with too many lines, especially if they overlap.
- Place time units on the horizontal axis.
- Start the vertical axis with zero and increase in units, without a break, to the top to adhere to graphical integrity.
- Place an Arabic number under the graph and include a title for the graph, also called a figure or illustration. For example, you might label a graph *Figure 3: Mid-level Management Turnover by Year, 2001 to Present.*
- Make sure the plotted line is the heaviest line; the x (horizontal) and the y (vertical) axes should be medium-weight lines; the grid lines, if used, should be the lightest.
- Keep all text in the same plane so that the paper does not have to be rotated to be read. That is, avoid text printed diagonally or angled 90 degrees from the main text.
- Label both the x- and y-axes to identify the individual items on the axis. Thus, the label *Years* would be used for 1998, 1999, 2000, and 2001.
- Make sure to include a legend (or key) when necessary, but keep it unobtrusive. The legend is there to assist in understanding the graph, not to steal attention.
- If you decide to box the graph, do not allow the box to clutter the impression. Use boxes on other graphs in the same presentation for consistency if you place a box on the first graph.
- When selecting a typeface for a graph, try to match the typeface of the text of the report. Keep type sizes consistent—or at least complementary—if possible.

See Figure 3.3 for an example of a multiple-line graph.

Bar Graphs Bar graphs are popular because they can present a variety of information. Their main application is in showing comparisons. A bar typically is two-dimensional, and may be filled with shading or color, and the number the bar represents may be placed on or above the bar. You should be able to move from the top of the bar to the appropriate axis to determine the value that the box represents. A bar that meets these criteria is clear and is not as subject to misrepresentation as three-dimensional bars are.

As you draw bars, keep these guidelines in mind:

- Draw bars so they are wider than the space between them.
- Prepare gridlines so they disappear behind the bars.
- Hold the maximum number of bars to 12.

FIGURE 3.3   **Multiple-Line Graph**

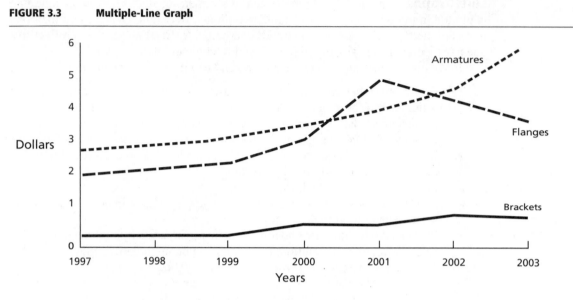

Figure 1: Development Cost History for Three Products

- Draw bars of the same width.
- Arrange the items so that the bars appear in increasing, or perhaps decreasing, order if the x-axis does not show a time element and there is no other logical order to the x-axis items. Be aware, however, of other graphs in the same presentation with the same x-axis items. It is better to have a consistent arrangement of x-axis items across graphs than to modify the x-axis items for each graph to accomplish increasing or decreasing bars.
- When using segmented bar graphs (graphs that divide individual bars into parts), place the largest portion of the bar at the bottom to give a feeling of a low center of gravity. Use dark colors or treatments on low portions for the same reason. Then work in the next largest portion. Avoid conflicting adjacent patterns for the segments.
- Do not use part of the y-axis to form the leftmost bar; there should be some space between the y-axis and the first bar. This space typically is one-half the amount of space between the other bars.
- Make bar graphs more precise by placing numerical values on or above the bars. The numbers should not be obtrusive. If the numbers are to be printed on bars that are black or patterned, they should be positioned within white boxes so that they can be legible.

The bars in bar graphs may be vertical or horizontal—decide which direction to place the bars by first placing the time units on the horizontal axis and then deciding whether you wish to portray a comparison by time (a vertical bar graph) or by another variable (a horizontal bar graph). If there is no time dimension, use a graph that employs vertical bars. Figures 3.4 and 3.5 illustrate vertical and horizontal bar graphs.

FIGURE 3.4   **Vertical Bar Graph**

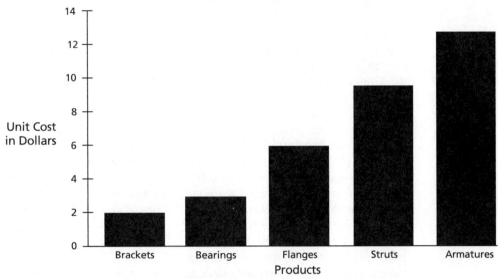

Figure 1: Unit Cost of Five Products

FIGURE 3.5   **Horizontal Bar Graph**

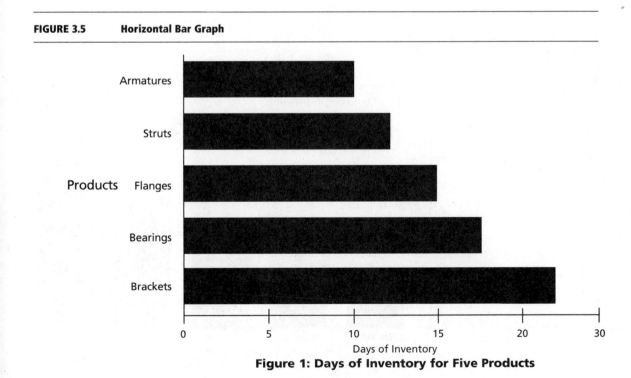

Figure 1: Days of Inventory for Five Products

When you break a single bar into components (which usually total 100 percent), it becomes a segmented bar graph. For example, a whole bar could represent income for 2001, but its segments could break income into taxable and nontaxable income. The bar for each year then would have two parts, each drawn to scale. Usually, the parts are treated in some fashion to differentiate them from each other, possibly using color or shading. The segmented bars may be vertical or horizontal. See Figure 3.6 for a segmented bar graph.

You may wish to group some bars together, especially when they, as a group, do not add up to 100 percent of something. For example, you may wish to compare three of five regions for net profit by year. Thus, you would cluster Regions 1, 2, and 3 as bars on each year. In drawing a clustered bar graph, the clustered bars should touch each other and there should be an equal amount of space between clusters. See Figure 3.7 for an example of this type of bar graph. Compare Figures 3.6 and 3.7. Each bar in Figure 3.6 correctly adds up to 100 percent (marketing investment, R&D cost, and production cost). In Figure 3.7 there are five clusters of three bars each. If the goal is to compare the five products by the three types of costs, this approach is best, since all bars share a common zero point.

When confronted with data that could be either a segmented or a clustered bar graph, ask what is the main purpose of the graph. If it is comparing the sum of the parts, select the segmented bar graph. If, however, comparison of the parts is the primary intent, pick the clustered bar graph. Each type of graph allows the secondary purpose of the alternative analysis.

FIGURE 3.6   **Segmented Bar Graph**

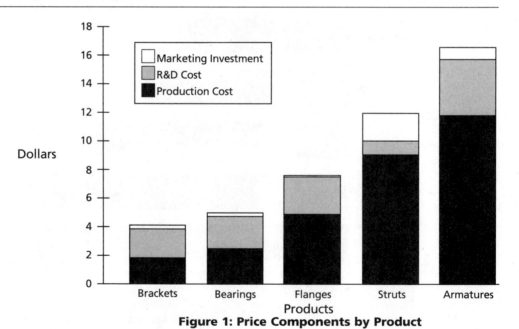

Figure 1: Price Components by Product

FIGURE 3.7   **Clustered Bar Graph**

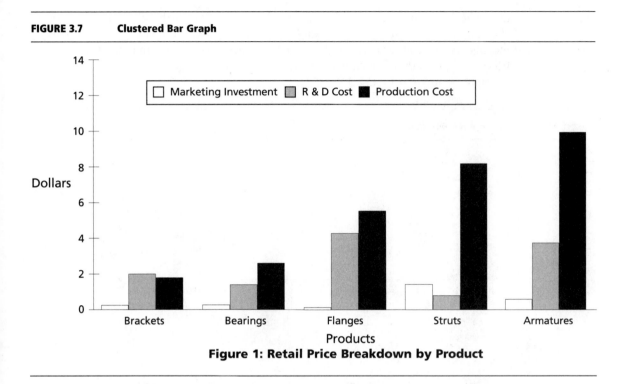

Figure 1: Retail Price Breakdown by Product

Most graphs are drawn in the upper-right quadrant (Quadrant 1) of the intersection of a vertical and a horizontal axis. This quadrant represents the positive half of the vertical line and the positive half of the horizontal line. Sometimes you wish to show negative numbers as well as positive ones, which means you must use more than one quadrant. A bar graph that uses two quadrants, such as the example in Figure 3.8, is a bilateral bar graph.

The reason most bilateral bar graphs use the upper-right and lower-right quadrants is that time is usually a variable, and thus plotted on the x-axis. Therefore, the other variable is the one with positive and negative values.

If there is no inherent order to the sequence of the bars (such as years), apply some order that enhances comparison, such as highest positive to lowest negative, or vice versa. An up-down-up-down approach may be visually pleasing and can stress the fluctuations.

Pictographs A pictograph is somewhat similar to a bar graph. Pictographs usually employ horizontal and vertical axes and plot data for comparison. However, instead of using bars to represent the amounts, symbols are used. For example, a picture of an oil drum might stand for 1,000 barrels of oil. Part of the symbol is used to show a fraction of the amount. Thus, in this example, half of an oil drum would represent 500 barrels of oil. Barrels stacked on top of each other show total amounts. Stacking symbols of equal size is better than increasing the size of just one item to show an increase, because most symbols represent three-dimensional things, and three-dimensional items increase in volume as they increase in height. In other words, showing a one-inch-tall oil barrel and a two-inch-tall barrel to suggest a 100 percent increase is misleading because the actual increase (in volume, and therefore perception) is 16 times that. This misuse greatly affects the lie factor. A correctly drawn pictograph is shown in Figure 3.9.

FIGURE 3.8   **Bilateral Bar Graph**

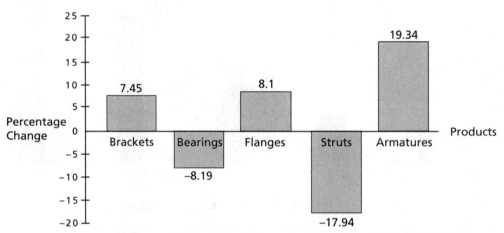

Figure 1: Percentage Change in Five Products' Co, 2000–2001

FIGURE 3.9   **Pictograph**

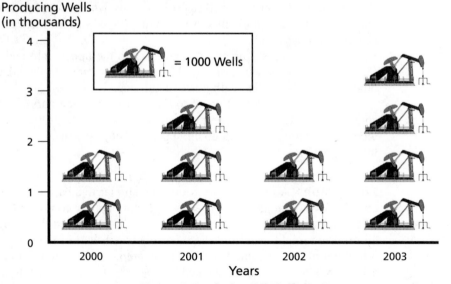

Figure 1: Producing Oil Wells by Year

Occasionally you may see a pictograph with no y-axis. The reasons are that the unit values normally on the y-axis are inherent in the symbol, and that if high accuracy was the intent, probably a bar graph would have been used.

Geographics Another graph that uses pictures—usually maps—is the geographic type. The value of geographic figures is to compare geographic divisions, such as states or regions, on some numeric variable. Sometimes states are enlarged or reduced and shown with other size-varied states to illustrate a quantity of something by state. For example, a geographic for population would reduce the relative size of Montana and enlarge Massachusetts. The intent is not to portray precise cartographic location or distance; that is the venue of maps, which will be discussed soon. A geographic visual is found in Figure 3.10.

Pie Graphs A popular but frequently boring and incorrectly prepared graph is the pie graph. Although commonly referred to as pie graphs or pie charts, note that they are not true graphs or charts. Pie graphs present data as slices of a whole, and the sum of the pieces totals 100 percent. According to William Cleveland,[6] author of *The Elements of Graphing Data*, these wedges are not an effective way to present percentages. His

FIGURE 3.10   Geographic Graph

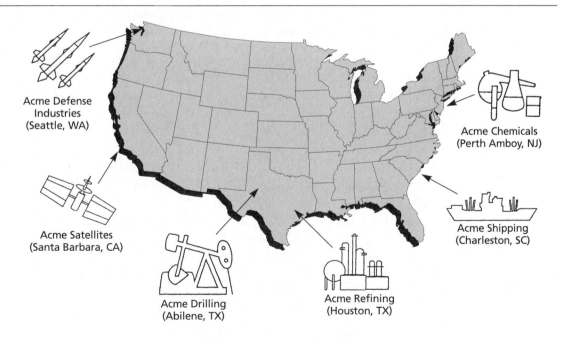

Figure 1: Primary U.S. Holdings

Source: Reproduced with permission from Computer Support Corporation.

research shows that visual perceptions of pie slices are consistently inaccurate. He is also concerned about the problem of labeling narrow slices. Tufte, too, is critical of pie graphs because they do not order numbers along a visual dimension.[7]

Be cautious; many of the computer software packages that facilitate preparation of pie graphs do not follow time-honored pie graphing rules. These rules include:

- Always show 100 percent of something.
- Start at 12 o'clock with the largest slice and move clockwise in descending size. An exception to this rule is to place an Additional or Miscellaneous slice, no matter what its size, as the last slice.
- Use a protractor to draw each slice if you are hand drawing the pie; each 3.6 degrees represents 1 percent.
- Consider using colors or patterns to visually differentiate the slices. Be careful, however, not to clutter the graph.
- Try to limit the number of slices to six. If you have only two or three slices, challenge whether you need the graph at all.
- Use the lightest color for the largest slice and move to progressively darker, smaller slices. Other alternatives are to move from darkest to lightest, or to alternate between light and dark to allow each slice to stand out. See which approach works best.

Try to make your software package agree with the rules above, but also be aware of its capabilities. For example, some packages allow you to "explode" a slice from the rest of the pie for emphasis.

Figure 3.11 shows six pie graph treatments of the same data. The author must decide which of the first four pies best supports the oral or written message; does identification of the slices by product, percent, price, or a combination make the most sense? Notice the uneven exploding of the slices in Treatment D, which starts to misrepresent the data. Going to a 3-D exploded pie, as in Treatment E, introduces some of Tufte's lie factor because the amount of thickness given to the slices is not equal. Treatment F, which exaggerates the 3-D effect, amplifies the lie factor.

3-D Graphs For variety and visual excitement, 3-D graphs are popular. On the other hand, 3-D representations can be misleading and are often difficult to draw. Software can facilitate 3-D graphs, such as the 3-D pie graph shown in Figure 3.12.

High–Low–Close Graphs Especially valuable for financial graphs is the high–low–close graph, such as the *Wall Street Journal* uses. Rather than show a single dot for a dollar amount, the high–low–close graph shows the dots (the high and the low) that indicate a range and are connected with a line. The close may appear as a point on the line between the high and the low. Or, the top of the line is the high, the bottom is the low, and a cross line or dot is the close.

Gantt Graphs The Gantt graph is used for event or production planning and process scheduling, such as for coordinating ordering, delivery, prefabrication, final

FIGURE 3.11   Pie Graphs

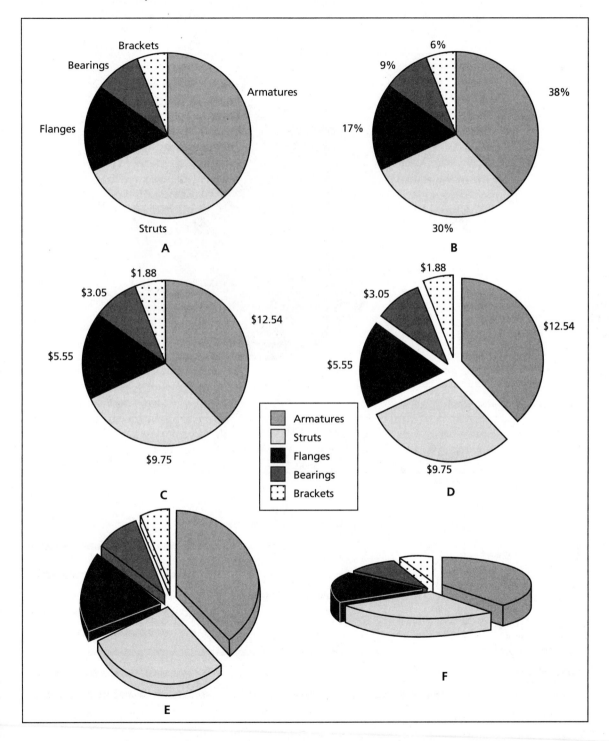

fabrication, packaging, and shipping of a product. Bars on the graph show initiation and completion dates. Many software packages ease the tedious or repetitious burden of preparing Gantt graphs, and their first cousins, PERT graphs. A Gantt graph is shown in Figure 3.13.

FIGURE 3.12   3-D Graph

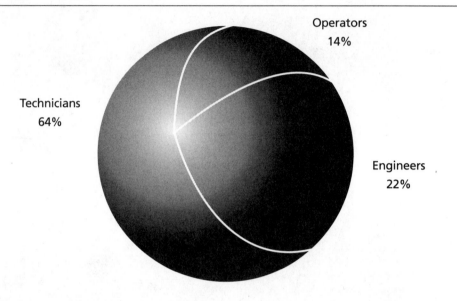

Operators
14%

Technicians
64%

Engineers
22%

FIGURE 3.13   Gantt Graph

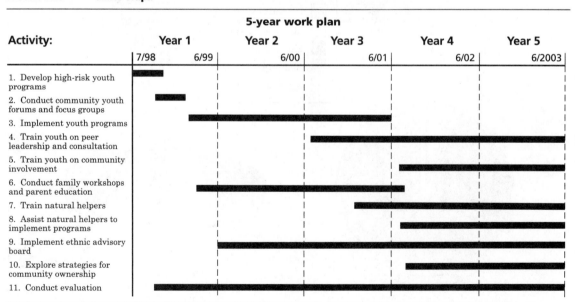

5-year work plan

Activity:	Year 1	Year 2	Year 3	Year 4	Year 5
	7/98 6/99	6/00	6/01	6/02	6/2003
1. Develop high-risk youth programs					
2. Conduct community youth forums and focus groups					
3. Implement youth programs					
4. Train youth on peer leadership and consultation					
5. Train youth on community involvement					
6. Conduct family workshops and parent education					
7. Train natural helpers					
8. Assist natural helpers to implement programs					
9. Implement ethnic advisory board					
10. Explore strategies for community ownership					
11. Conduct evaluation					

Source: Used with permission of Union of Pan Asian Communities.

Scatter Graphs A scatter graph presents dots on a two-dimensional matrix and is most often used with statistical data to show correlations. Lines may be drawn through clusters of dots to show trends or make forecasts.

Charts, Drawings, and Diagrams

Charts, drawings, and diagrams, as opposed to graphs, usually represent less precise data, relationships, and flows of activities.

Charts Charts often depict relationships, such as those in an organization. Within organization charts, solid lines usually connect line personnel and dotted lines link staff personnel. Organization charts show the channels that formal communication should follow. An organization chart appears in Figure 3.14.

FIGURE 3.14   **Organization Chart**

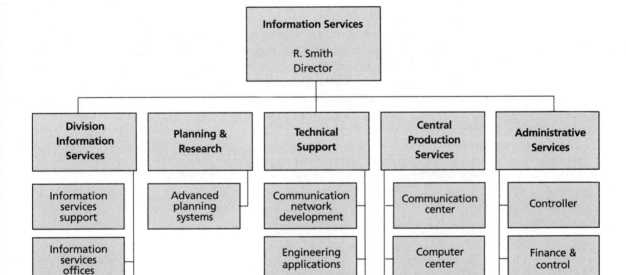

Figure 1: Information Services Structure

Source: Reproduced with permission from Computer Support Corporation.

Bubble charts present data, people, or departments inside circles (or bubbles) and then connect them with various thicknesses of lines to illustrate interrelationships. The size of the circles illustrates the amount of data or department size (see Figure 3.15).

Drawings Drawings are beneficial for accurate representation of images that do not lend themselves to verbal descriptions, such as blueprints and technical drawings. These drawings often use standardized techniques and symbols to facilitate understanding.

Diagrams Diagrams are often drawings, but diagrams usually show a flow between items, such as communication between people or the electrical current in a wiring scheme. Diagrams showing steps in information processing by computer hardware and software are flow charts. Figure 3.16 shows a diagram.

A Venn diagram uses overlapping circles to characterize mutuality and exclusivity. Venn diagrams can quickly illustrate what would often take many words to describe. See Figure 3.17 for a Venn diagram.

Maps

Maps are used when geographical precision is important, as opposed to a geographic graph, which might show a map but have the purpose of showing characteristics by section, such as product penetration by state. Identifying exactly where oil leases are on a piece of property may well call for a map (as well as a legal description of the location). See the map in Figure 3.18.

FIGURE 3.15   **Bubble Chart**

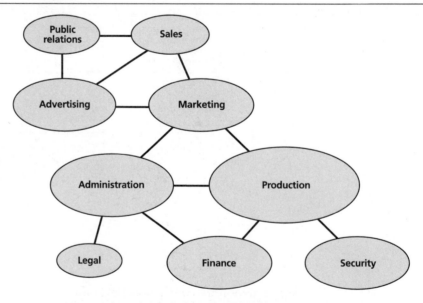

Figure 1: Relative Size of Departments

FIGURE 3.16   Diagram

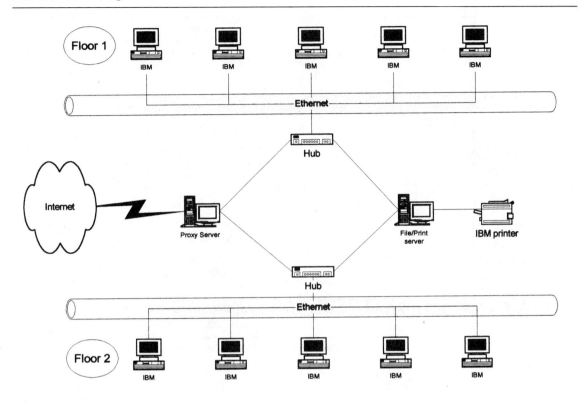

FIGURE 3.17   Venn Diagram

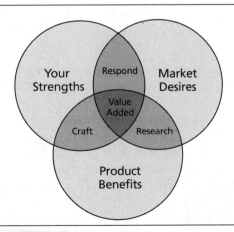

FIGURE 3.18   Map

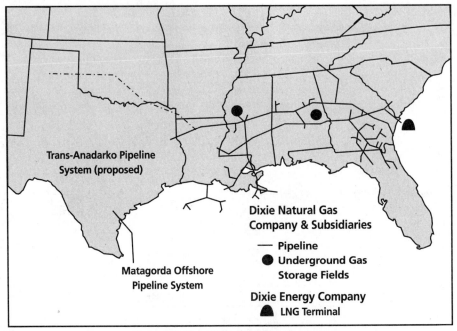

Figure 1: The Dixie Pipeline System

Source: Reproduced with permission from Computer Support Corporation.

Photographs

Most illustrations represent something; photographs often come the closest to representing what they stand for. Few people have the ability to describe a particularly beautiful sunset accurately; a photograph of the sunset can capture much of the emotion elicited by the original occasion. Photographs, then, not only effectively document a visual moment better than words but also improve on other visual means. They can, of course, be accurately duplicated as prints, prepared for print media, or scanned into a computer. A photograph that underscores these thoughts is found in Figure 3.19.

Text

Many visuals transmit only words. Quotes, outlines, and key thoughts are examples of text visuals. Because printed presentations, such as reports, are already heavy with text, text visuals are less likely to be used. In oral presentations, however, text visuals can show the direction of a presentation, give guideposts along the way, and pull together final conclusions. Text visuals can work in unison with the spoken word for emphasis or can stand alone. They are often used in 35 mm slides, overhead projector presentations, and computer slide shows. Figure 3.20 is an example of a text visual.

FIGURE 3.19   **Photograph**

Source: © PhotoDisc, Inc.

FIGURE 3.20   **Text Visual**

Steps in developing text slides

1. Select a background image
2. Select colors for text, back- and fore-ground
3. Type in text
4. Pick a "build" effect
5. Add flourishes as appropriate

Some guidelines for the preparation of text include:

- Use a mixture of capital and lowercase letters to enhance readability.
- Select a simple, readable typeface if possible. Serif typefaces are easier to read than sans serif faces. (Serifs are the little lines on the ends of letters.)
- Select bullets or symbols to make items in a list show up and to clarify relative importance among items.
- Use color, boldface, or large type to differentiate between levels or to make important items stand out.
- Keep the lettering style for titles, legends, tables, and other illustrations consistent.
- Use no more than three type sizes in a single visual. More than three becomes too complicated.

In summary, you can choose from many types of visual support, but you need to know the rules for preparation and design. Learn which support is best for certain types of data; see Table 3.3 for a comparison of the support types by strengths and weaknesses. You also need some common sense. It is easy to allow visual support to become complicated, particularly when you are working with involved data. Figure 3.21 illustrates a complex graph that shows the timed steps of building an ocean-going vessel.

WHEN TO USE VISUAL SUPPORT

As we mentioned before, visual support can improve most written and spoken interpersonal communications. Because visual support has the ability to enhance involvement, understanding, and retention, it is used in written business reports, procedures, statements, proposals, feasibility studies, memos, and letters. Oral communications, such as individual and group presentations, speeches, seminars, training sessions, and briefings also are enriched with visual support.

When should support be used within the oral or written message? As it is needed. Visual support is support, not just entertainment. There are precise moments that call for visual support; those are when to use the visual. However, because visuals do have some value in garnering attention and in breaking up long blocks of text or extended periods of less interesting information, you may be able to position them at a place or time when you need to rouse your audience.

As you decide whether to use visual support with your written or spoken communication, ask yourself these three questions:

1. Does the support increase efficiency?
2. Does the support increase effectiveness?
3. Does the support increase impact?

Efficiency reduces reading or listening time; effectiveness enhances understanding; and impact emphasizes the impression.[8] Your visual support should increase at least one of these qualities. If not, don't use it.

TABLE 3.3   **Visual Support Classification System**

Visual	Strengths	Weaknesses
Table	Shows precise numerical data	Tedious to prepare; slow to show relationships
Graph		
Line	Best for showing trends	Too many lines can be confusing; about 4 lines maximum
Bar	Best for comparisons; can be horizontal, vertical, segmented, clustered, or bilateral	Often incorrectly drawn; about 12 bars maximum
Pictograph	Visually interesting	Can be less immediately obvious than a bar graph; must stack numerous symbols rather than enlarge a single symbol
Geographic	Compares geographic divisions	Not drawn to scale
Pie	Popular; shows comparison of parts that total 100 percent	Wedges can be difficult to compare; too many wedges can be confusing
3-D	Visually exciting	Can be misleading
High–Low–Close	Best for financial data, such as stock prices	Complicated to prepare
Gantt	Excellent for scheduling events	Can be quite large and may need frequent updates
Scatter	Useful for statistical data and comparisons	Tedious; may require special software
Chart	Good for showing relationships; a bubble chart shows relative size or importance	Many items may require a large chart; a bubble chart is quite time consuming to prepare
Drawing	Beneficial for showing accurate representations of images, perhaps with standardized techniques	May require special knowledge or skills to prepare
Diagram	Best for illustrating flows; a Venn diagram efficiently shows overlaps of parts	May not accurately reflect relative importance of parts
Map	Shows geographic data	Relevant data can change over time
Photograph	Excellent for portraying pictures	Requires photographic ability or equipment
Text	Focuses attention on key words or phrases	Requires careful planning
Videotape	Shows motion; captures events, displays color	Requires special equipment to create and exhibit; carries high expectations by audience

FIGURE 3.21   A Complex Graph

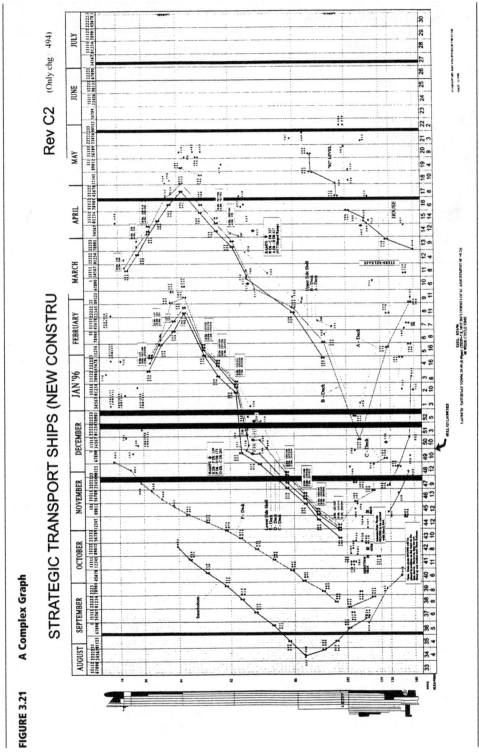

Source: Reprinted courtesy of National Steel and Shipbuilding Company.

Within business reports, illustrations follow their discussion in the text. If an illustration is small—one-half page or less—it may be placed on the same page as text, with the text above or below. Larger illustrations require their own page. A separate page illustration should be placed on the first page following its mention in the text. The text will run on from its mention of the figure to the bottom of the page. The next page will be the illustration, and the page after that picks up the text. If the illustration requires a horizontal display, place it sideways in the report so it is read from the outside edge rather than across the binding. Illustrations also can be placed in appendices at the end of a report. Rules for the preparation of illustrations described in this section apply.

In oral presentations, visuals supplement or complement spoken words. They generally are shown concurrent with verbal descriptions when they are used to explain or illustrate. Visuals may precede oral comment for striking effect or attention value. They may follow a description to emphasize a point or summarize.

Critical skills for effective communication, then, include knowing both the value of visual support and the formal and informal rules for when to use that support. You also need to know the media available to you and how to prepare the support.

MEDIA SELECTION, PREPARATION, AND USAGE

Many media are available for transmitting visual images. Paper handouts, flip charts, overhead transparencies, and slides are the most frequently used visual media. Other popular media include blackboards, electronic blackboards, computers, and videotape.

Paper

By paper, we mean visuals that are prepared for delivery on paper, which probably will be prepared with a computer or typeset for inclusion in reports or used as handouts. Written words often carry a connotation of more formality than spoken words; this feeling of formality is even stronger with typeset words than computer-printed text, though the difference in perception between the two is narrowing. Therefore, if a sense of formality is desired, consider text visuals. Further, printed visuals usually carry the assumption that the audience may keep the paper for documentation or later review. The audience, of course, has the visual in its original form, not one subject to redrawing or interpretation.

One drawback to handing out visual aids prior to a presentation is that you lose control of when and how the audience receives your message. The audience is likely to page forward to sections later in your presentation and may even raise questions about that information before you are ready to discuss it.

Preparation While the cost of black ink on white paper is relatively low, adding color to a visual increases the cost. However, the cost of high-quality color printers and copiers is falling rapidly.

Usage If you use visual support in reports or handouts, number your illustrations. Give them a title that accurately describes the data and their relationships. Visual support should stand alone and require little explanation; the support should be carefully integrated into the presentation. Keep illustrations neat and attractive, but not at the cost of misrepresenting information. Proofread for accuracy. Aim for consistency across illustrations.

Flip Charts

Flip charts are not charts but, rather, large paper tablets. Speakers can mark on the sheets with colored markers and can remove sheets or flip to the next sheet with ease. Flip chart tablets are usually supported on easels and can be moved easily. Expense is minimal, and no special skills are needed. Flip charts can help deal with unanticipated needs, such as recording an audience-developed list.

The impact of flip chart visuals often suffers, however, from incomprehensible writing, too many abbreviations, sloppiness, or audience frustration with someone slow at writing or drawing. Because most tablets are about three feet by two feet, viewers must be relatively close. You can't erase images; mistakes must be redrawn, crossed out, or ignored.

Preparation Speakers can overcome some of the disadvantages of flip charts if they can plan what images will be needed and can draw or print them beforehand. The corners of pages can be coded or stick-on flags can be used so the speaker can quickly flip to the correct sheet. Most audiences do not look unfavorably on this planning step. If there is reason for extemporaneous drawing or writing during a presentation, consider lightly penciling the words or images beforehand on the sheet and then darkening the words during the presentation. Most viewers will not see the pencil marks.

When you prepare text or images in advance of a presentation, consider leaving blank sheets after each prepared sheet. The blank sheets allow you to flip a prepared sheet out of sight, thus redirecting attention back to you. The blank sheet also allows you space to write about your topic during the talk, if the occasion arises, without having to jump to the end of your prepared sheets. For especially dark or bright images, the blank sheet avoids bleed-through, where the image on the next sheet can be seen.

If you prepare your charts beforehand, consider using color. Red catches attention for key words, for example. One source suggests a maximum of three colors per sheet.[9]

Obtain a rather professional impression by making a black-and-white transparency of an image you would like on a flip chart, such as a city skyline or the face of the president. Then project the image on the tablet sheet and trace the image with a marker.

For presentations that will be repeated and that rely on flip charts, consider investing in equipment that creates professional flip chart pages. This equipment can produce enlarged photocopies, laser output, drawings, and text with color images on easel-pad-size paper for about $2 a page.

Until you have substantial experience with flip charts—and perhaps even then—practice giving your oral presentation while using the flip chart to coordinate the delivery of text and visual effectively.

Usage Avoid standing in front of your flip chart, even as you write on it. A pointer can give you distance if necessary. Have a supply of markers available in case colors are unexpectedly needed or a marker runs out of ink. Consider having an audience member do the writing for you, which will free you to lead a discussion. Have plenty of paper available and do not put too much information on a single sheet. Sometimes when sheets are completed, they are posted about the room for re-viewing.

Overhead Transparencies

As the size of an audience grows, so does the need for a larger image. One popular and inexpensive medium is the overhead projector. The projector transmits images from a low-cost transparency to a projection screen. Users find the machine quiet, moveable, and efficient for large audiences. Most organizations have access to overhead projectors.

Preparation For a high-quality black-and-white overhead transparency, start with a black original image on white paper and, from that, make the transparency by one of several methods. In one method, the image is photocopied; then, the transparency film is placed over the photocopy and the pair are run through a transparency-making machine. Many machines use infrared technology. Alternatively, the original can be placed on some photocopiers and transparency film loaded instead of paper. Then the original is transferred directly to the film. Yet another method is to print a computer-prepared visual on a printer that accepts transparency film. This last alternative usually produces the sharpest image of the three techniques.

Computer software packages designed to facilitate presentations ease the burden and much of the expense of preparing overhead transparencies. These packages can automatically put the same border or background color on each visual, sequentially number them, size them appropriately, and allow for easy rearrangement or updating of the visuals. They can incorporate text, symbols, and graphics.

Several options for transparency film exist, including black or color images on clear film and black images on colored film. You can make transparencies of typed or drawn material in minutes with a photocopier, or you can use clear film on which you can write with special pens. If you must prepare or alter a transparency while it is being projected, use the special pens designed for this purpose. These inexpensive pens are available in erasable water-based ink and in permanent ink, both in a variety of colors. Color transparencies from color pictures are available, but they usually suffer in comparison to the originals. Computer programs can create color images and use color printers to print directly onto transparencies.

Key your colors in a series of transparencies to your main topics. Perhaps you will use blue for major topics and green for subthoughts. In this way your audience has a better feel for where you are in the presentation. Used effectively, color can accelerate learning, improve comprehension, and reduce errors. It can attract attention, create moods, and add vitality. You may wish to select colors based on their association in Western culture.

White	for clarity, purity
Red	for stop, hot, or danger
Yellow	for caution, happiness
Green	for growth, money
Dark blue or purple	for royalty

But be careful if your audience includes non-Western cultures; your colors may have different meanings elsewhere.

Some uses of color are to

- Emphasize words or lines
- Distinguish between parts of an illustration
- Show before-and-after changes[10]

To avoid mismatched foreground colors and background colors, apply the information in Table 3.4.

Transparencies carrying text often have too much text. Use the 7 by 7 rule for text transparencies: limit the number of words per line to seven and the number of lines per page to seven. Another guideline regarding the size of transparency images is to step away from the screen about eight times the distance from the projector to the screen to see if you can read the text. If you cannot, your image size should be increased.

For text transparencies, aim for consistency. For example, your template for a series of transparencies might include main titles in 36-point Helvetica type in all capitals; subpoints could be 24-point Times Roman in capital and lowercase letters, appearing after bullets.

Consider adding overlays to your transparencies. In this case, the transparency is encased in a frame, and the overlays are then attached to the frame; they are then folded over the main transparency as needed. You may have three or four overlays on one transparency. Overlays may add bars to a bar graph, lines to a line graph, or images to a map. What is added by the overlay can be in color by using transparent colored film. As we will see in the section on computerized slides to follow, this process can be much more professionally delivered with a computer if the equipment is available.

TABLE 3.4   Guides for Color Selection

Background Color	Lettering Color (most readable to least readable)
Light	Black, blue, violet, red, green, orange, yellow
Dark	White, yellow, orange green, red, blue, violet

Source: Minnesota Western Visual Support Systems, 1991, p. 202.

Usage Most users of overhead projectors quickly master the idiosyncrasies of the machine: move the transparency up to raise the image on the screen, but move it to the left to move the image to the right and vice versa. Most machines have an on–off or off–low illumination–high illumination switch and a knob for focusing the image. As the importance of the presentation increases, so does the need to have a spare bulb or an additional projector; some machines have a spare bulb in an alternate socket inside them.

Learn the correct use of the projector. Follow these guidelines:

- Place the transparency on the projector and then turn on the projector.
- Turn off the projector after the transparency has made its point or move to the next transparency.
- Try to switch from one transparency to the next quickly, since the projector is projecting light. If, however, you need to make comments before the next transparency, turn off the projector, remove the transparency, place the next one, comment, then turn on the machine.
- Consider using relevant clip art to spice up your transparencies. Possibilities include a corporate logotype, cartoon characters, or drawings of computers or people. The art should be related to the topic.
- Avoid or minimize looking at the projector glass or projection screen. Know the content of the transparency and be able to discuss it without relying on it too much. Keep to a minimum the time you spend reading what your audience can read for themselves.
- Consider pointing to items in a list or locations in a table or figure as you discuss them. Consider using a pen or pencil on the transparency surface as a pointer or using a pointer at the projection screen if you deem that sort of focus is needed.
- Consider using cardboard frames for your transparencies. Tape the frame on top of the transparency—that keeps the transparency as close as possible to the glass. Write notes to yourself on the frames—they cannot be seen by the audience. The order of presentation can be written on the frames too.
- Use a sheet of paper to keep the transparency from being projected and then remove the sheet a bit at a time to disclose your points, such as items in a list. If you place the paper between the glass and the transparency, you will be able to read the portion of the transparency yet to be uncovered.
- If you are right-handed, try to have the projector to your right as you face your audience so that you minimize blocking views when you write on or point to transparencies. This technique also improves your eye contact with the audience.

35 mm Slides

Another popular way to support oral presentations is with 35 mm slides. Slides convey a variety of information, including texts, graphs, and pictures. The slide can be the focal point of the presentation or can support a topic. A drawback to using slides is the requirement that the room be darker than for most other presentations.

One value of a slide presentation that may escape some presenters is its professional image. A study by the 3M Company and the University of Minnesota found that using 35 mm slides for graphics caused viewers to perceive the presentation as more professional.[11] With a potential for improving your image, careful planning should go into a slide presentation.

Preparation Text messages on slides follow the same guidelines as those for textual overhead transparencies, including the 7 by 7 rule.

As you prepare your slides, make a few black slides. These can be used in lieu of shutting off the projector during the presentation and are especially valuable when you are using multiple projectors simultaneously and wish to black out one projector.

Consider preparing the 35 mm-sized images with a computer presentations software package (as will be discussed soon). Then either mail or electronically transmit the file to an imaging firm that can create your 35 mm slides for you.

In planning your presentation, consider the possibility of outlining your talk for the audience with key words. First, prepare a slide (or slides) with the outline of your talk. Show only major topics. Perhaps you will have seven main topics, ranging from an introduction through conclusions. In addition to the master slide of your outline, make eight more copies. Pick a background color, such as blue, and a foreground color, such as orange. For the first slide, color all words orange. For the next, color the first heading (Introduction) orange and the rest red. Continue through the rest of the slides, moving down the outline. Conclude with another copy of the entire outline in orange on blue as a summary. In presenting your talk, first show your (orange) outline. Then, when you begin the Introduction, show the slide with that heading highlighted in orange. Continue to show your audience, as you progress through your talk, where you are. In between these slides, insert additional slides, as required. The result: a highly structured, clear presentation that will be remembered.

Because even single projector presentations can become complicated, you may find valuable a storyboarding technique that shows the coordination of slides and voice. If you are using two or more projectors and add music, the storyboard becomes a necessity in planning and a benefit in delivery. Figure 3.22 is a storyboard for a single projector presentation, and Figure 3.23 shows a storyboard for a more complicated presentation.

In planning your slide presentation, keep in mind that your audience grasps the point of a slide quickly. Change your slides often. A two-projector, five-minute presentation might easily consume 100 or more slides.

Usage Learn the operation of the projector well before your presentation; know how to focus, how to advance and reverse slides, and how to replace a bulb. Also pay attention to how the slides enter the projector. Many presentations have fallen victim to slides entered backwards or upside down. Look into increasingly sophisticated presentations as your needs grow, such as multiple projectors, fading in and out, and coordination with music or narration on several screens.

FIGURE 3.22   Single Projector Storyboard

TITLE: CABLEVISION: THE INSIDE STORY	Page 1 of 12
VISUAL	AUDIO

VISUAL:

text slides have blue background

CABLEVISION

The Inside Story

HORIZON

CABLEVISION

AUDIO:

Music is *"Stargazer"*

0:12   (time of frame)

Cable television has evolved with telecommunications and satellite technological advancements to the point where, today, 42 million people in the United States enjoy cable service.

0:12   (total time)

0:15

This program is presented by Horizon Cablevision to familiarize you with how this technology works and what it offers our community.

0:27

Source: Courtesy of Mark Baird.

FIGURE 3.23   Double Projector Storyboard

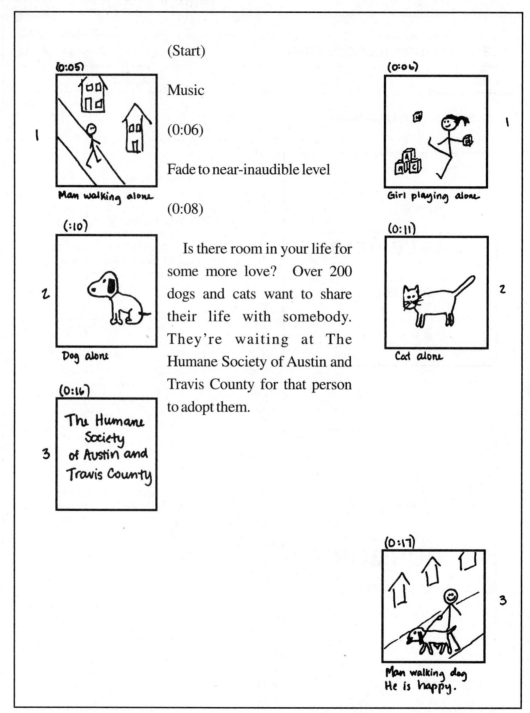

(Start)

Music

(0:06)

Fade to near-inaudible level

(0:08)

    Is there room in your life for some more love? Over 200 dogs and cats want to share their life with somebody. They're waiting at The Humane Society of Austin and Travis County for that person to adopt them.

Source: Courtesy of Laura Nichols.

Blackboards

Blackboards, now available in many forms, have many strengths. They are flexible, usually placed to be viewed by the entire audience, and can be changed easily. Colors add clarity and are especially easy to use with white boards.

Preparation Boards require little preparation beyond erasing them before use and perhaps putting complicated images or long passages on the board before a meeting. Make sure there are erasers and plenty of chalk or fresh markers.

Usage Boards are usually used to put information in front of an audience as it is generated by a speaker or from a discussion. In the haste of writing on the board and with an audience watching, many people write poorly. Take the time to write legibly. Avoid standing in front of what you are writing and what you have written. Erase unimportant messages. If what is being developed on the board requires dissemination, ask someone to take notes and duplicate them later.

Audio teleconferencing with eight to ten participants at each location has recently emerged as a mode of communication superior to a telephone conference call. Among the apparatus that enhance audio teleconferencing are a microphone that picks up only one voice at a time and the teleconferencing blackboard. Typically, two remote locations are connected by telephone lines, and each may have the teleconferencing blackboard and a television monitor. What is written on either board appears on both monitors simultaneously. Thus, as one group develops a forecasting model on the board, the second group can see it and modify it.

Yet another form of the blackboard is the electronic blackboard. This board is usually a white board that requires markers. Information that appears on the board can, at the touch of a button, be sent to a built-in photocopier. On some models, the screen rotates so that the message then appears on the back side, and a clean screen appears to the audience. Again, the touch of a button returns the first side to the front.

Computerized Visuals

Computers have emerged as a quick, easy, and inexpensive way to develop messages for other media, such as overhead transparencies. They have also become a medium unto themselves. In retail stores, training situations, displays, shopping mall kiosks, classrooms, and laboratories, computers present a programmed series of "slides" on computer screens. Such slide shows can be especially beneficial in business presentations. Readily available presentation software, a portable computer, and a computer-image projection system now combine to form a portable unit capable of flashy, professional messages.

The type of computerized presentation in which the presenter prepares a series of slides, adds photos, graphs, arrows, or clip art, incorporates fancy transitions from slide to slide, and adds movement by building a list item-by-item is so common that it is expected from many businesspeople and classroom instructors. Software packages such as PowerPoint facilitate development of professional, colorful, and stimulating presentations. Further discussion of these presentations appears in Chapter 10. To be consistent with the discussions of other forms of visual support preparation and usage already delivered, we do highlight some suggestions here.

Preparation Most computer slide presentations require developing a series of slides and then ordering and timing the slides. Individual slides may include text, graphs, still pictures, clip art, sound, video, or any combination. To develop text slides, follow these steps:

1. Select a background image and slide layout (template).
2. Select colors for text, foreground, and background.
3. Type in the text in outline form.
4. Pick a "build" effect for emerging items in a list.
5. Add flourishes, such as clip art or graphs, as appropriate.
6. Choose a transition to the next slide.

Clip art picture or symbol libraries, which may be part of a presentation software package or a stand-alone package, supply popular or difficult-to-draw pictures, old photos, cartoons, or audio or video clips. A user can search the library for a desired picture, select the picture, enlarge or reduce it, and add shading or patterns if desired. Libraries can be specialized, such as for computers or new technology (see Figure 3.24). Of course, huge amounts of supporting images, sounds, and motion can be found on the World Wide Web. As long as the addition is not gimmicky, the addition of a well-known voice saying something relevant or of a striking photo can add a professional feel.

When deciding which addition to use, ensure that it relates to your topic, matches the mood, and is compatible with other art and slides in your presentation.

Other hints for preparing computerized slide presentations include

- Consider having a blank slide in a single color with no images as your first slide.
- Start with a title slide.
- Consider a text slide with the outline of your presentation.
- Use graphs to help in visualizing tabular data.
- Select charts, diagrams, or photos for variety.
- Consider an occasional one-, two-, or three-word text slide for impact.
- Avoid too many text slides with lists.
- Each slide should have one—and only one—dominant visual effect which provides a starting point for the audience's eyes.
- Use color creatively.
- Add a conclusions slide that pulls together the main topic of the presentation.
- Seek a feeling of consistency for the entire presentation.
- End with a blank slide like your first one, or one that says "thank you" or "Questions?"[12]

Usage Computerized slide shows can demand attention, manage the information flow, and create a professional tone. However, they can also be boring, disorganized, or plagued by technical problems. Here are some usage suggestions:

FIGURE 3.24   **Clip Art**

- Keep the attention upon yourself and let the presentation support what you have to say; don't be left out of your own presentation.
- Be unobtrusive in your computer interaction during the presentation.
- Consider putting the presentation in automatic mode in which each slide (and even each item in a list) is assigned a specific and predetermined amount of exposure time.
- Don't leave simple, one-, two-, or three-word impact slides on the screen too long.
- Avoid reading what appears on the screen to the audience; paraphrase the thought.
- Consider using a remote control to forward (and perhaps reverse) the slides.
- Use the "rehearsal" option in some software to practice and perfect your timing.
- Explore the Internet for fresh templates, drawings, or photos, often at no cost.
- Anticipate problems. Consider having a backup of your presentation already prepared as 35 mm slides or overhead transparencies. The more important the presentation, the more crucial the backup.

Videotape

In the past 25 years, videotape usage has moved from an expensive, moderate-quality, black-and-white image to an inexpensive, high-quality, color image. Professional color cameras and studio-quality productions are still expensive, but the handheld camera and individual videotapes have become inexpensive. Many firms, such as travel agencies, real estate brokers, and producers of computer software distribute free videotapes of their products or services. As with other media, videotapes as part of business presentations require planning and experience.

PLANNING AND EXECUTION

Table 3.5 compares the seven media just discussed and lists their strengths and weaknesses.

The visual and verbal portions of a presentation should support each other as part of one package.

1. Define your topic. As discussed in the chapters on making presentations and delivering case analyses, you must first determine what topic you will be addressing.
2. Determine audience characteristics. Find out about your audience (characteristics, attitudes, and so on), and what they expect from your presentation. How are they likely to respond?
3. Set learning objectives or goals. What do you want your presentation to accomplish? Awarding of a contract, development of a new product, expan-

TABLE 3.5   **Media Selection Guide**

Medium	Audience Size	Formality	Strengths	Weaknesses	Cost
Paper	No limit	Formal	Inexpensive, flexible	Preparation required	Inexpensive
Flip charts	10–15	Informal	Inexpensive, flexible	Can be hard to read	Inexpensive
Overhead transparencies	100	Informal	Inexpensive, focuses attention	Easy to misuse; poor presentation skills	Inexpensive
Slides	Several hundred	Formal	Strong impact	Dark room required; preparation required	Moderately expensive
Blackboards	15–25	Informal	Inexpensive, flexible	Color seldom used effectively	Inexpensive
Computers	3–5 at a time (without projection capability)	Informal	Current, flexible, easy to use	Expensive; can appear childish	Expensive for hardware; software inexpensive
	100 (with projection) multi-media capable	Either	Focuses attention, flexible,	Takes time and expertise	Projection system can be expensive
Videotape	15–25 with single monitor	Varies with topic	Shows motion, can be quite professional	Limited audience size; no interaction	Can be expensive

sion into a new market, or expanding of personnel? The information should be geared toward accomplishing observable, measurable objectives.

4. Prepare the verbal content of the presentation. Many people prefer to outline their verbal presentation first.

5. Add the visual support. Add visual support where it would enhance your verbal presentation.

6. Pretest the package. Run through your presentation to make sure it is clear and accomplishes your goals. Practicing an oral presentation with all components in place, including the visual support, avoids awkward fumbling at a meeting. Bring in peers for their reactions and modify as necessary.

7. Execute your presentation. Deliver your report, presentation, or case analysis.

8. Evaluate your performance. How well did you do? What could have been improved if you had it to do over? What did you learn? Did some things work especially well?

SOME ADDITIONAL HINTS

Here are some additional hints to help improve your visual support.

Color

Adding color to chalkboards, handouts, 35 mm slides, computerized slide shows, or overhead transparencies can grab the audience's attention and, if used correctly, increase comprehension and understanding. However, colors can also detract from the message and even confuse or offend the viewer. In addition to the earlier comments about color, keep these hints in mind:

- Match the color to the presentation and to the audience. Members of the board of directors expect different colors than would be appropriate at a Cub Scout meeting or a garage sale announcement.
- Arrange heavier colors, such as blues and greens, at the bottom of illustrations, if possible, and move upward to lighter colors.
- Use colors in moderation. Limit the total number of colors to six.
- Select bright colors for special effects.
- Pick contrasting colors to set ideas apart.
- Choose shades of the same color to group items.
- Be aware of cultural differences in meanings of color.

Simplicity

Whether you prepare a graphical design, a text chart, or an entire presentation, keep it simple. Too many colors, too much clutter, excessive words, too many bars or pie slices, or too many numbers overwhelm the viewer. In a study by the University of Minnesota on graphics, researchers learned that the simple presentation works best.[13] As computers increasingly are used to design illustrations, it becomes easy to add textures, patterns, and colors to graph bars and slices, but be wary. Tufte refers to the overabundance of visual distinguishers as "chartjunk."[14] Most of the figures in this chapter represent simple presentations.

Repress the desire to fill an illustration with too much information. Use graphs to show trends and rely on tables when specificity is needed. As the data become more complicated, consider a series of graphs to depict the information.

Professionalism

The quality of the visual images supporting your oral presentations will enhance or detract from your professional image. Therefore, in addition to presenting data accurately, make sure it looks good. When the message is an important one and the visuals are not satisfactory, call in experts. Be aware, however, that many artists, designers, and media technologists are not familiar with the principle of visual integrity; you must make sure that the final image is appropriate and not just professional looking.

In oral presentations, it is important to keep your talk moving; all too often, the visuals become the centerpiece instead of support. If a lot of time must be spent discussing a single illustration, it probably should have been distributed prior to the talk.

Visuals are no place for misspellings, too much jargon, too many acronyms, or heavy reliance on passive voice. Further, ensure both word and nonword elements do not embarrass, belittle, or ridicule any member of the audience.

The Environment

Before making your presentation, become familiar with the environment. You should learn about the equipment and the availability of backup bulbs, chalk, computers, and projectors. Know the location of electrical outlets, light switches, microphone outlets, and controls for lowering and raising screens and adjusting amplifier volumes. You need to plan ahead if extension cords or three-prong adapters are needed. You may also need to arrive early to arrange chairs, erase blackboards, distribute handouts, or set up screens or flip charts.

You may also wish to know the location of the controls for dimming lights or adjusting air conditioners. Dimmed lights can focus attention on the screen even if darkness is not required. You may also need to know how to adjust window blinds to darken a room. An overheated meeting room distracts your audience; consider lowering the room's temperature just before the meeting begins. Conversely, a noisy ventilation system also can detract from your presentation. In that situation, cool the room first and then shut off the system for your talk.

Business Graphics Checklist

Sometimes the best way to ensure that you are abiding by the many rules for the preparation of business graphics is to follow a checklist. One such checklist, prepared by the Information Center Institute, appears in Figure 3.25.

FIGURE 3.25   The Information Center Institute Checklist for Justifying Business Graphics

The Information Center Institute Checklist for justifying business graphics

Computer graphics cover a lot of ground—business, engineering, manufacturing, medicine, and the arts. And the software applications to accomplish the various tasks in these fields are burgeoning at an ever-increasing rate.

The question now no longer seems to be will computer graphics help the business organization, but how much will they help and how will we measure it? In other words, how can we justify the increased use of computer graphic systems? What questions should be asked in order to start the justification process for the use of these systems? The following checklist is designed as a way to begin thinking about this process. A careful definition and understanding of needs will go a long way toward providing the information needed for justifying these graphics systems.

After determining user attitudes, especially those of management, the types of graphics needed for your situation, and the measurable and nonmeasurable costs and benefits, you will be much better prepared for the process of justifying the purchases of new graphics systems or the improvement of existing ones, and better equipped to decide on the kinds of hardware and software systems that you will need.

Note: For analysis, the estimates of the costs as well as the benefits should be divided into two categories: one-time and recurring.

No.	Item	Yes	No	N/A	Comments
	Management Attitudes				
1.	Is management interested in graphic rather than tabular presentations for decision-making tasks?				
2.	Is management comfortable with graphic presentations for spotting trends and making forecasts?				
3.	Is management satisfied with the quality, scale, and accuracy of graphs produced in the past?				
4.	Will management place a value on the availability of better graphics?				
	Use of Graphics Systems				
5.	Are business graphics desired primarily for: a. presentation of information for discussion and decision? b. summary and display of large quantities of information?				
6.	Are graphics applications already used for: a. observing statistical relationships and variable interactions? b. display of engineering results and designs?				
7.	Is there interest in image generation for: a. visualization of planned objects? b. illustration of presentation slides? c. eye-catching figures to include in presentations?				
8.	Have cost comparisons been made for: a. microcomputer-generated graphics? b. mainframe-generated graphics? c. graphics produced by specialized hardware? d. hand-generated graphics for comparison?				

FIGURE 3.25   Checklist for Justifying Business Graphics (Concluded)

No.	Item	Yes	No	N/A	Comments
	Uses of Graphics Systems cont'd.				
9.	Have costs been analyzed for downloading prepared files to minicomputers or microcomputers for graphic production?				
10.	Will the graphics costs be absorbed by information services or charged back to the users?				
11.	Have cost calculations for any software included the cost of needed modifications and extensions? Is the price of the graphics package competitive with similar packages when modifications and extensions are considered?				
12.	Are the total costs, including extra features, modifications, and maintenance, likely to remain within the budget limitations for the next three years?				
13.	Will overall costs be lowered by: a. reducing graphics production expenses? b. reducing graphics maintenance expenses? c. reducing manual effort and clerical expenses? d. reducing communications expenses?				
14.	Will controlling production costs reduce operational expenses?				
15.	Will there be faster turnaround for clients at same or reduced costs?				
16.	Will certain costs be avoided by: a. making personnel available for other work? b. employing fewer people for graphics production?				
17.	Can profit increases be estimated for: a. providing graphics for management? b. providing graphics for customers/clients? c. providing faster reaction and turnaround times? d. Improving the use of resources?				
	Intangible Benefits				
18.	Is there value in reducing errors that result in the manual production of graphics?				
19.	Is there value in having more checks and controls on designs and displays?				
20.	Are there operational cost advantages in the sharing of graphical information between files?				
21.	Are there operational cost advantages in improved planning and scheduling through the use of graphics?				
22.	Can a value be estimated for the reduction of problems and complaints?				
23.	Is there a business advantage in the improved timeliness of graphics production?				
24.	Can financial benefits be estimated for: a. improved business analysis? b. improved business control? c. improved responsiveness to customers?				

Source: Information Center Institute, a division of Chantico Publishing Co., Inc.

SUMMARY

In many ways, visual support can have a greater impact than the spoken or written communication it assists. However, you need to know how to correctly use visual support to make it valuable. Support should be clear, precise, and efficient and reflect integrity with what it represents. Knowledge of design considerations such as emphasis, unity, balance, scale, shade and color, and texture and pattern improves the process. You also need to know the type of visuals from which to select. Major types include tables; graphs; charts, drawings, and diagrams; maps; photos; and text. Each has rules for its preparation.

Some people overuse or misuse visual support. To test your decision on including support, ask yourself whether it is efficient and effective and creates impact. Valuable support should accomplish at least one of these three goals.

Presenters can choose from many media for oral and written delivery: paper, flip charts, overhead transparencies, slides, blackboards, computers, and videotapes. A system of planning and evaluation will assist your execution, as will review of the hints that conclude this chapter.

Applications

1. Create a visual aid that effectively gets across this message: "40 percent of the state's air pollution comes from 10 percent of the cars."

2. Using a computerized presentation program, create slides using builds and transitions. Try to include treatments that will hold interest without being overly glitzy. Discussion point: Where is the optimal point for a computerized slide show between bland on one hand and so glitzy on the other that the audience doesn't pay attention to the message?

3. Prepare a simple table containing data typical of your needs or of your familiarity with some topic. Put the data into a common spreadsheet format, such as Lotus 1-2-3. Now import the data into as many graphics software packages as you can. Output the data in the same form, such as a segmented bar graph, from each of them. Evaluate the outputs. Which have the lowest lie factors? How many forced you to change the default settings to avoid lying? Which were the easiest to use?

4. Use the Internet to obtain sample computerized slide shows. Compare the various products for entertainment, clarity, and ease of use. Which are best? Why?

5. Consider this statement: People 18 to 24 now want to live to 88, people 45 to 54 now want to live to 93, and people over 75 want to live to 96. Prepare a single illustration that quickly and completely captures the concept.

6. Prepare a supporting visual that makes the following point: "Research indicates that the amount of time spent in athletic exercise extends a person's life by about the amount of time spent exercising."

DISCUSSION QUESTIONS

1. Why is visual support so important?
2. What are the principles for the preparation of visual support?
3. What are the design considerations of visual support?
4. What is the lie factor?
5. What are the major types of visuals?
6. What are the similarities and differences between tables and graphs?
7. What are the main types of graphs?
8. How do you determine whether to use visual support?
9. What are the eight steps in planning and executing a presentation that is supported visually?

NOTES

1. David L. Wilcox, "The Boom in Business Graphics," *PC Magazine*, May 1985, pp. 282–287.
2. Edward R. Tufte, *The Visual Display of Quantitative Information*, Graphic Press, Cheshire, Connecticut, 1983, p. 51.
3. Dona Z. Meilach, "The Do's and Don'ts of Presentation Graphics," *PC Week*, August 6, 1985, pp. 47–50.
4. Tufte, *The Visual Display of Quantitative Information*, pp. 57–58.
5. See, for example, the parallel interviews in *Aldus* magazine, "Saying It with Images: An Interview with Edward Tufte," 2, no. 4, May–June, 1991, pp. 27–56, and "The Picturing of Information: A Conversation with Nigel Holmes," 2, no. 6, September–October, 1991, pp. 18–55. A more lengthy delivery of Tufte's views is found in Edward R. Tufte, *Envisioning Information*, Graphic Press, Cheshire, Connecticut, 1990.
6. Marilyn Stoll, "Charts Other Than Pie Are Appealing to the Eye," *PC Week*, March 25, 1986, pp. 138–139.
7. Tufte, *The Visual Display of Quantitative Information*, p. 178.
8. Robert Lefferts, *Elements of Graphics: How to Prepare Charts and Graphs for Effective Reports*, Harper & Row, New York, 1981, p. 5.
9. "Low-Tech Training," *Workforce Training News*, April 1995, pp. 13–16.
10. Minnesota Western Visual Support Systems, 1991, pp. 200–204.
11. Cheryl J. Goldberg and Gerard Kunkel, "Charting a Course Through Graphics Software," *PC Magazine*, March 10, 1987, pp. 113–117.
12. Robert T. Grauer and Maryann Barber, *Exploring Microsoft PowerPoint for Windows 95, Version 7.0*, Prentice Hall, Upper Saddle River, New Jersey, 1996.
13. Mary-Beth Santarelli, "The Zen of Business Graphics," *Information Center* 2, no. 11, November 1986, pp. 42–47.
14. Tufte, *The Visual Display of Quantitative Information*, pp. 107–121.

Written Communication

4

A Process for Advanced Writing

Effective writing has certain characteristics. Some of these characteristics relate to the overall writing process, such as conceptualizing, researching, drafting, and revising. Other characteristics focus specifically on formal features, such as organization, tone, and readability. In this chapter, we will examine both of these approaches to the writing process.

THE OVERALL WRITING SEQUENCE

You may be surprised to know how many people start writing without knowing where they are heading. Perhaps the assumption is that they will figure out their direction as they wander through various thoughts. In order to achieve efficiency and clarity of writing, however, avoid this method.

Most writing goes through many steps. Usually, the more complicated, lengthy, or important the project, the more steps you include. Here are the eight steps through which most of your written communications will go. The order is typical; however, you may relocate some steps.

1. Define your problem.
2. Determine and analyze your audience.
3. Do your research.
4. Consider your layout and elements.
5. Draft your project.

6. Revise, edit, and proof the written copy.
7. Produce the finished package.
8. Conduct a post-writing evaluation.

At various times in your college and business careers, you will probably place more effort or emphasis on some of these steps than on others. For example, as a first-year composition student, you may have wrestled with finding a topic and defining it. Later in college, you no doubt prepared a paper that called on you to do research. As a middle manager, you may not prepare the finished version of a report, which upper managers do, but you write the initial draft. As a top manager, you will revise and edit the work of others. Nevertheless, each of these steps plays an important part in effective business writing, and each deserves examination.

Define Your Problem

When a superior gives you a writing project, you probably know the parameters you are to cover. No doubt you have a specific goal. You may even have a formal letter of authorization. Occasionally, however, your assignment will be vague. For example, how would you react to these written directions from your boss if you were in the management consulting division of a major public accounting firm?

> Sorry not to be able to give you more lead time, but by the time you read this I'll be in Madrid working on a hot project. This trip will keep me from completing the proposal for Nelson National Bank that's due this Friday. I've been working on it alone, although Bill and Tracy supplied some data. I want you to finish it and submit it to Nelson by the deadline. This package could be quite lucrative for us now and in the long term.
>
> In the attached folder are most of the supporting materials and my text so far. My secretary Phyllis typed and formatted a proposal something like this once before, and you can ask her to work on this one.
>
> Wish I could be more available to help you on this. See you a week from Wednesday.

Your assignment is to prepare the proposal. To know how to accomplish that, however, you need to know topic-oriented answers to questions such as these:

- What are we proposing?
- What (and who) is Nelson National Bank?
- What level of profit do we seek now and in the future?
- What is the time period reflected by the proposal?

In determining your approach, you'll also want to know:

- How would your boss write the proposal?
- How badly does your boss want the contract?

Answers to these questions would guide you in approaching this assignment. Clearly, you would be wise to know your direction before you start writing.

Determine and Analyze Your Audience

To whom will the letter, report, or memorandum be sent? Will it be sent to a group? Will it be shared with others? What is your relationship to your audience? The answers to these and other questions may determine the response you receive to what you send.

As you identify your audience, here are some factors to consider:

- What is their position in the hierarchy and how does it relate to you? Subordinates write differently to superiors than superiors write to subordinates. Yet another approach is needed when writing to peers. Messages downward are often authoritative or motivational in tone, while those going upward may have a softer tone. When you share information with peers, you often do so (1) cautiously if you are protecting yourself or (2) quite openly if you anticipate an enthusiastic response. Also, be aware of whether the audience is inside or outside the organization. Messages going outside the organization differ from internal messages by being more formal.

- What medium is best for your audience? Skilled communicators are able to match the message to the medium from the audience's viewpoint. Some media are perceived as formal (scholarly thesis) or informal (comic book), others are quick (spontaneous meeting in the hall) or slow (printed annual report), personal (face-to-face discussion) or impersonal (to whom it may concern letter), friendly (Christmas party) or stern (disciplinary interview). Many other characteristics exist as well. Should the message be written or spoken? If it is to be written, for example, would a facsimile, e-mail, memo, letter, report, or printed document be best? See if you can match the messages to the media in Table 4.1. Make the best pairing you can. The suggested correct answers are, of course, open to interpretation.

TABLE 4.1   Match the Message to the Medium

Message	Medium
1. Your voice mail has a message from a colleague suggesting a lunch meeting tomorrow.	a. e-mail
2. Company president delivers appreciation to an employee for 25 years of service.	b. facsimile
3. You have been told that one of your direct report subordinates is stealing company supplies.	c. collaborative writing software on a computer network
4. Six company peers need to plan the organization's strategy for the next five years.	
5. A supplier in another state has misplaced your order form. He needs it now and must verify your signature.	d. business letter
6. College professor invites a businessperson to speak to her class in six weeks; this is the first contact and details are included.	e. videotape
	f. face-to-face group function
7. Four managers must co-write a report for the board of directors.	g. telephone
8. A student seeks feedback on her business presentation skills.	h. 1-on-1 interview
9. You must set forth the steps involved in submitting a request for business travel.	i. policy and procedure statement

Answers: 1=g, 2=f, 3=h, 4=a, 5=b, 6=d, 7=c, 8=e, 9=i

- How much does the audience know about the subject? Ideally, your message will be appropriate to their level of understanding. They will not be confused when you use relevant jargon or be offended when you define unfamiliar concepts or words. You do not want to waste their time sharing information they already know.

- What is the educational level of the audience? Often writing somewhat below the education level of your readers is desirable (as we will discuss a little further on in this chapter). However, you should not write much above their level. Target your audience level—substantial damage to accurate reception of the message may occur by writing above the audience's level.

- What is likely to be their reaction? If the content is heavy with negative information, think out the best organization for the message. Consider the indirect approach described in Chapter 6. Lay out a different plan if you anticipate acceptance of what you propose than if you expect resistance. Will the current economic environment affect their reaction? Are funds scarce or is the economy in decline, and might these conditions determine acceptance of your proposal?

- How will your message affect or be affected by organization politics? Are favors owed among the readership? Is there animosity between readers? Are you challenging anyone's sacred cow or pet project? Are you sure which members of the audience are nominal leaders and which are true leaders? What does the grapevine say about what you are proposing or sharing? Sometimes trying out your message on politically savvy colleagues can save embarrassment. Do not underestimate the strength of corporate power, political cliques, or old boy networks.

- Are there major differences in demographics you should take into consideration? If there are dramatic distinctions in religion, age, upbringing, values, income, or other background characteristics that will affect interpretation or acceptance of what you transmit, consider tailoring your message to those characteristics.

- Is this an occasion of cross-cultural communication in which your message will be translated into another language, or where the reader is using English as a second language? Keeping the message simple and avoiding Americanisms, idioms, and euphemisms will help the reader.

In our example of the unanticipated assignment to write a proposal, to identify your audience you would want to know such things as:

1. What is the size of the bank in numbers of employees, customers, profit, and assets? Are these characteristics improving or declining?

2. Who are the principal players for the bank? Who has the formal and the informal power? What do you know about them in terms of age, experience, education, and so on?

3. How do the bank representatives feel about what you are proposing? Is there a need for what you are proposing? How do they perceive your competition?

4. Who authorized the report? What were the directions regarding the contract? What do they expect?

Answers to these questions will have great impact on what you say and the tone you use to say it. You may need to review the corporate organization chart, make some phone calls to colleagues or secretaries, talk with others in your department, use the company library, or consult peers in other organizations to answer some of these questions.

Do Your Research

As an advanced student, you have learned efficient and effective research techniques. Some of those techniques will benefit you in the corporate world. Well-written reports and proposals, for example, are based on data from research, not opinion alone.

If necessary, refresh your memory of such research techniques as library usage; computer, Internet, and electronic database searches; unobtrusive observation; sampling techniques; experimentation; and interviewing. Do not neglect key corporate contacts who may be experts on the subject. Pay attention to company files and records for historical perspectives, guidelines, past mistakes, and suggestions made earlier by others.

Imagine the assignment of working on a feasibility study for a new shopping center on the outskirts of a major metropolitan area. Research results, more than intuition, will support your conclusions. Topics for research will include

- Competition
- Traffic patterns of potential customers
- Tax rates
- Potential customers
- Government influences
- Building costs
- Perception of your firm by others
- Labor force
- Financial considerations
- Anticipated profit

You may think of generating information on these ten topics as doing your job. It is also important research. Inaccurate, biased, or incomplete data will contaminate the quality of your study. The two main characteristics of solid research are reliability and validity. Reliability means that others researching the same topic in the same way would draw the same conclusions. Validity means that the research measures or reports what it is supposed to measure. Thorough research should lead logically to a proposed solution to a problem. The defense of your solution lies in the depth and quality of your research, as well as skills in argumentation.

The discussion that follows guides you in how to conduct electronic research.

Electronic Research Computers and new technology have redefined the way we do research. Much of your research can be done from a computer that is connected to the Internet, which has enabled access to an increasing amount of information. From that computer you can connect to a library's on-line catalog, review electronic databases, or search the World Wide Web for information on companies, products, statistics, pictures, or publications. Below is a discussion of some useful research tools.

Step 1—Using the library's electronic resources

On-line Catalog. The first place to start when researching a topic should be the library's on-line catalog. Most research can be completed using this resource alone. Typically, libraries have electronic card catalogs, which include automated systems that check availability, computerized searches of databases for author's names or key words, and regular reviews of periodicals.

Electronic Databases. Many large libraries subscribe to electronic databases that contain full journal articles along with bibliographical information and/or abstracts of articles. The fact that entire articles can be downloaded or printed from the computer decreases the amount of time spent retrieving information. Thus, to save time, many researchers will begin their search within electronic journal databases rather than look up articles via the library's catalog. These databases can be especially helpful if the library has a limited number of journal titles. Here is a list of some of the more popular electronic databases. (Note that there are dozens of specialized databases not mentioned. Also, availability of databases depends on the home institution's needs and resources.)

- Lexis/Nexis: Provides access to the complete text of national and international news articles, and to business, legal, and reference information.
- ABI/Inform: Contains articles in business research journals and important industry trade publications. Many of the articles are full text, while lengthy summaries exist for the rest.
- ERIC (Educational Research Information Center): Is a federally funded database of research-oriented documents intended for the educational practitioner and researcher.
- ProQuest: Provides access to articles across a wide range of academic disciplines. The database features the full text of articles from over 1,400 periodicals.
- Ebscohost: Contains many full-text journal articles.

All of these databases provide keyword search utilities that can greatly speed up data gathering.

Step 2—Employing Internet Resources

Access to the Internet provides the researcher with invaluable research tools that can locate information on practically all topics. The problem with Internet research is that many times the researcher must sort through extensive irrelevant information in order to extract the desired materials. Moreover, the Internet is not as well organized as the library. While many Web directories attempt to catalog each Web site, a single Web directory will never completely represent the entire Web. Thus, it is important to know which Internet tools to employ when trying to locate research materials on the Net.

Library Home Page. Often the best place to start is the home institution's library Web page. Every college/university library has at least an informative Web site, which often provides access to electronic journal databases as well as the school's on-line catalog. Most library Web sites will also include several links to Internet information resources and research tips/techniques.

Web Directories and Search Engines. It would be difficult to research and organize information on the Net without the help of some sort of Web directory or search engine. One popular place to start on the Web is Yahoo! Yahoo! is a useful search tool when looking for specific information such as company news or general reference. Yahoo! is more of a subject-oriented search engine in that all Web matches are placed into categories. Lycos is another such Web directory.

Search engines offer highly accurate findings, since keyword searches are applied to the full text of the Web site rather than just the title and/or description of the site. To gather information on more general or arcane subjects, such as how to buy a car, the following search engines offer better results:

- AltaVista (www.altavista.com)
- Excite (www.excite.com)
- HotBot (www.hotbot.com)
- Infoseek (www.infoseek.com)
- Northern Light (www.northernlight.com)
- Google (www.google.com)

All of these search engines operate in a similar fashion, although search options and syntax differ. It is best not to rely on just one search site, since all engines extract Web information differently. Therefore, a search on one site may produce results different from another.

Using all search engines in combination is probably the best research strategy. To save the researcher time and effort, a couple of search sites offer the ability to search several different search engines simultaneously. MetaCrawler (www.metacrawler.com) is the most popular meta-search engine. A simple search from MetaCrawler's interface will generate results from almost a dozen different search engines. While technically not a meta-search engine, Ask Jeeves (www.ask.com) is a convenient starting point when the researcher has no idea where to start looking for information because it offers plain-English searches. Thus, typing "where do I find a listing of jobs in Los Angeles" will yield useful results from many of the big search engines.

Search Techniques and Strategies. When using search engines to do research on the Web, practice a few effective strategies. Since Internet search engines cover literally millions of Web pages, the researcher must exert extra effort to narrow the search to relevant Web pages.

The first step of any Web-based search is the identification of appropriate keywords. If your topic is already distinctive, such as the Battle of Antietam, then typing the word *Antietam* or even *Battle of Antietam* will generate useful results from all search engines. However, many times your topic will not contain specific keywords. In this case, Web directories can be particularly useful in generating a list of related keywords. For example, if your topic is "travel trends in America," you can start with Yahoo! subject directories to take advantage of human indexing. Searching just within the travel directory will already eliminate millions of Web sites that contain the words *travel, trends,* and *America.* If the Web directory doesn't help, Ask Jeeves is also a good place to generate a list of keywords related to a certain research topic. Typing in plain-English searches such as "where can I find information on current travel trends in America" will yield helpful results while leading the researcher to more useful keywords.

The researcher can narrow down a search even further with the use of Boolean logic. Boolean logic simply allows the user to add search criteria to the array of keywords, using the operators *and, or,* or *not.* For example, to search for Web sites pertaining to "Mexican oil" you might search for:

Mexic	To allow selection of Mexico and Mexican
not New	To avoid selection of New Mexico
and (oil **or** petroleum)	To select both Mexic and oil, place the **and** between them; to allow selection of petroleum as well as oil, use the **or**. Note that the parentheses are necessary to group the last **or** statement together

When using Boolean logic in your searches, syntax may differ from search engine to search engine. Every search engine will have a search help page that can be found next to the search text box. Each search engine has an increasing amount of logic tools that can help you refine your search. Use these help pages as a tool to become a skilled Internet researcher.

There are a few other search features that may help narrow down a query. If you want to find Web pages that contain a specific phrase, for example, the use of quotes would limit the search to only those sites that matched the entire phrase. Thus, typing "give me liberty or give me death" as your search criteria will yield dozens of pages on Patrick Henry. As you can see, quotation marks can be useful when you need to cross-reference information such as direct quotes.

Many search engines offer the user advanced search options such as limiting the search to only specific parts of the Web document. For example, within Yahoo! it is possible to search only the Web title or the actual URL by typing in *t:* or *u:* respectively before the keyword. Sometimes you will want to search only within a specific company's Web site. In this case typing *u:cnn* followed by another optional keyword would search only within CNN's Web site. Many search engines offer these features, but be sure to check each site's help pages to determine the correct syntax (Infoseek uses *title:* and *site:* to limit the search to a document's title or URL) as well as additional search options.

Search engines are key starting points to finding items in different media such as an audio clip, an image, or a short movie clip. Some engines, such as AltaVista, have a special search page exclusively for audio, image, or video files. Thus, by selecting the image type, the searcher can type a keyword or two to find a particular picture. If the item searched is well known, such as the Grand Canyon, the engine may return hundreds of images to your liking. AltaVista is a particularly good site to find clip art and miscellaneous pictures, since your search will return pages of thumbnail images rather than just text descriptions. This gives the user quicker access to thousands of useful images. Thumbnail clips are also given when searching for video files, while audio searches will return a brief but useful description. Other search engines are adding such "visual" utilities, giving the user access to even more media files.

A final strategy when searching the Web is to seek useful niche sites whose main purpose is to provide the general population with useful information. Many of these sites can be found from major Web directories such as Yahoo! For example, a site that lists company information and stock quotes can easily be found by clicking on the *Stock Quotes* link on Yahoo! By surfing within subject directories, you will be able to find a number of informative sites. The next section describes just a handful of very useful sites on the Web.

Useful Web Sites. In addition to search engines, there are a number of large information portals on the Web worth mentioning. Getting to know the information on the following sites may speed up the research process:

- www.ipl.org—The Internet Public Library is dedicated to organizing the information on the Web, thus making it more useful to researchers. The site helps direct the researcher to relevant on-line magazines and newspapers while providing several helpful research tutorials.
- http://lcweb.loc.gov—The Library of Congress site offers on-line catalogs, journal collections, and numerous research services.
- www.census.gov—The Census Bureau is an excellent reference site in terms of specific statistical and demographic information.
- www.ed.gov—The Department of Education's Web page offers useful statistics and news related to education.

When you encounter a useful site such as those above, bookmark it for future reference. It may be helpful when researching a topic later.

Newsgroups. Depending on the research topic, newsgroups can be an excellent source of information. There are thousands of newsgroups covering every topic imaginable. These newsgroups hold on-going discussions that relate to topics ranging from the C programming language to teaching. Most of the information provided in newsgroups is unstructured and usually based on opinion. Thus, newsgroups do not make good references when writing purely academic papers. However, many times, newsgroup moderators can help steer the researcher to other useful and relevant sources. Currently, Liszt (http://liszt.bluemarble.net) contains an exhaustive directory of all known newsgroups. By employing Liszt's search utility, a researcher will be able to locate several newsgroups related to a certain topic. Deja News (www.deja.com) is also a valuable directory of newsgroups.

Step 3—Using Other Electronic Sources

Many commercial products, often produced on CD-ROMs, are available to enhance your research without connecting to a library database or using the Internet. Encyclopedias, such as the Encarta 2000 Encyclopedia, are rich with statistics, pictures, text, and sounds.

Consider Your Layout and Elements

Letters differ from memoranda in appearance. Procedure statements look different from justification reports. A research paper has different elements than a case analysis. As you think out your writing project, consider which elements, such as salutations, copy distribution notes, tables of contents, abstracts, or appendices will appear in your final presentation. These considerations affect the content and organization of your message.

Layout considerations recently have become especially important with the power contained in our word processing software. Here are some layout considerations that can affect the final appearance of your product:

- Color of ink and paper
- Size and length of finished package
- Quality of appearance, including such printing techniques as color ink jet versus black-and-white laser printer output
- Use of illustrations and graphics
- Image to project
- Established corporate guidelines
- Longevity of message
- Interaction with other messages, such as periodic reports or brochures
- Treatment of headings and subheadings
- Decision on if and where footnotes should appear

Just as decisions about layout are part of the overall writing process, so are decisions about which elements you will include in the finished package. As the length and formality of what you are writing increase, so will the number of elements you add. While a simple letter may have few elements beyond the body, a formal report will have many elements. Here, for example, are the required and optional elements that one university lists for the MBA professional report, a project often required in lieu of a thesis. Many proposals and government reports will have even more elements.

- Bound cover with author's name and report title on spine
- Fly page, blank
- Approval sheet, with original signatures
- Dedication
- Title page
- Preface or acknowledgments
- Abstract
- Table of contents
- List of tables
- List of figures
- Body of the report, with chapters and sections
- Appendices
- Bibliography
- Vita
- Fly page, blank

While these elements surround and package the main content of the report—the body—they also influence writing decisions on such things as tone and formality. For example, adding a List of Figures or a Bibliography may increase the formality, while inclusion of Dedication, Acknowledgments, and a Vita may affect the tone because of the personal nature of the content. Anticipate, then, which elements to include in your writing project.

Draft Your Project

For most people, effective writing takes more than one attempt. When the message you wish to transmit is simple, your familiarity with the situation high, the consequences unimportant, and the length short, you may be able to draft a finished letter or memorandum on the first try. However, as complexity, familiarity, consequences, and length change, you are more likely to draft and revise.

People approach drafting in different ways. For some, drafting is writing down main ideas, no matter how rough they may be, then adding lesser thoughts. Finally, these writers work on smoothness. Others place initial emphasis on careful word selection and sentence development, simply adding transitions by the completion of the finished draft. Few writers expect perfection after just one draft. There is no best approach. Stick with what works for you. Just keep in mind the main value of drafting: to start the writing process.

An initial and important decision has to do with organization of the information. Organization has various meanings. At one level, a message is organized if its main thoughts flow together well and it reaches its goal. (In Chapters 5 and 6 we will discuss, in depth, this type of organization from the viewpoint of direct and indirect message approaches. Because of this attention later, we discuss overall organization only superficially here.) Your first decision may well be whether to use

- Direct organization, when you expect little resistance from the reader.
- Indirect organization, when the reader is not disposed to do as you suggest or does not want to read what you write.

As you select an organization or format, plan to outline your message. Many effective writers work from an outline of important topics because they know an outline saves time and is more likely to produce a smooth, flowing final product. As you draft an outline, try to include as many main thoughts as possible. Add lower-level ideas as they occur to you, but do not let them get in the way of your planning. As you revise and edit your outline, you can add such outlining principles as parallelism (such as starting each item with a similar part of speech) and having at least two subdivisions under each heading.

While outlining works well for many writers, it may stifle creativity or lock the writer into a set format. Some writers, therefore, benefit from looser drafting techniques aimed more at idea generation than organization. Among these techniques are listing random ideas and using free writing, brainstorming, creativity matrixes, or idea trees.

Hints for overcoming writer's block appear later in this chapter.

Revise, Edit, and Proof

Having prepared a draft, your next step is to polish it. Realize that many writers spend almost as much time editing as they apply to the drafting process. Often, allowing some time to elapse between drafting and revising permits fresh thoughts and a different perspective to emerge. This may be the stage where you send your draft to an immediate supervisor, colleagues, or a content specialist to seek suggestions. The approach to having more than one pair of eyes look at the draft is especially valued here. Check to ensure that the manuscript still solves your definition of the problem.

One valuable editing technique is checking for good transitions from thought to thought. Lead thoughts, such as quantifying the points to follow (Four main criteria affect the decision), facilitate numbering the points as they occur (Second, next, then, or last). Help your reader by supplying phrases that connect thoughts, such as when you show addition (furthermore, additionally), contrast (but, however, nevertheless, on the other hand), concession (as you've stated, I agree, admittedly), or conclusion (in summary, to conclude). You may also assist your reader by clarifying causation (because, therefore), comparison (likewise, similarly), explanation (in other words, to state differently), or example (such as, for example).

Additionally, worthwhile revision steps include seeking out clumsy words, typos, misspellings, and overly long sentences. Many computer software packages can assist with the tedious chore of finding these elusive errors. For example, you can use software to scrutinize for spelling errors, grammar, punctuation, style problems, and readability level. The grammar, punctuation, and style checkers help you spot many of the writing and typing errors that work against clarity, coherence, tone, and other attributes of effective writing. It is also helpful to use a computerized thesaurus. While these various packages cannot guarantee perfect spelling or word usage, they can help you identify common problems. Personally proofread to catch the correctly spelled but out-of-context errors (*there* for *their*). In the absence of software, elicit the help of people whose writing ability you respect.

Next, work on the organization of sentences, paragraphs, and the message as a whole. Is there an inherent logic to the entire manuscript? Does it flow smoothly within paragraphs and from section to section?

Depending on the goal of the message and the medium selected, such as an annual report, letter to all employees, procedure statement, or sales brochure, extensive review by others may be needed. Legal experts, technical content specialists, and editorial reviewers may be part of the revision cycle, as will your immediate supervisor, who reviews the work.

Because editing and revising your own work and the work of others is so important, you may wish to examine the paragraphs in Figure 4.1. The shaded text is new; the strikeouts show what would be omitted. While it maintains the integrity of the original message, the revision is briefer, clearer, and more active.

Many people who edit someone else's writing prefer to do so in a pencil-and-hard-copy mode and use widely accepted notation. Figure 4.2 shows some of this notation.

✴ Produce the Finished Package

Final production may be the word processing of your manuscript or the sending of copy to a printer for design, layout, typesetting, and printing. Now may also be the time for you to confirm final layout and element decisions you made earlier. Perhaps

FIGURE 4.1   **Sample Editing**

Information Gathering

The ~~most important~~ key issues to ~~be addressed~~ address in negotiations should be ~~those sections of~~ the contract sections that surfaced most often ~~under the past contract~~ during the contract term. Typically, the negotiating teams ~~in the traditional environment~~ will ~~try to patch~~ focus on these areas ~~as a priority~~. ~~What is critical is to gain~~ Gaining feedback from ~~the~~ management, ~~and~~ especially ~~the~~ first-line supervisors, ~~as to what~~ concerning areas they wish to modify is critical. Any issues ~~that are brought forward by~~ the ~~bargaining unit~~ employees raised ~~is~~ are also key to understanding ~~what is really expected of~~ the union negotiators' role.

The ~~single~~ most powerful resource ~~you can possess~~ in any negotiation is superior information. This ~~information~~ should be ~~then~~ blended with ~~similar input from~~ the union leadership's ~~relative to their~~ desires. Through parallel, small group sessions ~~of small group sensing~~ with management and union leadership, many key issues will surface (see Appendix A). ~~Additionally, those areas that are of common importance~~ Common concerns will also ~~become obvious~~ emerge and should ~~therefore gain a high~~ command top priority ~~for resolution~~. ~~One should not rely on instincts when~~ When the long-term stakes are high, ~~for in the long run,~~ instincts are no match for accurate and accessible information.

Determining Causes and Effects

~~Once the assemblage~~ After a list of ~~contracual~~ contractual problem areas ~~has been accomplished, it now requires an analysis for the causes of the undesirable effects~~ has been compiled, analyzing why they created problems is the next task. This process will help to ~~bring out~~ emphasize the issues that are ~~key to making significant gains in~~ fundamental to productive negotiation. ~~It is advantageous to facilitate a~~ A joint review ~~of~~ by human resources and line management personnel will help to ~~clarify and delineate what~~ define the action ~~are really~~ needed ~~for problem resolution~~ to resolve problems. If ~~it is a common issue with~~ the union has similar concerns, then ~~they should also be requested to clarify~~ their ~~understanding of the causal factors~~ input is also vital.

During this ~~activity it may become apparent that~~ process some ~~of the~~ earlier issues ~~brought about by the initial feedback is less important than was expressed~~ may appear less significant. These data should be set aside in a follow up file for last minute review ~~prior to the beginning of~~ before negotiations begin ~~for any last minute concerns~~. They may be ~~of use~~ useful later ~~during negotiations if it arises during that time frame. Again, it noteworthy to remember that historical information gained must be accessible at all times. It is at this stage where~~ Now information sharing should ~~be initiated~~ begin. By distributing the information gained in the ~~sensing~~ parallel, group sessions, ~~the beginnings of collaboration and a trusting relationship~~ mutual collaboration and trust can ~~progress~~ develop. Openness and sharing also ~~facilitates the lowering of~~ help to lower barriers to communication that will benefit both parties ~~during the negotiation process~~ in negotiations.

FIGURE 4.2   **Common Correction and Proofreading Symbols**

Abv	faulty abbreviation	*DM*	dangling modifier	*jar*	avoid jargon
Awk	awkward	*frag.*	sentence fragment	*sp*	spelling error
(cap)	capitalize	∧	insert	*pv*	passive voice
⌒	close up	*mm*	misplaced modifier	*w*	wordy
e	delete			*wc*	word choice

you will use your computer to boldface text, switch among different typefaces or sizes, switch to multiple columns, or add bullets in front of items in a list.

Even today's low-cost word processors can deliver some features of desktop publishing, and the top-end word processors and desktop publishing programs have powerful control over the appearance of printed words. In addition to needing artistic understanding of style, balance, and unity, effective design and layout require knowledge of such elements as grid layout, headings, borders, columns, typography, white space, and graphics. Most desktop publishing and design guides stress the need to keep layouts simple, clean, and attractive while gaining experience. Novices all too often clutter their layouts with the many variables under their control and end up damaging the appearance of their documents rather than enhancing them.

Conduct a Post-writing Evaluation

Now that you have transmitted the message, how would you change it? What mistakes did you make and what did you learn that will guide you in the future? Too many of us complete a major project only to shelve it in relief. However, before separating yourself from the project completely, review it to help guide yourself in the future. The time to conduct your evaluation is now, while the rationale for your decisions is fresh in your mind. Ask questions such as these: What are the strengths and weaknesses of the manuscript? Are there any unusual or unique aspects of the finished product that might be used again? How did others perceive the manuscript, and what suggestions did they make?

While you may proceed through all eight steps in the writing sequence, doing so does not guarantee effective writing. Effective writing has other characteristics.

SPECIFIC WRITING FEATURES

Effective writing is achieved when it has certain features. Your writing will be effective if it is organized, has appropriate tone, and is readable.

Organization

As we briefly discussed in the section above on drafting, organization can mean direct versus indirect order. A second form of organization has to do with the flow of words within and between sentences. Of particular interest are coherence and emphatic sentences.

Coherence Coherence grows when sender and receiver perceive the transmitted thought in the same way. Unfortunately, often what we think we are sending does not resemble the interpretation by the receiver. Standard grammar often overcomes incoherencies.

Using words such as *it, that,* or *this* at the beginning of sentences frequently leads to confusion about the word's referent. For example:

> The value of the stock rose nine points and made over $2,000 for us. It was great! (Revision: The stock rise was great!)

A second grammatical contributor to incoherence is misplaced modifiers, such as in this sentence:

> The subordinate had a phone call talking to his boss. (Revision: While talking to his boss, the subordinate had a phone call.)

A third incoherency grows from lack of clarity between multiple subjects followed by a singular pronoun, such as:

> Seldom had Kristi experienced the friendship of a co-worker like Stephanie. She was delighted. (Revision: Kristi was delighted.)

Standard grammar often overcomes problems with indefinite meaning. Here is an example of such a problem:

> His mother had worked the dough into a thin pizza crust with her own hands. Have you ever seen such smooth texture?

> (Clarify: Did the crust or the mother's hands have the smooth texture?)

Emphatic Sentences Your writing style can increase the emphasis of your messages. When you seek to add emphasis to specific sentences, consider these techniques.

- Put the action at the beginning of the sentence rather than bury it. "Dierdre proposed . . ." gets things moving; " . . . as proposed by Dierdre" does not.
- Build to a crescendo. "The three regions report improvements in sales of 12, 21, and 37 percent" accomplishes this goal.
- Place emphasis on important words and create memorable statements, such as "We try harder" or "Your downtown bank."
- Show causation. "Because of his timely investment, he quadrupled his profit" is more emphatic than reversing the two thoughts.

In addition to writing coherent and emphatic sentences, you will improve your sentences and paragraphs with having effective transitions, as described earlier in the discussion of revising, editing, and proofing.

Appropriate Tone

The second major characteristic of effective writing is appropriate tone. Three main ways of affecting tone are (1) writing with the *you* attitude, (2) using positive phrasing, and (3) avoiding tactless wording. Readers are egocentric. They like to read about themselves and to see references to themselves. Conversely, readers lose interest and attention when the topic turns to others. Business writing shares with direct-mail advertising the technique of personalizing messages to audiences to obtain a desired response. When you employ words such as *you, yourself,* or the person's name, you are using the *you* attitude. On the other hand, words such as *I, me, myself, our, we, us,* or your company's name illustrate the *I* attitude.

To view how detrimental the *I*-ish orientation can be, read Figure 4.3, which delivers the body of a cold contact letter from someone seeking tax work.

Consider how easy it is to remove most *I* references and to either replace them with, or to inject, *you* references; it is surprising that more writers do not follow the *you* attitude. Effective writers learn quickly the positive response that the *you* technique elicits.

FIGURE 4.3   **Example of an *I* Attitude Letter**

Dear Taxpayer:

We all are willing to pay our fair share of taxes, but we don't want to pay more than is necessary. I can help avoid taxes through my expert planning and preparation.

I have the experience, knowledge, and background to do your taxes. I also have a Ph.D. in accounting. My fees are competitive while my service is excellent.

I invite you to enjoy the personal and professional service that I'm known for. I will be sending you more information soon. Call me at 555-1212 to make an appointment with me. Do so before March 1 and receive a 10 percent discount.

Sincerely,

Read Figure 4.4 to see how the body of Figure 4.3 could be improved through *you*-ish tone alone. Although other improvements can still be made, the change in focus from author to reader helps this message.

Another level of the *you* attitude is more elusive but perhaps even more important. Beyond just the inclusion or exclusion of key pronouns is the goal of applying the *you* attitude to make the message sound like it is written to the reader, not sent by the author. A message prepared for the reader conveys sincerity, personalization, warmth, and involvement on the part of the author. It is these and other attributes that can bring about a positive reaction.[1]

Positive versus negative phrasing also affects tone. If you regularly communicate negatively phrased thoughts, you project a negative and undesirable image of yourself. Most of us prefer to associate with winners and with those who hold an optimistic outlook. While the Pollyanna principle can be overdone, you are usually better off to transmit a message that the glass is half full, not half empty. Politicians, of course, are well known for seeing the bright side of things. Top-level managers, too, seldom associate themselves with losing ideas, projects, products, or people unless they must do so. Such associations can taint careers. Apply this philosophy (avoid the negative, seek the positive, phrase the negative from the positive viewpoint) to your business writing.

While you may think that negative situations call for negative phrasing, just the opposite is actually the case. Unpleasant messages are only exaggerated by negative

FIGURE 4.4   **Example of a *You* Attitude Letter**

Dear Taxpayer:

You, no doubt, are willing to pay your fair share of taxes, but you don't want to pay more than is necessary. You can benefit by not paying unnecessary taxes by using my expertise in tax planning and preparation.

You will find I have the experience, knowledge, and background needed to best serve your individual needs. You'll also benefit from my Ph.D. in accounting when tricky accounting questions arise. These abilities are available to you at competitive fees that include excellent service.

Please call 555-1212 to make an appointment. You'll experience my personal and professional service that will help you avoid unnecessary taxes. And if you make an appointment by March 1, you'll receive a 10 percent discount.

Cordially,

tone. A more desirable approach is to state the bad news as positively as possible. For example, compare these two sentences:

Your bid for the project was rejected.
We selected another firm for the project.

Both transfer negative information, but the second does so in a more appealing fashion.

A third way to affect tone is through tactful wording. Tactless writing offends the reader, perhaps by stereotyping, challenging intelligence, inappropriately referring to religion or ethnic background, or using humor in poor taste. Tactful writers appreciate the delicacy of a situation and say the fitting thing.

Even though most businesspeople have learned to identify and avoid inappropriate ethnic references, many still need to have their awareness raised in regard to sexist language. For example, as the percentage of women in business and in executive positions increases, there are more women who dislike receiving letters addressed "Dear Sir" or being referred to as one of the girls. If you are using gender-specific language that is offensive to the reader, that language may work against you. The trend in U.S. business is away from sexist and other forms of discriminatory language.

Readability

A third major component in the writing process is making the writing readable. Readable writing builds on some of the concepts discussed above but adds additional dimensions: clarity, conciseness, and activity.

Clarity Clear writing is coherent and avoids muddy, incorrect, overly complex phrases and jargon. Muddy phrases are those that cloud the issue or idea by using too many words or skirting the issue. Here are some examples of muddy phrases:

a number of	(use *many*)
at your earliest possible convenience	(use *soon*)
fullest possible extent	(use *fully* or *completely*)
it has come to my attention that	(omit)
it would be reasonable to assume	(use *I assume*)

Many nonstandard phrases are current in our language. Clear writing, however, shuns errors. Here are some examples of frequently used but nonstandard words and phrases:

irregardless	(use *regardless*)
enthused	(use *enthusiastic*)
impacted	(avoid; *impact* is a noun, not a verb)
interfaced	(avoid; *interface* is a noun, not a verb)
between (three items)	(use *between* when comparing two items)
among (two items)	(use *among* when comparing three or more items)
can't hardly	(avoid; double negative)
virtually	(means *essentially the same* and is not necessary)

Occasionally, people try to make their writing sound more impressive by adding to its complexity. Usually they fail in this attempt and detract from readability at the same time. Anyone who has taken a simple, direct sentence and looked up long, abstract substitutes knows the approach. Instead, try to use simple, familiar words. Here are a few examples:

as per this date	(use *today*)
attached hereto	(use *attached is*)
contact the undersigned	(use *write me*)
considerable magnitude	(use *large*)
inasmuch as	(use *since*)
utilize	(use *use*)
necessitates	(use *needs* or *requires*)
at the present time	(use *now*)
prioritize	(use *rank*)
it is worth remembering that	(use *remember*)

Jargon, too, can detract from readability. Within any organization there will be many buzzwords and acronyms. Sometimes using this jargon will simplify and shorten complex or lengthy terms; other times it will confuse or obscure meaning. For example, *FIFO* immediately means "first in, first out" to an accountant, but may be meaningless to nonaccountants. Try to avoid jargon; if the receiver is not familiar with the jargon, it makes the reader feel like an outsider or as if he or she is being used to make the author sound intelligent. Ask yourself, "Am I using jargon that is appropriate to my audience?" If in doubt, avoid the jargon.

Conciseness A second major determinant of readability is conciseness. Avoid wordy phrases and long, complex words; opt instead for short, familiar words. You can also improve conciseness by eliminating redundancies, such as:

the consensus of opinion	(use *the consensus* or *the opinion*)
the first and foremost	(use *the first* or *the foremost*)
over and over and over again	(use *over*)
near future	(use *future* or *soon*)
desirable benefits	(use *desirable* or *benefits*)
all in all	(omit)
in the week/month/year of	(omit)

You can also improve conciseness (and coherency) by avoiding oxymorons, combinations of two words with opposite or contradictory meanings. Here are some examples:

jumbo shrimp
almost perfect
intense apathy
silent scream
old news
pretty ugly

Activity You can make your writing more readable by using the active instead of the passive voice. The passive voice discourages the reader from becoming involved with your message. You can identify passive voice by finding a form of the verb *be* plus a past participle that often ends in *-n, -en, -t, -d,* or *-ed.* In your efforts to avoid passive voice, also try to use present tense; both aid readability. Here are some examples of passive and active voice:

Passive	*Active*
has been sent	I sent
it was discussed	we discussed
were brought by	someone brought
you were mailed a	I mailed you a
were studied by	someone studied

Sometimes passive voice is desirable, such as when you do not know who did the action (The electricity was installed in the plant about 1911), when you want to bury the identity of the doer (The funds have been misappropriated), or when the action is more important than who did it (Corporate profits were increased 72 percent).

Readability Formulas You may find the concept of readability—and even effective writing—to be elusive. Many scholars have tried to quantify readability; the outcome has been the creation of many readability formulas. Since the 1950s, when many such formulas were created, only a half dozen or so viable formulas remain. The survivors are similar in that most attempt to measure prose through a ratio of difficult words or syllables to total words or sentence length. Some computer word processors include a readability tool that will calculate the approximate reading level of a piece of writing.

If you wish to use a readability formula to guide your writing, you should write at a level appropriate for your audience, or lower. Most of us prefer to read easy writing if it still conveys what we need to know and does not sound like the author is writing down to us. Readability formulas deserve a word of caution: while they can effectively guide you in matching your writing to the level of your audience, they can be imprecise, or overly mechanical, and may overlook important aspects of style and content. Use them to help catch problems, but take personal responsibility for the final output.

As you approach your writing and revising, seek a balance among the three main writing process considerations just presented: organization (including ways of organizing the entire message, coherence, and writing emphatically), tone (including *I* versus *you* attitude, positive and negative phrasing, and tactful writing), and readability (including clarity, conciseness, active voice, and reading ease).

Getting Writing Started

The assumption so far has been that once you know what you need to write, you can write it. Unfortunately, some people have very real problems getting started, and others start but have difficulty finishing. Here are some suggestions for increasing your writing output.[2]

1. Schedule a regular writing time and place. Then, when in that place, you will fall into the writing mood. Some people find the habit of writing at a certain time—but not necessarily a place—is all they need to enhance the process. Little changes from your regular routine will emphasize that here and now is the time and place to write. Change to a different desk. Alter the lighting. Select different music. Focus more on the periodic aspects of writing rather than on setting aside large blocks of time. Efficient use of 30 minutes a day may generate better results than setting aside a single three-hour period in which you tire or your mind wanders.

2. Set a writing goal. Pick a realistic goal, such as writing five double-spaced pages of draft in two hours. Modify your goal if you find you easily exceed it or have trouble achieving it. Try not to fall below your goal. If you are experiencing a good session, do not stop. If you must stop, jot down the ideas still in your mind to help to pick up in the same place. Review your progress periodically. You will be surprised how productive you can be.

3. Use a buddy system. Identify good writers and involve them in your writing. Find peers in your study group or people at your level in your organization who will be willing to assist you in the writing process. Be willing to help them. As you share ideas about each other's writing, all will benefit.

4. Overcome your writing blocks. Break large writing projects into small chunks. In writing your professional report, thesis, or other major academic writing project, work on and complete one chapter at a time. Then start on another chapter. Avoid writing several chapters at once. If you have trouble getting started, consider freewheeling. This process stresses writing something, no matter what, for a period of time. Then go back and revise and expand what you have created. If this approach does not work, try talking to a tape recorder to capture your thoughts. Conversations with others may help you, too.

5. Employ time management concepts. Spend your time writing, not getting ready to write. Some people must first clean the desk, get out a favorite eraser, sharpen all pencils, and make other preparations. Instead, use this time to get ideas on paper or diskette. Prioritize your writing and work on the most important project first. Lay out a list each day of what you need to accomplish and start working on the first item.

Thus far this chapter has focused on when and how to write; we now turn to computer techniques that can enhance the writing process.

ELECTRONIC WRITING PROCESSES

Writing has two components: composition and transcription. Historically, in U.S. business, managers composed and secretaries transcribed. Managers may have started the process with dictation and asked for a typed rough draft. The revision process may have gone through several iterations and involved the editing of others before achieving a finished product. The personal computer (PC) has changed this process in several ways. First, secretaries save time by inserting changes into an electronic file, which avoids retyping copy that is correct. They also quickly and easily make changes in appearance, such as adjusting margins or spacing.

Second, PCs have facilitated the transcription of many messages by their authors rather than by secretaries. For an author who drafts on a PC, it may also be easier to make revisions and to print the finished product than to explain the desired changes to a secretary. Research suggests that more employees at increasingly higher levels of management are keyboarding their drafts themselves. They also are increasingly manipulating text and data in spreadsheets, databases, and financial and accounting packages before they start a draft. Not long ago, these duties were assigned to the people in charge of the computers.

Computers can help you identify, search, record, organize, and modify relevant literature. Computers can then help you write, edit, and revise your document. They can sharpen the skills discussed so far in this chapter; however, they cannot replace poor writing skills.

This next section shows you how computers can help you improve your writing output. The steps apply especially to longer writing assignments, such as a thesis, grant proposal, feasibility study, or case study, but they also relate to short writing situations.

Writing Using a Computer

Your use of the electronic writing process will be dictated by the facilities, hardware, and software available. The following steps incorporate computer equipment available at most universities and at most businesses. The order of the steps is not absolute, and steps may be skipped. (Refer also to the section earlier in this chapter on using the computer and the Internet to do research.)

Step 1—Note taking. Skeletonize your notes as you take them in the library (ideally on a laptop portable computer). Use abbreviations, such as *J.* for *Journal*. Then, on your personal computer, record the notes to a file. Next, use a word-processing feature called *search and replace* to search for each occurrence of *J.* and replace it with *Journal*. Do the same with your other abbreviations.

Step 2—Searching. Especially if you are writing a lengthy research paper or working on a long-term project at work, place your research data in a database. Put similar topics under one heading. Later, when you are writing, seek out that heading to see your sources. Careful entry of bibliographic information will almost eliminate typing a bibliography later.

A variation on using the computer to help with your research is the recent introduction of report-writing software. These packages help authors of especially complex reports, which may be periodical but whose data change, to generate reports without instructions on how to organize the report or what to include. The packages typically can search many database files, join the data into one file, and paste it in appropriate locations. Many users of these report writers note increased productivity.[3]

Step 3—Word polishing. If your word processor doesn't have a built-in dictionary, load separate packages now. *The American Heritage Dictionary for Computers* has a "wordhunter" feature that helps you find the right word when you are stumped. What's the right side of a ship called? Type in *right, side*, and *ship* and get *starboard*. What is the name of the boat used on the canals of Venice? *Boat, canals*, and *Venice* yield *gondola*. Pronunciation question? Have the computer say the word to you.

Now also is the time to load stand-alone grammar and style checkers if your word processor doesn't have them. Be careful, however, of too much reliance on these checkers. Spelling checkers typically are unable to interpret context and therefore would not catch this misspelling: "I have two left feat." Grammar, style, and punctuation checkers have different capabilities; they seldom catch the same errors. You need to know the rules and then use checkers to help you uncover the problems. You, however, are the final editor.

Step 4—Outlining. Another valuable attribute is an outliner, which may be a separate program or part of a word-processing package. Outliners allow you not only to outline your thoughts quickly but also to rearrange sections rapidly, change levels, and so on. Usually you can import text from other files to the outliner, and you can send the outline to other files.

Step 5—Changing defaults. Enter your word processor. Do some setting up as you create your new file. This setup will enhance document appearance on your screen and layout later. These commands either alter the appearance both on the screen and for the printer, or affect only the printed output. Some word-processing packages allow definition of a template or master page that automatically carries such information as margin widths, typeface and size requirements for body and heading text, headers and footers, and page numbers to each page of the document. If your word processor can automatically correct typing errors, such as TWo INitial CApital letters, noncapitalized days of the week, or *don;t* for *don't* and *teh* for *the*, turn it on. Also, if available, turn on controls for widows (the first line of a paragraph that falls on the last line of a page) or orphans (the last line of a paragraph that appears at the top of a page). Now may also be the time to decide whether your finished manuscript needs a table of contents or index, since it is best to start your writing with special instructions to prepare these elements.

For a professional look with little effort for long documents, make the right headers list the chapter number with the page number, such as *Page 4-19*, and format the left header to carry the title of the chapter, such as *Data Analysis*.

Step 6—Using multi-screens. If your word processor supports division of the screen into two or more parts (called windows), split your screen and place your outline in one window. Then start writing your draft in the other window. Split windows also work well for entering superscript numbers for citations with the text in one window and entering the footnote or endnote in the other window.

Consider creating a "fast draft." Research indicates that some writers are held back by watching the monitor as they draft. Turn down the brightness on your monitor so you cannot see any display, check that your fingers are on the right keys, and start typing. For some, this approach helps to get them started. Any errors can be cleaned up later.

Remember that when you draft, you do not have to start at the beginning of your manuscript. If you have outlined your report, you know where you are and where you are going. Often, starting some place other than the beginning is easier, more logical, or more desirable. Start anywhere you wish. Your computer will help you assemble the parts later and you can then add transitions.

Step 7—Searching and replacing. As you edit or revise, take advantage of the search-and-replace function of your word processor. Find a word you now realize you misspelled, such as *convence*, and replace it with *convince*. Most search-and-replace functions allow you to choose between individual decisions on each occurrence or an entire text search and replace.

Step 8—Linking. Data in your database can be transferred to another program—say a spreadsheet—for statistical analysis and graphical presentation. While these statistical analysis and graphical presentation steps should occur before you start writing, the results of the steps find their way into the manuscript initially as you draft and later as you revise. You can ask some "smart" word-processing software to realize you are updating data in a spreadsheet and to automatically bring that new data to the manuscript as you work on it over time. Some software isolates the graphical presentation from the text portion.

Step 9—Adding attribution. Most word-processing software facilitates adding footnotes or endnotes. For example, a superscript number is inserted into the text and then the footnote or endnote is filled in for insertion at the correct location. Users can later add a new citation within the text and the other citations will change number and reposition. Other software allows the user to switch among major citation styles, such as MLA or APA, in a single keystroke.

Step 10—Using e-mail. In the last few years e-mail has moved from being a convenience for a few people to a necessity for most people. According to Hamilton, e-mail ranks with the printing press, telephone, and television in mass impact.[4] Just a decade ago hard-copy letters and memos were the primary written medium for most businesspeople. Today, receiving 25, 50, or even 100 e-mail messages a day is not uncommon. Growing out of the three billion plus e-mail messages a day is the prediction of 1,000 e-mail messages per person in ten years.[5]

Generally speaking, e-mail is much quicker to deliver, cheaper to send, and more formal in perception than hard-copy messages such as letters and memos. Unfortunately, the widespread use of e-mail has allowed many to become lazy. Business letters and memos in hard copy were expected to be letter perfect; e-mail messages, however, often contain spelling and grammar errors. Even worse, we seem to be growing complacent about these errors.

For all the many benefits of using e-mail, authors still must judge when an alternative medium would be more appropriate. Where, for example, would you "draw the line" and not use e-mail exclusively in the examples below?

1. Announce that part of the parking lot will be out of use for the next three days.
2. Congratulate a subordinate for a success and share the message with the department.

3. Ask a group of subordinates, peers, and superiors to let you know their availability for a meeting next Thursday or Friday.
4. Send a message of inquiry to a company to see if they have job openings.
5. Apply for a job and include your résumé as part of the message.
6. Send a formal thank-you message to a person who had publicly bestowed an honor upon you.

E-mail messages can also overlap with ethical and legal considerations. While we may think that we discard or erase our e-mail messages, many businesspeople are learning, to their dismay, that old messages can have a long life. Retrieved messages have been used to show company harassment against employees, for example. Microsoft chairman Bill Gates's e-mail containing the sentence, "Do we have a clear plan on what we want Apple to do to undermine Sun?" stands as an example of how high up in an organization a retrieved message can be found.[6]

Desktop publishing, which uses computers to design and prepare camera-ready copy, facilitates this gathering of text and nontext (such as graphics) and then shows the page on a screen as it would appear when printed. The finished product can look quite professional and be relatively inexpensive. See Figure 4.5 for an example of how desktop publishing software can manipulate graphic images. Figure 4.6 illustrates how text can flow around a graphic image through the power of desktop publishing.

Apply these ten steps to your writing projects and you will see, with a little experience, substantial improvements in the speed with which you write, the quality of that writing, the quantity of output, and the appearance of the finished product.

A final computer technology that involves communication and is becoming a major application area is multimedia presentations. These computer programs, which combine graphics, text, colors, animation, picture blends and dissolves, high-resolution photos, or sound, generate dazzling sales pitches and brilliant proposals. They can appear as a slide show on a computer, include video clips with motion, and incorporate interactive features for the viewer to respond to. They often use CD-ROM and stereo sound. Multimedia has uses in education, training, advertising, retail merchandising, and public access in addition to its obvious business presentation uses.

Because good etiquette in business and social settings enhances the communication exchange, and because rules for electronic etiquette are still emerging, you may wish review the suggestions found in Table 4.2.

Three final writing concepts that have become important recently, largely because of new technology, are collaborative writing, ethical considerations, and international communication.

Collaborative Writing

For years some businesspeople have co-authored text, edited each others' writing, and worked on the same projects concurrently. As they did so, they learned that there are as many different ways of writing as there are facets to interpersonal behavior. Within a writing team there may be different approaches to writing (each person does a part versus all work together on all), hierarchical influences, ability and knowledge dif-

FIGURE 4.5   **Illustrations of Graphic Image Manipulation with Desktop Publishing Software**

A: The original

B: Pulled horizontally

C: Pulled vertically

D: Selecting part of the original

Source: Logotype courtesy of MBA for Executives Program, San Diego State University.

FIGURE 4.6 **Flowing Text Around a Graphic Using Desktop Publishing Software**

To customize the shape of an existing graphic boundary:

❶ Select the graphic to display the graphic boundary.

Graphic handle ⊢

Graphic boundary ⊢

Graphic boundary handle ⊢

Lorem ipsum dolor sit amet, consectetuer adipiscing elit, sed diam nonummy nibh euismod tincidunt ut laoreet dolore magna aliquam erat volutpat. Ut wisi enim ad minim veniam, quis nostrud exerci tation ullamcorper sus- cipit lobortis nisl ut aliquip ex ea commodo consequat. Duis autem vel eum iriure do- lor in hendrerit in vulputate velit esse moles- tie consequat, vel illum dolore eu feugiat nulla facilisis at vero eros et accumsan et iu- sto odio dign- issim qui blandit praesent lupta- tum zzril delenit augue duis dolore te feugait nulla facilisi. Lorem ipsum dolor sit amet, consectetuer adipiscing elit, sed diam nonummy nibh euismod tincidunt ut laoreet dolore magna aliquam erat volut- pat. Ut wisi enim ad minim veniam, quis nostrud exerci tation

❷ Create new graphic boundary handles as necessary by clicking boundary.

New graphic boundary handle

❸ Drag the handles to change the shape of the boundary. To keep PageMaker from reflowing text until you have finished reshaping a graphic, hold down the spacebar while you drag the graphic handles. The text will reflow when you release the spacebar.

❹ Drag graphic boundary handles to outline shape of graphic.

❺ The text flows around the customized graphic boundary.

Lorem ipsum dolor sit amet, consectetuer adipiscing elit, sed diam nonummy nibh euismod tincidunt ut laoreet dolore ma- gna aliquam erat volutpat. Ut wisi enim ad minim veniam, quis nostrud exerci tation ullamcorper suscipit lobortis nisl ut al- iquip ex ea com- modo consequat. Duis autem vel eum iriure dolor in hendrerit in vulputate velit esse molestie consequat, vel il- lum dolore eu feugiat nulla facilisis at vero eros et ac- cumsan et iusto odio dignissim qui blandit praesent luptatum zzril de- lenit augue duis dolore te feugait nulla facilisi. Lorem ipsum dolor sit amet, consect- etuer adipiscing elit, sed diam nonummy nibh euismod tincidunt ut laoreet dolore magna aliquam erat volutpat. Ut wisi enim ad minim veniam, quis nostrud exerci tation ullam- corper suscipit lobortis nisl ut aliquip ex ea commodo

TABLE 4.2   **Suggestions for Electronic Etiquette***

e-mail   Avoid words all in capital letters; in e-mail it is the equivalent of shouting.

Avoid writing things you may regret if seen by other than those anticipated. Most e-mail is not confidential.

Proofread your message before sending it, since few e-mail messages are printed first and then proofread, spell-checked, or grammar-checked.

Avoid sarcasm and satire; they don't translate well over e-mail.

Use *urgent, priority,* or *receipt requested* judiciously—only when necessary.

Don't overload or intrude by "dumping" long articles or questionnaires that haven't been asked for.

If a message is unusually long, tell your reader early so he or she can decide how to handle it.

Respond quickly, but after you have had time to consider your response.

Use valuable, descriptive subject lines, since recipients may decide whether to read your message based on them.

Ensure the message is relevant to your audience. Because it is so easy to send a message to multiple receivers, people often send messages that are of no interest or value to some on the distribution list.

Be watchful of your tone. People tend to be harsher with e-mail messages than when face-to-face.

Don't write in anger. Put your response aside for a day or two and then send it if you still feel the same way.

If sending a message to a large number of people, put that list in the blind carbon copy (bcc) file and send the message to yourself. Then they see the message only, not the list.

Be judicious in keeping preceding message as part of new messages.

Only use abbreviations such as "LOL" for "laughing out loud," or emoticons, such as 0-: or the ubiquitous "smiley face."

Don't forward chain letters or the joke-of-the-day to a list of friends.

Keep signature lines brief; four lines is the upper limit for most people.

voice mail   Give your name at the beginning of your message. Spelling it out is valuable when you normally speak quickly, don't enunciate, or your name is spelled in an unexpected way.

Share the main point of the message early. This gives the listener a framework upon which to "hang" your comments.

Give your phone number(s) next, clearly and slowly. Include when you are available.

Next, give details, if necessary, regarding the message.

Keep your message as brief as possible.

Be sure to give the time of day and date of your call.

fax   Do not tie up the receiving fax machine for long periods of time.

Do not send junk faxes (of potentially little interest) to lengthy distribution lists.

Do not send private messages over organization fax lines.

Call first before sending a long fax or send it after hours.

Don't use faxes for personal notes of thanks, congratulations, or condolence.

cellular   Unless absolutely necessary, don't take them to public places.
phones and   Don't use phones in restaurants, concerts, or church.
pagers

speaker   Use only for conference calls; tell the other person before turning on the speaker phone.
phone

* For additional information about business etiquette, see the special issue of *Keying In,* the Newsletter of the National Business Education Association, January 1996; Michelle V. Rafter (Reuters News Service), "E-mail Etiquette Addresses Many Complaints," *Computerlink* supplement to *San Diego Union Tribune,* December 25, 1995, p. 4; Jean Mausehund, R. Neil Dortch, Paula Brown, and Carl Bridges, "Business Etiquette: What Your Students Don't Know," *Business Communication Quarterly,* 58, no. 4, December 1995, pp. 34–38; and Stephen Silha, "A Network of Conversations," *CreativeLiving* (Spring, 1995), p. 2–7; e-land, inc., "U.S. Net Users, Projected," 1999. e-marketer. Retrieved 5/6/99. <http://www.emarketer.com/estats/nmsg_usf.html>; Sally Hambridge RFC1855: Netiquette Guidelines. Retrieved 5/6/99. <http://www.dtcc.edu/cs/rfc.1855.html>.

ferences, time or job pressures, and various political effects. Sometimes the output of collaborative writing is a beautifully crafted message that is the result of team synergy, balanced abilities, a common goal, and plenty of effort. Often, however, the result pits writers against each other, takes too much effort, lacks seamless writing, and is at the level of the lowest contributor, not the group average or the highest contributor. Writing collaboratively can be challenging.

However, computers and computer networks can enhance this process. Because using computers for this process can increase quality and quantity and improve decision making, writing with others is becoming commonplace.

Collaborative writing goes well beyond trading diskettes containing text files. Today, group-oriented software tracks changes to files and records who made the changes. Queries to others can be implemented, and reactions to proposed alterations can be shared. Some software even allows as many as 16 writers, all writing on one document at the same time if they wish, to generate a group document. Using e-mail to transmit attached documents is a common way of sharing manuscripts. Other hardware and software permits many participants at one time, in one location, at individual PCs, to brainstorm a topic, share reactions, statistically chart members' deviations from the group, and make a record of all comments.

Collaborative writing is enhanced when as many of these conditions exist as possible:

- All authors are equally competent with the hardware and software.
- Each author's contribution can be tracked.
- Each revision is shown along with the original, and the author making the change is identified.
- Authors realize that not all authors need to work on the document at once.
- Authors can add comments and questions to other authors.
- Authors work well together and are willing to give and receive constructive criticism.
- Authors meet agreed-upon deadlines.
- All authors agree upon the goal of the writing assignment from the outset.

Both academic writing experts and business practitioners see collaborative writing as a technique that will increase in value. Today's advanced business writer needs to be aware of the move toward this writing process.

International Communication

As was discussed briefly in Chapter 1, communication across cultural boundaries is becoming increasingly important. Indeed, Victor states that "the ability to compete in the world economy is arguably the single greatest challenge facing business at the end of the twentieth century."[7] Tung adds, "With the globalization of the world economy, it is imperative that managers, both present and future, be sensitive to differences in intercultural business communication."[8] To this Victor adds, "Few things, in turn, are more important in conducting business on a global scale than skill in communication."[9]

Victor sees seven main variables in international communication: language, social organization, contexting, authority conception, nonverbal behavior, temporal conception, and environment and technology. Of these factors, the last is changing most quickly and in many ways making the greatest impact.[10]

Communicating internationally has always been a slow or expensive proposition. Letters were slow, long-distance phone rates were exorbitant, and time changes were inconvenient. Several technological innovations, however, are changing this situation. Electronic mail via computers, either through a central computer clearinghouse such as CompuServe or an international network such as the Internet, now deliver inexpensive messages quickly throughout the world.

These e-mail messages are often limited to text, though attachments to e-mail contain colors, files, or pictures. Facsimile (fax) machines, on the other hand, send and receive any black-and-white image, including drawings, handwriting, and graphics. Further, the price of color fax machines is decreasing rapidly. Part of the reason for the heavy use of fax machines at the international level is that the price of a long-distance phone call, which carries the fax message, is decreasing. Such relatively new technologies as fiber optics and satellite transmissions help bring the price of a five-minute morning phone call from California to Japan to $5.40.

As U.S. businesses continue to seek out international markets, international branches, and foreign business partners, and as technology continues to make communication less expensive, quicker, and easier, one can see why international communication is such an important topic. Most business schools are readjusting their curriculum to include global trade, and international communication is a major element of that interaction.

SUMMARY

Advanced writing calls on many skills. At the composition level, you will need awareness of the writing sequence, from defining the problem through performing a post-writing evaluation. You will also employ techniques that relate directly to writing. For example, organized writing follows some logical approach to the goal of the message, is coherent, and uses emphatic style efficiently. Another skill involves applying appropriate tone through such techniques as the *I* versus *you* attitude, positive phrasing, and tactful wording. Skill is also needed to write readable text; attention to writing with clarity, conciseness, and activity influence readability.

To make the most of your time, follow the suggestions for efficient writing, which include some time-management principles. Conducting research electronically is both time efficient and powerful; knowledge of this skill can produce thorough research results with ease. Further, the electronic writing process can dramatically influence the quality and quantity of your output. By using shortcut techniques, selected software, and the power of the computer, you can enhance the transcription level of advanced writing.

In addition to the process of writing, the advanced business writer needs to be aware of how technology is affecting communication and business through collaborative writing, ethics, and international communication.

DISCUSSION QUESTIONS

1. What are the steps in the writing sequence?
2. Are some steps in the sequence more important than others? Why?
3. What are the three main characteristics of effective writing?
4. What are some ways to organize your message?
5. What is meant by coherence?
6. What are emphatic sentences?
7. In what ways can tone be modified?
8. How much would you use e-mail in communicating with a company about possible employment? Applying? Sending a résumé? Following up with a thank-you note? Accepting the job?
9. What is the electronic writing process and how can it influence communication?

Applications

1. Visit a computer store and ask for a demonstration of the latest, most powerful computer. In what ways would such a computer affect your writing?

2. Invite an expert on desktop publishing to visit your class to explain the desktop publishing process and its principles.

3. Research the latest computer magazines to find articles that predict the future for personal computers. What is the writing process likely to look like in five years? In ten years? Will the quality of writing change through increased reliance on computers?

4. Select a paper, letter, memo, or report that was written without using a computer and input it into your word processor. Analyze, critique, and check the message with such tools as spelling, grammar, and punctuation checkers. Test the readability using a computerized readability formula. Revise the paper, letter, memo, or report and then compare it to the original.

5. Divide a writing project, such as a group report, among group members so that each person writes a section using the same word-processing program. Give each team member a hard copy of each section for editing. Unite the sections into one document. Working together on the same computer, edit and smooth out the flow so the document has consistent tone and coherency. Evaluate the document against the writing skills described in the chapter.

6. Discuss with your classmates how you would go about searching for information on the Internet for the following items:

    a. A map of your state taken from space
    b. Quotes relative to the value of information by Thomas Jefferson
    c. An audio clip of Richard Nixon relative to criminal activity
    d. Information on how to put together a crisis management plan
    e. Three years of financial performance by company #23 out of this year's Fortune 500
    f. The highest and lowest elevations for the alphabetically 42nd state
    g. The latest scholarly article on communication apprehension
    h. The ethnic breakdown of the freshman class at your university for last fall

NOTES

1. For a thorough review of dimensions of the *you* attitude, see Annette N. Shelby and N. Lamar Reinsch, Jr., "Positive Emphasis and You-Attitude: An Empirical Study," *Journal of Business Communication* 32, no. 4, October 1995, pp. 303–328.

2. Marilia D. Svinicki, "Increasing Written Output," *Newsletter of the Center for Teaching Effectiveness*, 8, no. 1, September 1986, University of Texas at Austin, p. 1.

3. A. DelRossi, "SQL Report Writers Collect Information from Your Database and Make It Presentable," *Infoworld*, September 27, 1993, pp. 83–95.

4. Joan O'C. Hamilton, "Like It or Not, You've Got Mail," *Business Week*, October 4, 1999, pp. 178–184.

5. Hamilton, "Like It or Not," p. 184.

6. Hamilton, "Like It or Not," p. 184.

7. David A. Victor, *International Business Communication*, HarperCollins, New York, 1992, p. xiii.

8. R. L. Tung, in L. H. Chaney and J. S. Martin, *Intercultural Business Communication*, 2nd ed., Prentice Hall, Upper Saddle River, New Jersey, 2000, p. ix.

9. Victor, *International Business Communication*, p. xiii.

10. Victor, *International Business Communication*, p. 14.

CHAPTER

5

Writing Direct Messages

Written business messages vary in directness. For instance, most congratulatory messages should be direct. In terms of directness alone, you may wish to start with your main idea (such as congratulations). In other cases, such as in most persuasive messages, you may work up to your primary thought carefully by preceding it with other information; this is an indirect organization. You should consider your message's goal and your audience, among other things, as you select between the two organizations or pick a different approach altogether.

While many messages clearly fall into either the direct or indirect categories, others do not. Examples of those messages that do not fit the direct or indirect organizations are messages that combine aspects of both, such as those that place the main point at both the opening and closing, and messages that are neither, such as those that have more than one main thought. This book uses the term *situational message* for those messages that do not overtly apply the direct or indirect approaches.

The purpose of Chapters 5, 6, and 7 is to discuss the writing of direct messages (Chapter 5), indirect messages (Chapter 6), and situational messages (Chapter 7). Of the three, Chapter 7 is probably the most important for advanced writers for three reasons: because many messages are situational; because complex audience analysis and message skills are involved; and because the higher the writer is in the organizational hierarchy, the more likely this category of message will be required. But because the logic behind preparing many situational messages grows from concepts associated with direct and indirect organizations, we will explore those approaches first. In this chapter, we will examine message formats briefly and then turn to writing direct messages.

MESSAGE FORMATS

Once you delete the inside addresses, attention lines, or dates, the bodies of letters, memoranda, and e-mails are organized in much the same manner. Further, as electronic message systems such as e-mail continue to pervade the business environment, content receives more emphasis than does appearance. For these reasons, this book does not differentiate between direct organization letters, direct organization memoranda, or direct organization e-mail messages. Most companies will dictate the desired format for their letters and memoranda. However, if you are in doubt about the appearance of most business correspondence, see Figure 5.1 for a letter and Figure 5.2 for a memorandum.

While the preparation of the bodies of memoranda, letters, and e-mail is similar, differences between the three do exist. Memoranda tend to get down to business more quickly than letters. Their *To, From, Subject*, and *Date* approach streamlines important information for the reader and creates a different visual impact. A *Recommendation* section may lead off a memorandum to quickly clarify its goal.

Another approach to writing direct memoranda is the simplified format, which delivers three main sections: *Facts, Discussion,* and *Recommendations*. As an internal, brief, and focused message for the busy executive, this order of information presents background, interprets it, and draws a logical recommendation for action. Although building to the recommendation suggests an indirect orientation, the straightforward delivery and short length, coupled with no intention to hide or manipulate the recommendation, identify this message as plainly direct.

Memoranda and e-mail messages tend to be rather informal, internal messages that use a format different from that of a letter; they also vary in length and distribution. While letters are usually only one page, memoranda and e-mail range in length from one or two sentences to many pages. Memoranda often are distributed to entire departments or groups, while letters typically go only to certain individuals. E-mail messages carry the additional distinction of being able to have attachments, such as electronic letters, scanned images, pictures, or audio or video clips.

Of the three media, letters are perceived as most formal; thus, certain messages should always be delivered by letter.

Before you can prepare effective written messages you must be aware of the available approaches, the reasons for their organizations, and the appropriate occasion for each.

THE DIRECT APPROACH

In the direct approach, the sender's primary goal agrees with the receiver's primary goal: what is foremost in the mind of the recipient is what the author most wishes to transmit. The direct approach immediately and clearly presents your main or most important thought. Additional thoughts follow by order of importance.

Substantial research exists to support the logic of the direct approach. For example, McGuire has found that presenting desirable information first, followed by less

FIGURE 5.1 **Example of an Effective Positive Information Letter**

The Computer Source
278 Electronics Avenue
La Costa, CA 93008
February 12, 200X

Jorge Hernandez, President
Chips and Stuff, Inc.
1093 Upper Knob Drive
San Francisco, CA 96060

Dear Mr. Hernandez:

Thank you for your recent bid to supply us with 256 mb P" C-100 32 x 64 Dimm memory chips—we have decided to accept it. Yours was the lowest bid we received, and we very much want you to sign the enclosed contract pertaining to supply of these chips.

You may be interested to know that you are being awarded this contract not only because of your competitive pricing, but even more because of the availability of these 256-megabyte units. These chips are crucial to us, and your competition would not guarantee delivery within 30 days on orders of 1,000 units, as you do.

This new business venture should be rewarding for both of us. We look forward to developing a close working relationship with you and to many mutually beneficial contracts. Please sign and return the contract by March 1.

Cordially,

Hans Sturgeon

Hans Sturgeon
President

HS/gw
Enc.: contract

FIGURE 5.2   Example of an Effective Direct Positive Memorandum

INTEROFFICE MEMO

To: All Employees
From: Quentin Harris, Senior Vice President
Subject: Appreciation
Date: November 23, 200X

Yesterday, Francine Smith, management consultant with Long Beach Management Consultants, won the coveted Consultant of the Year award from her national association. Please join us in extending our appreciation and congratulations by signing the 2' x 3' congratulations card that we will send her on Tuesday. The card is in the reception area.

Francine has spent the last 11 months, as most of you know, reviewing our structure, financial position, and movement toward our goals. Her recommendations have been insightful. The restructuring has improved production and accountability, our profits are on the rise, and we're now moving aggressively toward our corporate goals.

Sh-sh-sh-sh! Please keep this quiet. She doesn't know we are sending her the card.

desirable information, produces more change than would presenting information in the reverse order.[1] Janis and Feierbend also have found that when a message has both positive and negative content, the positive content should appear first.[2]

Some writers enjoy building up to the delivery of the most important information. However, while this indirect approach may be rewarding to the author, it is frustrating to the reader and does not evoke as beneficial a reaction as the direct approach.

Three main categories of information that can be delivered with the direct organization are:

1. Positive information, which pleases the reader.
2. Neutral information, which may not elicit either a positive or negative reaction but which may have strong information value.
3. Negative information, which the reader will not want to read.

Assumptions about your audience and your tone are likely to vary with these three categories. Therefore, we shall review each category individually.

DELIVERING POSITIVE INFORMATION

When you have only positive information to present, rank your information with the most positive first, followed by the next most positive, and so on. Work your way down to the least positive details.

When reading the most positive information first, the reader encounters the next thought in a more receptive mood. Assuming the second thought is the second most positive comment, these thoughts combine to place the reader in an even more favorable frame of mind for the third thought, and so on. This cumulative effect helps the reader receive the message with a better overall reaction than would be derived from an indirectly organized message.

Because substantial positive feelings can reflect well on the sender, you should make optimal use of this message category. You can achieve even more benefit by using direct statements that follow a subject/verb–first organization, selecting active voice, picking present tense, using strong verbs, organizing sentences for emphasis, and involving the reader through the use of the *you* tone. Here is an example of such a message:

> Congratulations! Your proposal for the restructuring of the R&D team is right on target. You saw the heated personality conflicts sooner and more clearly than anyone else. We're adopting your proposal effective immediately.

The positive messages you deliver will vary greatly from extremely positive (You're hired!) to only slightly positive (Here's our regular quarterly parts order for the usual items). The more positive your information is, the more positive and strong your language should be, and vice versa.

With positive content messages, the most difficult writing steps are: (a) correctly ranking the importance of the various items from the reader's viewpoint; (b) omitting extraneous information; and (c) writing transitions from thought to thought.

Business messages that typically provide positive information include those granting requests, announcing favorable information, extending credit, showing gratitude, and accepting or sending invitations.

DELIVERING NEUTRAL INFORMATION

Neutral messages can carry information of equal or even higher importance than positive messages, but their emotional content and involvement is usually lower. Order acknowledgments, inquiries, requests for credit information, personnel evaluations, and compliance with requests can be neutral messages. The distinction between neutral and positive messages is open to interpretation; one person may see the information as positive while another perceives it as having so little positive information as to place it in the neutral camp. The perception by the receiver, not the sender, is crucial.

Use the direct approach with neutral messages. Instead of placing the most positive information at the top, however, report the most important information first. Smooth transitions from thought to thought will be necessary for coherence. Occasionally, you will need to place the less important information earlier in the message to avoid illogical or awkward construction. For example, you may need to discuss your firm's recent name change before you request an extension of credit. Figure 5.3 illustrates an effort to organize the most important facts first while still incorporating the needed yet unimportant facts as transitions.

You are likely to write many neutral internal messages to accompany other written information. These messages often are transmittal messages. Letters and memoranda transmit reports, illustrations, internal proposals, and other data from sender to receiver. They briefly explain the content of and reason for transferring the data. In some cases, they summarize the conclusions or recommendations of the report. These messages usually end with an offer of availability for questions. Chapter 9 discusses transmittals. As mentioned above, e-mail messages can carry attachments, such as reports or proposals. While it might be inappropriate to send an e-mail message with a formal proposal attached in response to a Request for Proposal, this process might be quite efficient and desirable for circulating the draft of the proposal internally among co-authors.

DELIVERING NEGATIVE INFORMATION

A decision that is often difficult is whether to use a direct or indirect organization to carry information with negative content. Do you agree with these views?

1. "I'll bet I've received 20 job rejection letters this semester. At first I appreciated the gentle letdown, but now I just wish they'd tell me the bad news up front."
2. "Sure, I want the contract. I also know from the return address who the letter is from and, therefore, the general topic. So just tell me: did I get the contract?"
3. "Don't try to placate me. I'm a big person. I don't need a wishy-washy indirect opening. Get to the subject. That's the way I like to be handled."

You can probably see some logic in these views. The problem for the writer is that most people do not feel these ways all the time. Many people prefer all job rejection letters, contract denials, and negative information to follow an indirect order. Your challenge, then, is to decide:

1. Does this information or occasion justify a direct approach?
2. Does this person prefer a direct approach?
3. Is this a routine message, one that is "business as usual"?

FIGURE 5.3   **Example of a Direct Neutral Message**

Dataproducts Corporation
6200 Canoga Avenue
P.O. Box 746
Woodland Hills, California 91365-0746
(818) 887-8000   Telex 67-4734

Thank you . . .

for your recent request for information regarding products manufactured by Dataproducts Corporation. We are enclosing
descriptive literature and hope it will answer any questions you
may have.

Dataproducts manufactures a broad range of computer printers,
printer components and supplies, and telecommunications
equipment for the computer industry.

If you would like to discuss pricing and/or technical details
please telephone us at (800) 258-1386, and we will provide
you with the telephone number of the Dataproducts sales or
distributor/dealer office nearest you.

We would also appreciate your completing and returning the enclosed postpaid reply card. The information you supply will be helpful to us in providing you with additional literature and service.

Sincerely,

Keith Bauserman
Vice President
North American Sales

KB:adk
Enc.

Source: Reproduced with permission from Dataproducts Corporation.

If your answers to all three questions are yes, use the direct approach. If the answer to any one of these three questions is no, pick the indirect approach. If you are unsure of the answers, you are probably safest with the indirect approach because inappropriately using the direct organization can create strong antagonism toward the author and the author's business.

Inappropriate use of the indirect organization, on the other hand, may cause the reader some frustration but is unlikely to bring about extreme negative reactions. (More discussion of the indirect approach appears in Chapter 6.)

Prepare your negative messages that follow the direct organization with these thoughts in mind:

- Place the negative information first because you assume it is the most important information to the reader. Do not try to gloss over the bad news.
- Deliver the negative information gently. The passive voice may be appropriate. Use some finesse. Be tactful. Do not dwell on the bad news.
- Give reasons that support the decision, if possible. Avoid saying that you are sorry; instead, let the rationale of the decision work for you. Give selected details but do not pass the buck or blame company policy.
- Try to include some positive information, particularly at the end.
- Sound sincere. Insincere-sounding messages, especially carrying the negative information, can be destructive.
- Work for continued goodwill.

Accomplishment of this last objective may take the form of describing what you have done to avoid similar problems in the future, offering personal attention to the customer, or providing some free service or replacement. See Figure 5.4 for an example of an effective negative message that uses direct organization.

Additional Direct Negative Message Considerations

Sometimes you will want to use the direct negative approach, such as when writing to friends who might be offended by an indirect approach. Here is an example:

You're a good friend, but I still need payment for the money I loaned you last month so you could take advantage of your company's stock investment program. Please send me the $500 right away.

You may also wish to use the direct negative approach when trying to avoid a patronizing tone, which most of us dislike. When we are clearly at fault for something, sometimes we would rather just hear the bad news instead of being toyed with. Here is an example:

The Yellow River Project report was due yesterday. We both know how important the completion of the report is to the overall strategic plan. Submit the report to me no later than 5 p.m. tomorrow.

FIGURE 5.4   **Negative Message Using Direct Organization**

From:server@net.com
Date:Tue, 08Nov 200X 011:51:06 -4000
Organization:@net.com.net
X-Mailer: BX 98.7 [cba] V-atnet.com.net 0773 (Win2000; U)
X-Accept-Language: cba.774
FROM: Samantha Chen <samchen@net.com>
TO:ExecManTeam.list@net.com
SUBJECT: This weekend's Executive Management Team retreat

This past weekend's retreat at the Big Pines Resort was,
in my mind, a big flop. We had hoped to emerge from the
two days of meetings and discussions with a firm business
strategy for the coming year in place, a decision on
whether to move ahead on production of the X-14 or Z-19
audio chips, and a clearer understanding of the role
electronic commerce should play in our future. We did not
achieve the first two and made only slight progress on
the last goal.

In retrospect, I think there are several reasons why the
outcomes were not better. First, rather than functioning
as a committee-of-the-whole and seeking consensus on
every decision, we needed more structure. Second,
inviting our spouses, while most enjoyable for us, seemed
to interfere with our getting to sessions on time and
staying focused. Finally, the afternoon of golf on Sunday
afternoon cut into our total time together, and occurred
just as we were close to accomplishing our goals.

Therefore, I'm calling a day-long work session for
Saturday, the 23d of this month, in our executive
conference room, starting at 8 a.m. to complete our work.
I've arranged for Bill Finegar to serve as facilitator.

You know the issues, so be thinking about them. The
sooner we meet our objectives for the meeting, the sooner
we can join our spouses for the balance of the weekend or
get out to the golf course.

ADDITIONAL DIRECT INFORMATION MESSAGES

In addition to the positive, neutral, and negative information types of messages that use the direct organization, there are two others. Routine messages and directives may carry any of the three information types, but they have some unique characteristics as well.

Routine Messages

Routine messages occur at periodic intervals, such as quarterly reports, or regularly, such as in progress reports. See Figure 5.5 for an example of a routine form letter.

Here are two provisos exclusive to routine messages:

- First, if the routine message has negative content, it is often wise to emphasize the routine aspect of the message. For example, you might emphasize that this is your regular semiannual product order, that you plan to pay for it within 30 days after billing as usual, that you want it sent to your St. Louis plant as before, and that you appreciate the excellent service you have come to associate with the supplier. An example of routine negative information in such a message might be that your orders vary in size dramatically during the year, and this happens to be an order much smaller than the last two orders.
- Second, there are occasions where it would undercut your objective to inform the reader of your regular writing of this type of message. "This invitation goes out to all persons whose names appear in the weekly listing of 'Marriage Certificates Approved' for a special 10 percent discount" misses the opportunity to focus on an event that is for the reader infrequent and individually exciting.

Routine messages may appear as form letters or may be individually prepared as the occasion requires. Form letters, of course, often are impersonal and mass produced. Nevertheless, time and cost considerations frequently dictate the form message.

The messages discussed so far—especially the rather similar positive, neutral, and routine messages—and goodwill messages to be discussed in Chapter 7, have an interesting, complex relationship, as can be seen in Figure 5.6. Some of the information in a positive message (most likely the portions further down in the message) may be neutral; some early portions of a neutral message might be perceived as positive by some people. When you, as an insurance agent, send a Christmas card to your policyholders, you are sending a routine goodwill message that is also positive. When a person automatically places orders for parts with you each three months, it is a routine neutral message. Envisioning the relationship of these four message categories will help you to prepare any one of them.

Directives

Directives are internal messages issued to employees to identify desired or undesired behavior. As a manager, you will write directives not only for the obvious reason of

FIGURE 5.5   **Example of a Routine Form Message**

EMMAUS, PA 18049

Welcome!

Dear Subscriber,

Thanks for your subscription order to NEW SHELTER
Magazine. Enclosed you'll find your FREE booklet which comes
as part of your subscription to our magazine.

Your first issue should be arriving shortly. Once you've read
through it, you'll agree that a subscription to NEW SHELTER is
a great investment for any homeowner—one that's sure to pay
for itself many times over in the course of a single year!

NEW SHELTER is really the complete home magazine. If it's home
improvement you want, you'll find lots of help in enhancing the
value . . . the beauty . . . and the overall "liveability" of your home.

You should really be congratulated on the wise decision you've
made! We thank you again for subscribing to our magazine,
and we're confident you'll be glad you did and will want to
stay with us for many years to come! Again, welcome to NEW
SHELTER—it's nice to have you with us!

Sincerely,

Ed Fones

Ed Fones
Circulation Manager

EF:iss
Enc.

Source: Reproduced with permission from Rodale's *New Shelter* magazine.

FIGURE 5.6   **Relationship of Some Messages Using Direct Organization**

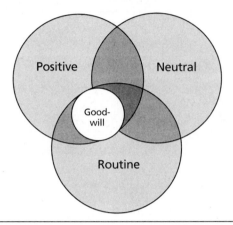

giving direction but also to provide a written record to which employees can be held accountable and to which they can refer over time for details. You may also use directives to establish or reinforce your authority or to build a framework of policies and procedures.

Many directives follow the direct approach. Your main purpose is to direct behavior; identify that behavior clearly and firmly at the beginning of the message.

Effective directives do more than just direct; they also present the rationale behind the directive. Therefore, your second step is an explanation for the desired behavior. Support your explanation with reasons when appropriate. Your explanation and reasons are your second most important information.

Finally, you may wish to include a motivational thought, such as "Let's follow safety rules for our own protection and for the good of the company." Be careful, however, not to undermine your authority, lose your tone of firmness, or appear too warm or friendly. Warmth and friendliness are valuable commodities to share with employees, but not in every communiqué; omit them from your directives. You seek compliance without emotional involvement. To avoid involving your readers too much in the message or even offending them, use an impersonal tone with relatively few adjectives, adverbs, similes, metaphors, or other colorful language.[3] See Figure 5.7 for an example of an effective directive.

Another direct message type is the direct persuasive message. This message is so unique, however, that it receives special attention in Chapters 6 and 7.

FIGURE 5.7 **Example of an Effective Directive**

```
From:server@comcom
Date:Wed, 08Dec 200X 011:41:06 -8000
Organization:@comcom.net
X-Mailer: MX 4.7 {xn} B-atcom.net 0443 (Win2000; U)
X-Accept-Language: xn
FROM: William C. Griggs <wcg@comcom>
TO:employeeslist_all@comcom

DATE:  December 8, 200X.

Many employees have been bringing privately owned
portable computers to work and have been using these
computers on the job. While employee involvement
and dedication are valuable assets, please do not
demonstrate them by bringing computers to work,
effective immediately.

The presence of non-company-owned computers has
created problems of control of confidential company
data, has wasted work time while employees
demonstrated the machines to colleagues, and has
caused compatibility problems in the steno pool,
where the word-processing specialists are familiar
only with Microsoft Word and WordPerfect on IBM PCs.

To involve computers more in your tasks and to assist
those of you familiar with computers, we are exploring
a bulk purchase of compatible computers for use by
salaried employees. Your suggestions regarding which
equipment best meets your needs, and assignment of
these machines, if purchased, would be appreciated.
```

SUMMARY

In business writing, you can choose between direct and indirect approaches. Go directly to the main message (a direct organization) if your information is positive or neutral in nature. Consider a direct organization for negative information only if the information or occasion calls for it, if you think the reader prefers it, or if the message is routine.

The direct approach assumes there will be little or no resistance from the reader and that what is most positive or most important to the sender is also most positive or important to the reader. Thus, the direct approach orders thoughts from most positive to least positive (or, for the neutral message, from most important to least important). For the transmission of negative information in a direct order, be gentle in your language and use logic to your benefit. The direct organization also can be used effectively with two other types of messages: routine messages and directives. Sometimes it is advisable to indicate the routineness of the message and other times it is not. With the directive, information is firm and clear about desired behavior on the part of employees.

Because a variety of message types appear in this chapter, Table 5.1 summarizes the three major message types (positive, neutral, and negative) and shows subcategories and additional categories.

Memoranda, letters, and e-mail messages using the direct organization are relatively easy to organize and write. But despite their ease in preparation, these messages—especially the positive and neutral ones—sometimes go unwritten because they are often not a response to a request. These messages are, therefore, not missed if not received. Because of their perceived expendability, they are among the first messages neglected by the overworked writer. This neglect is unfortunate because these messages reassure, reconfirm, and give attention to existing clients, employees, and customers.

As a portion of the total writing effort, direct messages are a mainstay—one often skipped by less-concerned communicators and weaker managers. These messages can help distinguish you as a person who makes the extra effort to send such often-ignored communications as congratulations or acknowledgments. Enhance your image with these messages.

This chapter introduces aspects of another major organization: the indirect approach, which is the subject of Chapter 6. Chapter 7 goes on to examine situational writing, which brings together many of the underlying concepts supporting direct and indirect organizations.

DISCUSSION QUESTIONS

1. What are the two main organizational approaches to written business communication?
2. Are there content differences between memoranda and letters?
3. How do you organize a message that contains positive information?
4. How do you organize a message that contains neutral information?
5. How do you organize a message that contains negative information?
6. How do you organize routine messages?
7. How do you write directives?
8. How would you write a message to a close friend who works for you but (a) needs to be disciplined, (b) is to be congratulated, (c) is to be relocated to an equally attractive location within the same city?

TABLE 5.1   **Summary of Direct Message Approaches**

Major Message Type/Subcategory	Goal	Example
Positive	Reception of positive information by receiver	Extension of long-term financing for a major project
Letter of Recommendation	Help someone obtain a job	Recommend employee or friend for employment
Goodwill	Elicit positive reaction back to sender	Appreciation for continuing business
Neutral	Reception of neutral information by receiver	Acknowledge reception of order
Transmittal	Transport other written media	Transmittal letter in a report
Negative	Clear, immediate delivery of negative information	Rejection of a bid
Additional Types		
Routine	Transmission of frequently recurring information	Sending clients a reminder that you need their tax information by February 1
Directives	Internal messages to direct behavior	Changing the time of coffee breaks

Applications

1. Gather business letters you receive over a week or more. How many do you classify as direct messages? Of those, how many are positive, neutral, negative, or persuasive? Do the results of your survey agree with what is suggested in the text?

2. The next time you need to prepare a direct negative message, try out a draft of the message on some colleagues. Do they agree with you that it should be written in a direct organization?

3. Locate an example of a direct negative message. Use these questions to critique it: Is the topic handled well? Should this message have been written directly or indirectly? How would the audience feel about this message? What could be done to improve the message?

4. Conduct a survey of business e-mail users. What percentage of their messages are formal versus informal, internal versus external, one screen in length versus longer, have attachments, and are sent to a distribution list of five or more people?

NOTES

1. William J. McGuire, "The Nature of Attitude and Attitude Change," *Handbook of Social Psychology*, 2nd ed., vol. 3, Addison-Wesley, Reading, Massachusetts, 1969, p. 212; and William J. McGuire, "Order of Presentation as a Factor in 'Conditioning' Persuasiveness," in C. I. Hovland (ed.), *The Order of Presentation in Persuasion*, Yale University Press, New Haven, Connecticut, 1957, pp. 98–114.

2. I. L. Janis and R. L. Feierbend, "Effects of Alternate Ways of Ordering Pro and Con Arguments in Persuasive Communications," in C. I. Hovland (ed.), *The Order of Presentation in Persuasion*, Yale University Press, New Haven, Connecticut, 1957, p. 23.

3. Ronald E. Dulek and John S. Fielden, *Principles of Business Communication*, Macmillan Publishing Co., New York, 1990, pp. 283–284.

'6'

Writing Indirect Messages

In Chapter 5, we explained that when the writer expects the reader to agree with the contents of a message, it is best to present the message directly. In business, you may also select the direct approach because you think the occasion dictates it or the reader prefers it, because the information is routine, or because it is easy to write—direct messages usually take relatively little planning. There is no resistance to overcome in direct messages. Resistance means that the reader may be opposed to what you are proposing (or to you or your company), may be disinterested, or may not be able to comply. You will encounter many other occasions when resistance is likely—for instance, when transmitting strong negative information or when persuading someone to act. This chapter presents writing approaches for these two message categories, both of which usually use an indirect organization. Chapter 7 discusses those messages for which there are no clear-cut formulas.

If positive messages with direct organization are among the easiest to write, then those with negative information or persuasive content are among the most difficult. The difficulty of writing a negative message stems from its bipolar objectives: (1) to transmit the bad news clearly and (2) to maintain the reader's goodwill. Picture, for example, writing a supplier to reject a bid but trying to maintain interest so that the company will continue to bid in the future. To accomplish either objective by itself is fairly easy; to accomplish both takes skill. Persuasive messages, too, are usually indirect messages because they try to overcome a reader's resistance. Using the approach that we outline below for a negative or persuasive message often makes the writer's job less burdensome.

Writing effective indirect messages entails understanding the rationale behind the indirect approach. The rationale emphasizes the steps in the formula.

NEGATIVE MESSAGES

The formula for negative messages grows from the dual objectives of transmitting bad news and maintaining goodwill. Occasionally, maintaining goodwill is not of primary concern and is even subordinate to the message delivery. Such an occasion might be the fifth in a series of progressively sterner letters seeking payment for goods or services. For most of us there is a point at which positive perception of us or our business is no longer a primary goal. Occasions such as these either use direct organization or are handled in a situational approach.

The pattern for transmitting negative messages has four steps: (1) a delaying opening, (2) the reasons for the upcoming bad news, (3) the bad news itself, and (4) a positive ending. These steps follow an indirect organization, which means that the primary reason for the message—the bad news—receives a location of low emphasis. Opening sentences and paragraphs carry high impact (that is why in positive messages the most positive thought is placed there), and so does the ending of a message. Using the principle of place emphasis, bad news most often appears in the middle of the message to diminish its impact.

The underlying logic supporting the indirect approach is that preparing the reader for the message can determine to a great extent the reader's perception of the message. While the reader will not be happy hearing the bad news, the reader may at least understand the writer's position if the information appears in such a way that the recipient reads all the message and if the reasons are believable, realistic, and logical.

Understanding the rationale behind the order and preparation of the four steps is useful not only in preparing negative messages but also in writing more complicated messages, such as situational messages.

The Delaying Opening

The purpose of delaying the opening is to present the general topic without hinting about the upcoming negative news. Writing a delaying opening that does not sound like it is delaying the bad news can be difficult. If you have ever read an opening that you recognized as a delaying tactic, then you have read an ineffective opening. For example, this opening is weak because it leaks the upcoming bad news: "Over the last year you've met most of the essential deadlines." Other characteristics of weak openings are those that start too far from the general subject and those that have too positive a tone.

Because many negative messages are in response to earlier messages or inquiries, the readers of those messages often eagerly anticipate the answers. This anticipation puts pressure on the delaying opening. For example, how would you react to this opening?

Thank you for your recent letter of application for our position of management consultant. You were correct in your observation that our consulting division is one of the largest and best of the major public accounting firms. Because of this size and quality we always carefully review the education, experience, and other characteristics of job applicants.

If you are especially eager for this job, you might find the delay of the important news, whatever it may be, frustrating. On the other hand, you might find the personal references a positive way to get in the mood of the topic. At least the opening does not give away the upcoming bad news or start too far from the subject.

The astute reader may well argue that any response that does not immediately state the good news must be delaying the bad news. If all messages were prepared following either the direct or indirect organizations and were written effectively, this observation would be correct. However, there are many writers who inappropriately apply the indirect organization to positive messages and still others who use a direct organization for strong negative content. In other words, there are enough writers who are poor at organizing messages that most readers will not see through your intentions when you write an effective delaying opening.

Writing an effective delaying opening is often the most difficult of the four steps in the negative message formula. For many writers, starting with a more positive opening than is necessary is easier than the neutral-to-slightly-positive delaying opening. However, an opening that is too positive forces awkward transitions to the rapidly approaching bad news. For example, "You have consistently prepared better marketing analysis than others in your department" makes difficult the switch to negative information.

Another reason—a major one—that delaying openings are so difficult to write is that they often appear manipulative. As soon as your reader thinks he or she is being tricked or coerced or is receiving biased or one-sided information, he or she will reject your message. (Indeed, this reaction applies to indirect messages as a whole!) Strictly speaking, you are manipulating the reader as you make such decisions as word selection and order, message organization, format, and delivery timing. However, if the reader does not recognize your manipulation, you probably will achieve your goal.

The Reasons

Probably the most crucial step in the negative message formula is the second, which establishes the reasons for the upcoming bad news. The goal of the step is to seek reader acknowledgment of the reasons; acknowledgment at this point establishes a relationship with the yet-to-be-announced decision. Returning to the example of a response to a job application, does this example accomplish the step's goal?

> Because of the fine reputation of the Management Consulting Division, our well-known training program, and the firm's solid national standing, many dozens of applicants—a large percentage with MBAs—are seeking positions. Both the large number and the high quality of the applications make our job of selecting the top interviewees difficult. Our strong appreciation for experience in consulting guides us in our selections.

The example presents three reasons: the number of applications, the quality of the applications, and the focus on applicants with experience.

In preparing your reasons, empathize with your reader—the reasons should be logical to the reader and not just to you. Avoid reliance on such weak reasons as company policy. Instead, explain the reasons for the company policy. Do not pass the buck, blaming someone else for the decision. As the author of a letter being sent to someone outside the company, you represent the company; it is poor form to transfer the decision elsewhere. If possible and appropriate, each reason should build on preceding reasons.

If the reasons step appears logical, the upcoming bad news will emerge naturally. Further, this second step also should not leak bad news, even though that news is the next step.

The Bad News

Step three in the indirect organization of a bad news message delivers the negative information. While the delaying opening and the development of the reasons may take from several sentences to a paragraph each, this third step can be quite short, sometimes taking only a part of a sentence. The bad news often follows from and can be appended to the reasons step. Avoid putting bad news in a separate paragraph. A stand-alone paragraph, such as "For the reasons stated above, we must sever our contract," is undesirable because it receives too much emphasis.

In appending the bad news step to earlier steps of the sample message, the goal is the reader's agreement with your decision.

> Applicants other than you, ones with equally solid educational background but extensive consulting background, have been selected to be interviewed.

Despite its relatively short length, this third step is still important and requires careful wording. Too blunt a negative message can destroy effectively prepared earlier steps. To maintain the goodwill of the reader, it is necessary to present the negative news as positively as possible. Sometimes you can leave the interpretation of the bad news to the reader by establishing what you are doing as opposed to not doing. For example, stating that you are awarding a bid to another firm tells the reader that he or she did not receive it.

Most often the active voice is best for business writing to add interest, clarity, and movement. In the third step of a negative message, however, the active voice may be too forceful; the passive voice may be softer. For example, the passive "Your firm's services are no longer required" is softer than the active "We no longer want to employ your firm."

The negative step can also be too personal. Seek an impersonal style by avoiding people's names and personal pronouns. Be especially cautious of first names, *I*, and *you*. Some writers, in an attempt to show personal involvement with the decision, declare their sympathy or extend an apology. Such statements weaken the strength of the earlier logic and usually add little to soften the bad news. An "I'm sorry" is likely to elicit a "me, too" or a bitter "I'll bet you are." Further, the unnecessary sympathy or apology only underscores the bad news, thus emphasizing it.

Once you deliver the negative message, leave it. Do not dwell on it. Change the subject to something more positive, such as the topic of the positive ending.

The Positive Ending

The last step seeks to change the tone from negative to positive. The reason for this step is to maintain goodwill. Positive information at the end allows the writer to end on a nice note, avoids closing on bad news, and uses the location—at the end of the message, which provides emphasis—to push a positive overall tone.

At a minimum, the ending can extend thanks for the offer, the bid, the suggestion, the application, the idea, the message, or whatever you have decided to reject. Make sure that this thanks sounds sincere; even heartfelt appreciation stated as, "Thanks again, and don't hesitate to write," will make little impact on the reader. The phrase sounds insincere and overused. The same idea, rephrased to sound sincere and individualized, might be, "Perhaps your next idea will be the award winner, so don't hold back on sharing other suggestions with us in the future."

Look for stronger endings than just thank you. Perhaps you can alter the declined inquiry so that you can give an affirmative answer. For example, if asked for reprints of an article, respond by saying, "If photocopies of the report rather than reprints are acceptable, we can mail them immediately." You may also be able to suggest an alternate source for something you could not provide: "We no longer manufacture the pressed glassware you seek; Art Products bought the molds; they may be able to help you. Their address is . . . ."

A third technique for stronger positive endings is suggesting that in the future you might be able to extend a yes. To exemplify this approach, we again turn to the response to a job application:

> As our Management Consulting Division continues to grow, we expect to have new openings. As you acquire additional accounting experience elsewhere, please keep us in mind as a possible employer.

Resist the desire to toss in a final reference to the bad news such as, "Again, know that we're as sorry about this as you are." Once you deliver the negative in the third step, do not resurrect it. End on a positive thought.

The four steps in the negative message should flow from idea to idea. Let's look again at that letter responding to a job application with its parts consolidated.

> Thank you for your recent letter of application for our position of management consultant. You were correct in your observation that our consulting division is one of the largest and best of the biggest public accounting firms. Because of this size and quality we always carefully review the education, experience, and other characteristics of job applicants.
>
> Because of the fine reputation of the Management Consulting Division, our well-known training program, and the firm's solid national standing, many dozens of applicants—a large percentage with MBAs—are seeking this position. Both the large number and the high quality of the applications make our job of selecting the top interviewees difficult. Our strong appreciation for experience in consulting guides us in our selections. Applicants other than you, ones with equally solid educational background but extensive consulting background, have been selected to be interviewed.
>
> As our Management Consulting Division continues to grow, we expect to

have new openings. As you acquire additional accounting experience elsewhere, please keep us in mind as a possible employer.

Transitions are important in all writing. Negative messages are no exception. A smooth transition is especially crucial between steps one and two. Look for a phrase that links thoughts occurring at the end of step one to the first thoughts in step two. (A discussion of writing transitions appears in Chapter 4.)

Avoiding such reversal words or phrases as *on the other hand, however*, or *unfortunately* will smooth the transition from step one to step two, as well as avoid alerting the reader to the upcoming bad news.

As discussed, the transition from step two to step three is usually an easy one. Although there is a major tone change from step three to step four, the transition is not as important because the tone is now positive. The author may even wish to accentuate the change by starting step four with a reversal word or phrase, such as "In the next few months, however, . . ." This technique serves to tell the reader, "the bad news is over; now we're changing to more pleasant topics." See Figure 6.1 for an effective indirect negative message.

Not all negative messages nor all companies follow the steps described here. A few years ago one of the largest merchandisers in the United States, in rejecting requests for credit, responded with computer-generated form letters that started

Dear Credit Applicant:

Thank you for the opportunity to consider your request for credit. We regret, however, that we cannot, at this time, accommodate your specific credit needs.

As noted below,

    <u>ACTION TAKEN</u>

Application for credit denied.
You have the right to . . . .

Place yourself in the position of the applicant. How would you feel toward the company that sent this letter?

PERSUASIVE MESSAGES

The second major category of messages that relies on the indirect organization is persuasive messages. Most business writing tries to persuade others to act in a desired way. Those who are successful at altering the behavior of others make their readers want to take the proposed action. If the reader already wants to do what you propose, you should not resort to a persuasive message. Write a direct request to act. When it is necessary to change an opinion toward an action or product, however, work up to the request. You are guaranteed a rejection if you start with a request when resistance is present. Therefore, build your message following the indirect organization, which saves the request for the desired action until last. (Request messages that do not fit the concept are discussed in Chapter 7.)

FIGURE 6.1 **Example of an Effective Indirect Negative Message**

First National Bank
P.O. Box 987
Ft. Worth, TX 78206

April 23, 200X

David Hertfelder, Executive Director
Substance Abuse Program for Children
Dallas–Ft. Worth Region
P.O. Box 2322
Ft. Worth, TX 78210

Dear David:

Thank you for your letter describing the substance abuse program. While I was aware of the existence of your program, I had not realized the extent of your services. Your request for financial support for your upcoming Awareness Fair honors us. As you mentioned in your letter, we do believe in community duty and seek out those programs that focus on children. That you know of our involvement is reassuring to us. As part of our giving program, each January we establish our contribution budget and then, in February, we announce our contributions to the public. Our contributions for 200X already have been announced and distributed.

If you decide to hold your Fair next year or wish to be considered for a contribution to another aspect of your program, please submit a proposal before January 1, 200X. Your proposal will receive careful consideration.

Thank you again for thinking of us. Good luck with your program and your Fair.

Cordially,

Traci Petalek

Traci Petalek
Director, Community Relations

Writing persuasively usually follows a series of specific steps; these steps parallel the behavior we follow each time we take an overt action. For example, analyze this vignette:

You need some parts for your old car, so you go to the dealer. The parts department is closed for another ten minutes so you decide to wait in the showroom. You immediately notice a bright red, new BMW 325i in the middle of the room. You admire the sleek lines and take in the rugged, powerful beauty. "Now there's a car," you say to yourself.

As is usually the case, you have been near the car for only a short time when you are greeted by a salesperson: "Great little car, isn't it?" he says. "Just check this baby out!"

"You're right, it's a beauty. How much is it?" you respond.

"It's probably the best buy we have. Here, sit behind the wheel in the real leather seats. Have you ever seen a better dash? Looks like the car was made for you," he responds.

"It's comfortable, all right. I'll bet it costs a fortune. How much is it?" you query again.

For the next few minutes the salesperson continues to sidestep your inquiries about price. Instead, he maneuvers you around the car, getting you to look here, feel there. His conclusion of each exchange with a question such as, "Feels great, doesn't it?" or "How does that compare to any other car you've seen?" eludes you. Next, there's a transition in his comments. He now tries to get you to say in a different way how much you want the car. "Picture yourself pulling into the parking lot at work. Everyone's looking at you. Feels good, doesn't it?"

"Sure does," you reply. "There's no doubt I'd love to have the car. I just can't afford it."

"Hey, wait a sec. We've just announced a new, low 9 percent interest rate, and this car is on special this month, as well. Payments can be made over 48 months, so that they're so small you barely notice them. What? You have a car you could trade in? So much the better. Let's go back to my office and run some scenarios on my calculator."

Your head is spinning, but you know you're under no obligation yet. This is exciting.

Concurrently, the salesperson is planning his strategy; he's moving in for the kill. He punches the calculator for a while, looks at some tables, hits the calculator some more, smiles, and says, "We can put you in that new BMW today so you can drive back to work in it today for under $400 a month. Of course that includes full warranty and service for 50,000 miles, and we'll take your old car off your hands. Let's go ahead and sign the contract; what do you say?"

Whether you sign the contract now, wait weeks or even years to buy a similar car, or never buy the BMW, you still have been through a common behavior process. Something caught your attention—in this case the bright color of the car shining in the showroom's spotlights. In other cases, advertisements or jingles might be the attention getter.

Next, and quickly, your interest was piqued. In the vignette, the salesperson spoke of general and major attributes he felt sure you would acknowledge affirmatively.

Third, the salesperson created in you a desire for the car. He listened to your needs and filled them with his product. You started to feel you needed the car. At the same time, hesitations emerged in your mind—cost, payments, trade-in, and so on. But before these thoughts were verbalized, he struck them down with counter-arguments and opposing logic. Having convinced you not only that you needed the car, but also that you were willing to make certain trade-offs to get it, he moved to the final step: action. The concluding step reiterated some strengths, made it easy to say yes to the request, and contained the big question: would you sign the contract?

As an advanced business communicator, your application of persuasion will have little to do with buying or selling cars. Nevertheless, as you will see, the steps are important to writing effective persuasive messages in other aspects of business. The vignette exaggerates the five steps we go through with each major action we take: attention, interest, desire, conviction, and action. Just as these are the steps we follow to action, they, too, are the steps of a persuasive message.

As we examine the writing steps in a persuasive message, be aware that there are other elements in the persuasive encounter that need consideration, such as perception of the sender, hierarchical differences, the context, nonverbal factors, degree of rapport, and so on.

The Attention Step

The less disposed your reader is to respond favorably to your request, the stronger and more highly defined should be the attention step. Conversely, the more likely your reader is to act as desired, the less you need an attention-getting opening.

When writing strong attention getters, several techniques may be applied. Questions are good openers because they involve the reader. Few of us can resist answering even the silliest rhetorical question. Perhaps because of the effectiveness of the question as an attention getter, questions are prevalent.

Attention-getting devices include making a startling statement, using mechanical or printed grabbers, focusing on a single word, giving something away, stressing low cost, describing some enticing mood or situation, or personalizing with the reader's name or address. Often, even the envelope is treated in such a way as to encourage the recipient to read the information inside.

No rule exists about how closely related to the ultimate action the opener should be. Many magazine subscription mailings, for example, open with contests and give-aways even though these devices have no apparent connection to the action they want you to take. Compare these three openings by how they relate to the action step:

Unrelated to action "Would you pick the $100,000 house or the year-long vacation around the world if you won this contest?" Action: subscribe to magazines.

Semi-related to action "For only one penny you can have any 12 CDs or tapes from the hundreds listed." Action: join a CD/tape club.

Related to action "Just as the bright, shiny penny that is glued to this letter says, 'In God We Trust,' we trust you to support our Children's Hospital." Action: financially support a children's hospital.

The goals of an attention step are (1) to get the reader's attention and (2) to develop enough attention to carry the reader into the next step. Those attention getters that do not accomplish both objectives are in a message that will probably not result in success.

The Interest Step

The interest step is one of transition; it carries the reader from the attention-getting opening to the desire step. The interest step also starts to give some direction to the message (if the opening did not do so). The step takes the undirected momentum of the attention getter and points toward the ultimate action. The step also encourages some involvement by the reader. Interest develops through blending the strengths of the opening and the enticements of the upcoming desire step. The interest step often is relatively short.

Avoid just telling the reader to become interested; give information that creates interest. Replace "You'll be interested to know that . . ." with "Five of seven people in your job classification are desperately untrained in using a computer spreadsheet."

The Desire Step

The third step develops desire in the reader for the ultimate good, service, or action. The desire grows solely from positive attributes. The goal is for the reader to feel that he or she would like the service or product. The attributes of the service or product will determine how much information to include in this step. At this step, there is no concern with the counterarguments or hesitancies against what will be proposed. These are handled in the next step.

Here's an example of a desire step that pushes the positive attributes without yet talking about their cost: "Successful business people at the beginning of the twenty-first century—those making the big salaries and having job security—will have technological competence, entrepreneurial skills, and international business expertise."

The Conviction Step

Before the reader has a chance to organize arguments against the upcoming action, the conviction step lays out the counterarguments. While these may sound like positive attributes, similar to those in the desire step, they actually are positive ways of looking at the action's weaknesses. For example, saying that time payments are available may disguise an unusually high price, or that the position holds great opportunities and a promising future offsets its long hours and low starting salary.

The desire and conviction steps are closely related and should flow together. Both will sound positive, but desire is inherently positive information while conviction may be seen as displacing negative information and using positive tone.

Central to all persuasion is the concept of need. A reader must feel the need to take the suggested action to satisfy some personal motivation. Without the feeling of need, the persuasion is likely to be hollow and short lived. Need is developed across several of the steps of the persuasive message but is primarily in the desire and conviction steps. The wording of the presentation of the attributes creates the feeling of need. Sometimes effective need development is as simple as employing empathy and using *you* words and the *you* attitude. For example, look at these statements:

Positive but impersonal and ineffective "Underwriting this venture will be financially rewarding."

Positive, personal, and need-developing "Enhance your image as a venture capitalist by taking advantage of this opportunity."

While the use of the *you* attitude is desirable in most forms of communication, including written and spoken, you will find its use especially fruitful in developing the need in the desire and conviction steps.

The Action Step

Only after you are sure that the reader is convinced of the need to take the action that you plan to propose should you propose it. An action statement that occurs too early will meet defeat. Each of the first four steps sets up the next one; if any one is ineffective, the reader will not be carried to the culmination of the message. The reader may stop somewhere in the sequence or read the balance of the message but decide not to accept the proposed action.

Not only does the action step build on earlier steps, it also uses selected information from them. This last step reemphasizes the reader's benefit from taking the proposed action, makes it easy for the reader to do as suggested, and asks for the action. These three parts may be in any order within the action step.

Here's an example of an action step that incorporates the three parts:

So, start your membership in the City Club, where the Dallas business and financial world conducts the real transactions. To qualify for the special rate, just complete the brief application form and mail it in. Your membership starts once we receive your form.

The benefits are (1) to have access to critical events, (2) to pay a special rate, and (3) to begin membership soon. Ease of response is shown by the short form that is mailed back. The action request is simple: "complete the form . . . and mail it in."

Ways to Stimulate Action

Two main categories of techniques to stimulate action are (1) punishment and reward and (2) emotional and rational appeals. Both are used in business.

You can change behavior by threatening punishment: "If you don't pay the balance due by March 1, we'll contact our lawyers." Or you can change behavior by offering a reward: "If you pay your balance by March 1, your credit rating will remain unblemished." While these approaches may both be successful, the positive tone of the reward approach is preferable in business settings. Long-term business relationships especially benefit from the reward approach.

In developing persuasive messages, you may also pick from emotional and rational appeals. Emotional appeals seek a quick action based on limited thought and perhaps incomplete logic. See how this example works on our emotions:

> Select us as your management consultants. We've had a long-term relationship with your firm that dates to its founding by your father, the insightful Mr. John Jones.

Rational appeals, on the other hand, seek a stronger commitment and one the reader is likely to feel comfortable with for a longer time. Rational appeals are based on logic. Here is the example above, rewritten with a rational appeal:

> The proposal to serve as your management consultant satisfies the three needs you have identified: sharing of intensive experience on a temporary basis, acting as a catalyst to complete the Smith project on schedule, and providing impartial advice.

Some topics, such as children or animals, are rich with potential emotional content. Other topics, including many in business, rely more on logic. Be aware of your message's strengths and weaknesses and of your goals as you select between rational and emotional appeals. Either can be effective depending on the content. Of course, a single persuasive message can hold punishment, reward, logic, and emotion. Take care, however, not to clutter the message with divergent thoughts.

Hard Sell Versus Soft Sell

Not all persuasive messages can be characterized as the hard-sell type that push magazine or record club subscriptions. When you describe a promising new product to a regular customer, your job is easier than if the reader is unfamiliar with you. Writing a reminder to place a periodic order would be even easier. Some persuasive messages are soft sell. In preparing soft-sell messages, you must make judgments about whether the goals of the early steps can be assumed. If, for example, you think you already have the reader's attention, you will check off this step and move on to the next one. If you have the reader's interest, you will go to the desire step. When you check off the first two steps, you start your letter with the desire step and then complete the message with the rest of the steps, in their correct order. As a manager, you are more likely to write these more subtle, softer persuasive messages.

Figure 6.2 illustrates the relationship among the five persuasive steps and hard- and soft-sell messages. The hard-sell message, such as a magazine subscription letter, will have all five steps. An extremely soft sell letter might have only the action step: "You're invited to the office holiday party next Tuesday at 3 P.M. Hope you can be there." Other persuasive messages fall between these two extremes.

FIGURE 6.2   **Steps in Developing Hard- and Soft-Sell Indirect Messages**

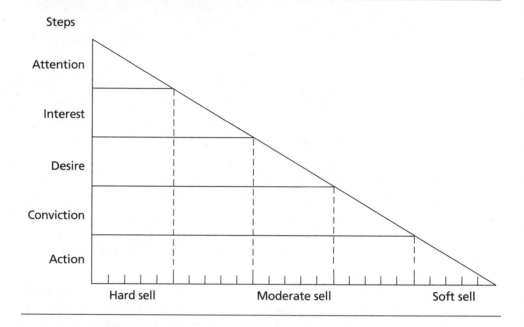

Although the illustration represents the five steps as being of equal size, that is seldom the case. The characteristics of the reader and of the proposed action will dictate the extent to which each step is developed. In one letter, there may be a brief paragraph that combines the attention and interest steps followed by well-developed desire and conviction steps. Another letter might reverse the emphasis. There is no rule regarding length of the steps.

The harder the hard-sell message, the more emphasis (and probably the more space) is needed for attention. In other words, as you move in Figure 6.2 to the left, you increase the attention step and then write the remaining steps.

One of the major problems in writing an indirect persuasive message is deciding where on the spectrum between hard and soft sell your reader and the message fall. If in doubt, it is better to include an earlier step rather than assume that it has already been met. Further, reiteration usually does not hurt persuasion other than by lengthening message.

Hints for Writing Persuasive Messages

Other hints may ease the task of writing persuasive messages or make the message more effective.

1. Although the steps dictate the order of information, you still need to organize your thoughts. Be careful not to let your steps overlap too much. Each step has its own goal and content. To intermix the content dilutes the impact.

2. Seek a blending from one step to the next. While each step has its own content, use transitions from step to step. Doing so will unify the entire message.

3. Consider writing your action step first. Preparing this punch line may guide the development of the earlier steps.

4. Finally, in general, try not to let your desired action leak out until the action step. In the vignette about buying a car, the salesperson avoided answering questions about cost until closing the deal. Had he told you the BMW cost $37,000 at the beginning, or even in the middle, of the conversation, he might have lost the sale. The price was so close to the desired action that the salesperson sought to hold it until the end.

When we read typical mass mailings, many of us speed through or omit passages and search at the end for what it will cost. This cost usually appears graphically with a dollar sign and some numbers. This characteristic behavior has not gone unnoticed by mass mailing experts. They counter by hiding the dollar amount. Often you will find that they spell out the word dollar and the numbers so that we will have to endure the entire persuasive spiel to learn its cost.

Although we may be frustrated by the quantity of direct mail we receive that does not apply to us, much of it is quite sophisticated in design and employs techniques that may be adaptable to even our soft-sell messages. For example, direct-mail advertisers know that the more involvement on the reader's part, the greater the likelihood that their message will be successful. How do they involve us? By getting us to put paper coins or keys into slots, to paste music or magazine selections on a card, to pick a potential prize from a list, or to scratch gray ink to disclose a sweepstakes number. For the manager, this may translate into seeking involvement through appreciation for a job well done, mentioning a common and important goal, or occasionally using the person's first name.

Second, these experts at persuasion recognize that the more time and effort we expend, the more likely we are to keep working our way through the message. For example, how often would we admit to ourselves that we have wasted 30 minutes placing keys, pasting stamps, or picking prizes and then not mail in the gift entry form—the form that can also be used to order a magazine subscription?

Third, these advertisers know that usually they have but one moment of your time to persuade you. If you stop to answer the phone, put the information away until later, have to search for your credit card number or checkbook, or have to look for a stamp for the envelope, you will probably not return to complete the action. Therefore, these advertisers employ techniques to encourage immediate action. For instance, they include a small pencil in the packet, supply the postage stamp, or offer to bill later. They also know an interesting thing about human behavior: once the return information is completed and sealed in the envelope, few people have second thoughts and decide not to mail the envelope.

In addition to Figure 6.1, which relates to negative messages, see Figure 6.3 for an example of an effective, moderate-sell, persuasive message. Figure 6.4 shows a well-written soft-sell message.

Finally, personalization of form letters can enhance positive responses. As a reader, you like to see your name and comments about yourself. Computers that integrate lists of names with form letters, inserting personal references from the database, make personalization easy. Letters appear individually typed with such techniques as

FIGURE 6.3   **Example of a Moderate-Sell, Persuasive Message**

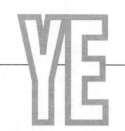

YOUNG EXECUTIVE MAGAZINE

Editorial Offices:
680 Northland Blvd. / Suite 107
Cincinnati, OH 45240-3137
(513) 825-0309   Fax: (513) 825-0220
e-mail: yexec@young.com
http://www.yexec.com

Dear *Young Executive* Reader:

As a subscriber to *Young Executive* you are aware of the magazine's uniqueness. Only *YE* meets the interests and needs of America's aggressive, educated, fast-track young executives. You've seen such articles as "Investing in Condos," "Using Nonverbal Communication to Exert Your Power," and "Mexico's Best Executive Vacation Spots." You're familiar with our popular columns: CEO Gossip, Power to the Women, and Dressing the Part.

Your subscription ends in six weeks. You can continue to receive *YE* for another year with no break in your subscription, and at a $3 savings, by returning the enclosed card right away. Just check the number of years you wish to extend your subscription and mail the card. More great *YEs* will be on the way.

Executively,

Harrison Christopher

Harrison Christopher
Subscription Manager

Enc.

the inclusion of phrases using the recipient's name or address. The efforts are especially likely to appear at places where the reader may lose interest: the very beginning, at the bottom of pages, and at the request for action. While the techniques may differ, knowledge of such elements of human behavior and persuasion as these can assist you in your persuasive writing.

FIGURE 6.4   **Example of a Soft-Sell, Persuasive Message**

Dear Customer,

Typically, our policy is to keep all boats until we have received payment for the work done on them. Since we have extended the courtesy of delivering your boat and then mailing your bill, please help us keep our costs down by mailing the payment today. Perhaps you selected Bitsy Boats to detail your boat because, as a small firm, we focus on a select clientele. As a small business, we will notice and appreciate your help.

Thank you.

SUMMARY

Many messages are those that receivers do not want to see. Most negative and persuasive messages typify such messages. For the negative message, because the goals of the sender (to maintain goodwill as well as to transmit the negative news) differ from the desire of the receiver (to hear good news), use an indirect approach. For the persuasive message, when you expect to encounter resistance, use the indirect approach.

The indirect approach to a negative message has four steps: (1) an opening that delays discussion of the bad news, (2) a presentation of the reasons for the upcoming bad news, (3) the bad news, and (4) a positive ending. The first step is difficult to write because often it comes across as a delaying tactic and thus reduces its value. Instead, it should prepare the reader for a discussion of the topic and the reasons behind the decision.

Often the second step is the most important of the four. If you do not have good reasons for the bad news or if you do not present those reasons well, the reader is unlikely to accept the news or the logic of it. However, well-developed reasons will encourage acceptance of the news without hostility. Readers may not like the decision, but at least they will understand your reasoning. Further, well-planned and well-explained reasons, written with the reader's viewpoint in mind, make the delivery of the bad news much easier. After relating the bad news, change the subject to a more positive one. Do not go back to the bad news. Close on a pleasant note.

Persuasive messages follow the steps of overt behavior: attention, interest, desire, conviction, and action. Some persuasive messages are hard sell and therefore require development of each of the five steps. Soft-sell messages may assume attention and interest on the reader's part and can start with desire. Authors of persuasive messages need to calculate carefully where on the spectrum between hard and soft sell their messages fit.

Indirect message organization delays the main message component—the bad news or the request for action—because resistance is anticipated by the sender. Other message organizations that do not fit the criteria for either direct or indirect organization appear in Chapter 7.

DISCUSSION QUESTIONS

1. What is the indirect approach?
2. How are negative messages presented in the indirect organization?
3. What are the problems associated with writing delaying openings?
4. What is the most difficult step of a negative message?
5. What are the steps in a persuasive message?
6. What is the difference between hard sell and soft sell?

Applications

1. Critique some of the hard-sell direct mail that you have received. Does each piece follow the five steps presented in the text? Do different products and services require different treatments of any steps?

2. Think about a time when you were searching for a job. How would you feel had you received a direct negative message? Why is the job-getting process such an ego-involving one, and why are feelings so easily hurt? Is this why almost all job rejection letters are written indirectly?

3. Place a call to an expert on direct-mail advertising whose advertisement you just received. Inquire about what techniques were employed, and why. If the person is unwilling to disclose this information, consider an alternative expert, such as an advertising or journalism professor.

4. Locate a written proposal from a manager. Evaluate it on its effectiveness in presenting the persuasive message's five steps. Where does it fall between hard and soft sell?

5. Survey some colleagues or classmates on this thought: "How often do you prefer to receive a negative message in a direct organization?" How many said "often"? Do you believe them? How much chance is there that they think they prefer the direct organization until the message is *really* negative to them?

Writing Situational Messages

Many written messages can be classified as positive, neutral, negative, or persuasive and can follow the direct or indirect organizations described in Chapters 5 and 6. Others, however, cannot be classified so easily; they combine two or more of the four formulas or fall outside the formulas altogether. They are called situational messages. Although situational messages may account for only a small percentage of all messages, they deserve careful attention from the advanced business communicator because they are difficult to prepare.

Many executives forget that a well-written situational message can distinguish its author and its company from competitors. Situational messages often require deeper understanding of the business organization and of the environment than do other messages. Important concerns such as tone and audience analysis play an even more crucial role in situational messages, where achieving a goal is particularly difficult. Standard instruction in business writing usually stops with the four basic categories of messages. This chapter will help you develop a more sophisticated approach, one more suitable for advanced managerial communication.

This chapter divides the discussion of situational messages into two parts: those messages that are a combination of formulas and those that fall outside the formulas. The chapter also examines selected memoranda as unique applications of situational writing.

SITUATIONAL WRITING THAT COMBINES FORMULAS

As we discussed in Chapters 5 and 6, a direct organization is usually applied to positive and neutral messages, but either a direct or an indirect organization may be applied to negative and persuasive messages, depending on many variables. The steps in writing these messages create formulas for their construction; a formula-based situational message rearranges the steps and principles of the individual formulas in a manner appropriate for an individual, specific situation.

Because of the great similarity between the positive and neutral formulas, for instance, it is quite easy to prepare a message that contains both positive and neutral information. Indeed, the positive formula, which prioritizes information starting with most positive, would place neutral information immediately after the last bit of positive information. To show you techniques for writing effective situational messages, this chapter focuses on the more difficult-to-write combinations of direct positive and indirect negative and persuasive messages. While other combinations exist, your understanding of these combinations will prepare you for writing the others.

The four combinations that we will discuss are (1) positive/negative, (2) positive/persuasive, (3) persuasive/negative, and (4) positive/persuasive/negative. These four represent most of the situational messages you will write and capture the technique of generating a plan for how to organize these messages.

In reading this discussion, refer to the summary in Table 7.1, which presents the organization of the five main message types we have already examined. Additionally, whenever you write situational messages using a combination of formulas, keep these principles in mind:

- Identify your goals and prioritize them.
- Empathize with your reader. What reaction will be likely? As with other messages, carefully analyze your audience.
- Try to maintain the integrity of the formulas; there are reasons for the order of the steps in each formula.
- Employ effective writing rules and techniques, as with any other written message, by making it readable, using the *you* tone, and including smooth transitions.

The Positive/Negative Combination

A message containing both positive and negative information is difficult to prepare because of the opposite approaches for negative and positive messages. Poorly prepared good-news/bad-news messages receive regular attention from many comedians with their line, "I have some good news and some bad news." To be effective, this combination needs to apply principles from the respective formulas.

In deciding how to mesh the two formulas, it may be helpful to place them side by side, as in Table 7.2. Positive information appears in two places in the negative message formula—at the beginning and at the end. They are the two most likely places to report your good news. In deciding where to place the positive information, consider the following:

- Is the information so positive that if placed first, it will make the transition to the negative information extremely awkward? If so, move the positive information to the end.

TABLE 7.1   **Formula Message Steps**

	Positive Message	Neutral Message	Negative Message	Negative Message	Persuasive Message
Organization	Direct	Direct	Direct	Indirect	Indirect
Principles	Positive impact is additive; most benefit occurs when starting with most positive information	Send important information first (unless negative); seek clarity and write to avoid follow-ups	Reader prefers the direct explanation of the bad news or occasion calls for direct organization	Deemphasize the negative by placing it in middle of message; maintain goodwill; precede negative with explanation	Persuasion to action requires movement through all steps; softer-sell messages can assume early steps; action must come last
Steps	Most positive information	Most important information	Negative, presented gently	Delaying opening	Attention
	Next most positive information	Next most important information	Details	Explanation	Interest
	Next most positive information	Next most important information	Positive closing	Negative message	Desire
	Next most positive information	Next most important information		Positive closing	Conviction
					Action (request, easy to do, reader benefit)

TABLE 7.2   **The Mixed Direct Positive/Indirect Negative Message**

Positive Message Steps	Negative Message Steps	Positive/Negative Mix Formulas
Most positive information	Delaying opening information	Positive opening
Next most positive information	Explanation	Explanation
Next most positive information	Negative message	Negative message
Next most positive information	Positive closing	Positive closing

- Is the positive information only moderately positive? If so, start your message with it.
- If you do not place the positive information first, will the receiver read the message? If not, present the positive information first. (This might occur when you are responding to a direct request from the reader.)
- Is the negative information only slightly negative? If so, it is easier to start with the positive and make a smooth transition to the negative. If the negative message is very strong, then start with a delaying opening and move to the explanation and the bad news before presenting the positive information.

In Chapter 6, the discussion of the indirect organization negative formula includes two important principles: bury the negative information in the middle of the letter, and always precede the negative information with an explanation. Adhere to these rules in your positive/negative combination message.

Table 7.3 highlights the four steps in a positive/negative message through an example that indicates the person may receive venture capital but not at the amount requested. The two formulas retain their identity while accomplishing their goals.

The Positive/Persuasive Combination

While the direct organization of the positive message and the indirect organization of the persuasive message conflict, the clash can be resolved by using the positive information as an attention-getting opening. Even in soft-sell persuasive messages, little harm is done by starting with positive information and then turning to interest, desire, or even conviction. Table 7.4 compares the two formulas and shows a resulting situational formula. Table 7.5 illustrates how the steps of the two formulas can be combined effectively.

The Persuasive/Negative Combination

Persuasive and negative messages share the indirect approach but follow different formulas. Table 7.6 compares the steps of these two formulas. In developing the situational message, retain the principles of both formulas: place the negative in the middle

TABLE 7.3	**A Sample Positive/Negative Message**
Positive/Negative Mix Formula	Example Thoughts from Steps
Positive opening	You are being considered for $200,000 in venture capital.
Explanation	XYZ Co. has limited assets available now; the economy is tight; others are also seeking our support.
Negative message	You are not receiving the full $250,000 you requested.
Positive closing	Entering into this venture will be to our mutual benefit; the project is promising.

TABLE 7.4   **The Mixed Direct Positive/Indirect Persuasive Message**

Positive Message Steps	Persuasive Message Steps	Positive/Persuasive Mix Formula
Most positive information	Attention	Positive attention-getter
Next most positive information	Interest Desire	Desire
Next most positive information	Conviction	Conviction
Next most positive information	Action (request, easy to do, reader benefit)	Action with emphasis on reader benefit

TABLE 7.5   **A Sample Positive/Persuasive Message**

Positive/Persuasive Mix Formula	Example Thoughts from Steps
Positive attention-getter with interest	Congratulations on being nominated for this year's Grant Wolford Young Manager Award.
Desire	Each year the Little Rock Jaycees select one of their members for this award; you are one of five nominees; the winner of this prestigious award receives $500.
Conviction	Each nominee must complete a seven-page questionnaire and take part in a 30-minute interview with the selection committee.
Action with emphasis	Complete the enclosed questionnaire and call us to schedule your interview. This is an impressive award.

TABLE 7.6   **The Mixed Indirect Persuasive/Indirect Negative Message**

Persuasive Message Steps	Negative Message Steps	Persuasive/Negative Mix Formula
Attention	Delaying opening	Attention/interest opening serves as delaying opening
Interest Desire	Explanation	Explanation
Conviction	Negative	Negative message
Action (request, easy to do, reader benefit)	Positive closing	Desire, conviction, and action steps, with stress on reader benefits, form positive closing

of the message after its explanation and end with a request for action after preparing the reader for that request.

The attention and interest steps of the hard-sell persuasive message can serve as the delaying opening of the negative message. The same is true if the persuasive message is softer in nature; still, use the desire or even conviction steps to delay the bad news. Follow with an explanation and the negative information. Once you present the negative information, leave it. Switch tone to the conviction or action step. Place special emphasis on the portion of the action step that reiterates the reader benefits. These benefits then serve as your positive closing. Table 7.7 shows one scheme for combining the steps of these two formulas.

The Positive/Persuasive/Negative Combination

When you combine three of the formulas, it becomes more difficult to incorporate individual steps and principles. Table 7.8 shows positive, persuasive, and negative formulas and illustrates one situational approach that might grow from a need to combine them.

As with earlier combinations, positive information appears in the positions of primacy or recency, negative information follows the explanation, and the required persuasive steps are woven into the message prior to the action step. Depending on the relative strengths of the positive and negative information and the degree of persuasion required, you can design various situational formulas. Table 7.9 uses the situational formula from Table 7.8 and illustrates its steps with sample phrases.

If these various formulas and mixes seem confusing, there is a general technique you may use to generate your own situational formula. This technique has four steps:

1. Is the occasion indeed one that can be answered with a basic formula, or is a situational message necessary? If a simple formula can be used, apply it. Otherwise, go to step two.

TABLE 7.7   A Sample Persuasive/Negative Message

Persuasive/Negative Mix Formula	Example Thoughts from Steps
Attention/interest opening serves as delaying opening	You've worked for us before and have submitted bids for contracts to us.
Explanation	Oil prices are down; prospects for prices increasing are poor for the immediate future; as oil speculators, we are being hurt by the economy too.
Negative message	We need to pay less than usual for oil-well drilling.
Desire, conviction, and action steps, with stress on reader benefits, form positive closing	There's still money to be made in oil; it's important to keep people on the payroll, to keep the equipment active, and to maintain a cash flow.
	Please submit a bid for drilling the nine shallow wells described in the attached specifications sheet; we both can benefit from you giving a low bid.

TABLE 7.8 **The Mixed Direct Positive/Indirect Persuasive/Indirect Negative Message**

Positive Message	Persuasive Message	Negative Message	Positive/Persuasive/Negative Mix Formula
Most positive information	Attention	Delaying opening	Positive attention getter with interest, delays negative message
Next most positive information	Interest Desire	Explanation	Desire and explanation serve as second most positive information
Next most positive information	Conviction	Negative message	Mention negative and weave in counterarguments for upcoming action
Next most positive information	Action (request, easy to do, reader benefit)	Positive closing	Request action with emphasis on positive aspects

TABLE 7.9 **A Sample Positive/Persuasive/Negative Message**

Positive/Persuasive/Negative Mix Formula	Example Thoughts from Steps
Positive attention-getter delays negative message	About a century ago, Butch Cassidy was offered amnesty; recently illegal aliens were also offered amnesty.
Desire and explanation serve as second most positive information	Amnesty can take on various forms; we need customers and payment for goods delivered; we dealt with you in good faith; you need our goods and a good credit rating.
Mention negative and weave in counterarguments for upcoming action	Pay us what you owe us; your credit rating is in jeopardy; we may need to contact credit services.
Request action with emphasis on positive aspects	We'll grant you amnesty on the penalty portion of your bill if you'll pay by Nov. 1; no questions will be asked, and you'll keep your credit card; mail your remittance today.

2. If a situational message is required, which of the types of formulas are present?

3. Of the various types of formulas present, which one is the primary thrust of the message?

4. Using the primary message formula as a skeleton, apply the elements of the remaining message formulas to it. These elements may be inserted between steps of the primary formula or appended to the end, depending on the situation.

NONFORMULA SITUATIONAL WRITING

Not all situational messages are combinations of formulas—some reside outside the sphere of the formulas. As an advanced business communicator, you will need to follow formulas and write nonformula messages. Over time, your instincts will develop; you will gain experience and acquire knowledge from reading well-written nonformula situational letters written by others. Examples of nonformula situational messages are those that transmit goodwill, serve as a reference, encompass the collection letter series, present negative-only content, serve as complaint letters and responses to complaints, deliver disciplinary reprimands, and are overt requests for action.

Goodwill Messages

Goodwill messages are a unique category of positive message. Like other positive messages, goodwill messages carry information likely to elicit positive responses from their readers; but with goodwill messages, the author makes an extra effort to garner an affirmative reaction from the reader that will benefit the author. This ulterior motive usually takes advantage of some pleasant event; letters or cards are sent to clients, customers, or employees for birthdays, promotions, reasons for congratulations, thank you's, appreciations, anniversaries, special programs or sales, and holidays. These messages may benefit the author through increased business or strengthened loyalty. For similar reasons, it can be good business to send messages to new residents, new customers, regular customers, or prompt payers. As a manager, you are more likely to direct others to write goodwill messages than to prepare them yourself.

The goodwill message follows the same direct organization as other positive information messages by presenting the most positive information first. Figure 7.1 presents the body of a goodwill message.

A special case of the goodwill message is the extension of sympathy as a matter of course to a regular customer or employee on the occasion of a family member's illness or death. Clearly the topic is unpleasant. What sets this direct message apart is the potential for indirect reward, perhaps in the form of appreciation, on the part of the sender. As with other direct messages, start with your main thought.

The Reference Letter

In applying for jobs, usually you are asked to supply a list of references, as well as names of past and present supervisors or employers. If people on your list of references are contacted, assuming you sought their permission to supply their names, they most likely will deliver positive comments written in a letter of recommendation. Supervisors and employers, on the other hand, write letters of reference. Letters of reference often are unbiased and may be directed To Whom It May Concern. These two terms often are confused with each other. (Chapter 16 discusses various aspects of written information that pertain to obtaining an advanced job.)

FIGURE 7.1   **Example of an Effective Goodwill Message**

Gardner, Givens
Certified Public Accountant
P. O. Box 1423
La Jolla, CA 98192

November 23, 200X

Professor Adrian McGuffey
San Diego State University
San Diego, CA 92183

Dear Professor McGuffey:

This is just a quick note to thank you for inviting Gardner, Givens into your classroom. We very much enjoyed describing our percep- tions of the importance of communication to the accounting profes- sion. The feedback received on this end from the students has been quite positive. We hope you, too, feel the time invested was worth- while. I welcome any comments you wish to share about the speaker or presentation.

Gardner, Givens looks forward to participating in your classroom activities again. Such discussions afford us an excellent exposure to your high-caliber students.

For your leisure reading, I've enclosed our hot-off-the-press brochure describing the accounting services we provide.

Cordially,

GERALD GIVENS

Gerald Givens

GG: cs
Enclosure

As a supervisor, you may receive requests for letters of recommendation after having allowed your name to be supplied by former or current employees who are applying for jobs or school. Your loyalty to former and current employees is likely to travel the grapevine; you will want to save copies of these letters. After having written a few letters of reference, you may find yourself following a certain pattern, in which case you may wish to develop a letter outline template that can be used for other employees. These outlines can be filled in with individualized information for each employee. Each letter—including those that follow your own form—should be individually typed and personalized to the applicant.

When you write a letter of reference, you should (1) directly state the purpose of the letter, (2) explain the conditions and time frame of the acquaintanceship, (3) describe the applicant's attributes that would be of both general and specific value to the position, and (4) end with a willingness to expand on comments or answer questions.

You help an applicant the most by giving relevant examples of his or her skills (the third step above). Rather than say, "She's a good manager," for example, say:

> She has demonstrated a superior ability to work with peers. Her colleagues cite her understanding of human nature, ability to direct subordinates, and achievement of high productivity. They say she is a team player.

Further, a comparison of the applicant to others can be beneficial. Generally, the more relevant information you write about the applicant, the more favorable the reaction. Readers know these letters take time, and they view your efforts accordingly. Conversely, a few checkmarks on a form and no responses to open-ended questions, such as "What makes you think this applicant might have a future with us?" do little to help the applicant. See Figure 7.2 for an example of a letter of reference.

In some letters of reference, of course, you will find it necessary to be less than positive about the applicant. Not all the employees—current and past—under your supervision deserve glowing recommendations. You do little to enhance the image of your organization to another firm by exaggerating positive attributes of an ineffective or fired employee. Your message, therefore, is likely to carry less enthusiasm and fewer examples of positive behavior.

The question of ethical messages, in light of today's frequent unethical behavior by some in business, places renewed importance on saying what is accurate and can be defended.

Collection Letters

The collection letter is another message type that can benefit from an understanding of situational writing. As a manager, you may direct the writing of collection letters. Collection letters do not fit the recommended indirect approach to negative message writing because they usually consist of not one message but a series of messages, often moving from light in tone in the first message to stern in later messages. Many businesses prepare a series of three, four, or even five messages. Frequently the series starts as a gentle, direct message, progresses to an indirect message, and concludes with a strong direct message. The first message may take the form of a card with a

FIGURE 7.2   Example of an Effective Letter of Recommendation

Adams Advertising
Baton Rouge, LA 52063

May 7, 200X

Scott Burkette
Accounting Supervisor
3-A Advertising
845 Lost Creek Road, Eleventh Floor
Dallas, TX 75213

Dear Mr. Burkette:

Thank you for the pleasant opportunity to recommend to you Mr.
Bill Andersohn for your position of Account Executive. Not only is
he one of our top Assistant Account Executives, he is also an
especially mature, personable, and insightful individual. It is only
because our comparable positions are and will continue to be
filled for some time that we are not promoting him.

Two years ago Mr. Andersohn joined us as an intern; six months
later I enthusiastically recruited him to assist me with consumer
research. In evaluating consumers by a variety of characteristics,
he showed an understanding of advertising and marketing and
exhibited particular skill in working with sales and persuasive
materials. These latter skills also have served him well in his
pursuit of becoming an Account Executive.

He is a self-starter and a person who predictably meets deadlines. I often notice his impressive creativity—a characteristic he
has applied in the design of some brochures.

I most sincerely believe that you would benefit from the abilities
Mr. Andersohn has to offer. I enthusiastically recommend him.

Sincerely,

Jackson Adams

Jackson Adams
President

thought such as, "Oops, I forgot to make my payment!" A second message may still be slightly positive and relatively direct, such as the main thought, "It's now been 45 days since your payment was due."

A third letter in a series probably stresses the positive reasons for making the payment, such as maintaining a good relationship, keeping a credit card, or avoiding complications.

In a fourth letter, the tone of the reasons may change to more negative thoughts: avoiding legal issues, returning the goods, and so on. A final letter, no matter how many letters are in the series, will be the most firm. If the company has decided to take the matter to court, this letter will present that decision. On the other hand, if the decision is to give up on the effort, perhaps because the legal case is weak or the amount small, the final letter might be a letter that says, in effect, "return your credit card, and don't shop here anymore."

Figures 7.3 through 7.7 deliver the bodies of five messages in a collection letter series. Note the progression toward sternness. These letters are adapted from a software package that contains dozens of collection letters and facilitates the merging of mailing lists containing tagged, delinquent addresses with various categories of letters.[1] In addition to many other letters from which to choose, the software includes a spelling checker, ample control of the messages, and a wide variety of applications, such as service, professional, product, or trade businesses.

FIGURE 7.3   **First Notice Letter in a Collection Series**

Dear   :

Everyone forgets once in a while. Or perhaps our bill is buried in a pile of paperwork. However, now that I have brought it to your attention, perhaps you could dig it out right now and take care of it. The total balance due is $_____.

As a reminder, our credit terms are net 30 days. Past due balances are subject to a finance charge of 10 percent a month. I'm sure you'll want to avoid any additional finance charges and get your account back into good standing by taking care of your balance now. I know we would appreciate it, too.

Thank you for your prompt response to this payment request. If you have any questions about your account, please call.

Sincerely,

FIGURE 7.4   **Second Notice Letter in a Collection Series**

Dear   :

In scanning our accounts, we noticed that yours is still carrying a past due balance. We had to double check, because that seems out of character, but there the balance was.

Right now, you owe us $_____, including finance charges. You probably realize that past due balances incur finance charges at a rate of 10 percent a month if they are not paid within _____ days.

Please take just a moment right now to find your checkbook and write us a check. You would be saving additional finance charges and resuming your usual good standing.

Thanks for taking care of this right away. If you have any questions about your account, please give us a call.

Sincerely,

FIGURE 7.5   **Third Notice Letter in a Collection Series**

Dear   :

Can you help with something? I've been trying to collect a past due amount on your account, and up to now I haven't had much luck. Could you look into why the payment is being held up? Our records show you owe us a total of $____.

You are in business, too, so I'm sure you can understand our concern. This matter really needs clearing up and you need to get your account back in order.

We would be happy to answer any questions you have about the charges and will work with you to get your account up to date. We expect either a check or a phone call in the next few days. Thanks.

Sincerely,

FIGURE 7.6   **Fourth Notice Letter in a Collection Series**

Dear   :

Something must be terribly wrong. Your account is delinquent and has been for several months. We really need your help to get this straightened out.

As things now stand, you owe a total of $_____. We have made several efforts to collect, but to date they have all been ignored.

It is very important that you forward your payment immediately, or get in touch with us to tell us when you will be able to pay us. Obviously, if you fail to do so, there are alternative ways of making our point. However, I can't believe that will be necessary.

If you value your good name, personally and professionally, you will make good on this obligation. I'll be expecting your call or your check.

Sincerely,

FIGURE 7.7   **Fifth Notice Letter in a Collection Series**

Dear   :

Your account is now seriously delinquent. You owe a total past due amount of $_____. We must receive payment in full immediately.

Your negligence in this matter is of great concern to us. You have ignored numerous requests for payment and failed to contact us to explain the circumstances that have held up your payment.

You are legally and morally obligated for this bill. Further delay may force us to take legal action to collect what is owed us. This could prove embarrassing and damage your personal and professional reputation.

Please do not let this problem come to that. Write out the check now, or pick up the phone and call. Do it today. Do it now.

Sincerely,

Negative-Only Messages

Sometimes you will want to disregard the goal of maintaining goodwill evident in the indirect negative formula and assumed in the direct negative formula and focus on the bad news. We've just seen how a collection letter series typically begins positively and progresses to increasingly firm letters. By the time you have mailed three, four, or even five reminder letters, you have probably lost your patience. The payment, and not customer goodwill, is now the most important issue. A negative-only message conveys the extreme urgency and severity of the situation. A negative-only message differs from a direct negative message in its lack of concern for the feelings of the receiver. The body of such a message follows:

> Over six months ago you made purchases at our store totaling $795. Because of your disregard for our requests for payment and your lack of explanation, we must turn over your account to a collection agency. While its techniques for obtaining payment often are not as understanding as ours, you have left us no other option. Further, as spelled out in the state's civil code, we have the legal right to require the return of your charge card. We are exercising that right. Return your card in the enclosed envelope by April 9. Otherwise the matter will be remanded to the county sheriff's office for action, as prescribed by law.

The reader of this letter will have little doubt that the company is no longer gently seeking payment. The gravity of the situation is conveyed by the negative-only message.

Most businesspeople resist writing negative-only messages unless absolutely necessary.

Complaints and Responses to Complaints

Another type of nonformula situational letter is the complaint letter and its counterpart, the response to the complaint. While, as a businessperson, you are more likely to be writing responses to complaints or directing others to do so, both situations are common in business.

The Complaint Letter Companies today are much more open to customers' inquiries than in past decades. Nevertheless, not all complaints produce satisfactory results. The likelihood of receiving your desired response largely depends on the quality of your complaint letter.

Typically you initiate your complaint with the seller of the product or provider of the service. Next you complain to the manufacturer, perhaps several times and to increasingly higher levels of management. Finally, you may seek satisfaction by going to trade associations, national headquarters, consumers' rights organizations, or even to the courts. The complaint letter is an important part of this process.

Complaint letters, of course, can be from individual customers or from companies complaining about products or services supplied by other companies. While the content may vary, the principles are the same. Here are some suggestions for a complaint letter written by a customer.

Begin your complaint letter with details, not angry criticisms. Explain what you purchased in detail—give serial and model numbers. Tell when and where you made the purchase. Be precise. What was the location of the store, and what was the exact date? You may wish to include a salesperson's name, if available. If this letter is part of a lengthy complaint process, give the history of your complaint. While you want to be complete and to give important detail, do not overburden the reader with unnecessary information.

Next, explain the problem. What went wrong? What were the conditions at the time? Were you following the manufacturer's instructions? How long after the purchase did this occur?

Third, verify your purchase with copies (not originals) of sales receipts, checks, and guarantees. Check the guarantee to see if there are specific steps or information that you have forgotten, such as handling or postage charges.

Fourth, state specifically what you want. Do you seek reimbursement or replacement? By what date do you want action? Only if you have no other recourse should you threaten legal action.

You may reorganize these steps, depending on the situation, to be even more effective. However, all four thoughts are likely to appear somewhere in your message.

In writing this letter, do not be sarcastic, aggressive, or negative. Let the facts present your case. Keep a copy of the letter you write as documentation of what you said, to whom, and when.

Picture the complaint letter as a mix of the negative and persuasive categories. The information has a negative component, and you are seeking action from the company. The negative information is in the middle of the message, and the action request appears at the end. Beyond this similarity, however, a complaint letter does not follow the two formulas. See Figure 7.8 for the U.S. Office of Consumer Affairs' sample complaint letter.

The Response to the Complaint Letter Responding to a well-written complaint letter—one that has presented evidence in a logical format—can be quite a challenge. In so doing, consider the following:

- Can you do what the writer is requesting? If so, use the positive formula and relate the good news immediately.
- Do you need more information? Use a neutral approach. Be pleasant but do not be too positive; you do not want to get the reader's hopes up and then dash them with your next letter.
- Should you turn down the request? Consider writing a standard negative formula letter.
- Do you have both positive and negative messages to relay? Apply the principles of each as discussed in formula-based situational letters.
- Is this response outside the formula-based situational letter approach? If so, why? Is a nonformula situational letter needed?
- What images are you projecting? You are the company, and the reader's image of the company may well depend on how you write this letter. Avoid

FIGURE 7.8   Sample Complaint Letter

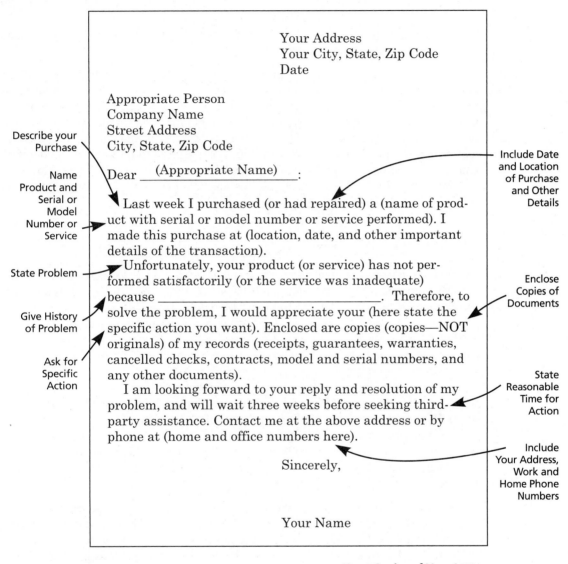

Your Address
Your City, State, Zip Code
Date

Appropriate Person
Company Name
Street Address
City, State, Zip Code

Dear _____(Appropriate Name)_____ :

Last week I purchased (or had repaired) a (name of product with serial or model number or service performed). I made this purchase at (location, date, and other important details of the transaction).
Unfortunately, your product (or service) has not performed satisfactorily (or the service was inadequate) because _____. Therefore, to solve the problem, I would appreciate your (here state the specific action you want). Enclosed are copies (copies—NOT originals) of my records (receipts, guarantees, warranties, cancelled checks, contracts, model and serial numbers, and any other documents).
I am looking forward to your reply and resolution of my problem, and will wait three weeks before seeking third-party assistance. Contact me at the above address or by phone at (home and office numbers here).

Sincerely,

Your Name

Labels (left):
Describe your Purchase
Name Product and Serial or Model Number or Service
State Problem
Give History of Problem
Ask for Specific Action

Labels (right):
Include Date and Location of Purchase and Other Details
Enclose Copies of Documents
State Reasonable Time for Action
Include Your Address, Work and Home Phone Numbers

Keep Copies of Your Letter and All Related Documents and Information

Source: United States Office of Consumer Affairs, Washington, D.C.

hiding behind such weak phrases as company policy. Use solid reasons, such as expired warranties or lack of proof of purchase.

- Is an apology or indication of sympathy appropriate? Although your reasons should generally speak for themselves, there are times when you should express sympathy or state an apology.
- Is the message tailored for the individual, if possible? A form response can be irritating in and of itself.

You may need to respond with a *yes, but* letter that agrees with many of the author's points but disagrees with one or more other crucial points. For example, if you received a complaint letter from a firm that was rejected from the proposal process because their submission missed the deadline, you might agree with their points, stressing the importance of doing the best job possible in writing the proposal, that writing proposals takes time, and that it is a service to hire college students as couriers, even though they sometimes make deliveries at the wrong address. However, you must explain the reason for deadlines and that you always adhere to them, as stated in your Request for Proposals.

Disciplinary Reprimands

Another message type with negative content that you are likely to encounter is the disciplinary reprimand. Written reprimands usually follow spoken reprimands and may substantiate some disciplinary problem. Managers typically place copies in the offenders' personnel files. As a manager, you may find writing reprimands an unpleasant but necessary activity. Although a reprimand may appear to be a situation that calls for an indirect negative formula, reprimands usually avoid that formula and use a more direct approach. Follow these three steps.

First, begin the message with a direct statement of the action you are taking and why you are taking it. Explain what behavior prompted the reprimand, and why. Tell the reader what action can help correct the problem. Be firm.

Second, support the situation with specific facts. When and where did the offense occur? What were or might have been the consequences of this behavior?

Finally, explain the consequences if your instructions are not followed. Here is the body of a sample reprimand:

Because of your misuse of company telephone facilities, your access code to the long-distance network is being revoked. Calls made on your access code during November totaled $83. A check of the numbers shows calls placed to your relatives in New York, to the resort in North Carolina where you recently vacationed, and to several private residences unknown to the company.

When you were given your access card, you signed a statement that long distance calls would be made for business only. Last August, you were reminded of the company policy regarding long-distance calls when three questionable calls appeared on your record.

The company places repeated telephone misuse in the category of disciplinary problems that can lead to termination. You are advised to reread our telephone policies. A copy is attached.

Overt Request for Action

A final type of nonformula situational message is the overt request for action. Using the persuasive formula, you first decide where on the spectrum of hard to soft sell the message should fall and then begin with the appropriate step that leads to action. In a moderate soft-sell message, for example, you might assume that you have the reader's attention and interest and, therefore, begin with the desired step.

A direct, overt request for action disregards the persuasive formula and opens with request for action. This may be appropriate when the requested action embodies the attention through conviction steps. The following opening illustrates such an occasion:

> Your address places you in the North Shore Subdivision. As a North Shore resident, you are no doubt aware that no full-service banking facility exists in the neighborhood. Until now, that is. To introduce you to North Shore Bank, we'd like you to . . .

Other occasions for the overt action request are with directives and reprimands, as discussed above.

Two Examples of Nonformula Situational Writing

As you gain experience writing your own situational letters, you will begin to notice the effective style of others. Here are two examples.

Rise in Insurance Costs In Figure 7.9, a letter from a boat owners association informs members of a rise in insurance costs. The letter is unusual because it presents the bad news (rise in costs) at the beginning and even in negative terms (unpleasant, and none of us like that). The second paragraph explains the true goal of the letter: not to deliver the news of a rise in costs but, rather, to promote understanding of the reasons for the rise.

The letter switches from the explanation to a more upbeat persuasive twist to help sell the insurance program and concludes on a positive note.

Order Canceled Figure 7.10 illustrates a beautifully written situational letter. Unknown to many people, there is a law that requires mail-order houses to either fill orders within a prescribed time period or refund money. This letter is written to a customer to conform to this law. Read the message and note the tone: concern by the company for the customer, emphasis on high-quality products, adherence to the law, and desire for additional business.

The first paragraph provides background in a positive tone. Paragraph two establishes the concept of quality and mentions the law. Before the reader can complain, however, mention is made of the refund check. To maintain the order, the reader learns how to reorder and receives a prepaid envelope. The letter concludes with an unnecessary apology for the poor service, even though the service appears quite good. This self-effacing phrase emphasizes the company's concern for the customer.

The letter breaks most of the rules established for formula messages, yet suc-

FIGURE 7.9 **Example of an Effective Situational Letter**

BOAT OWNERS ASSOCIATION of THE UNITED STATES

Washington National Headquarters
880 South Pickett Street, Alexandria Va. 22304

(703) 823-9550

Dear Member:

This year we are faced with the unpleasant fact that insurance rates are rising. None of us like that. I, for one, have never filed an insurance claim on my home, autos, or boats, pay my premiums faithfully every year, and see my rates going up with everyone else's.

It is only natural to want to know why, and the purpose of this letter is to provide some of the answers.

The reasons are both complex and simple. Complex because they involve concepts such as increasing numbers of lawsuits and society's view of legal liability. Complex because they involve an insurance company philosophy called "cash flow underwriting" (pursued for the past seven years) that depends on high interest rates and return on investments to cover claims and make profits. Simple because for several years now insurance companies have not been making profits.

Insurance companies won't continue business as usual when they lose money in successive years. They are going to make changes. The question is what do they change and how? In most cases, the answer is higher rates. In a few, it is cancelling or non-renewing coverage.

Inevitably the question arises, why not have those that filed claims pay the increase. In fact, those with claims at BOAT/U.S. do pay a heavier price as they lose their 10% "no loss" credit for one year. Repeat claimants whose claims reflect a lack of reasonable care are refused future participation in the Group. Since we do not know which of us will suffer an accident in 200X, everyone must share to some extent in the increase. We truly regret the necessity of the increase and hope for your continued support and participation.

On the good side, 200X saw a record number of Members participating in the BOAT/U.S. Marine Insurance Group, over one billion dollars worth of boats insured, loss prevention material distributed on hurricane preparation and avoiding sinkings at the dock, and thousands of boats assisted with problems.

Your Association staff is committed to being there to assist when you need help. We wish you a safe and enjoyable year on the water.

Sincerely,

William M. Oakerson

William M. Oakerson, Director
Marine Insurance Division

Service, Savings, and Representation for the Nation's Boat Owners

Source: Used with permission of Boat Owners Association of the United States.

FIGURE 7.10   Example of an Effective Situational Letter

L.L.Bean
FREEPORT, MAINE 04033
Outdoor Sporting Specialties
TEL. (207) 865-4761

Dear Customer,

Thank you for your order for the Pathfinder Pants. Your request for the purchase of this item is very much appreciated and our being able to ship it to you in a timely manner is important to both of us.

L.L. Bean is very concerned with providing quality merchandise. The fabric quality on the initial shipment of these pants was not satisfactory and shipment had to be returned to our supplier. The Federal Trade Commission requires that we fill your order within 60 days. For that reason we must cancel your order for the above item. Your refund check is enclosed.

We expect our shipment of the Pathfinder Pants by late September. You are welcome to reorder by returning the enclosed order blank; please include the stock #, color, size and method of payment. A postpaid envelope is provided for your convenience.

I apologize for this poor service. Your patronage is valued here and we look forward to providing you with fine quality merchandise and service in the future.

Sincerely yours,

Marj Porter
Customer Service
Manager

MP/klr
Encls:

Source: Reproduced with permission from L.L. Bean.

cessfully creates a positive perception of the company. It also serves as a reminder that breaking rules can sometimes be quite effective.

WRITING MEMORANDA

As mentioned in an earlier chapter, there are few differences in the organization of e-mail messages, memoranda, and letters. Further, the principles of the direct, indirect, and situational organization of messages apply equally well to all three. Hard-copy media such as memoranda and letters differ somewhat in appearance. *To:* and *From:* replace a letter's inside address and signature block, for example. Further, letters usually are sent outside the organization while memoranda usually are internal messages. As internal messages, memoranda tend to be more informal and more direct than their letter counterparts.

One survey of 800 business people showed they spent from 21 to 38 percent of their time writing memoranda.[2]

There must be a lot of executives overwhelmed by the number of memos they receive! Competition for the reader's time places importance on directness and clarity. More so than with letters, memos should start with a statement of the purpose early in the message. In other words, memos are more likely either to be direct messages or to bend the formula steps of the indirect organization to become situational messages.

Memoranda also need special visual treatment. Keep paragraphs short, much like newspaper articles. Consider using bullets (asterisks, lowercase o's, or large dots) in front of items in a list. A recent approach to typing memoranda—probably enhanced by software packages and computers—places the main text of the memo in a narrow column and then, to the left of it, adds notes summarizing the content to the right. In the last several years, college textbook designers have learned that readers prefer this approach for its ease of understanding, organizational clarity, and speed of review. These same attributes hold true for memoranda preparation. An example appears in Figure 7.11.

As more mid- and upper-level managers prepare their own memos on computers without secretarial help, standard memo forms are modified. These modifications grow out of ignorance of correct memo form on the part of some managers and overt disregard of the form by others. If you prepare your own correspondence, realize the importance of dating your messages. Knowing precisely when you recommended, ordered, signed, or asked about something often is crucial. Computers often can date (or time stamp) information for you easily.

Another characteristic that can set memoranda apart from letters is the inclusion of humor. Humor—or attempts at it—requires judicious use in both memos and letters. However, when the internal message is lighthearted and relatively unimportant, humor in a memo can distinguish its author as a person with personality and depth. As long as humor is on target, does not embarrass others, is not overdone, and is not too frequent, it can reflect positively on its author. A word of caution is needed, however; what is funny to you may not be funny to others. You may wish to test your message on a neutral friend. Figure 7.12 presents a lighthearted e-mail message.

FIGURE 7.11   New Memorandum Format Option

Memo

To: Regional Managers
From: Fred Gilley, Vice President, Planning
Subject: Improving Regional Meetings
Date: December 3, 200X

Managers, I have a few thoughts for you:

AMENITIES AT MEETINGS   One of the objectives of regional meetings should be to provide opportunities for attendees to meet and talk with one another. Our decentralized organization does not lend itself to intraregional communications. Therefore, we should make the most of our regional meetings by providing the following.

- a reception for everyone the night we arrive
- a luncheon for everyone on Friday
- a reception for VIPs and speakers on Friday night
- coffee midmorning Friday and Saturday
- coffee and soft drinks midafternoon Friday.

Minimal cost is involved in providing these amenities and they provide the occasions for informal visits.

JOINT MEETINGS   Last year the Southwest region and the Southeast region met in New Orleans for a joint meeting. The regions shared common discussions for the first day and then split into their respective groups for the next two days for topics relevant only to themselves.

Those in attendance agree the sessions were valuable and that it was enjoyable interacting with those from another region. Maybe other regions should consider having joint meetings.

FIGURE 7.12   Humorous Message

X-Originating-IP: [142, 221, 198, 916]
FROM: Alex Bartholemew <abart76@fastnet.com>
TO: Brand Management Department
<dept.list.serv@fastnet.com>
SUBJECT: Season Football Tickets
DATE: May 1, 200X

For the past few years, several members of the Brand
Management Department have banded together to submit
their season football ticket applications as a group. As
a result, we have been able to secure a large block of
seats.

This procedure has the advantage of (a) securing a very
good location, and (b) allowing you to enjoy the fine
company of your colleagues, and (c) providing the opportunity to speculate as to who Jenny Carnahan's date will
be. It has the disadvantage that arises from the fact
that Bill Maldando and I almost always show up.
Furthermore, you might be located between me and the concession stand, a "high traffic" area.

All this notwithstanding, if you are interested, just
deliver your application and your check to my mailbox by
May 13, 200X. On May 14, depending on how many applications I receive, I will either deliver them to the ticket
office and demand with righteous fervor that we be given
preferential seating, or head for Rio.

Remember, we play A&M here next year, so this offer is
not for the squeamish.

If you have any questions about the procedure or whether
you'll ever see the money or your tickets again after you
place your check in my hands, feel free to ask.

Source: Reproduced with permission from Robert Prentice, MSIS Department, University of Texas–Austin.

SUMMARY

Situational messages require advanced levels of planning and audience analysis because they do not clearly fit either the direct or indirect organizational approaches. Instead, they piece together the steps and principles of other messages to create a unique approach to a specific message. This chapter illustrates the combination of a variety of message types to create plans for situational messages. The main focus of this chapter, then, is illustrating the thinking that supports the planning and writing of messages that are not obviously direct or indirect.

Several types of situational messages do not follow the combination-of-formulas approach. They include goodwill messages, the collection letter series, negative-only messages, complaints and responses to complaints, disciplinary reprimands, overt requests for action, and selected memoranda.

The experienced writer uses the principles of writing discussed in Chapters 5, 6, and 7 to prepare specialized messages to well-defined audiences. With experience, you will learn to write according to the situation and to place less emphasis on the steps of the formulas.

Applications

1. Perhaps you have saved some of your better-written memos or letters. If not, do so. Then examine them from the viewpoint of an organization. Were some situational? What mix of formulas was used? Did they follow the principles established in this chapter?

2. Research the underlying concepts that support the various message types, such as the indirect persuasive. (The notes section in the preceding two chapters can help you get started.) How strong is the research support? From what disciplines does this support come?

3. Interview or invite a social psychologist to visit your class or business. What does he or she think of the approaches to situational messages? What suggestions beyond those in the text can he or she share?

4. Locate an example of a goodwill message and critique it. Was it successful? Why? How could it be improved?

5. Examine a block of messages, such as a group of e-mail messages after an extended absence. What percentage are of direct organization? Indirect organization? Situational messages?

DISCUSSION QUESTIONS

1. What are situational messages?
2. What approach might you take to write a positive/negative message?
3. What approach might you take to write a positive/persuasive message?
4. What approach might you take to write a persuasive/negative message?
5. What are goodwill messages?
6. How might you write a negative-only message? What are your assumptions?
7. Discuss the collection letter series and why it is approached as it is.
8. What are the difficult aspects of preparing a response to a complaint?
9. When might you use humor in a business message?

NOTES

1. Get Paid Plus software, Great American Software, Nashua, New Hampshire, 1991.

2. Neil Chesanow, "Re: The Office Memo," *New Woman*, February 1987, p. 47.

The Planning and Writing of Persuasive Proposals

No matter what profession or area of business you enter, you will probably write a proposal. Proposals make money for a company or organization by recruiting customers, winning contracts, or closing sales. Proposals are so important that you may one day receive a promotion because of your ability to write them effectively. For these reasons, and many more, it is important that you understand what a proposal is and how to prepare one.

A proposal is a marketing tool that sells your ideas to others. It is a persuasive document that

- Communicates what you plan to do or offer.
- Explains how you will implement what you propose.
- Convinces the potential customer that your organization can better meet his or her needs than the competition.
- Stresses your organization's unique qualifications to do the job or provide goods or services.
- Often stands alone in selling your solution or services.[1]

This chapter is divided into four main sections: the major purposes of proposals, classification of proposals, the planning process, and the writing process. Sample proposals appear at the end of the chapter.

TWO MAJOR PURPOSES OF PROPOSALS

While all proposals are selling documents, what they sell varies. The purpose of a commercial proposal is to sell a specific product or solution to meet a particular need.

For instance, you may write a proposal to provide 20 hours of training on how to motivate employees as your solution to a decrease in a manufacturer's production rate. Or you may propose to sell 50 computers to an engineering firm that wants to automate its office function. Perhaps you will prepare a qualification proposal, in which you seek to sell yourself or your organization as the best qualified to solve a potential client's problem or meet a need. A qualification proposal does not offer a concrete solution but, rather, attempts to demonstrate that whatever the need, you can devise and implement the steps to an effective solution. Advertising agencies, public relations firms, and political consultants often use qualification proposals to establish agency relationships. For other types of proposal situations, refer to Figure 8.1.

CLASSIFICATION OF PROPOSALS

Proposals can be internal or external; they can be solicited or unsolicited; and they can take different forms.

Internal Versus External

Proposals can be aimed at audiences inside or outside your organization. Internal proposals usually are directed at a specific level of management within your organization. They can be relatively simple, such as suggestion box ideas, or they can be time-consuming and lengthy and can have the potential to radically change the organization, such as proposals to reorganize the company or build new facilities. On the other hand, external proposals are a marketing tool aimed at current or prospective customers. One company or organization proposes to satisfy another organization's need. External proposals are more common than internal proposals and are the main subject of this chapter.

Solicited Versus Unsolicited

Proposals either identify a need and propose to meet it (unsolicited) or respond to a request (solicited). The proposal writer initiates the unsolicited proposal; it is usually

---

FIGURE 8.1   Types of Proposal Situations

Proposals are written for the following activities or situations:

To pitch advertising campaigns
To bid on construction or landscaping projects
To provide temporary help services
To provide consulting services to political candidates
To conduct issue analyses for governmental entities
To provide office furnishings
To install computer equipment
To provide employee training programs
To win contracts to write companies' business plans, marketing plans, or strategic business plans
To seek approval of academic research, such as for a doctoral or master's thesis

---

the more difficult type to write because the target audience must first be convinced that a need exists and then that the response is worth the time and money required. Preparing and presenting unsolicited proposals generally requires exceptional persuasive skills.

When a company requests a proposal to supply specific goods, to solve a problem, or to exploit some situation, the proposal is solicited. There are two types of solicited proposals. Advertised proposals are requested when the desired product or service can be defined concisely and quantitatively. Potential suppliers learn of the requirements in a detailed Invitation for Bids (IFB). These proposals favor the lowest bidder. Another type of solicited proposal is the negotiated proposal, which allows the writer to specify a proposed solution to the need. The negotiated proposal originates with a Request for Proposals (RFP) from the potential customer, which explains the need and seeks responses. Negotiated proposals usually are not awarded on the basis of price, but on the quality of the solution and the ability to implement that solution.[2]

Forms of Proposals

Proposals are delivered orally, in writing, or both. Even if a simple proposal is generated by a conversation, do not neglect the important task of spelling it out in writing. A written proposal minimizes misunderstandings or disagreements about the type, quality, and cost of goods or services provided. Many proposals constitute the basis of legally binding contracts. There are four forms of proposals, which differ by the extent of work required to prepare them rather than by their content.

Letter proposals are brief proposals written for projects that are not complex or expensive enough to warrant a longer document. Use this form to present either qualification proposals or commercial proposals.

Preliminary proposals (sometimes called short proposals) find application in service areas such as public accounting, advertising, or communications or in technical areas such as research and development. They may be either qualification or commercial proposals.

Detailed proposals (sometimes called formal proposals) are the longest and most complex proposals. They are usually commercial proposals and contain precise implementation plans and cost estimates.

Oral presentations generally accompany written qualification proposals but should not take the place of them. An oral presentation is an opportunity for experts to explain their areas of knowledge and experience, to detail the services they can provide, and to give immediate feedback to questions.[3]

THE PROPOSAL PLANNING PROCESS

Planning is the most crucial stage in preparing a proposal and, if done properly, will greatly increase your company's chances of producing a successful proposal. Thorough planning will make the actual writing of an effective proposal easy; view the effort as an investment in success. There are four major steps to the planning process: (1) screening, (2) creating a capture plan, (3) formulating solution and implementation strategies, and (4) budgeting and scheduling the proposal effort.

Screening: The Bid/No Bid Decision

Within the planning process, screening is perhaps the most important aspect. Omission of this task can cost your company time and money. When your company receives a Request for Proposals (RFP) or an Invitation for Bids (IFB), you must screen the document as soon as possible. Do this even if you have discussed the project with the potential client. Screening involves asking yourself whether your company should consider competing for the job. You should read the RFP or IFB thoroughly to determine if your firm qualifies. Many government RFPs contain special requirements for firms, such as having company headquarters located in specific states or having full-time engineers on staff. Read the RFP carefully, including the fine print.

You must also determine if your company is capable of doing the work. Do you have the resources and expertise necessary to bid on the job? If not, can you obtain the resources to enable you to meet the requirements? Many companies waste time and money bidding on work of which they are not capable. Consider how taking the job will influence your staff's workload and the work being performed for your other clients. Other strategic questions that you should ask are whether taking this job will enhance your reputation and what your chances of winning are.

A final and essential step in screening is to determine the total value of the project or sale to your company. Will this opportunity reap an adequate return or profit for your company? If not, look for a higher-value project on which to bid.[4]

Creating a Capture Plan

A capture plan is an analytical planning document prepared for internal use to ensure the creation of a winning proposal. Preparation involves careful planning to review whether all variables that might affect the proposal have been considered. The capture plan entails conducting a customer analysis and a situational analysis.[5]

Conduct a Customer Analysis The customer analysis step, much like the audience analysis step discussed in Chapter 4, involves researching the entity that is requesting the proposal to discover facts that will help you formulate a proposal that responds to their needs and has a high probability of being selected. The customer analysis is analogous to doing your homework and is essential preparation for the later writing of the proposal. A customer analysis is composed of four parts:

1. *Problem Identification.* Although most requests for qualification proposals outline the problem to be solved, you should not take for granted that this is the primary problem. The problem stated in the RFP may be a symptom of a greater, underlying but unstated problem. What does the customer perceive as the solution to the problem? Can this be improved on while staying within the scope of the RFP? In the case of a commercial proposal, the type of goods

the potential customer is requesting may not be adequate for the desired tasks. The best way to get clarification is to ask questions. Meet with the contracting agent in charge of receiving proposals. In addition to obtaining valuable information for identifying the problem, formulating your strategy, and writing your proposal, by having such a meeting you let the organization know of your intention to submit a proposal. Furthermore, the meeting may provide some hints of the contractor's expectations on some issues about which you cannot ask direct questions. For example, a nonverbal cue such as tone of voice may inadvertently reveal an estimate of the amount budgeted for the project.

2. *Needs Analysis.* If a formal RFP (or an IFB) is issued, be sure that you understand what the potential customer is asking for. Do not rely on previous discussions with the customer. Do not read just the Statement of Work section in the RFP or IFB. Examine the entire document, including the attachments and exhibits, which may contain important information that is not presented elsewhere. What assumptions are inherent but not stated explicitly? Are these realistic assumptions? Restate exactly what you believe the customer is requesting in the RFP or IFB and ask why.

3. *Customer's Previous Procurement Background.* Know the buying behavior of the potential customer. Conduct research to determine

   - Current suppliers
   - The goods or services purchased
   - The quality of goods or services purchased
   - The price paid for the goods or services
   - The customer's satisfaction with the goods or services

   Use the results of your research when you formulate a solution to the problem. The information could spare you from proposing a brand of product or solution that is not satisfactory, a product that is priced too high, or one that is of inappropriate quality.

4. *Proposal Evaluator.* Find out who in the requesting company will evaluate the proposal. An individual or a team may serve as evaluators. Either way, a formal list of criteria is likely to be used in the evaluation. These criteria can serve as a checklist for tailoring your proposal. If the evaluator is an individual, knowledge of personal background can reveal information that might help you. For instance, if the evaluator has an accounting background, you can anticipate concern about the financial aspects and cost containment of your proposal. Knowledge of evaluation criteria for previous projects may prove useful as well. Does the company usually award contracts or jobs to the lowest bidder, or to the bidder that offers the best solution to the problem, or to the company that offers the highest-quality goods? Are bids evaluated according to a combination of factors, and if so, what are the weightings?

Conduct a Situational Analysis As the second portion of the capture plan, the situational analysis scrutinizes the internal and external environment to make the proposal more persuasive. It supplies the groundwork for turning your proposal into a competitive marketing tool by providing information to outdo your competition, emphasize your strengths, and highlight major selling points. There are three components to the situational analysis:

1. *Competitor Analysis.* Know your competition, their strengths and weaknesses, and what they are likely to propose or offer. In most cases, you will not be able to find out which companies are submitting proposals, and you will have to assume that all firms similar to yours will submit proposals. However, you may learn who bids on similar projects by examining public records. Especially if you are trying to win a state or federal contract, previous bids are probably in the public record. As you analyze bids in these records, keep in mind that some companies bid at a loss to gain knowledge in a new area or to establish a reputation. Wasson contends that each bidder tends to follow a consistent pattern in estimating cost. Knowing your competition can influence your final product and your chances of being awarded the job.[6]

2. *Internal Analysis.* A winning proposal convinces the proposal evaluator that your company is the one to implement the solution to the problem. Conduct an internal analysis of your firm with this criterion in mind. What strengths does your company possess that should be played up in the proposal? Are there weaknesses that will hamper your ability to perform the work? How is your company uniquely suited to perform the work required for this proposal? Do you have previous experience in this specific field? In the proposal, use the strengths identified in this analysis to demonstrate that your firm has performed well in the past and can do so in the future. Build on or sell your company's reputation.

3. *Theme Development.* Themes are major selling points that run through your proposal. Develop a few major themes that communicate that your ideas are better than everyone else's. Label your themes with key words and weave these words into your title, headings, introduction, and text. Examples of themes are high quality, cost justification, efficiency, reliability of your research, major benefits of your plan, and return on investment.

In summary, a capture plan forces a proposal team or writer to analyze crucial strategic issues before writing the proposal. Perhaps the greatest benefit of a capture plan is that it helps identify the nuances of the proposal environment as well as the major themes to which one must be sensitive in order to write a winning proposal.

Formulating a Solution and Strategies

Once you have decided to submit a proposal and have evaluated the customer and the situation, the next step is to formulate a solution. The capture plan helped you understand strategic issues and identify the problem; now use these issues to devise a solution to the problem. For instance, if the problem is that a company needs some software that doesn't exist, the proposed solution might be that your staff could prepare such software. With a solution prepared, you need to devise strategies for implementing it. An effective proposal contains these three kinds of strategies:

1. *Technical Strategy.* Your technical strategy explains the solution (be it a product or service) that is being proposed and how the solution will be implemented. The goal is to convince the reader that your solution best meets the customer's need. If you are preparing a qualification proposal, you will discuss your proposed research methodology or type of analysis. Readers usually evaluate this section first to ensure that a feasible solution is being proposed.

2. *Management Strategy.* The management section establishes your company's ability to carry out the solution proposed or to deliver the goods promised. Whether you are writing a commercial or a qualification proposal, you must establish your firm's ability to implement the proposed solution through expert personnel, experience, insight, facilities, internal organization, and quality control as well as a schedule or a timetable for implementation. Customers that are governmental agencies may want to review your company policies, finances, or personnel records.

3. *Cost Strategy or Cost Estimate.* Your reader needs information to assess if his or her company can afford your products or services and if your offering is reasonably or competitively priced. Many simple commercial proposals are evaluated on the basis of cost after the evaluator determines that the offering meets the company's need. The technical and cost sections of a qualification proposal carry equal weight to the proposal evaluator.

For lengthy, detailed proposals, each of the three strategies may be presented as a separate section or even as individual volumes, as in the case of large government contracts. Letter or memo proposals devote a paragraph or two to each strategy.

Budgeting and Scheduling the Proposal Effort

The final step in the planning process is budgeting and scheduling the proposal writing process. Because some proposals take months to prepare and require considerable financial investment, it is necessary to prepare a proposal cost budget and a proposal schedule. A proposal manager monitors and controls proposal costs. Calculations in employee-hours ensure that all members of the proposal team are performing their assigned tasks.

Preparation and use of a Gantt chart (see Chapter 3, Figure 3.13) aids scheduling your proposal effort. Schedule all proposal activities to meet crucial deadlines and to ensure that all aspects of preparing the proposal have been delegated to a proposal team member. Scheduling has the positive by-product of forcing you to be organized.

THE PROPOSAL WRITING PROCESS

If you were thorough in your planning, writing the proposal should be relatively easy. In this section, we will examine three topics: the writing process, additional types of proposals, and proposal formats.

The Writing Process

The writing stage requires strict attention to detail. The written proposal must reflect all the work you have done to this point. It is a tragedy to have a brilliant solution disqualified because of dull text, poor writing skills, lack of organization, or use of an ineffective or inappropriate format. Your proposal package requires persuasion, effective writing, and appealing graphics.

Be Persuasive Your goal in writing a proposal is to win—to be awarded the project or job. You are selling your solution and your organization. Some suggestions for being persuasive include:

- Open with a persuasive and conclusive summary. The proposal evaluator exhaustively analyzes every detail of your proposal, but the final selection decision may be made by a busy executive who can spend only a few minutes reviewing your proposal. A concise but thorough summary that is hard hitting will appeal to his or her needs. (This opening is often called an Executive Summary.)
- Use a hook or attention-getting device to begin your proposal. Choose your words carefully; maintain a business tone. For businesses, the most effective attention-getting device is often to focus on profits. Governmental agencies show more interest in competence and reliability.
- Use the themes you formulated in the capture plan.
- Back up your statements with facts, statistics, and expert testimony to be convincing and to build credibility for your solution.[7]

Write Effectively Your writing should be clear, concise, attractive, and free of spelling and typographical errors. Readers interpret writing ability as an indication of how well you can do the job, especially if the job involves writing.[8] In addition to following the suggestions for effective writing in Chapter 4, you should take care to organize your proposal well. Organization is especially crucial if you are not well known by your audience; the clarity of your language and organization are the best—sometimes the only—ways your target can judge your thinking and organizing ability.

Near the beginning of your proposal place a specific statement of what you propose. Organize your writing for maximum clarity and psychological effect. Avoid the tendency to write in chronological order; starting with remote causes can be boring and appear irrelevant. Save the background details for middle paragraphs. Locate the most important unknown information at the beginning—the proposal evaluator needs the specific details of your solution as early as possible. Consider summarizing highly detailed portions in the body of the proposal and relegating the details to an appendix to avoid a dull text.

Use Graphic Appeal Graphic appeal refers to the look of your proposal. For better or for worse, your reader gains a first impression of your work before reading a single word of it. Several graphic features determine whether the piece invites or discourages reading, places emphasis efficiently, or adds clarity. Some graphic considerations are:

- Provide adequate margins and white space on each page. If the proposal looks tight and jammed on the page, it does not draw the reader in and could even be viewed as a chore to read.
- Construct paragraphs that vary in length and are no longer than one quarter of a page. Long, heavy-looking paragraphs discourage reading. Short paragraphs invite reading and emphasize content. Keep opening and closing paragraphs pleasingly short.
- Break up the text by section, subsection, and paragraph headings; use headings as often as possible—in every paragraph if appropriate. Exhibit an array of headings in contrasting type styles. For example, use bold capitals for major headings and lightface capitals for subsections for two degrees of emphasis. Avoid the use of too many different styles of type, though, and use consistent type styles for headings of the same level.
- Use appropriate graphics to illustrate, clarify, and summarize. Place the graphics to break up larger blocks of text.
- Employ desktop publishing techniques to add additional levels of professional impact at relatively low cost.

Additional Types of Proposals

The type of proposal prepared depends on the proposal's purpose. Three of the most common types are the sales proposal, the procurement proposal, and the grant proposal. A sales proposal sells a product, service, or idea and is primarily used for business-to-business transactions. Procurement proposals are solicited by federal, state, or local government agencies seeking to obtain goods or services. They are usually longer than sales proposals and their contents are usually specifically dictated in an RFP. Nonprofit organizations write grant proposals to obtain funding from businesses, foundations, and governmental agencies. Because the latter two types of proposal are written so frequently and have unique features, we will discuss them individually.[9]

The Procurement Proposal Solicitations for proposals issued by government entities specify a tremendous amount of detail, and thus the process of preparing the proposal requires a special degree of care in every stage. Procurement proposals usually state who qualifies to submit a proposal, what form the proposal is to take, what specific information should appear in each section of the proposal, and many more requirements. These proposals and the subsequent work usually entail substantial paperwork. For large government procurements, your proposal may encompass three or more volumes. In preparing your proposal, use graphs, charts, and time lines to simplify complexities.

A common problem in proposal writing is nonresponsiveness—being disqualified because you did not follow the RFP or IFB directions or guidelines exactly. Review your proposal carefully to ensure that you have met all requirements. One omitted detail could disqualify you. Imagine a proposal that took three months to produce being disqualified because you did not include one topic. It is helpful to prepare, in advance, a checklist of the details so that you will not overlook any.

Finally, keep in mind that you may be required to show your accounting books to federal auditors. Be aware also that there is a plethora of government regulations that you must follow if you are awarded the contract.

The Grant Proposal Most nonprofit organizations obtain funding by applying for grants-in-aid from foundations, governmental agencies, and businesses. Before you prepare a grant proposal, your organization must qualify by proving its nonprofit status. Next, your project must be eligible to receive the grant. Funding sources usually specify the characteristics that establish eligibility.

It is important to demonstrate your credibility in the introduction. Build credibility by explaining your history, your organizational goals, what support you have received from other sources, and your previous accomplishments.

When explaining the reason for seeking aid (the *Need* or *Problem Statement* section of the proposal), define the problem narrowly. Do not attempt to solve all the ills of society with this additional funding. Document the problem with research and statistics. Demonstrate your depth of understanding of the problem.

Propose a specific objective that is measurable and realistic. If you intend to request additional funding in the future, the funding source will want to know what you have accomplished with the resources granted in the past. They will want tangible statements, such as: "purchased three buses for the disabled and transported 25 wheelchair patients to the physical therapy facility each day" or "renovated 22 homes for occupancy by low-income families."

Your proposal should have a special section entitled *Future Funding*. Funding sources will want to know how you will continue your program when their funding runs out. You should present a plan for obtaining additional funding in the future.[10]

Proposal Formats

There is little agreement about what format to give proposals or what to name the various subject headings.[11] Often, RFPs or solicitation packages suggest an outline or contain a Business Proposal Instruction section. If so, follow that format. In following a dictated organization, your persuasiveness and the quality of your solution will distinguish your proposal from the others submitted. In the absence of such guidance, you may be able to follow a standard format that your company uses. Perhaps you will be fortunate enough to be able to design your own format. Designing your own format is your opportunity to be persuasive and creative, but do not deviate too far from the traditional format. Effective proposals, at the minimum, include a summary, a statement of the problem or need, the proposed solution, how the solution will be implemented, and what it will cost to implement the solution. The following is a suggested format that will be appropriate for many proposals.

1. *Cover Materials.* Include a letter of transmittal, a title page, and a table of contents.
2. *Executive Summary.* A persuasive summary briefly states the need or prob-

lem, the solution, the implementation plan, and the costs and resources required. Use an attention-getting device to open your summary and highlight the themes or strategy you will discuss throughout the proposal. Make the summary persuasive and concise enough for your reader to make a decision about your offer on reading your summary, without having to read the entire proposal. At the same time, draw in and make your reader want to read the rest of your proposal.

3. *Introductory Materials.* The introduction can include the background to the situation or problem which the proposal is addressing, the most immediate cause of the problem, the purpose for studying the problem or submitting the proposal, the goals of the proposal, or the benefits to be derived from adoption of the proposal.

4. *Need or Problem Statement.* State the problem concisely. Differentiate between symptoms of the problem and the root problem.

5. *Technical Solution or Methodology.* This section is the heart of your proposal. Present your solution and prove that it is not only viable but that it is the best alternative for solving the customer's problem or meeting the need. Convince the reader of the strengths of your proposed solution. Demonstrate that your solution is based on the latest research findings and the most current or most appropriate technology. It is not enough to just state your solution; you must sell your solution. Use facts, figures, and expert testimony.

This section also outlines the implementation of the technical solution. Discuss the methods. Identify major and minor tasks. Provide a time line for completion of each task. Give the specifications of materials and products used or produced.

If you are writing a qualification proposal, describe how you will accomplish the work, how you will conduct the study, what research techniques will be employed, why they are the most appropriate measures to use, and how you will analyze the data.

Finally, many customers want to know how you will evaluate yourself and track your progress to completion. If the job will be lengthy, the customer may ask you to periodically report on the progress of the project and to evaluate your company's performance.

6. *Management Profiles.* First, introduce the individual or team who will be implementing the solution. Describe qualifications and related backgrounds. Include résumés of key personnel in an appendix. Tailor the résumés for the specific proposal. Highlight your company's previous experience or specialization in the area. List work done for other clients in the area of interest and the scope or depth of the work performed.

Second, describe how you will organize the project. Delineate lines of authority and responsibility. Design the workload and structure from start-up to completion. Create an organization chart. Include all resources and facilities to be used.

Next, present the management policies and administrative methods applicable to the project. For example, describe quality control, cost accounting, payroll, time-keeping, and reporting methods.

End the Management Profile by demonstrating that your company is stable, financially viable, and reputable. Include financial statements, letters of reference from satisfied customers (in an appendix), and awards. Close by selling your company's strengths.

7. *Budget*. Provide a thorough breakdown of costs and differentiate between direct and indirect costs. List any subcontractors and give their qualifications and costs. Describe the method of payment that will be followed and clearly state any penalties prescribed for late payment.

8. *Conclusion and Recommendations*. The conclusion is your last chance to sell your solution. Make it persuasive. Summarize the problem and your solution. Bring in key themes and strategies and highlight the strengths of your solution and your company. If the proposal would benefit from a recommendation, include it.

9. *Bibliography*. If you did research and want to project a scholarly or authoritative image, include your sources.

10. *Appendices*. Include résumés of key personnel, letters of reference, highly specific details of implementation that you summarized in the body of the proposal, and any other relevant material.

FINISHING TOUCHES

Some finishing touches include packaging, evaluating, and delivering the proposal.

Packaging

Does your proposal have a professional appearance? Type should be clean and easy to read. Avoid dot matrix printers for final drafts; the clean type of a laser printer is preferable. Print your proposal on white paper that is smooth, crisp, and heavy enough not to look cheap. Use 25 percent cotton content (rag) bond, in 20-pound weight. External proposals should always be enclosed in a binder. While bindings should be attractive, avoid obvious extravagances, such as submitting your proposal in a leather binder. You do not want to give the impression that you spend resources needlessly.

Evaluating the Proposal

After you have completed writing the proposal, evaluate it in light of the RFP or IFB to ensure that it is complete. Have you correctly identified the problem? Have you offered a solution that is feasible? Were you effective in selling your solution? Have you met all the requirements? Does the text flow smoothly? Read the proposal as if you were the evaluator; is it concise and competitive? Now read it from the viewpoint of the busy decision maker; is it a persuasive document if skimmed?

Delivering the Proposal

If you are rushed to complete the proposal, you are likely to overlook crucial last minute details. Be sure that you are submitting the correct number of copies of your proposal. Is a transmittal letter enclosed? Is the proposal addressed properly? Are all the required forms enclosed? Careless omission of any one of these details could cost you the job.[12]

Often when a customer has narrowed the choice to two or three companies, the companies are asked to present their proposal orally. Be prepared to make an oral presentation by referring to Chapter 10 on effective presentations.

SUMMARY

A proposal is a persuasive document that makes an offer to provide goods or services to a potential or existing customer. The effective proposal convinces the customer that you are the best qualified to meet the customer's needs. Commercial proposals sell a specific product or solution. Qualification proposals sell skills, experience, knowledge, and creativity as the most capable in implementing an effective solution.

Proposals may be prepared for those inside your organization (internal) or outside (external). The writer initiates an unsolicited proposal. An entity that has need for goods or services may solicit proposals when it issues an Invitation for Bids (IFB) or a Request for Proposals (RFP). IFBs usually specify the solution the solicitor wants implemented. Negotiated proposals, on the other hand, allow the proposal writer to create a unique solution to the customer's need; RFPs are often of this type. Proposals take many forms including letter proposals, preliminary proposals, detailed or formal proposals, and oral presentations.

The planning stage of the proposal preparation process is crucial. First, screen the RFP and decide whether to submit a proposal. Second, create a capture plan that analyzes the customer and the proposal situation. The customer analysis step evaluates the need (as stated in the RFP), the problem, the customer's buying behavior, and the proposal evaluator. The situational analysis step examines the competition, your strengths and weaknesses, and major themes. Third, create a solution to the problem that consists of technical, management, and cost strategies.

When writing the proposal, be persuasive, write effectively, and make your proposal graphically appealing. Use appropriate content and format, depending on the type of proposal you write (sales, procurement, or grant proposal). All types of proposals should include the following: cover materials, executive summary, introduction, need or problem statement, a technical solution or methodology, management profiles, budget, conclusion, and appendices (if needed). Your proposal should have a professional appearance. Finally, evaluate the finished product carefully.

DISCUSSION QUESTIONS

1. What are the two major purposes of proposals?
2. What are the ways of classifying proposals?
3. What are the four steps in the proposal planning process?
4. What is a capture plan and what does it entail?
5. What are three strategies for formulating a solution?
6. What is involved in the proposal writing process?
7. What is an executive summary?
8. What should the technical solution or methodology section of the proposal accomplish?
9. What is a procurement proposal?

Applications

1. Most large, daily newspapers have a section for Announcements, Request for Proposals, or Bids. Find the appropriate section and scan some of the RFPs. Based on the discussion of proposals presented in Chapter 8, what specific classification of proposals do you see? How specific are the requirements, such as length, headings, page limits, or deadlines?

2. Contact a local governmental agency and ask permission to review some submissions in response to RFPs. Many of these will be public record once a decision has been made regarding the winner of the bid or proposal. Examine the proposals for such things as length, quality, attractiveness, depth, and persuasiveness. What conclusions can you draw about those that seem especially strong versus those that were obviously weak?

NOTES

1. William H. Roetzheim, *Proposal Writing for the Data Processing Consultant*, Prentice-Hall, Englewood Cliffs, New Jersey, 1986.
2. Roetzheim, *Proposal Writing*, Chapter 3.
3. Joel P. Bowman and Bernadine P. Branchaw, *How to Write Proposals That Produce*, The Orynx Press, Phoenix, Arizona, 1992, pp. 171–184.
4. Bowman and Branchaw, *How to Write Proposals*, p. 31.
5. Both of the above-mentioned books deal thoroughly with the planning process and strategic issues to consider when planning your proposal.
6. C. R. Wasson, *Understanding Qualitative Analysis*, Appleton-Century-Crofts, East Norwalk, Connecticut, 1969.
7. John Schell and John Stratton, *Writing on the Job: A Handbook for Business and Government*, New American Library, New York, 1984, p. 126.
8. Anne Simon Moffat, "Grantsmanship: What Makes Proposals Work?" *Science* 265, September 23, 1994, pp. 1911–1912.
9. Schell and Stratton, *Writing on the Job*, Chapters 11, 12, and 13.
10. Norton J. Kiritz, "Proposal Planning and Proposal Writing," *Grantsmanship Center News*, Los Angeles, 1987.
11. All of the above sources discuss proposal formats extensively.
12. Roetzheim, *Proposal Writing*, Chapter 10.

Appendix:
Sample RFPs and Proposals

This chapter concludes with an example of an unsolicited, brief, internal proposal for a new computer (Figure 8.2), and a Request for Proposals and the response to that RFP (Figures 8.3 and 8.4). You will find that the latter proposal follows most of the observations and suggestions presented earlier in this chapter. Keep in mind, of course, that there are many forms of proposals, that authors have their favorite writing styles, and that evaluators have differences in what they expect. These proposals, then, are just two of many alternatives that could have been prepared.

FIGURE 8.2   Example of a Brief, Unsolicited Internal Proposal

Small Products World
Yuma, AZ 89947

INTEROFFICE MEMO

TO: Caroline de Rosa
FROM: Carmine Vasquez
SUBJECT: Proposal to purchase new computer
DATE: January 12, 200X

The purpose of the memo is to propose that we purchase a Delta 5000 computer workstation. The number of orders for our products has been increasing over the last four years, and the increase is dramatic for the last two quarters. This increased business has reached the point where our current computer is holding back the shipment of goods. The Delta 5000 would overcome these problems. Immediate approval of this proposal is requested.

The Current Situation

Our reputation for importing high quality international goods and for having exceptional service and delivery systems has resulted in a positive growth pattern over the last four years. However, orders are pouring in so fast that we are unable to give customers our usual quality service or expected delivery times. Complaints are on the rise as well.

The Problem

The reason for our slow delivery times and most of the complaints lies with the overwhelmed, slow, outdated computer we use for our customer database, billing information, and shipping information. This computer has served us well, but now, because of the amount of data submitted, the ongoing process of backing up our hard disk, and new software we've installed, the computer can no longer keep up with our demands. Updating it is cost-prohibitive.

The Analysis

As you can see from the data illustrated on the next page, 2001 showed increased profit, but at a cost of dramatically increased complaints.

FIGURE 8.2   **Example of a Brief, Unsolicited Internal Proposal (Concluded)**

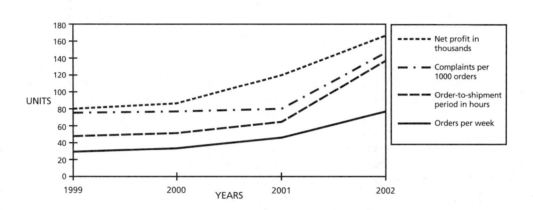

The trends of the last four years, and especially this last year, require increased computer use. Upon investigation of information in our database, I note the following inverse relationship between average order amount in dollars and number of orders per week. I believe our customers are spending less money per order because the quality of our service is slipping.

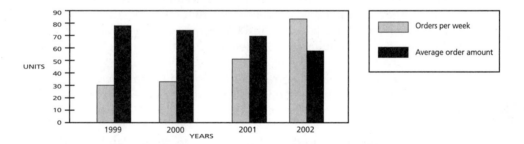

In sum, because of change in our business and because of the age of our current computer, we are offending more customers and flirting with losing some of them.

The Solution

We should purchase and install the Delta 5000 workstation (for $8,799) immediately. I forecast it will meet our needs well into the twenty-first century. I'll be pleased to meet with you if you have any questions.

FIGURE 8.3   **Sample Request for Proposals**

REQUEST FOR PROPOSALS

Financially well-backed private investor seeks proposals to start a rubber stamp vending business. The purpose of the business is to solicit orders for rubber stamps and then to prepare and deliver those stamps, to retail already prepared stamps, and to vend related materials, such as ink pads, business forms, and so on. Types of business stamps would include individually prepared Paid, Received, Filed, and Date stamps. Boutique aspects of the business would include many forms of household use stamps, such as This belongs to Mary, A recipe from Mary, A note from Mary, animal and cartoon caricatures for children, and envelope return addresses.

Details: A storefront in Horton Plaza in downtown San Diego is under lease by the investor and is of adequate size for this business. A written business proposal should be delivered to Union-Tribune, P.O. Box 1234, no later than the 10th of next month. Proposals should address these issues: proposed vendors for prepared stamps and office materials, cost of equipment for preparation of stamps, anticipated profit margin for various products, further description of products to be offered for sale, size of workforce with salaries, and background of the person proposing to be selected as the manager of the store.

The investor has access to store fittings, such as display cases and computerized cash registers; do not discuss these needs or the monthly lease fee. The store would be open from 10 A.M. to 9 P.M. daily.

Proposals should be limited to 12 pages, single-spaced, and include a cover page as part of the 12 pages. An executive summary and table of contents are not needed. Content should reflect the degree of business opportunity available based on research or substantiated facts. A 50 percent interest in the business will be awarded to the winning proposal. The proposer may be, but is not required to be, the manager of the store.

Opportunity: For the right person, this is the opportunity to establish a financially rewarding business with no personal financial obligation and to become a store manager in a promising field.

FIGURE 8.4   **Sample Proposal**

<u>Proposal</u>

A Business Opportunity:

Starting a Rubber Stamp Business

Prepared by:
Susan Jones
January 200X

FIGURE 8.4   **Sample Proposal (Continued)**

Proposal for a Rubber Stamp Business

Introduction

A financially well-backed private investor is planning to start a rubber stamp vending business. The business would sell custom-made rubber stamps, traditional rubber stamps, and related supplies. The business would be located in Horton Plaza in downtown San Diego, in a storefront leased by the investor.

The investor has issued a Request for Proposals to provide an analysis of the business opportunity and an implementation plan.

Purpose

The purpose of the business is to sell rubber stamps and related office supplies to businesses, households, and tourists in the San Diego area. The business would actively solicit orders for custom-made rubber stamps and manufacture and deliver those stamps. The business would also sell traditional business and household stamps containing phrases such as "Paid," "Received," and "A Note from Mary," as well as related supplies such as ink and ink pads.

This proposal presents a business overview, implementation strategy, and financial analysis. The implementation strategy includes the proposed rubber stamp vendors, the cost of equipment for making rubber stamps, the anticipated profit margins by product type, the products to be offered for sale, the planned workforce, and the background of the proposed store managers.

This proposal demonstrates the viability of the rubber stamp business and substantiates that we should be selected to initiate the business and bring it to profitability. We suggest the name "Stamp It Out" for the business.

Business Overview

Rubber stamps and associated supplies are used routinely by most businesses and many households. Businesses frequently stamp forms or checks as "Received," "Filed," "Processed," or "Paid." Households often stamp envelopes with return addresses and label personal property with name and date stamps. Rubber stamps can be customized with a company name or logo for business use or with a personal note for household use. Rubber stamps with attractive designs are often purchased as gifts.

FIGURE 8.4   Sample Proposal (Continued)

San Diego's Horton Plaza is a particularly attractive location for a new rubber stamp business. San Diego is the sixth largest city in the United States with a population of 2.8 million as of July 1998 (U.S. Census Bureau, 1999). According to the California State Board of Equalization (1999), there are approximately 80,000 businesses in San Diego County with a total taxable sales revenue of $32 billion per year. About half of this business occurs in the City of San Diego. Horton Plaza is located next to the historic Gaslamp Quarter in the center of downtown San Diego. Horton Plaza is a major shopping attraction in downtown San Diego and hosts over 140 specialty stores (Westfield Shoppingtown Horton Plaza, 1999).

Horton Plaza is located a few blocks from the San Diego Convention Center, making it a prime attraction for convention attendees. San Diego's Convention Center was recently named one of the top three convention centers in the world by Europe's largest meetings industry trade publication (San Diego Convention Center Corporation, 1999a). During fiscal year 1999, the convention center hosted 210 events, attracted 362,034 out-of-town delegates to San Diego, and contributed $543 million to the local economy (San Diego Convention Center, 1999b). Conventions are a particularly attractive source of customers because convention organizers tend to give small gifts, coupons, and shopping recommendations to attendees as part of the conference registration process. Contracts with a few large conventions could provide significant revenue for this business.

To target convention attendees, we plan to work with the San Diego Convention Center Corporation to offer customized stamps, key chains, magnets, signs and other personalized items to convention attendees. We also plan to target local businesses by attending trade shows and career fairs. Businesses at these events may have a particular need for rubber stamps to properly label the resumes and business cards they receive.

Implementation Strategy

This section includes the details of establishing the operation.

Proposed Vendors for Prepared Stamps and Office Materials

We propose two major vendors and other smaller niche vendors for the products.

FIGURE 8.4   **Sample Proposal (Continued)**

Simon's Stamps

Our primary vendor for prepared stamps, inkpads, ink, and related materials will be Simon's Stamps in Amherst, MA. Simon's Stamps has been in business since 1989 and has several hundred wholesale accounts (Simon's Stamps, 1999). Simon's sells self-inking push-down stamps, traditional wood-handle rubber stamps, and three types of metal frame self-inking date stamps. Simon's provides both custom-made stamps and off-the-shelf stamps. Orders can be placed on-line, and net 30-day credit terms are available. On-line orders are shipped within 24 hours, including orders for custom-made stamps.

Simon's Stamps is our first choice because it focuses on rapid service and provides an attractive wholesale dealer discount program. This program provides a 40 percent discount off suggested retail prices for traditional wood-handle stamps, Kwik and Trodat brand stamps, and a 25 percent discount for inkpads, ink, date stamps, numbering stamps, and heavy-duty stamps.

JLS Rubber Stamp Co.

Our second major supplier will be JLS Rubber Stamp Co., Inc. of Redding, CA. JLS has been in the rubber stamp and office supply business for 35 years (JLS Rubber Stamp, 1999). JLS manufactures and sells several types of self-inking rubber stamps, embossers and seals, engraved signs, name badges, and stencils. JLS also sells a variety of gift products such as engraved luggage tags and key chains, custom metal license plate frames, and custom name stamps. JLS specializes in serving commercial and industrial accounts.

Other Stamp Vendors

Two other stamp vendors can bring a variety of stamps to our customers. Rubber Stamps of America features over 1,000 stamps designed by graphic artists; specialties include wildlife and exotic art (Rubber Stamps of America, 1999). The Doodle Art Rubber Stamp Company provides a variety of special occasion stamps. Their Christmas stamps include pictures of trees, snowmen, Santa Claus, reindeer, and many others (Doodle Art Rubber Stamp Company, 1999).

Backup Suppliers

AllMark Identification Systems can provide rubber stamps and ink pads, and FormsPlus can supply a wide array of business forms. Both companies are located in San Diego. While they cost more than the vendors we propose, we need backup suppliers in case of emergencies.

FIGURE 8.4   **Sample Proposal (Continued)**

<u>Cost of Equipment for Stamp Preparation</u>

Rubber stamps can be produced at least six different ways (Forks Web, 1999). The most common and least expensive method is to use a hand-set foundry. This process involves positioning individual letters of printer's type into a holder and then creating the rubber stamp with a heated press. For this process, the necessary equipment and supplies cost about $500. Because of the smell of heated rubber associated with this process, special city permits would be required or an alternative site needed.

The newest method of producing rubber stamps uses photographic processing (Forks Web, 1999; Insider Reports, 1994) to make stamps from laser-printed artwork. Prices for the photoprocessor vary by the manufacturer, but Grantham's Polly Stamp of E. Grand Forks, MN sells one for $1,095 (Insider Reports, 1994). In addition, J. R. Martin (1999) offers a four-day training course on making rubber stamps.

For this business, we recommend the photographic process because it can produce stamps from any picture or drawing, not just words and letters. This flexibility is particularly important in our proposed business because we plan to sell stamps with company logos, hand-written signatures, and personal photographs or drawings that would be difficult to produce with the foundry method. Permits would not be required.

Once the rubber portion of the stamp is completed, it must be attached to a stamp molding and handle, usually made of natural wood. A description of this process is given by rubber stamp making organizations (Happy Rubber Stamps, 1999). Moldings and handles can be purchased cheaply in volume. Pictures of the major categories of stamps appear below.

Traditional   **Self-Inking**   **Pre-Inked**

Source: www.ams-stamps.com

FIGURE 8.4   **Sample Proposal (Continued)**

The equipment used for making rubber stamps can also produce a variety of other custom-made gifts. We plan to make key chains, refrigerator magnets, and name plates from the same material.

To provide the best service to Stamp It Out customers, we plan to have a computer at the store displaying a variety of possible stamp designs. Our employees would then be able to work with our customers to add names, logos, or other personal items to existing designs. The customer's modified stamp would then be printed on-site and used in the photographic process. Similarly, a customer would be able to bring in an existing design, scan it into the computer, and modify it as necessary. The proposed store manager for this business offers to donate a Dell computer and a Hewlett-Packard Printer/Scanner/Copier (PSC) for this purpose. If purchased new, the Dell computer would cost approximately $1,500 and the PSC would cost $400.

Anticipated Profit Margins

Industry data for office supply firms indicates an average gross margin of 30 percent (Market Guide, 1999c). We anticipate that we will obtain a similar average margin on most previously prepared stamps, ink and ink pads, note paper, and gift items. Based on discounts provided by Simon's Stamps, we anticipate a margin of 40 percent on traditional wood-handle stamps, Kwik stamps, and Trodat stamps, and a margin of 25 percent for inkpads, ink, date stamps, numbering stamps, and heavy-duty stamps.

Custom-made stamps can be ordered from Simon's Stamps or produced directly. If ordered from Simon's, we estimate a potential profit margin of 25–40 percent, based on the type of stamp ordered. Much higher margins are possible for stamps that we produce ourselves. Ignoring labor costs, we estimate that the stamps can be produced for $5–$10 and sold for $12–$30, implying a gross margin of about 60 percent. Based on our prior experience and unobtrusive observation of similar businesses in the Los Angeles area, we estimate that about half of our business will be custom-made stamps and the other half will be previously prepared stamps and supplies.

Further Description of Products

We plan to market a variety of custom-made and off-the-shelf stamps for business and household use. The custom-made stamps will be produced in the back of our store within 20 minutes of the customer's order. The customer may provide the design for the stamp or customize one displayed on our computer screen.

FIGURE 8.4   Sample Proposal (Continued)

The computer can display thousands of images and designs for traditional business-use stamps as well as household-use stamps. The business-use designs will give the customer the opportunity to add a company name or logo to traditional stamps such as "Received" or "Paid." The household-use designs will allow the customer to add a name or slogan to stamps such as "A Note from Mary" or "Property of John Smith." We can also easily create a rubber stamp of the customer's signature.

We plan to sell all six basic types of rubber stamps marketed by Simon's Stamps. The six types include both traditional stamps and self-inking stamps, as listed below:

- Trodat Self-Inking Printer. Push-down model. Efficient and convenient. Available in seven sizes. Suggested retail price: $12.50 ($\frac{3}{8}$" × $\frac{11}{32}$") to $24.75 ($1\frac{1}{2}$" × $3\frac{1}{16}$").
- Kwik Stamp Plus Self-Inking Stamp. Push-down model. Available in four sizes. Suggested retail price: $12.95 ($\frac{5}{8}$" × $1\frac{3}{4}$") to $19.95 ($1\frac{1}{4}$" × 3").
- Traditional Wood-Handle Stamp. High-quality commercial-grade. Used with ink pad. Suggested retail price: $6.90 ($\frac{1}{2}$" × 1") to $27.00 ($3$" × 5").
- Metal Type-Band Die-Plate Dater. Changeable date stamp, custom text available. Used with ink pad. Suggested retail price: $29.75
- Heavy Duty Self-Inking Dater. Super heavy-duty stamp. Durable, nickel-plated steel construction. Suggested retail price: $38.40 ($1$" × $1\frac{5}{8}$") to $69.95 ($2$" × $2\frac{3}{4}$").
- Metal Frame Self-Inkers. Super-heavy duty stamp for bank tellers, tax collectors, and receiving clerks. Suggested retail price: $31.38 ($1$" × $1\frac{5}{8}$") to $56.45 ($2$" × $2\frac{3}{4}$").

These rubber stamps will include the words "Received," "Faxed," "Paid," "Billed," "Replied," and "Filed." We will also sell ink and ink pads, business forms, and note pads to go with these stamps. We will also provide customers with the opportunity to order custom-made embossers and seals from JLS Rubber Stamp Co.

For household use and for gifts, Stamp It Out will sell a variety of rubber stamps and other custom-designed products. These products are listed below:

- Custom-made name stamps, for both adults and children.
- Custom-made key chains, luggage tags, and refrigerator magnets.

FIGURE 8.4   Sample Proposal (Continued)

- Customized license plate holders from JLS Rubber Stamp Co.
- Over 1,000 rubber stamps from Rubber Stamps of America (RSA), including wildlife, exotic art, and cartoons for children. We will purchase a sample of about 50 of these from RSA and provide the full catalog to customers for special orders.
- Several hundred stamp designs from Doodle Art Rubber Stamp company, including a variety of holiday and seasonal stamps. We will purchase seasonal stamps during the holiday shopping periods and provide the catalog to customers throughout the year.
- Other specialty stamps include alphabet, recipe, and hobby stamps.
- Books on stamping.
- Stamp ink (all colors, permanent and water-based).
- Embossers and desk plates.

Size of Workforce

The business will begin operations with four employees: the store manager, an assistant manager, and two sales clerks. We anticipate that the store will be open when Horton Plaza is open: 10:00 A.M. to 9:00 P.M. Monday through Friday, 10:00 A.M. to 7:00 P.M. on Saturday, and 11:00 A.M. to 6:00 P.M. on Sunday (Westfield Shoppingtown Horton Plaza, 1999). This is a total of 71 hours per week. We require that at least two employees be present in the store at any time, including the store manager or assistant manager and at least one sales clerk. We currently plan to hire two full-time (40 hours per week) cashiers but may choose to hire four half-time cashiers instead, based on labor availability. As the business grows, additional full-time or part-time sales clerks will be hired as necessary, particularly during peak hours.

The store manager will be responsible for overall store operations, including hiring of additional employees as necessary, ordering supplies, and marketing the company's products and services to convention planners. The assistant manager will be responsible for store operations when the store manager is not present and will assist in ordering supplies and training sales clerks. Sales clerks will be responsible for helping customers to find products, collecting orders and payments, and making custom stamps.

We propose an initial annual salary of $50,000 per year for the store manager and $40,000 per year for the assistant manager. Sales clerks will be paid $6–$7 per hour, or about $13,000 per year for full-time work. Thus, we anticipate total salary expenses of $116,000 per year. Adding an additional 20 percent of salary for benefits such as health insurance and workers' compensation insurance, we estimate initial total labor costs of $140,000 per year.

The main duties of the store manager would be inventory, bookkeeping, personnel management, and daily store operations. The assistant store manager will focus on customer service, new product selection, and marketing, and will assist with daily store operations.

FIGURE 8.4   Sample Proposal (Continued)

Background of Store Managers

The store manager will be Susan Jones. Susan recently graduated from San Diego State University with an MBA, specializing in finance and entrepreneurship. Prior to getting her MBA, Susan worked for Staples for two years as a store manager and for Wal-Mart for three years as a department manager. During her two years at Staples, Susan initiated a marketing campaign with small businesses that increased sales by 30 percent.

The assistant store manager will be Sandra S. Davis. Sandra is currently the assistant manager of an arts supply store in Solana Beach, CA, where she has been employed for the past three years. Her duties include ordering supplies, assisting customers with special orders, and training sales clerks. Sandra was previously self-employed creating arts and crafts and selling them at craft fairs. Forty percent of Sandra's craft business came from customizing existing items for individual customers by adding names or slogans. She has a bachelor's degree in business.

Financial Analysis

According to the California Board of Equalization (1999), total taxable sales of office supplies in San Diego in 1998 were approximately $470 million for 500 stores, or average sales of almost $1 million per store. To confirm that this estimate applies to stores of our proposed size, we obtained annual revenue estimates for Staples and Office Depot stores and scaled these numbers downward. This calculation is shown in Table 1 and confirms that a $1 million estimate is reasonable.

The annual revenue given in this table is taken from the firms' most recent financial statements (Market Guide, 1999a and 1999b). Revenue per store averages about $10 million for these large chains. To adjust the revenue to a store of our size, we computed the revenue per employee for these chains, and used this to estimate the revenue for a comparable four-person store. These values are given at the bottom of Table 1.

Table 1.
Sales for Office Supply Stores
(dollar values in thousands)

	Staples	Office Depot
Total annual revenue	$7,820,000	$10,028,200
Number of stores	913	800
Revenue per store	$8,565	$12,535
Number of employees	21,580	44,000
Revenue per employee	$362	$228
Estimated Revenue for four-person store	$1,449	$912

FIGURE 8.4   Sample Proposal (Continued)

There is sufficient demand for rubber stamps, related office supplies, and related gift items in downtown San Diego to support these estimates. As mentioned earlier, San Diego Convention Center brings 326,000 people to San Diego every year. Based on our contacts with convention organizers, we believe we can sell a $20 rubber stamp, key chain, or other gift item to at least 10 percent of convention attendees. This alone would produce revenue of $652,000. In addition, as mentioned earlier, there are about 80,000 businesses in San Diego County. If we could generate sales of $100 per year from 5 percent of those businesses, we could produce additional revenue of $400,000. These two target markets combine to provide over $1 million of revenue, before including sales to households for general use and for gifts. Thus, we believe that we can achieve $1 million of annual revenue within a year or two of starting this business and still have future growth prospects.

Based on an annual revenue of $1 million, the estimated profit for our proposed rubber stamp business is given in Table 2. We used a gross margin estimate of 45 percent in this analysis, assuming that half of our sales will be custom-made products at 60 percent margin and half will be off-the-shelf products averaging 30 percent margin. As shown in Table 2, we estimate a pretax profit of $310,000 per year based on this initial business size.

Table 2.
Estimated Profit for Rubber Stamp Business
(dollar values in thousands)

Estimated Revenue	$1,000
Gross Margin	45%
Gross Profit	$450
Labor Costs	$140
Net Profit (before taxes)	$310

Conclusion and Recommendation

Horton Plaza provides an ideal location for a rubber stamp business, since it is close to downtown businesses and to San Diego's Convention Center. Estimated demand for rubber stamps and related materials in the downtown San Diego area indicates that we should be able to achieve sales of approximately $1 million per year. A small four-person store can generate pretax profits of approximately $310,000 and has the opportunity to expand into related office supplies and custom gifts. The proposed management team has significant experience and a track record of success in managing similar retail stores.

This proposal demonstrates that initiating a rubber stamp business in downtown San Diego can be financially rewarding. We believe Stamp It Out can be operational with six week's notice. We encourage you to select us to bring this profitable venture to fruition.

FIGURE 8.4   Sample Proposal (Concluded)

References

American Marking Systems, (1999). 15 Dec. 1999 <http://www.ams-stamps.com/index.htm>.

California State Board of Equalization. (1999). "Taxable Sales in California." 26 Nov. 1999 <http://www.boe.ca.gov/tsalescont.htm>.

Doodle Art Rubber Stamp Company (1999). Home Page. 21 Nov. 1999 <http://www.doodle-art.com>.

Forks Web. (1999). "All About Getting into the Rubber Stamp Business." 21 Nov. 1999 <http://www.forks-web.com/freeinfo.htm/business.htm/pah5.htm>.

Happy Rubber Stamp Club. (1999). "How to Mount Your Rubber Stamp." 21 Nov. 1999 <http://www.happyrubberstamps.com>.

Insider Reports. (1994). "Start Your Own Rubber Stamp Business." 21 Nov. 1999 <http://www.insiderreports.com/bizrprts/r21.htm>.

JLS Rubber Stamp Co., Inc. (1999). Home Page. 21 Nov. 1999 <http://www.jlsrubberslamp.com/default3.htm>.

Market Guide. (1999a). "Snapshot Report for Staples, Inc." 26 Nov. 1999 <http://www/marketguide.com/mgi/snap/83812.htm>.

Market Guide. (1999b). "Snapshot Report for Office Depot, Inc." 26 Nov. 1999 <http://www/marketguide.com/mgi/snap/65440.htm>.

Market Guide. (1999c). "Performance Comparison Report for Staples, Inc." 26 Nov. 1999 <http://www/marketguide.com/mgi/ratio/83812.htm>.

Martin, J. R. (1999). "A Rubber Stamp Shop." 21 Nov. 1999 <http://homebizexpert.com/ideas.html>.

Rubber Stamps of America. (1999). Home Page. 21 Nov. 1999 <http://www.stampusa.com>.

San Diego Convention Center Corporation. (1999a). "San Diego Convention Center Named One of Top Three Convention Centers in the World." 26 Nov. 1999 <http://www.sdcc.org >.

San Diego Convention Center Corporation. (1999b). "FY 99 Record Breaking Year." 26 Nov. 1999 <http://www.sdcc.org >.

Simon's Stamps. (1999). Home Page. 21 Nov. 1999 <http://www.simonstamp.com>.

Westfield Shoppingtown Horton Plaza. (1999). Home Page. 26 Nov. 1999 <http://www.hortonplaza.com>.

US Census Bureau. (1999). "County Population Estimates for July 1, 1998." 30 Nov. 1999 <http://www.census.gov/population/estimates/county/co-98-1/98C1_06.txt>.

Report Writing: From Formal Documents to Short Summaries

In the business world, report writing is a common activity. Reports may cover short meetings, analyses of customers' relationships with your company, problems your company may be facing with manufacturing, or they may summarize the work your company accomplished under a contract won by a proposal.

At first the job of writing a report may seem overwhelming. Like other types of writing, however, it becomes easier if it is broken into small parts. This chapter introduces you to report writing and discusses several report forms, ranging from formal documents to short executive memos. After reading the sections of this chapter on the preparation and writing of reports, you will find that the job of report writing will become much easier.

UNDERSTANDING THE NATURE OF A REPORT

What Is a Report?

A report is the compilation of information that has been sought out, collected, sifted, organized, and written to convey a specific message. The objective is generally either to present information or to analyze a particular situation. Consequently, reports can be broadly categorized into information reports and research reports.

The Information Report An information report may present a record of previous events, or it may periodically cover past and new information that will allow readers to stay current on a topic, see progress on a project, or gain insight on product development. The purpose of the information report is to convey ideas and data as clearly, concisely, correctly, and quickly as possible.

The Research Report A research report is concerned with analyzing information. The writer looks at a problem that needs to be solved, gathers data, analyzes the data that are available, arrives at a decision, and then makes recommendations. The analysis process is much like that described in Chapter 14 on the case study method. Research reports may solve merchandising or production problems, offer remedies for better ways of financing an organization, or give insight into anticipated acts by competitors. The objective is that the reader of a research report will desire to take some action as a result of the new information disclosed in the report.

What Initial Questions Should You Ask?

There are several questions that you should ask in the preparatory stages.

What Is the Purpose of the Report? Your first task is to determine the objective of your report. Understanding your assignment should help you decide whether the report will be informative or research oriented, and its specific purpose.

Who Will Read the Report? After determining the purpose of the report you should then determine who will read the finished product. Knowledge about your readership will help you research and write the report. In addition to your primary readers, you should also consider any secondary readers to whom the report may be distributed.

Upward reports carry information such as progress on production facilities or product lines, status factors, anticipated problems, requests for personnel or budgetary support, financial data, and projected business conditions. Downward reports more often take the form of policy statements, procedures of action, and decisions of which employees need to be aware.

If you find that the primary readers are on your organizational level, the report is likely to contain information to be used by others in preparing additional reports. This situation often occurs in marketing and production realms. Finally, reports are often intended for other companies, competitors, and the public.

Once you know the audience for your report, you can then determine what they will want to read, why they want it, and what your responsibility is in fulfilling their needs. This information will help you analyze, organize, and write the report. But before you start the research and writing of your report, it is important to know how a report should look. This information appears in the next section.

THE FORMAT OF A REPORT

To get a better understanding of how a finished report will look, you must determine how formal it will be. This section covers the different levels of formality: the formal report, the semiformal report, the consultant's report, the informal report, and the executive memo.

The Formal Report

Formal reports are usually long; they can contain several of the traditional parts listed in Figure 9.1.

Formalities The various elements listed below all serve a distinct purpose for the formal report. The *cover page* lists the title and name of the producer. The *letter of transmittal* sends the report to the reader. It can be either attached to the outside of the cover page or placed immediately inside the cover.

The *title page* gives the full report title, the names of the authors, the name of the company or person for whom the report was prepared, the date of transmission, and any related information.

The *authorization letter*, if included, is a copy of the letter that requested the report. It serves as an authorization document to any secondary readers.

The *table of contents* presents the parts of the report along with page numbers on which each part begins. It is usually produced last so that the pages can be listed accurately.

An *abstract* (also sometimes called *synopsis, epitome,* or *précis*) is typically written by the author. For most reports, the abstract is limited to about one-half page,

---

FIGURE 9.1   **Possible Parts of a Formal Report**

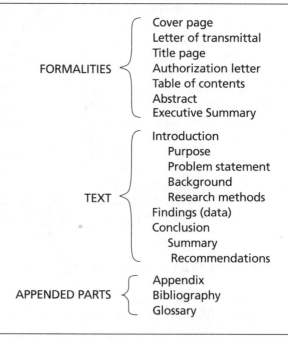

FORMALITIES
- Cover page
- Letter of transmittal
- Title page
- Authorization letter
- Table of contents
- Abstract
- Executive Summary

TEXT
- Introduction
  - Purpose
  - Problem statement
  - Background
  - Research methods
- Findings (data)
- Conclusion
  - Summary
  - Recommendations

APPENDED PARTS
- Appendix
- Bibliography
- Glossary

---

single spaced. An *executive summary*, which may be longer but seldom more than ⟨ page in length, may be written by either the author or someone else. There are tw̶ approaches to writing either an abstract or executive summary. The first approach i̶s most widely used; the writer prepares a miniature edition of the body of the report—concepts appear in the same order and in the same relative proportion as in the body. The second approach, which is more likely when a person other than the author is writing, is interpretative. The writer might point out strengths, flaws, new information, or important implications of the report and may connect to other issues outside the report.

The abstract (in any of its configurations) exists outside the body; it stands alone. The abstract is all some people will read. Since it presents the main points discussed in the report, it often communicates succinctly all the news a reader needs or wants. Illustrations and footnotes are not used. The abstract acts as an enticer for the report and gives highlights that draw the reader toward what is contained in the body of the report. In professional journal articles, the abstract appears under the title.

Text   The formal report text is normally divided into three parts: the introduction, findings, and conclusion.

The *introduction* prepares the reader for the report by describing four parts of the project: purpose, problem statement, background, and research methods. The *purpose* encompasses both the thesis and the objective of the study. The *problem statement* condenses the purpose into a succinct description that gives a boundary to the scope of the research. The *background* helps orient the reader to any information needed to understand the investigation and analysis to follow. This area includes important definitions, qualifications, and assumptions. The *research methods* section describes the process by which the author collected the report data and any analytical procedures that were used to show that the findings are significant. Research limitations are also important to note; they give the reader insight into how additional research might be conducted.

Within the *findings* section, all the report data is disclosed and discussed. Occasionally, statistics too detailed to be included in the body of the text are moved to charts or graphs in the appendices.

The *conclusion* brings a finish to the report by way of summary and any recommendations. A good *summary* highlights, in a logical sequence, the purpose of the study, problem statement, relevant background, research methodology, and findings. The *recommendations* direct the reader toward behavioral action.

Appended Parts   Three items commonly appear in the appended area: appendices, a bibliography, and a glossary.

In an *appendix,* an author can place a variety of items—charts, exhibits, letters, and other displays—that are too lengthy or inappropriate to include in the text.

The *bibliography* is normally found in research reports that draw on a number of secondary sources. Bibliographies are helpful in directing readers to places where additional information can be obtained.

A *glossary* is often found in technical reports where a reader might be unfamiliar with certain words.

Final Product Formal reports generally are bound, expensive to produce, and attractive to view. They sometimes contain illustrations or photographs. While formal reports may never be read in their entirety (as a result of their length and formality), the information is usually important for both the present and future readers. Usually, the primary reader learns what the writer has written through an oral briefing. The public is often a secondary reader of the formal report.

Figure 9.7, found in the Appendix to this chapter, contains several front pages from a formal report, "Report of the Special Bid Oversight Commission." This report was the final product of a special oversight group commissioned in 1999 by Bill Hybl, the president of the United States Olympic Committee. The commission was created following months of allegations regarding improprieties in the International Olympic Committee's (IOC) controlled bid processes. Most notably it was alleged that the Salt Lake City Bid Committee for the Olympic Winter Games provided IOC members with gifts and other personal benefits in order to influence the selection process for the 2002 Olympic Winter Games.[1]

The formal parts of the sample report in Figure 9.7 include a cover page, a lengthy executive summary, and a detailed table of contents that summarize the findings and recommendations.

The Semiformal Report

The semiformal report is shorter and is sometimes typed and stapled together instead of bound. The readership is also smaller. This type of report has a highly organized structure and outline, and employs major headings like those of the formal report; but overall it carries a more informal tone and look. This report style is more commonly used in daily business settings.

Figure 9.8 contains a report that follows a letter style. The "Big Eight Management Company" report was actually produced by a major consulting firm for a client, although the individual and company names have been changed. The report is short and to the point. A *summary,* which briefly reviews the findings and recommendations, follows the opening sentences of the letter. A brief statement describing the *scope of the work completed* is next. The report moves quickly into three pages of *findings and conclusions* and four pages of *recommendations* along with the *recommended implementation approach.* It is evident from reading the recommendation section that the Big Eight Management Company wants to continue its work with Hydroplex Industries. The last three pages of the report describe the *method* Big Eight would use to staff the new work and the *cost* for the new project.

The Consultant's Report

This style of report can take either the formal or informal format. It is presented here because many advanced business students become consultants and because the internal design of the report is different from both the formal and informal.

Consultants are professional people who give expert advice. As Peter Block says in

Flawless Consulting, they are in a position to have influence on individuals, groups, or organizations, but they have no direct power to make changes or to implement programs.[2] The consultant's job is to identify client problems, determine reasons for the problems, decide the effect that the problems are having on the client's organization, create a vision for the organization's future without the problems, decide upon possible solutions, determine the value of the solutions, develop and refine recommendations for solving the problems, and finally, prepare and present the deliverables to the client.[3]

A consultant's deliverables consist of a final report and an executive presentation. The report is written and contains significant detail. The presentation is oral, more graphical, sequenced differently than the report, and designed to stress such areas of importance as findings, recommendations, value statements, and priorities. Figure 9.2 shows the difference in the parts of the project report and the executive presentation.

The project report starts with a *cover page* like that of the formal report. An *executive summary* then gives an overview of the report along with conclusions and recommendations. Next is the list of *team members* who were responsible for researching the project. The *table of contents* lists every part of the report, along with page numbers. The *scope definition* states exactly what the client and consultant agreed upon at the start of the engagement. It identifies what is and is not included within the project boundaries. The *objectives* state why the project was conducted. The *methodology* identifies how the project was done. The *findings* indicate what the project team identified as problems and/or opportunities for improvement. The *recommendations* indicate what needs to be done. The *business impact* describes the value to the organization if the recommendations are implemented. This usually includes benefits to be derived and costs to be implemented. The *implementation considerations* describe the requirements or barriers to implementation and what dependencies upon other projects may be evident. The *next steps* list things like the recommended priorities, sequences, and funding requirements for implementation. This usually includes a pro-

FIGURE 9.2 **Format Comparison Between the Consultant's Final Report and the Executive Presentation**

The Final Report	The Executive Presentation
Cover page	Title slide
Executive summary	Team introduction
List of team members	Session agenda
Table of contents	Project scope definition
Project scope definition	Project objectives
Project objectives	Approach or methodology
Methodology	Recommendations
Findings	Business impact
Recommendations	Implementation issues
Business impact	Next steps
Implementation considerations	Wrap-up
Next steps	Support documentation
Conclusions	
Appendices	

posed schedule that shows things like time frames and dependencies. The *conclusion* brings the entire report together. The *appendices* give all supporting documentation and other appropriate materials.[4]

The Informal Report

The informal report is the report most frequently used in business. This report form can extend from a one-page letter or memo to several typed pages that are produced inexpensively for distribution. The topics are usually less important events, e.g., status reports, trip evaluations, training analysis, and minor requests. The writing style is informal and carries more of a conversational tone than either formal or semiformal reports. Informal reports generally stay within the organizational setting.

Figure 9.3 displays an informal report in which the author details the month's activities of the personnel in his service area. The memo format is one of the most common forms of informal reports. Often, informal memo reports are handwritten or e-mailed.

The Executive Memo

While most reports can be categorized as formal, semiformal, or informal, another type of popular report can take the form of any of these styles. The executive memo has become a standard means by which subordinates communicate with their superiors.

Long formal reports use an inductive process that many refer to as suspense oriented. Starting with an introduction, it weaves through a purpose statement, methodology description, data findings, conclusions, and recommendations. The real news of the report arrives for the reader in the conclusion and recommendation stages. In some reports, this may not be until page 200 or 300.

Since most managers are burdened with too much to read, they need a method of receiving information quickly. The indeductive method of starting with the news first and then giving general information is favored by many today. The semiformal report in Figure 9.8, from the Big Eight Management Company, uses the deductive process. The author started with a summary, gave some general information on the scope of the study, and then spent most of the report time on findings and recommendations.

An executive memo can take either the inductive or the deductive approach. The real purpose of the memo is to present the most information possible in an abbreviated and condensed fashion. Lengthy detailed explanations are eliminated; only the main points are presented.

Technical writing teachers often tell their students that the first step in writing the summary for a paper is to list all the topic sentences for all the paragraphs in the paper. The second step is to weed out the sentences that carry relatively little information (every report contains empty paragraphs; they may serve bridging or summation functions). The third step is to add new sentences to supply essential facts and smooth the whole.[5]

On the following pages there are examples of two executive memos. Figure 9.4 uses the deductive style and puts the recommendations at the beginning. Figure 9.5 uses the inductive style by putting the recommendations at the end of the memo.

FIGURE 9.3   **A Sample Informal Report**

MID-STATE POWER & LIGHT COMPANY

Interoffice Correspondence

Date: April 10, 2001

To: Mr. R. E. Jones

From: William C. McGill

Subject: Monthly Activity Report

The following is a report of the activities of the Technical Services Division for the month of March 2001.

Ben Nielson visited Berkeley, California, as a member of the ASHRAE Task Force number 3, evaluating some infiltration studies for DOE. Apparently, several people with technical experience are involved in this project, but very few have practical work experience.

David Odan spent the major portion of the month planning, coordinating, and conducting the New Employee Training Meeting held in Richardson. A total of seventy-four Customer Service employees attended all or part of that meeting.

Marvin Smith met with Eastern Division and district personnel in Rockwall to review two solar-powered water-heating systems for the REC Rider. One is a Sun-A-Matic system from Butler in Mineral Wells, and the other is a Grumman system. The recorders are to be installed in April.

Tech Services inspected Jim Miller's polycel home under construction. We intend to install recording equipment on this house, since he is designing it to the exact Arkansas standard. Our first inspection revealed that he needs to put in considerable caulking in his home to stop up the holes.

Tech Services has visited with Bruce Hart, president of Sun Spot Systems, and Milton Nichols, publisher of *Solar Science and Technology* magazine. Mr. Hart is constructing a 4,500-square-foot house in Lansing that will have solar-powered water heating and cooling. The cooling system will utilize the Japanese Yasaka absorption system and could possibly be a project to be used in some manner for high-profile solar advertising. The Yasaka absorption machine has been improved to utilize lower temperature water, and there are only a few of these units in the United States at present.

FIGURE 9.4   **An Executive Memo Using the Deductive Style**

September 3, 2000

Western Slope Unit
DFF Justification
Drill Four Development Wells

RECOMMENDATION

We recommend approval of Mile High Oil Company's proposal to drill
four Western Slope development wells (Wells No. 17, 18, 19, and 20)
for a total of $1,795M gross ($395M net). The project will increase
field recovery by 595 MBO. Economics are a PW10 of $250M, an IE of
0.7, an IROR of 35, and a payout of 2.7 years. Infill drilling at the
Western Slope Unit is successful.

DISCUSSION

The four proposed wells will develop the northwest portion of the field
in a five-acre pattern. The infill drilling program of 1992–1993
reduced spacing to five acres. Production increased by 1675 BOPD
and reserves by 7.2 MMBO.

The wells are in an area of low water-cut producers. Pressure buildup
and falloff tests have shown the western portion of the field to exhibit
homogeneous, single porosity characteristics. The eastern portion of
the field exhibits nonhomogeneous, dual porosity, fractured characteristics. The eastern portion of the reservoir has seen very active water
encroachment due to the fractures in the reservoir. The location of the
wells in the northwestern portion of the field will be near the crest of
the structure. The crest is the area of lowest water cut.

RESERVES

Reserves for the four proposed wells assumed a drainage area of five
acres, phi-h values from logs, a FVF of 1,015, and a water saturation
of 12.5%. Decline analysis on the production profile before and after
the 1992–1993 infill drilling program is 17%. The 17% RF is more
conservative than the 22% RF used by Mile High. Reserves for the
project total 635 MBO gross and 133 MBO net to ARCO.

ECONOMICS

The economics assumed an initial production rate of 120 BOPD/well.
The last two wells drilled in the field produced over 120 BOPD. The
production rate declined at 18% a year. Incremental operating costs are
$.5M per well, per month. The project has an 86% chance factor. The
project remains economical at the contingency price forecast at a PW12
of $104M, an IE of 0.3, an IROR of 22, and a payout of 3.3 years.

FIGURE 9.5   **An Executive Memo Using the Inductive Style**

Date: March 17, 2001

To: Executive Managers

From: Ben Petty

Re: Customer Surveys for Final 2000 Quarter

This report reviews our present offering of distinctive products, services, and systems as described in customer surveys collected during the final quarter of 2000.

Future Customer Desires

Our customers told us that to be a valued supplier we need to:

1. Be quality oriented
    –provide quality products
    –provide quality service
    –provide quality information
2. Be distinctive
    –offer products, services, and information not currently available from our competitors
3. Be aware of our customer's needs
    –continually monitor the desire for product change and the specifics of that change
4. Be educationally oriented
    –constantly educate and train the distributors to represent the merchandise and its potential use

Current Customer Perceptions

1. Our product is the highest quality, our service dependable, and our information reliable . . . although not always current.
2. We are not distinctive in our products and information. The same merchandise is available from our competitors. The only area of distinction is our reliable and friendly service.
3. We are fairly good about maintaining an awareness of our customers' needs. More frequent drop-by visits, however, can ensure that this awareness remains high.
4. Better education of our distributors is needed. They know the product and price, but they do not adequately convey our heartfelt philosophy.
5. We are rapidly losing ground on the best price advantage. Currently many of our prices are higher than those of our competition. In fact, our competitors are using pricing as their primary sales tool.

FIGURE 9.5 **An Executive Memo Using the Inductive Style (Concluded)**

Recommendations

Our philosophy is sound. We must ensure that every person who represents us understands and follows our philosophy of providing the best products, service, and information. It is especially important that we meet with distributors more often, after monthly training sessions, to keep them up-to-date on product changes and to furnish the most current information available.

The work that production is doing on the Quality Management Program will improve our inventory control and our costing and pricing problems. This must be monitored closely to ensure that problems are truly solved. Such a resolution should enable us to reduce prices in graduated stages to meet that of our competition by the second quarter of 2001.

THE PROBLEM-SOLVING PROCESS

Now that you have an idea of five different formats for producing reports, let's look at the process of problem solving. In most instances, you will have an understanding of the problem you desire to analyze. In your classroom assignment, it may be the major issue presented in the assigned case. At work, it may be a new product on which you are seeking to eliminate the design problems. Regardless of the situation, most problems that we encounter can be solved with a five-step process: define the problem, determine possible solutions, pick out the best solution, implement the solution, and evaluate the results of what happens. We will discuss the first three here. Step four, implementing the solution, involves the actual writing process. Evaluating the results takes place as we receive feedback from readers.

What Is the Problem?

The process of defining a problem situation can be simplified considerably if you ask certain stock questions in the course of the analysis.

- What is the nature of the problem?
- What is the extent of the problem?
- What are the causes of the problem?
- What means have been employed to correct the problem?

As you start asking your questions, decide on the research tools that you will use.

Deciding on Possible Research Tools Often an analytical study requires surveys to collect data that will yield understandable and useful information. Many of the analytical tools discussed in the chapter on cases (Chapter 14) are useful in analyzing the data for a research project. More academic statistical analyses are also available to crunch numbers for a final conclusion.

Gathering the Data Report writing often becomes time consuming because of this particular step. Gathering sufficient data can take hours and even days. Thomas Edison once advised on the place to start: "The first thing is to find out everything everybody else knows, and then begin where they left off." Your data may come from personal observations, experiments, books, questionnaires, interviews, financial records, or a variety of other sources.

The data may be primary—those generated by the researcher for the explicit purpose of the research, or secondary, any material already generated for another purpose but usable for the research. Discretionary readers are concerned about the sources that a writer uses. Primary documents can include items like surveys, questionnaires, observations, and scientific experimentations. All secondary sources—items like company records, current business survey conclusions, or census information—depend on the accuracy and validity of their sources for credibility. Always remember that the statements you make are only as strong as your source. As you gather your data, constantly analyze and question the interpretations that you find. Question your material: Is it relevant? Is it accurate? Is it fairly representative? Is it timely? And most important, Is it necessary?

In the Big Eight Management Company report the writer describes the process taken to define the problem areas and the methods used in gathering the data. This information is described on page 231 under "Scope of our Review" and "Findings and Conclusions."

Electronic Information Sources Excellent electronic information resources are available in the libraries of most colleges and universities. Most of these resources allow for quick and extensive searches on a wide variety of topics.

Electronic resources change continually. Depending upon your institution, you may access the identical information using a Web browser, such as Internet Explorer or Netscape, or you may use an interface designed by the database producer or third-party database provider. A local or remote computer may store the information.

Database providers and your institution's library or information center will offer training sessions, either as workshops or in conjunction with your courses, to help you get started searching. By taking the time to participate in even brief workshops, you will save hours of time in the future—time you can devote to analyzing data and developing reports, papers, and presentations.

It is also helpful to realize that electronic information resources are similar. Before you begin using a new service or searching a new database, you need to ask these questions: What is the content of the resource? Does it provide full-text information or only references to resources? Is the full text only text or are materials such as tables, graphs, and illustrations also available on-line. If you need retrospective information, how many years of information are available? How do you narrow or broaden a search? Does the system support Boolean operators (**and, or, not**) and truncation? In what order do your search results display: by relevance, date, alphabetical order?

The following list can serve as a starting point for your next research project.

Aggregated Databases

- **Bloomberg.** This provides live, around-the-clock coverage of national and international governments, corporations, industries, and financial markets. *Bloomberg* transmits 3,000 news stories daily and appears in over 160 newspapers throughout the Americas, Europe, the Middle East, and the Pacific Rim. It is designed so that researchers can instantly access all news, research, securities, pricing, and research reports directly through a single source.

- **Dialog.** This comprehensive information resource, computer-based, on-line system contains over 450 separate databases. The databases contain more than 120 million records and provide information ranging from a directory-type listing of companies, associations, or famous people to in-depth financial statements on a particular company. Citations, abstracts, conference papers, and complete texts of journal articles are available. *Tradeline* is available through *Dialog.*

- **Dialog Business Connection.** This service allows access to more than 11 million U.S., Canadian, and European companies. About 40 of these databases have been pulled together to form the *Dialog Business Connection.* Financial profiles, late-breaking news stories, investment research reports, and more are brought together in a menu system. The information in this service can be accessed by industry, product, or company. There is no subject approach. On-screen and written instructions guide you through this database.

- **Dow Jones News/Retrieval.** This service provides business and financial data on nearly 10 million U.S. and international companies in more than 80 industries. Researchers can review financial reports on public and private companies, research corporate families and ownership structures worldwide, access SEC filings, 10Ks, and 10Qs, track the activities of the major stock exchanges, and gain insight into emerging markets information. *Dow Jones* provides access to more than 3,900 business, trade, and general publications, including the *Wall Street Journal.*

- **FirstSearch.** This offers access to a number of business and economic databases useful to business researchers: *Articles 1st, Contents 1st, ERIC,* the *GPO Monthly Catalog,* and *WorldCat,* an electronic card catalog of 24 million bibliographic records representing the holdings of 13,000 libraries worldwide.

- **Lexis-Nexis.** This service provides full-text access to business and legal information. The total system provides access to approximately 22,000 sources but institutions may subscribe to subsets of the database. Most institutional subscriptions will provide full-text access to national and international newspapers, business periodicals including magazines, regional business journals, trade publications, newsletters, company and financial information, statistical sources, and business directories.

- **Million Dollar Database Premier.** This subscription by Internet site is used to search public and private companies, specific companies, or specific industries. You can search by size or new markets by using multiple selection criteria. It will list potential prospects or prospective employers in a targeted market, identify key decision makers so you can contact them directly, and search executive biographies for hard-to-find information.

- **Moody's Company Data Direct.** This link provides immediate access to fully searchable data on more than 10,000 NYSE, AMEX, NASDAQ, and other select regional exchange companies. All financials are "as reported," providing balance sheets, income statements, expenditures, assets, liabilities, and cash flow performance trends.

Databases

- **ABI Inform.** This database, updated monthly, indexes approximately 1,000 worldwide business and management periodicals. Subject areas include accounting, banking, data processing, organizational behavior, management science, marketing, advertising, sales, real estate, public administration, new product development, and telecommunications. It is backfiled from 1985. Full citations and abstracts are available for all references. Full-text articles are available for approximately 500 publications.

- **Business Dateline.** This product is updated monthly and provides access to hard-to-find, regional business information. It covers most of the same subject areas as *ABI Inform* from 535 local, state, and regional business publications. These articles are the full text of the publication. Press releases from "Business Wire" provide a corporate perspective on events and people. Back files to 1985 are available. It is updated weekly.

- **Disclosure SEC Database.** This product consists of business and financial information extracted from 10K reports which public companies file with the SEC. It includes all financial statements (three to seven years for comparison purposes), subsidiaries, description of the business, officers and directors, stock information, president's letter, and management discussion for over 11,000 public companies. Financial data can be converted to files that can be imported as numbers directly into spreadsheets.

- **Compustat PC Plus.** This source contains 20 years of annual reports, 12 years of quarterly reports, seven years of business and geographic report segments, and 240 months of stock prices and dividend data for over 10,300 U.S. and Canadian companies. It also has data for over 7,600 inactive companies no longer filing with the SEC due to merger, liquidation, or bankruptcy.

- **Dun's Million Dollar Database.** This database provides comprehensive business information on 1,260,000 U.S. public and private companies. Lists are limited to companies with $25 million or more in sales, or 50+ employees, or a net worth of $500,000 or more. File records can be searched by geographical area, primary and secondary SIC codes, annual sales, and number of employees. This is a useful tool for job searching.

- **Hoover's Inc.** *Hoover's* offers basic directory information, public domain materials such as 10K reports, and in-depth analysis of both public and private companies. A unique feature is the list of competitors accompanying each profile. Hoover's on-line on the World Wide Web provides direct links to company sites and recent newspaper and magazine articles about the company.
- **InfoTrac Business ASAP.** This product contains bibliographic references to and abstracts of articles from more than 400 business, management, and trade publications, including the *Wall Street Journal, New York Times, Asian Wall Street Journal,* and *Financial Times of Canada.* Full-text access is provided to approximately 50 percent of the periodicals indexed. It is updated monthly.
- **Moody's Investors Services.** This service provides information on national and international companies. Information available may include company histories, products, income sheets, and balance statements. The breadth of resources available at a single location is subscription based.
- **Morning Star Mutual Funds Ondisc.** This product provides such items as description and analysis, basic operating facts, and several years of statistics for total return, income, capital gains, and performance/risk factors.
- **Standard & Poor's Stock Corp.** Publications such as the *Industry's Surveys, Corporation Records, The Outlook, Stock Reports* and various guides to stocks and bonds are available electronically. The breadth of resources will vary with an individual institution's subscriptions.
- **Wall Street Journal.** This is a full-text product containing every article including daily stock market reports, finance, investment, and business-oriented news. Its coverage is from 1989 and is updated monthly. Full-text access is not available via third-party database services; a direct subscription is required.

Writers who frequently produce reports should be aware of one major problem with the use of secondary material. This problem arises frequently, particularly in management and engineering consulting firms. The problem is called "boiler plating." Boiler plating occurs when individuals do similar work for different clients. Once a report is produced for one client it is filed, only to be reviewed later, and often borrowed from so heavily that the new product does not fully communicate the message the writer wants and needs to convey.

Today, managers no longer have to save the hard copies of memos and reports and labor over them, gleaning the data they need to make reports. With computers and central integrated databases, information can be stored in single files and used in numerous ways.

Grammas describes three basic types of reports that can be generated by a computer and by the use of a database: performance analysis reports, exception reports, and special analysis reports. Periodically scheduled performance reports for marketing, finance, and manufacturing can be automatically accessed, processed, printed, or electronically distributed to readers. With graphics software, the data can even be organized to show interrelationships.

Database analysis also makes it easy to pull out "exceptional" information that falls outside the norm of usual business activity. Exceptionally high or low performance by individuals, lack of inventory movement, and wide fluctuation of prices are a few examples of the reporting possibilities in this area. Computer programs can be written to automatically generate reports when exceptional information becomes available. Likewise, managers can use databases to create special analysis reports on a wide variety of subject areas.[6]

What Are the Possible/Best Solutions?

After the problem is defined and the data gathered, the researcher must analyze and order the data in such a way as to arrive at as many solutions as possible. Once all the possible solutions are determined, the best can then be selected.

Once the analysis is complete, you should arrive at several conclusions. Always ask yourself, though, whether other conclusions about the data are possible. Do loopholes or inconsistencies appear in your line of thinking? Do the facts suggest other alternatives for action? What is the order of importance for these facts? Sometimes a good guide sheet, like that found in Figure 9.6, helps the writer to order data in a manner that will make writing easier.

In the Big Eight Management Company report, the writer arrived at several solutions and presented these in the form of recommendations. As a consultant wishing to continue the working relationship with the client, the author then proceeded to make a recommendation, or communicate the writer's logical way of implementing the approach. Because the various recommendations made in this report are lengthy, they are not reported here. If you would like to read them again they are found in Figure 9.8. "A Sample Semiformal Report."

The problem-solving stages are normally the most time consuming and important in the report-writing process. If you have done a sufficient job of preparation, the actual writing of the report should be relatively easy.

WRITING THE REPORT

After you have analyzed and ordered your data and identified your solutions and recommendations, you are ready to write the report. Writing a report is very similar to writing a proposal (Chapter 8) and case analyses (Chapter 14). Consider the particular format you want to follow in regard to formality, then condense your information into the necessary parts of the report.

You should produce both an initial draft and an edited version. Strive to make your writing complete, concise, and clear, using some of the tips outlined in Chapters 4 to 6.

Reports have always employed a variety of graphic materials. Basic graphs include bar graphs (segmented, group information, simple listings), line graphs, and pie charts. Graphics are used to help present information for quick comprehension and to clarify ideas that are difficult to convey with words alone. As you read in Chapter 3, with the use of computers, databases, and numerous software packages, a writer's job in seeking and presenting information has been made considerably easier.

FIGURE 9.6   **Guide Sheet for Ordering Data More Easily**

Writer's Guide Sheet

Title of report: _____

Primary reader designation: _____

Secondary reader designation: _____

Formality level of report: formal _____ semiformal _____ informal _____

Reader's need for report:

_____ obtain information   _____ self-instruction

_____ participate in decision   _____ refer to as needed

_____ pass up the line   _____ file

_____ make change   _____ take action

_____ part of longer report

_____ other:_____

What action will reader(s) take?_____

What terms, formulas, principles, or policies may require some definition or explanation?

_____

What other obstacles may hinder the message being received?_____

_____

Probable length of report:

_____ 1 page   _____ 2–10 pages   _____ 10–50 pages

_____ 50–100 pages   _____ 100–150 pages   _____ 150 pages or more

Type of reproduction_____

Type of cover_____

Types of illustrations or visuals_____

_____

Will the organization be inductive _____ or deductive _____ ?

What will be the sequence of the material?

_____ chronological   _____ problem/solution

_____ reverse chronological   _____ cause/effect

_____ space   _____ pro/con

_____ advantage/disadvantage

_____ other _____

_____

SUMMARY

Report writing can be frustrating and time con-suming unless it is approached in a systematic way. Reports come in several types, ranging from formal documents to short executive memos. Various exhibits were displayed to show examples of reports.

As a report writer, you should begin by asking: What is the purpose of my report? Who will read my report? Reports have one of five levels of formality: the formal report, the semi-formal report, the consultant's report, the infor-mal report, and the executive memo. The major divisions of a formal and consultant's report are formalities, text, and appended parts.

After you decide what your problem is, you need to gather and analyze your data. A variety of electronic sources available to most advanced business students will make your research easier. From the analyzing stage, you move to reviewing possible solutions and pick-ing the best solution. Finally, you offer recom-mendations for further action.

Once the writer has collected and analyzed the material, the actual writing of the report is relatively easy. Of course, the basic steps of editing and striving for completeness, concise-ness, and clarity should not be ignored.

DISCUSSION QUESTIONS

1. What, in your words, is a report?
2. Before a person begins the task of accumulating data or of writing a report, some important questions need to be asked. What are these questions?
3. What is the difference in the format of the formal, semiformal, consultant's, informal, and executive memo reports?
4. What are the possible parts of a formal report?
5. How does a writer coordinate the problem-solving process into writing a report?
6. What are the steps of the problem-solving process that a writer must follow?
7. What is the purpose of the "Writer's Guide Sheet"?

NOTES

1. George J. Mitchell, "Report of the Special Bid Oversight Commission," United States Olympic Committee, March 1, 1999. (Executive Summary of the Report is found in Figure 9.7.)
2. Peter Block, *Flawless Consulting: A Guide to Getting Your Expertise Used,* Pfeiffer & Co., San Francisco, California, 1999.
3. Burton S. Rafuse and Robert E. Loth, "Management Consulting: A Skills-based Workshop for Success," presented to the Southern Methodist University MBA program, January 18–19, 1996.
4. Burton S. Rafuse and Robert E. Loth, "Manage-ment Consulting."
5. Thomas A. Easton, "Summarize, Remember, and Use Your Reading," *Handbook of Executive Communication,* John Louis Di Gaetani (ed.), Dow Jones–Irwin, Homewood, Illinois, 1986, p. 41.
6. Gus W. Grammas, "The Management of Communication Flow," *Handbook of Executive Communication,* John Louis Di Gaetani (ed.), Dow Jones–Irwin, Homewood, Illinois, 1986, p. 63.

Applications

1. Try to obtain a formal report that you can review. If you can obtain one from a business colleague, use it. If you are unable to get one from a colleague or friend, go to the career center on your campus. Look through the material from various companies. Compare the reports that you find to the discussion of format that begins on page 203. Do the reports match the format in the book? If not, how do they differ?

2. Connect to the Internet. Search for a sample report like that of "The Special Bid Oversight Commission." See how the parts compare with those highlighted in the text.

3. For your next book report or topic review, use the executive memo format described on page 208. How does this format compare to the format that you normally use?

4. Attempt to use the "news first" writing approach described in this chapter. One method requires reading articles in magazines and newspapers and practicing writing the real news in the first paragraph of an analysis of the articles. Try it and see how your writing is more concise and direct.

Appendix:
Sample Report Pages

This chapter concludes with examples from two different reports. The first (Figure 9.7) shows the front pages from a formal report: title page, executive summary, and table of contents. The second (Figure 9.8) is a sample of a semiformal report. Both of these reports were described earlier in this chapter. Keep in mind that the parts of reports represent general ways that authors assemble information. You will find a variety of different forms available in different business settings.

FIGURE 9.7   Sample Pages from a Formal Report

REPORT

of

The Special Bid Oversight Commission

Senator George J. Mitchell, Chair
Kenneth Duberstein
Donald Fehr
Roberta Cooper Ramo
Jeffrey G. Benz

Counsel:
  Richard A. Hibey
  Michael K. Atkinson
  Jared R. Silverman
WINSTON & STRAWN   March 1, 1999

FIGURE 9.7   **Sample Pages from a Formal Report (Continued)**

EXECUTIVE SUMMARY

This Commission was created by Bill Hybl, the President of the United States Olympic Committee (USOC). He promised us full support and total independence and he kept his promises. For that we thank him.

Throughout this process, the USOC has demonstrated a deep concern for the problems facing the Olympic Movement and a willingness to learn from the mistakes of the past, including its own. For that we commend them.

The findings and recommendations in our report are exclusively those of the members of this Commission and its counsel. We are unanimous in our conclusions; there is no disagreement among us. Each member of the Commission volunteered many hours of time and effort. Counsel worked exceptionally hard to complete this report in a tight time frame.

The troubling events in Salt Lake City, and other host cities, are attributable to the fact that ethical governance has not kept pace with the rapid expansion of the Olympic Movement. The Olympic Games have become big business for sponsors, host cities, athletes, and the organizations that make up the Olympic Movement.

The intense competition to host the Olympic Games, coupled with the multi-billion dollar enterprise that results from winning that competition, have exposed the weaknesses in the Movement's governing structure and operational controls. Despite the fact that everyone recognizes the Olympics to be a huge commercial enterprise, the IOC and its constituent organizations lack the accountability and openness in keeping with the role the Olympic Games play in the world today. The commercial success of the Olympic Games creates both the opportunity to better the Games and the potential for abuse. To preserve the integrity of the Olympic Games, especially with the public, there must be reform at every level of the Olympic Movement.

It was wrong for Salt Lake City officials to give money to IOC members and their families to win their votes. But what happened in Salt Lake City was not unique. In 1991, Toronto officials reported to the IOC an experience in the Olympic site selection process. In strikingly prophetic language, they warned of the consequences of such improper behavior. The Toronto prophecy has come true. As a result, credibility of the Olympic Movement has been gravely damaged.

FIGURE 9.7 **Sample Pages from a Formal Report (Continued)**

As the organization with exclusive responsibility over the conduct of the Olympic Games when held in the United States, the USOC shares responsibility for the improper conduct of the bid and organizing committees in Salt Lake City. This responsibility stems from its failure to assure that United States candidate cities not seek to influence IOC members in the selection process by improperly providing them with things of value. This responsibility also extends to the USOC by virtue of the admitted recognition by certain USOC personnel that the bid and organizing committees were using the USOC's International Assistance Fund to influence or pay back IOC members for their site selection votes.

We were asked to review "the circumstances surrounding Salt Lake City's bid to host the Olympic Winter Games," and to make recommendations "to improve the policies and procedures related to bid processes." We have done that. In the process, we have concluded that it will be impossible to improve such policies and procedures unless there is significant change by and within the IOC. That is because the activity in which the Salt Lake committees engaged was part of a broader culture of improper gift giving in which candidate cities provided things of value to IOC members in an effort to buy their votes. This culture was made possible by the closed nature of the IOC and by the absence of ethical and transparent financial controls in its operations.

In each improper transaction, there was a giver and a taker; often the transaction was triggered by a demand from the taker. We do not excuse or condone those from Salt Lake City who did the giving. What they did was wrong. But, as we have noted, they did not invent this culture; they joined one that was already flourishing.

The rationale behind the governance changes proposed by the Commission is that the integrity of the Olympic Movement must be restored and protected. Reform and restoration will be effective only if they reach the entire Olympic Movement. The IOC must be reformed. For too long, it has tolerated the culture of improper gift giving, which affected every city bidding for the Olympic Games.

The Commission's call for reform is rooted in the concept of fair play. Competition should not be weighted in favor of a city that spends the most on IOC members and should be made, instead, on the basis of which city can best stage the Olympic Games.

We believe those concerned about the future of the Olympic Games must recognize that true accountability for this mess does not end with the mere pointing of the finger of accusation at those who engaged in the improper conduct. Those responsible for the Olympic trust should have exercised good management

FIGURE 9.7   Sample Pages from a Formal Report (Continued)

practices, should have inquired into the purpose and propriety of programs, should have followed expenditures, and should have set a proper framework for those competing to host the Games.

In our Report, we make a series of recommendations. Principal among them are:

1. Bid cities should be prohibited from giving to members of the USOC or the IOC anything of more than nominal value, and from directly paying the expenses of members of the USOC or IOC. Travel to bid cities and other expenses should be paid out of a central fund administered by the USOC in the selection of a United States candidate city, and out of a central fund administered by the IOC in the selection of a host city;

2. The USOC must strengthen its oversight of the site selection process by:

   (a) establishing an independent Office of Bid Compliance;
   (b) prohibiting bid and candidate cities from having or participating in any international assistance program;
   (c) strictly applying the criteria for the award and administration of its International Assistance Fund; and
   (d) strengthening its Bid Procedures Manual and its Candidate City Agreement.

3. The IOC must make fundamental structural changes to increase its accountability to the Olympic Movement and to the public;

   (a) a substantial majority of its members should be elected by the National Olympic Committees for the country of which they are citizens, by the International Federations, and by other constituent organizations. The athlete members should be chosen by athletes. There should be members from the public sector who best represent the interests of the public.
   (b) Its members and leaders should be subject to periodic re-election with appropriate term limits;
   (c) Its financial records should be audited by an independent firm, and the results of the audit disclosed publicly, at least yearly; and
   (d) appropriate gift giving rules, and strict travel and expense rules should be adopted and vigorously enforced.

4. The USOC should request the President of the United States to consider, in consultation with other governments, naming the IOC "a public international organization" within the meaning of Foreign Corrupt Practices Act, as amended.

FIGURE 9.7   Sample Pages from a Formal Report (Continued)

The IOC should not award the Olympic Games to any city whose country has not taken steps to enact a law that applies the principles of the Anti-Bribery Convention of the Organization for Economic Cooperation and Development, signed by 34 governments, including the United States. Of the twenty-one nations that have hosted or are scheduled to host the Olympic Games, nineteen are signatories to the OECD Convention. Only the cities of Moscow and Sarajevo are located in countries that are not signatories to the Convention. The Convention entered into force on February 15, 1999.

Timely, aggressive reform goes hand-in-hand with acceptance of responsibility. It is the true measure of commitment. Each Olympic entity has pledged to reform. The seriousness of that commitment and the credibility of the Olympic Movement turn on the extent to which that reform is undertaken. The Olympic flame must burn clean once again.

FIGURE 9.7   **Sample Pages from a Formal Report (Continued)**

Table of Contents

FIGURE 9.7   **Sample Pages from a Formal Report (Continued)**

FIGURE 9.7   **Sample Pages from a Formal Report (Concluded)**

1.   Members of the Commission and its Counsel

2.   Time Line of Milestone Events in the Selection of Salt Lake City and the Applicable Governance

3.   Governance Applicable to IOC, USOC and SLOBC/SLOC

4.   Report to the International Olympic Committee by the Toronto Ontario Olympic Council on the Candidature of the City of Toronto to Host the Games of the XXVIth Olympiad

FIGURE 9.8   **Sample of a Semiformal Report**

BIG EIGHT MANAGEMENT COMPANY
One Main Place
Suite 1990
Dallas, Texas 75206

March 31, 2001

Mr. Andrew Wallace
Vice-President-Controller
Hydroplex Industries, Inc.
75230 Statesman Avenue, Suite 251
Washington, D.C. 20062-0251

Dear Mr. Wallace:

The purpose of this report is to present our findings and recommendations from the review of the associated systems and procedures manufacturing operations and computer capability at the Hydroplex Industries plant in Duluth, Minnesota.

This report is divided into the following sections:

- Summary
- Scope of our review
- Findings and conclusions
- Recommendations
- Recommended implementation approach
- Staffing

SUMMARY

Our summary findings are:

- Present data collection procedures for labor and materials appear to be adequate to provide usable information to an inventory cost system.
- Accounting procedures are unable to produce accurate inventory balances on a timely basis.
- There is significant processing time available on existing equipment; however, present storage capacity is limited.

We recommend the following:

- A standard cost system should be installed at Hydroplex. We believe the most effective approach to implementing this recommendation is the acquisition of suitable packaged software. This belief is based upon the lack of local resources for programming and maintenance of systems and

FIGURE 9.8   Sample of a Semiformal Report (Continued)

upon the likelihood of the existence of packaged software that would conform to Hydroplex requirements.

- The EDP processing alternatives for all the Hydroplex manufacturing plants should be evaluated as a part of the decision to implement a computerized standard cost system. Several cost-effective alternatives may be available to maximize the use of existing purchased equipment among facilities at your three manufacturing locations.

The remainder of this report contains our more detailed comments and presents a work plan for implementing our recommendations.

SCOPE OF OUR REVIEW

We reviewed the cost accounting procedures and records for the Hydroplex iron manufacturing plant in Duluth, Minnesota. A walk-through of the factory operation was performed including shipping, receiving, raw material stores, repair and maintenance, the brass foundry, the cast iron foundry and cleaning operations, assembly, and the finished goods warehouse. We also reviewed the payroll and incentive pay accounting procedures and the procedures for maintaining factory incentive pay standards. Finally, we reviewed the computer systems and discussed available capacity on existing computer equipment. We were unable to make an evaluation of the quality of cost information because useful cost reports are not presently produced.

FINDINGS AND CONCLUSIONS

This section includes findings from the review and provides some basic information with respect to the cost system. We found that the processing procedures for maintaining inventory cost records are very inefficient and cumbersome. As a result, the inventory cost information is out-of-date and cannot be used to develop inventory costs on a current basis. Further, it appears that little or no useful cost reporting is produced from the cost records. In terms of potential improvements, however, data collection procedures for labor activity and material costs appear to be adequate to provide reliable information to an inventory cost system.

Following are our findings about specific areas within the cost system:

- Payroll/Labor Costs—It appears the payroll procedures are well controlled and accurate. Many direct labor employees are paid on a piece rate (incentive) basis and for this reason work-order numbers, labor operation numbers, piece counts, and elapsed time are reported daily for each employee. This information is used to charge work-in-process (WIP) work order accounts for labor costs. Labor time reported is reconciled weekly for each employee to his or her time card. Procedures for charging labor to WIP include manual sorting of approximately 3,000 labor tickets monthly by

FIGURE 9.8   Sample of a Semiformal Report (Continued)

work order and labor operation for recording to WIP. These postings to WIP cards are at least one month behind the current period.

- Raw Materials/Purchases—Purchases of raw materials are posted to raw material ledger cards. Raw materials are charged to work-in-process from material requisitions. It appears some materials may be charged to WIP based upon the standard bill of materials (BOM) maintained in accounting rather than actual material requisitioned. The BOM is believed to be different from that maintained in production because it is not as frequently updated.

- Standards—A standards book is maintained that lists all assembly part numbers and the individual labor operations required to make the part. While standards set for each labor operation are for piece rate incentive pay purposes, they may be suitable for inventory costing if they have been set according to appropriate engineering criteria. There do not appear to be material usage standards or overhead rates set by department or for the factory. Material usage standards may be determinable for inventory costing purposes from historical production records and production BOM's. The development of overhead rates would require detailed cost analysis work.

- Clerical Procedures—A number of clerical procedures presently in use are very cumbersome and prevent the efficient and timely maintenance of cost records. Nearly 3,000 inventory cards are maintained and posted using Burroughs posting equipment. Labor is posted at least one month later than the month incurred because of the effort required to manually sort and balance thousands of labor tickets by work order and operation before the data can be posted. Material costs are not posted to work-in-process until a job is completed, which may be 8 to 12 weeks or more after material is used. Therefore, it is not presently possible to compute the cost of work-in-process until a job is completed. At the time of our visit in February, 2001, work orders had only been closed through November 30, 2000.

Some additional findings are:

- It appears the production BOM's may reflect actual manufacturing processes while the BOM used for cost accounting is out-of-date.

For payroll purposes, seven factory departments are defined.

- We noted instances of excessive production of some parts, evidently resulting from long production runs made ostensibly for efficiency purposes. This practice may be building excessive inventory and allowing payment of inordinate incentives.

FIGURE 9.8   Sample of a Semiformal Report (Continued)

Findings with respect to computer operations are as follows:

- The IBM system is utilized 3 to 4 hours per weekday on the average and somewhat more during month-end. The only system presently running on the computer is accounts receivable and invoicing. While considerable processing time is available, the present data storage capacity of the equipment is very limited. Until increases are made, this condition will severely limit the implementation of any major new systems. Additional storage capacity has been ordered and is expected to be available in late summer, 2001. No programming or systems design capability is present at the Hydroplex facility.
- The compatibility of the IBM equipment and software programs allows the consideration of a number of alternatives. For example, the PC can be connected via network to other PCs that could receive and process data for retransmission for printing. This configuration would reduce the need for local programming and design support at Hydroplex. Also, programs that run on all PCs, such as that at your Detroit facility, can be adapted to the current machine, although processing efficiency would be reduced. If organizationally appropriate, a combination or integration of hardware and software resources may present an opportunity for cost saving. Your Worland, Wyoming plant has no computer capability at present.

RECOMMENDATIONS

We understand management is at this time primarily concerned with the development of reliable inventory costs and the timely closing of Hydroplex's books for financial reporting purposes. Both current costs and LIFO costs would be required. We believe adequate cost information to report performance, at least by department, and the ability to report product line standard costs would be desirable. We recommend an automated standard cost system meeting these requirements be developed and installed at Hydroplex.

The development of a standard cost system would involve:

- Labor—The automation of labor cost distribution to produce information by work order and operation, for maintenance of standards and for capturing units of production. The automation of payroll would be desirable but not critical for cost system information.
- Inventory Records—The automation of inventory records and reporting for raw materials, WIP, and subassemblies/finished goods.
- Standards—The development of usable material cost standards, material and labor usage standards, and departmental overhead rates.

We further recommend an evaluation be performed to determine the most cost effective combination or integration of existing hardware and software.

FIGURE 9.8   **Sample of a Semiformal Report (Continued)**

The similarity of Duluth, Detroit and Worland's operations and reporting requirements may provide a unique opportunity to reduce costs while improving the quality and timeliness of accounting information. Should a hardware/software combination or integration not be deemed appropriate now, we would recommend the work proposed accommodate such a possibility at some future date.

In addition to improvements in the inventory and cost systems, we recommend that, in the future, management consider automating other important accounting and operating functions such as general ledger, purchasing/accounts payable, and production control and scheduling. Below we present a suggested approach to evaluate the EDP processing alternatives, and to implement an improved inventory cost system at Hydroplex.

RECOMMENDED IMPLEMENTATION APPROACH

Presented below is a summary work plan outlining an approach to implement our recommendations. Since there are two basic processing alternatives to be considered, we have included a task (Task 3) in the approach to develop a recommendation as to the most viable alternative for systems development and processing. Subsequent tasks would be dependent upon the recommendation developed and adopted during Task 3.

Summary Work Plan

Task 1: Project Initiation

> This task includes the finalizing of the project objectives, the assignment of manpower, and the development of a project timetable and work plan. Hydroplex management prior to work beginning would approve the work plan.

Task 2: Requirements Definition

> The work in this task would be directed toward the definition of general system requirements in terms of output reporting, input requirements, and processing. This task would also allow us to determine basic accounting requirements, such as the alternative methods available for LIFO inventory accounting, and to determine the approach to developing standards for material, labor, and overhead to be used in the standard cost system. The output of this task would be a written requirements definition that would be submitted for approval by management. In developing this requirements definition, consideration would be given to the needs of Duluth for inventory management and costing, and also the needs of Hydroplex's office in Washington, D.C. for top level summary reporting.

FIGURE 9.8   Sample of a Semiformal Report (Continued)

A written requirements definition would be used in Task 3 work to evaluate the most effective implementation approach.

Task 3: Evaluate EDP Processing/Systems Development Alternatives

The purpose of this task is two-fold: to evaluate packaged software versus development of proprietary software through design and programming; and, to determine the most cost effective equipment utilization approach.

We will conduct a review of commercially available packaged software which meets the key user requirements developed in Task 2. Recommendations from this review will be based upon the suitability of such packages to Duluth's requirements and Hydroplex's management's concerns with the following:

- development and implementation timing;
- relative costs;
- extent of need for specific unique capabilities; and
- need for and capability of providing ongoing in-house system maintenance.

We will perform an evaluation of the EDP hardware processing alternatives available to Duluth, Detroit and Worland. Our evaluation will be directed towards maximizing the use of existing EDP purchased hardware and will focus on modifications or additional features that could significantly improve the effectiveness of the equipment.

The output of Task 3 would be written, definitive recommendations on equipment utilization and recommendations to either acquire a specific packaged software product or develop proprietary systems. Relative costs for alternatives would be presented. The completion of this task would be a major checkpoint requiring approval of our findings by Hydroplex/Duluth management before work would continue.

Task 4: Package Acquisition, Modification, and Enhancement.

This task assumes that the purchase of commercially available software is the alternative chosen. To complete this task we will:

- analyze the selected software package to identify necessary modifications or enhancements;
- define these modifications or enhancements in sufficient detail to allow the software vendor to program them; and,
- assist management and legal counsel as appropriate in the development of an agreement with the software vendor. We would expect the software vendor to program the necessary modifications and enhancements, provide systems and operations documentation for the package, train

FIGURE 9.8   **Sample of a Semiformal Report (Continued)**

Hydroplex/Duluth personnel, assist in implementation, and provide ongoing maintenance.

Task 5 Implementation

Our participation during implementation of the purchased software package will be to monitor the activities of the software vendor and Duluth personnel. Our participation would also include technical assistance to Duluth employees in modifying manual procedures for data collection and for input preparation. In addition, we will review test results during system implementation and review the output expect Duluth employees to prepare all input, including standards, necessary to begin the system's operation and to perform work necessary for monthly processing.

STAFFING AND COSTS

The project would be staffed with experienced consulting personnel from Big Eight Management Company with appropriate experience in the design of cost and inventory accounting systems and in data processing. Several individuals from your Duluth plant should be designated to participate in the implementation work. Specifically, this should include individuals from payroll, accounting, and manufacturing. Some limited participation may also be needed from individuals in such areas as purchasing or marketing. Continuing access to knowledgeable personnel in Duluth will be necessary throughout the project.

We estimate our fees to complete the requirements study, evaluate hardware/software integration and select a software package from $30,000 to $34,000. In addition, our-of-pocket expenses incurred in completing our work would be billed at cost. It is difficult to precisely estimate the costs of providing assistance during the implementation phase (Task 5) without knowing which software vendor and package will be selected. A number of factors will affect the level of our support during implementation:

- how closely the software vendor package matches Duluth's needs;
- what level and complexity of modifications or enhancement are desired;
- reputation of vendor;
- number and quality of individuals Hydroplex will assign to implementation activities, including the intensity of supervision they would expect to provide to the effort;
- quality of vendor training; and,
- special problems anticipated, such as file conversion, etc.

Since these factors cannot be defined precisely at this time, we recommend our services only be engaged at this time for the $30,000 to $34,000 explained above. However, for budgeting purposes consulting assistance during implementation could run an additional $8,000 to $14,000. Following Task 4 and the

FIGURE 9.8 **Sample of a Semiformal Report (Concluded)**

selection of a software package, we could jointly determine what participation we should provide to be most cost effective during implementation. We note that our fee estimates have been made predicated on the assumption that the software vendor selected would perform his responsibilities in a businesslike and timely manner.

* * * * *

The project work plan described above assumes the alternative selected in Task 3 would be the purchase of a software package. If instead the alternative selected is the development of proprietary software, Tasks 4 and 5 would be redefined accordingly. In this case, we believe our fees would be higher than under the software package alternative, but we cannot make a meaningful estimate until Tasks 1, 2, and 3 are complete.

We are pleased to have the opportunity to provide you with our findings and recommendations concerning the Hydroplex/Duluth operation and would be pleased to participate in implementing our recommendations. We will be available to answer any questions that you may have at your convenience.

Very truly yours,

William A. Davenport
Consulting Partner
Big Eight Management Company
WAD/aa

cc: Mr. John Craine
     Executive Vice President
     Hydroplex Industries, Inc.

     Mr. Alex Burton
     President and Chief Executive Officer
     Hydroplex Industries, Inc.

Oral Communication

′10′

The Business Presentation

In this chapter, we will consider business communication situations in which you must make a presentation before an audience, usually a small group of decision makers.

TYPES OF PRESENTATIONS

While some presentations can be classified as primarily informative, most presentations are persuasive in nature. They seek agreement with a position on an issue or approval for an action proposal. Common presentations within the organization include briefings, status reports, and budget or project proposals. Outside the organization, presentations are typically occasions for selling to groups of clients or customers.

To highlight the diversity of presentations made in a typical large organization, a group of managers attending a training session conducted by one of the authors suggested the following typical presentations in their organization:

"Results of Engineering Evaluations"
"Status Report on Affirmative Action Program"
"Budget Proposal"
"Forecast Projection"
"Systems Demonstration for Upper Management"
"Briefings for Vendors"
"Briefings for Senior Executives on Community Issues"
"Orientation for New Employees"

"Quality Assurance Orientation"
"Company Position at Arbitration Hearing"
"Recruitment Talk at a College Career Day"
"Briefings for Senior Executives on Labor Relations"
"User Briefing on New Computer System"
"Talk at Company Training Seminar"
"Contract Award Recommendations"
"Briefings on Technical Subjects for Nontechnical Audience"

This list reflects the range of presentations made by middle managers in most companies.

FIVE PROPOSITIONS ABOUT PRESENTATIONS

Despite the obvious differences among specific types of presentations, five propositions apply to all types.

1. Presentations are made before small audiences, which are often composed of decision makers. By decision makers, we mean people such as your boss and other senior executives who might be considering your budget proposal or status report. Or the decision makers might be your clients and customers considering your pitch on behalf of the services or products of your firm.

   Even when a presentation appears to be informative rather than persuasive (a briefing or an employee orientation talk), your audience will also be making an evaluation—an evaluation about your competence and, frankly, your future prospects with the firm.
2. Presentations are usually delivered extemporaneously. By extemporaneous, we mean that the presentation is prepared and delivered from an outline. While some executives like to deliver memorized presentations (without an outline), reading the complete text of your presentation to a small group is almost always viewed as inappropriate. The balance of this chapter presents detailed guidelines for preparing and delivering the extemporaneous presentation.
3. Presentations usually complement some type of written communication. Oral presentations rarely assume the full burden of communication on the subject. The typical oral report, for instance, complements and reinforces a longer, more detailed written report. The same can be said for proposal presentations, budget presentations, project presentations, or sales presentations.
4. Presentations usually employ some type of visual aid, typically computer-generated presentation graphics (e.g., PowerPoint), overhead transparencies, or slides. (See Chapter 3 for a detailed discussion of these visuals and others.)

   Although visuals serve the important purposes of highlighting main points or conclusions and clarifying statistics and financial information, they also make the presentation more interesting for the audience. Later in this chapter, we will consider some guidelines for using visuals in presentations.
5. Presentations usually have a question-and-answer session. You rarely escape a presentation without some questions from members of the audience. This

is to be expected. After all, whether you are sharing important information, seeking approval for your pet project, or selling the services of your firm, the decision makers sitting before you will probably need some clarification or elaboration of points you have made in your presentation.

TYPES OF DELIVERY

As we noted in the second proposition, business presentations are nearly always delivered in an extemporaneous style. Before describing the extemporaneous style in some detail, let us consider the three other types of delivery: manuscript, memorized, and impromptu.

The Manuscript Delivery

A manuscript presentation is delivered from a full text. It is read word for word from a typed manuscript or from a TelePrompter. There are occasions when a manuscript delivery is appropriate, such as when presenting testimony at a hearing, delivering a major policy statement before a large public audience, or taping a message for broadcast. Manuscript delivery offers precision and control over content.

The cost of these two benefits may be high, though. First, most managers read manuscripts poorly (without sufficient vocal expressiveness and emphasis). Second, because they are busy reading their manuscripts, they eliminate virtually all eye contact with their audiences. Third, a manuscript presentation is relatively inflexible; it is difficult to adapt to a speaking situation and depart from the prepared text. Most importantly, however, reading from a text is considered inappropriate for most presentations in business, especially those before small groups. Thus, the manuscript presentation is not a serious option for most presenters.

The Memorized Presentation

The memorized presentation also requires that the presenter write out the content word for word, but rather than reading it to the audience, the presenter memorizes the presentation in advance and then recites it. Naturally, some managers make brief or recurring talks that are suitable for memorization, but too many managers create unnecessary problems for themselves by memorizing long presentations.

First, as a method of delivering presentations, memorization places considerable pressure on those giving the presentation because they fear that they will forget their lines. They worry what will happen if their minds suddenly go blank, or if they lose their chain of thought. Frankly, they're in big trouble. Consider this hypothetical situation. You memorize your presentation. Midway through the presentation, you are interrupted by a question. Startled by the interruption, you momentarily forget where you are in the presentation. Unfortunately, when you resume, you skip over an important point. This creates confusion for your audience—and more questions, too.

Second, memorization of a presentation is time consuming. Along with the time it takes to plan, compose, and practice a presentation is the time spent memorizing it. Although we recommend, below, that presenters do some memory work when preparing an extemporaneous presentation, we do not feel that the time required to memorize a full presentation is justified, especially in light of the other problems associated with this style of delivery.

Third, memorized presentations tend to sound memorized. There is a canned, mechanical, self-conscious quality to many memorized presentations. In fact, some speakers, eager to get through the presentation before they forget something, resemble Las Vegas slot machines, with words instead of coins spilling out of their mouths.

Fourth, the memorized presentation is as inflexible as the manuscript delivery. Speaking from a script, albeit memorized, the presenter will find it difficult to respond to the audience and the occasion.

The Impromptu Presentation

The impromptu presentation is unprepared, spontaneous, off-the-cuff. Although there will be situations in business when you will have to speak in an impromptu manner, you place your professional reputation at risk if you fail to prepare for those situations you can foresee. Unlike carefully prepared presentations, impromptu speaking tends to be relatively disorganized, imprecise, and repetitive. It is not the stuff of which successful careers are made.

Impromptu presentations, therefore, are justified only by necessity. For example, you are asked unexpectedly by your boss at a meeting to give a briefing on some problem or a status report on some project; you are asked at a presentation before some prospective clients to address an issue that you had not planned to talk about; or you are asked a rather sophisticated and unexpected open question on an employment interview, one that requires a response of several minutes.

Try to minimize these situations by anticipating them. For example, if you plan to attend a meeting, prepare for the possibility that you might be asked to speak. Then, if you are asked, what you say will be cogent. That is the stuff of which successful careers are made.

Extemporaneous Speaking

An extemporaneous presentation is carefully prepared and delivered from notes or an outline. Although the method is not without disadvantages, it is clearly superior to the manuscript, memorized, or impromptu deliveries. Once mastered, the extemporaneous method of speaking will serve you well any time you make a business presentation.

The goal of extemporaneous speaking, as a style of delivery, is to be conversational. You appear to be conversing with the audience in a natural and spontaneous manner. Although you consult your notes occasionally, you spend most of your time looking at the audience. Your voice is expressive and emphatic.

Most audience members prefer this style of communicating because you appear to be conversing with them rather than talking at them. Your image is enhanced as well.

Unlike the case in a manuscript presentation, you are relatively free of written material, suggesting that you have a greater command over the content of your presentation.

Furthermore, the extemporaneous delivery provides flexibility. Given that you are speaking from an outline, it is relatively easy to adapt and modify your presentation as the occasion and audience may demand. Content may be added, deleted, expanded, or reduced without the audience becoming aware of any changes. This is much harder to do with a manuscript or memorized presentation, for reasons discussed above.

The audience-pleasing style of delivery, the flexibility it offers, and the enhanced credibility it confers on the presenter are the major advantages of the extemporaneous method of delivery. But there are a few disadvantages that arise from the nature of the extemporaneous method, which asks you to look at your outline, construct the message in your mind, and speak to the audience.

First, there is a degree of stress associated with the process. Because you are not working from a complete text, you may worry that you will misspeak or leave something out of your presentation. These are reasonable concerns.

Second, the method sacrifices a degree of precision and conciseness compared to the manuscript presentation. Over the course of the presentation, you may make minor errors in grammar or diction, leave out an important detail, or make an error in fact. It is in the nature of the method of delivery.

Third, the extemporaneous method may be too flexible for a presentation giver. You may find it difficult to resist the opportunity to digress, to ad-lib, or to exceed the time limit assigned to the presentation. Here, again, the manuscript and memorized presentations offer an advantage.

Nevertheless, the advantages of the extemporaneous method, when compared to the other three methods of delivery, outweigh its disadvantages. In the next section, as we describe the process of preparing and delivering the extemporaneous presentation, we will suggest a number of devices that will minimize those disadvantages.

THE SEVEN-STEP PROCESS OF PREPARING AND DELIVERING EXTEMPORANEOUS PRESENTATIONS

Step One: Plan and Organize the Presentation

You may recall from your basic undergraduate speech course that a speech consisted of three parts: an introduction, a body, and a conclusion. The introduction was said to have three primary functions: to gain the attention of the audience, to state a thesis or purpose, and to offer a preview of the main points to be covered. The body of a speech was the presentation of the main points backed by supporting material. The conclusion was said to be the obverse of the introduction: first, it reviews the main points of the speech; and then it closes with another attention-getting device. This basic plan applies to presentations in business with a few modifications.

Plan and Organize the Introduction of the Presentation Obviously, in most cases you will plan and organize the introduction last—that is, after you have prepared the body of the presentation. Otherwise, how will you know what you are introducing? But for the purposes of this discussion, we will first consider how to plan an introduction.

As we noted above, a presenter needs to accomplish three major goals in the introduction: get the attention of the audience, state the thesis or purpose of the presentation, and preview the main points.

Attention   A number of techniques may be employed to secure the attention of an audience. Common attention-getting devices are a startling statement or statistic, an anecdote or story, a rhetorical question, a quotation, and humor. Such attention getters must be related, of course, to the thesis or purpose of the presentation.

But be careful here. Many of these devices may be inappropriate to presentations made to decision makers. First, you usually have the attention of such an audience— your problem will be to keep it! Second, attempts at storytelling or humor may seem frivolous and a waste of time to an audience of senior executives or even to a group of important clients. Remember, too, that humor is highly subjective. What is funny to you may not be funny to your audience. It is a lonely feeling to be in front of an audience when your attempt at humor falls flat. A third reason to avoid an attention getter when presenting to decision makers is that the device may backfire. Suppose you pose this rhetorical question to a group of senior executives: "Why have benefits risen 20 percent this year?" You risk the following response from a crusty senior executive: "Why the hell are you asking us? You're here to answer questions, not ask them. C'mon, get to the point."

Often the best way to begin a presentation before decision makers is to skip the attention-getting device and move directly to a statement of thesis or purpose, followed by a preview of the main points of the presentation. Often the thesis will be sufficient to elicit the attention of an internal audience of decision makers: "Over this year and next, the cost of our benefit program will increase 50 percent." If that does not get their attention, check for pulses! See Figure 10.1 for a good organization for an in-house speech by a benefits manager.

Still, some presentations may benefit from a clever attention-getting device. Typically, such presentations will be before somewhat larger groups of peers and subordinates or before public audiences outside the company. See Figure 10.2 for such a use of an attention getter.

Thesis or Purpose   A presenter may or may not choose to state a thesis or main point in the introduction. If a direct plan is chosen, then the thesis will be stated in the introduction; if an indirect plan is chosen, the thesis will not be stated there. As you have read in earlier chapters, the direct plan is commonly employed when presenting information that does not evoke a strong negative response from the audience, whereas the indirect plan is used to present negative information and in cases where persuasion is necessary. The outlines in Figures 10.1 and 10.2, both of which follow the direct plan, include a clear thesis statement.

Preview   The preview prepares the listeners to consider the main points to be covered in your presentation. A preview is especially useful to an audience listening to an oral

FIGURE 10.1   **Outline of Presentation by Benefits Manager to Company's Executive Committee**

Introduction
    Attention-getting device: None
    Thesis: Over this year and next, the cost of our benefit plan will
    increase by 65 percent.
    Preview: I'll proceed by addressing the projected cost of benefits for
    2000 and then offer a projection of costs for 2001.

Body
I.   The projected cost of the benefit plan in 2000 is 25 percent over costs
    for 1999 due to increase in employees and premiums.
    A.   Ten percent increase in employees
    B.   Increased premiums for medical/dental plan
II.   The projected cost for benefit plan for 2001 is likely to be additional 30
    percent over costs for 2000 due to further increases in employees and
    premiums.
    A.   Projected 20 percent increase in employees
    B.   Projected increase in premiums for medical/dental plan

Conclusion
    Review: Actual and projected increases in both the number of
    employees and the medical/dental insurance premiums for 2000 and
    2001 will likely increase the cost of our benefit plan by 65 percent over
    1999 costs.
    Attention-getting device: None

presentation, since they usually do not have a text to follow. The outline in Figure
10.2, however, shows that a preview can be omitted when the main points are easy to
follow and recall.

Plan and Organize the Body of the Presentation   Conventional wisdom among
speechwriters is that you should plan to cover no more than three main points in an oral
presentation. We agree. Most listeners find it difficult to juggle more than three main
ideas in the air over the course of a presentation. If you can limit the main ideas to two,
especially when speaking to nonprofessional audiences, consider doing so.

    If the presentation is informative, the information in the body of the presentation
may be organized as suggested in Chapter 2. Topical, chronological, cause-to-effect,
effect-to-cause, and spatial organizations are most common. (Analyze the plan of
organization used in Figures 10.1 and 10.2.)

    If the presentation is an oral report, you may choose to follow a specific report
format, especially if the oral version is based on a written one. For example, an oral
progress report may organize the body of the presentation as follows:

FIGURE 10.2   **Outline of Presentation by President of Small Computer Firm to a Group of Industry Analysts**

Introduction

Attention-getting device: You'll read tomorrow in the *Wall Street Journal* that J.D. Power & Associates has ranked our firm first in customer satisfaction among all firms in the computer industry based on their survey of mail-order customers.

Thesis: We've topped $3 billion in sales because our prices are competitive and customer service is superior.

Preview: None

Body

  I.   Our prices are competitive.

     A. We're able to bypass the high-cost dealers and deal directly with the customer through the mail.

     B. We're able to pass on our lower costs in the form of lower prices to our customers.

 II.   Our customer service is better and faster.

     A. We customize and ship an order in five days.

     B. We guarantee next-day, on-site service.

     C. We provide replacement machines by overnight delivery.

Conclusion

Review: We offer competitive prices and superior service.

Attention-getting device: Let me leave with a statistic that I'm most proud of: 70 percent of our buyers are repeat customers.

  I. Progress to date

 II. Problems encountered to date

III. Projected completion date

An oral presentation of a proposal might follow the format described in Chapter 8. If the presentation is persuasive, the problem–solution plan works well, along with an approach similar to the approach described in Chapter 6. Known as the motivated sequence (an approach introduced in 1935 by the late Alan Monroe), the presentation is organized in terms of these five steps:

1. An attention-getting step—Secure the attention of the listeners.
2. A need step—Show the audience that there is a need to be satisfied.
3. A satisfaction step—Propose a way that the previously identified need may be satisfied; offer a plan of action.
4. A visualization step—Assist your audience to visualize the results of satisfying the need.
5. An action step—Tell your audience what action they must take to put in place the plan you have proposed.[1]

When you organize a persuasive presentation using the motivated sequence, place the attention step in the introduction; the need, satisfaction, and visualization steps in the body of the presentation; and the action step in the conclusion of the presentation. See Figure 10.3 for an outline that follows this approach. It is taken from a sales talk to prospective buyers of condominiums.

Plan and Organize the Conclusion Do not neglect the conclusion of your presentation. It is the last thing the audience will hear; it is the last impression you will make. Ensure that the conclusion leaves your audience with a positive impression.

Use the conclusion to review and restate the main points of your presentation when presenting information. Use it to call for action when you are making a persuasive presentation. (See Figures 10.1 and 10.2.)

Finally, if appropriate, end your presentation with another attention getter. But as we noted in our discussion of attention getters for introductions, consider whether or not such a device is really necessary. For many presentations before decision makers, a summary or restatement may be sufficient to conclude the presentation. For other types of presentations, a concluding attention getter will have some impact. Use any of the devices described in the discussion of introductions. (See Figure 10.2.)

FIGURE 10.3   **Outline of a Persuasive Presentation Employing the Motivated Sequence**

Attention-Getting Device:	What if you could sell your home in New York, buy a condo with half the proceeds, invest the balance, and warm your bones in the sun 12 months a year while living in a secure and elegant retirement community?
Need:	While you sit on the equity of your home, your taxes keep climbing, the winters get colder, and life in the big city seems more threatening.
Satisfaction:	Buying a condo at The Vineyard, South Carolina's newest retirement community, will fortify your financial position, allow you to escape the harsh Northeast winters, and live the good life.
Visualization:	Just think of it: Sun warming your shoulders in January, an elegant condo in a secure community, low taxes, and your money invested and working for you.
Action:	Accept our offer to fly down as our guest and visit South Carolina's newest retirement community: The Vineyard.

Step Two: Compose the Content of Your Presentation Word for Word

Once you have decided on the essential content of your presentation, compose your oral presentation word for word as though you were preparing a manuscript speech to read.

Executives who are skillful and experienced speakers may wish to skip this step and simply prepare an outline. This may work well for some executives, but inexperienced and nervous speakers will find this extra step well worth the effort. Here is why.

When you actually make the presentation, you are likely to find that the pressure of the moment will make the process of speaking from an outline more difficult than you anticipated. As we noted before, there is likely to be a loss of precision and conciseness as you extemporize from your outline. But if you have previously prepared the full text of the presentation, looking down at the outline will trigger in your mind many of the carefully chosen words and well-crafted phrases that you had composed earlier. In short, you will sound more articulate.

As you compose the content of your presentation, since it will be an oral presentation, you should bear these four suggestions in mind regarding style and organization:

1. Use relatively short sentences, and avoid overly complex sentence constructions.
2. Be especially careful not to use technical expressions or acronyms unfamiliar to your audience.
3. Employ such techniques as summarization, restatement, enumeration, and transitions to help your audience follow your presentation.
4. Round off numbers and statistics, and avoid throwing too many figures at your audience. (Use handouts and other visuals to present complex quantitative data.)

In short, edit for the ear.

Finally, if you plan to speak to an international business audience composed mostly of non-native speakers, consider these four suggestions from Patricia L. Kurtz as you word your presentation.[2]

1. Consider using more repetition (identical words) than restatement (use of synonyms) as you summarize and recapitulate main points of your presentation to avoid confusion and compensate for the relatively less rich vocabulary of a non-native-speaking audience.
2. Avoid English idioms and slang or explain what they mean (e.g., "the 'fast-food' market—that is, food such as hamburgers cooked rapidly and uniformly . . .").
3. Avoid Anglo-Saxon phrasal verbs (a verb used with an adverb particle). This type of verb is difficult for non-native speakers to understand because the meaning of the phrasal verb is often different from the meaning of the words considered separately (e.g., "make up," "bring up," "stick to," etc.) and will change meaning depending on the context in which it's used. (Kurtz relates the anecdote of a presentation to an international audience in which the American speaker referred often to "sticking to the plan." During a break in the meeting the host, a non-native speaker of English, arranged to have the conference table wiped clean, fearing that food or drink had made the "plan" (document) "stick" to the table.

4. Use examples and analogies that are indigenous to the audience; an analogy to baseball may be appropriate to the United States or Japan, while an analogy to soccer is more appropriate to a European audience.

Step Three: Construct Your Presentation Outline

Your outline should serve as an aid to effective delivery. Therefore, after you are satisfied with the content of the presentation in manuscript form, you should reduce the manuscript to an outline.

Outlines may be alphanumeric or decimal; outlines may be full sentence, key phrase, or key word. (Figure 10.4 offers examples of the various types of outlines.) We recommend full sentence outlines and key phrase outlines. The key word is a bit risky, since it leaves out so much information.

After you have developed your outline, you should prepare the materials in a form suitable for delivery. First, type the outline on either 8½ × 11-inch stationery (20 lb.) or index cards, using a large type size—for example, 18-point computer output. (If you plan to speak from a lectern, either the stationery or the index cards will work well. If you must speak without a lectern, the index cards will be easier to handle.) Double-space between lines, allowing for 1½- to 2-inch margins at the top, bottom,

---

FIGURE 10.4   Types of Outlines

FULL SENTENCE OUTLINE (PARTIAL)
1.0 The cost of benefits has increased by 25 percent in 2000.
    1.1 The primary reason is the new employee dental plan.
    1.2 Another reason is the 5 percent increase in employees.
2.0 The cost of benefits will increase by 30 percent in 2001.
    2.1 The new employee medical plan will increase costs by about 20 percent.
    2.2 We estimate a 10 percent increase in employees.

KEY PHRASE OUTLINE (PARTIAL)
I. Benefits increased by 25 percent in 2000.
    A. New employee dental plan
    B. 5 percent increase in employees
II. Benefits will increase by 30 percent in 2001.
    A. 20 percent increase for new medical plan
    B. 10 percent increase in employees

KEY WORD OUTLINE (PARTIAL)
I. Increased
    Dental
    Employees
II. Increase
    Medical
    Employees

left, and right of each page, and number the pages. If (when) the pages or cards fall to the floor, you will find the numbers a blessing as you hurry to reassemble the sheets in their proper sequence.

Many speakers find it helpful to write reminders about effective oral delivery in the margins of the outline. Some examples are:

SLOW!
LOOK AT THE AUDIENCE!
SPEED UP!
PAUSE HERE!
RELAX!
SMILE!
WATCH POSTURE!
GESTURE!

Along with comments about delivery, important instructions for the presentation such as these should also be included:

SHOW SLIDE #1 HERE
USE TRANSPARENCY #2 HERE
START INTRODUCTIONS OF GUESTS STAGE RIGHT
ADJUST MICROPHONE

If it is important, write it on your outline.

Step Four: Memorize the Beginning and the End of the Presentation

Although we do not recommend that you memorize your entire presentation, we do recommend that you employ some memory work to enhance the effectiveness of the presentation.

We propose that you memorize the very beginning of the presentation. By doing so, you will be able to begin your presentation without looking at your notes. Instead, you will walk to the lectern, look directly at your audience, pause a moment, and begin to speak. After your opening remarks, naturally, you will glance at your outline. But the first impression you give will be one of confidence and command over the content of the presentation.

At the end of your presentation, do the same in reverse. Look up from your outline, pause, and speak directly to your audience as you conclude the presentation. Your last impression will also be one of confidence and control.

Step Five: Practice Your Presentation

You would be astonished at the number of managers who neglect this step or simply pay lip service to it. Except with a few gifted people, practice will always improve one's actual performance. You also run the risk of wasting any efforts expended on the first four steps if you do not practice your presentation.

Here are some suggestions for practicing your presentation:

- *Practice from the Beginning to the End* Start at the very beginning of the presentation—practice even an acknowledgment or an anecdote. Continue to practice with your outline until you have worked your way through the conclusion. Do this a minimum of three times to attain command over your material and to increase your self-confidence.
- *Practice the Use of Your Visual Aids* If you plan to use visual aids (e.g., PowerPoint, overhead transparencies, slides, and so on), practice using them in your presentation. Be sure to follow the advice in Step Three and indicate in your outline when to use each visual aid.
- *Time Your Presentation* Be sure to time your presentation as you practice. Given the nature of extemporaneous speaking, you will find that the time will vary a bit from practice session to practice session. If you are an inexperienced presenter, allow your presentation to run a little longer rather than a little shorter in your practice sessions. You will find when you stand before your actual audience that your rate of speech will increase somewhat due to nervousness. Therefore, a 16-minute practice session may well be a 15- or 14-minute presentation.
- *Use Audio-Visual Feedback While Practicing* If possible, tape your delivery during practice on a tape recorder or videocamera to provide feedback. Listen to your vocal delivery; observe your body language. Use the discussion on effective delivery (Step Six) and the checklist in Figure 10.5 as a basis for self-evaluation.
- *Ask for Feedback from Colleagues and Superiors* After a few practice sessions by yourself, ask a colleague to watch another practice session and offer some constructive criticism. This step is especially valuable if the presentation is a major one. If the presentation is to be made before your boss's superiors or some major clients, you might consider asking your immediate superior for some feedback, too. Be sure, however, to ask for specific, constructive criticism.

Step Six: Deliver Your Presentation

Your audience will both hear and see you: what they will hear is your vocal delivery, and what they will see is your body language. Let's consider both in turn and then discuss the effective use of visual aids in the delivery of a speech.

Vocal Delivery The key factors in vocal delivery include expressiveness, emphasis, rate and volume, and articulation and pronunciation.

Vocal Expressiveness To create the conversational style that we associate with the extemporaneous method of delivery, your voice must convey expressiveness. Simply put, vocal expressiveness is variation in the pitch, rate, and volume of your speaking voice. To sound expressive, your voice should move up and down in pitch, increase and decrease in rate of speech, and increase and lower in volume. Although you should make a conscious effort to vary these three vocal elements, an easy way to

FIGURE 10.5 **Checklist for an Effective Extemporaneous Delivery**

KEY ELEMENTS OF DELIVERY	EVALUATION			
Sufficient eye contact?	W	A	G	E
Appropriate gestures?	W	A	G	E
Appropriate facial expressions?	W	A	G	E
Poised and confident?	W	A	G	E
Vocal expressiveness?	W	A	G	E
Vocal emphasis?	W	A	G	E
Appropriate rate of speech?	W	A	G	E
Sufficient volume?	W	A	G	E
Clear articulation/correct pronunciation?	W	A	G	E

KEY ELEMENTS OF CONTENT				
Appropriate introduction	W	A	G	E
Appropriate pattern of organization	W	A	G	E
Appropriate supporting materials	W	A	G	E
Appropriate use of visual aids	W	A	G	E
Appropriate use of language	W	A	G	E
Appropriate conclusion	W	A	G	E

E = excellent; G = good; A = adequate; W = weak

remember how to sound is to model your vocal delivery on an animated conversation. Listen to two people engaged in a lively conversation. You will hear the vocal expressiveness. That is how you should sound.

Vocal Emphasis All words are not created equal; some are more important than others. When you write, you have a number of devices at your disposal by which you can emphasize a word or phrase—for example, underlining (italics in the printed page), bullets, indentation, and so forth. Obviously, these devices are of no help in an oral presentation. Instead, you must employ vocal emphasis.

Vocal emphasis is achieved in three ways: by the use of the pause, by variation in rate of speech, or by variation in volume. If, for example, you wish to emphasize an important phrase in a presentation, do any or all of the following:

- Pause before or after a key word
- Slow down when you reach an important passage
- Increase or decrease volume

These three techniques, simple as they seem, will effectively convey to your audience the following message: this is important!

Appropriate Rate and Volume Along with vocal expressiveness and emphasis, you must be careful to avoid two common problems among inexperienced presenters: speaking too rapidly and speaking too softly. Rapid speech is often caused by nervousness. Nervous speakers, perhaps seeking relief from the stress of delivery, seem compelled to race through their presentation, sacrificing both vocal emphasis and the comprehension of the audience. Resist the temptation. If you tend to speak too quickly, write yourself a note or two in the margins of your outline to remind yourself to slow down. A caution, however: some speakers overcompensate by speaking too slowly, a sure recipe for boring your audience. Try to speak at about 150 words per minute, slowing occasionally to emphasize a key word or phrase.

Speaking too softly is a serious problem as well. If members of your audience cannot hear you, or can hear you only part of the time, your presentation is doomed. Avoid this problem by projecting your voice with sufficient loudness so that all members of the audience are able to hear you. If volume is a problem for you, write yourself a reminder on your outline to project. You might also consider asking someone in the audience to signal to you if your volume is too low.

Articulation and Pronunciation Pay careful attention to articulation and pronunciation as you make a presentation. By articulation, also referred to as enunciation, we mean the precision and crispness of your spoken words; by pronunciation we mean the sounds assigned to a given word. Sloppy articulation and errors in pronunciation create a poor impression. Make a conscious effort to articulate clearly, without over-articulating. When in doubt about the standard pronunciation of a word, check with a dictionary. Be especially careful about the pronunciation of names; people are not amused when they hear their names mispronounced.

Body Language Eye contact and body movement are the two major categories of body language to consider.

Eye Contact Eye contact—looking at members of your audience—is essential to any effective extemporaneous presentation. Here are some suggestions for effective use of eye contact:

Because presentations are usually given to small audiences, establishing eye contact from time to time with all members of the audience is expected. We recommend, however, that you linger a bit on each audience member—do not gaze rapidly around the room like a surveillance camera at a bank.

If you are speaking to a large group, it is wise to break up the audience into four sections. As you speak, shift your gaze from section to section, looking at individuals in each section. Again, linger.

Be careful with supportive and friendly audience members. Some presenters see someone in the audience smiling and nodding approval and direct the bulk of the eye contact to that person. Avoid the temptation.

Body Movement Your body language should reflect your expressive and emphatic vocal delivery. Here are some suggestions:

- Use facial expressions to forecast and reflect the tone of your presentation.
- Gesture naturally as you speak.
- Stand with an appropriate, relaxed posture.
- Project a high energy level.
- Move with poise and confidence.
- Do not adopt a deadpan expression or a fixed smile.
- Do not employ gestures that will distract the audience.
- Avoid touching your hair, mustache, etc., while you speak.
- Avoid a rigid posture.
- Control such unmotivated body movement as swaying, shuffling your feet, pacing back and forth, or playing with coins or keys in your pocket.

In short, allow your body movement to convey a positive, professional image.

Visual Aids Here are three suggestions for the effective use of visual aids during your extemporaneous presentation:

First, do not display your visual aid until you are ready to refer to it in your presentation. Otherwise, the audience will be distracted by the visual.

Second, allow your audience sufficient time to look at the visual before you remove it or replace it with another. It is most annoying for audience members to have a visual whisked away before they have fully read or understood it.

Third, do not talk to the visual aid; talk to your audience. To avoid the problem of turning your back to your audience as you point to a visual, use your inside arm.

Translation Finally, if you find it necessary to have your presentation translated to an international audience as you speak, consider these four suggestions:[3]

1. Plan to meet with your interpreter prior to your presentation to ensure that he or she will be familiar with your phrasing, accent, pace, and idioms.
2. Review all technical terms with your interpreter prior to your presentation.
3. Insist that the interpreter translate in brief bursts and not wait until the end of a long statement, to ensure both the accuracy of translation and to sustain the interest of the audience.
4. Make a special effort to use visual aids, since the combination of both the interpreter's words and the visual message will enhance audience comprehension and accurate communication.

Step Seven: Evaluate Your Presentation

After a presentation, evaluate your performance. What did you do well? What aspects of your presentation, content, or delivery were ineffective? What feedback have you received from audience members? (Consider both positive and negative feedback.) Use the checklist in Figure 10.5 as a basis for your evaluation.

SUMMARY

Oral presentations in business and industry are common. They may be internal or external, informative (a briefing) or persuasive (a sales presentation). The preferred style of delivery for nearly all business presentations is extemporaneous—that is, the speech is carefully prepared and delivered from an outline. The effective extemporaneous presentation is characterized by such conversational qualities as vocal expressiveness and vocal emphasis, good eye contact, and appropriate body language. This chapter has outlined seven steps to follow as you prepare, deliver, and evaluate your oral presentations.

Applications

1. Listen to a live or taped presentation or speech and analyze the speaker's introduction and conclusions.

   - Was an attention getter used? Which type was it?
   - Was the thesis stated and restated?
   - Were the main points previewed and reviewed?

2. For the same presentation or speech that you analyzed above, analyze the body of the presentation or speech.

   - How many main points were there?
   - How were they organized?
   - How were they supported?
   - Were any visual aids used? What kinds of visuals were they?

3. For the same presentation or speech, analyze the speaker's delivery.

   - How was the vocal delivery in terms of expressiveness, emphasis, volume, rate, pitch, articulation, and pronunciation?
   - How was the body language in terms of eye contact, facial expressions, gestures, posture, and movement?
   - How was the use of visual aids?

DISCUSSION QUESTIONS

1. Recall some oral presentations to which you listened recently. How effective were they? Be specific.
2. Why is the extemporaneous method of delivery superior to the other three methods for most business presentations?

3. What specific aspects of your extemporaneous speaking style need improvement?
4. Have you made a presentation to an international (non-native-speaking) audience? Was it successful? Were there problems? Explain.

NOTES

1. Joseph A. Devito's discussion in *The Communication Handbook*, HarperCollins, New York, 1986, pp. 204–205.
2. Adapted from Patricia L. Kurtz's excellent primer, *The Global Speaker*, AMACOM, American Management Association, New York, 1995, pp. 40–49.

3. Adapted from the writing of R. E. Axtell, cited in Lillian H. Chaney and Jeanette S. Martin, *Intercultural Business Communication*, Prentice-Hall, Englewood Cliffs, New Jersey, 1995, p. 105.

ʻ11ʼ

Meeting Management

Effective meeting management is an essential business communication goal. In this chapter, we will consider the reasons for meeting, review common complaints about meetings, and offer some sensible advice for planning and leading face-to-face meetings.

REASONS FOR MEETING

Think of the last meeting you attended. What was the reason (assuming there was a reason) for the meeting? Was it to make a decision? Was it to solve a problem? Or was it for another reason? The 3M Meeting Management Team has identified 13 of the most common reasons for calling a meeting (see Figure 11.1); the reason for your meeting will probably be on its list. We will consider each reason in turn.

To Accept Reports from Participants

Many organizations schedule meetings on a weekly or monthly basis to allow managers to report on the activities of their departments or divisions, including an account of positive or negative developments. Usually led by a senior executive, the meetings serve three vital organizational communication functions: upward communication (information is shared with superiors), downward communication (superiors provide feedback on the reports), and horizontal communication (colleagues in different departments or divisions are kept abreast of developments throughout the firm). Such meetings have a

FIGURE 11.1   The 13 Most Common Reasons for Holding a Meeting

Reasons for meeting

1. To Accept Reports from Participants
2. To Reach a Group Judgment or Decision
3. To Analyze or Solve a Problem
4. To Gain Acceptability for an Idea, Program, or Decision
5. To Achieve a Training Objective
6. To Reconcile Conflicting Views
7. To Communicate Essential Information to a Group
8. To Relieve Tension or Insecurity by Providing Information and Management's Viewpoint
9. To Ensure That Everyone Has the Same Understanding of Information
10. To Obtain Quick Reactions
11. To Reactivate a Stalled Project
12. To Demonstrate a Product or System
13. To Generate New Ideas or Concepts

Source: 3M Meeting Management Team, *How to Run Better Business Meetings: A Reference Guide for Managers,* McGraw-Hill, New York, 1987, pp. 8–13.

disadvantage; they run the risk that participants have little to report, especially if the meetings are biweekly. This leads to trivial presentations and wasted time.

In addition to such periodic meetings, there are ad hoc meetings called to receive reports on the status of various projects within an organization. Again, ad hoc meetings serve an important organizational communication function.

To Reach a Group Judgment or Decision

Should we discontinue a product line? Should we approve a loan to a corporate customer? Should we reorganize the Human Resources Department? Should the firm move from a decentralized to a centralized word-processing system? Should we approve a new company-wide medical benefits plan? These are some of the many types of decisions that might be decided at a meeting of executive decision makers.

Decisions may be made in the following five ways:

1. Unanimity—All participants agree on the decision.
2. By consensus—Although some members have reservations about the decision, all participants support the decision.
3. By majority—More than 50 percent of the participants agree on the decision; it is understood, however, that the minority will support the majority's decision once it is made.

4. By a plurality—The decision supported by the largest number of participants is adopted even if the number is less than a majority.

5. By fiat—The boss makes the decision; other participants are expected to endorse it.

To Analyze or Solve a Problem

Why has our software lost 20 percent of its market share? Why is turnover so high at one of our subsidiaries? How can we reduce the cost of our liability insurance? How can we improve our recruitment of MBAs from the most prestigious business schools? A meeting allows the knowledge and experience of participants to be pooled and applied toward the analysis and solution of problems such as these.

Meetings called to analyze and solve a problem often adopt the following well-known approach:

1. Define the problem (as an open question).
2. Assess the significance of the problem.
3. Analyze the problem (duration, causes, effects).
4. Establish criteria for evaluating solutions.
5. Generate possible solutions.
6. Evaluate solutions (using the criteria from Step 4).
7. Select the best solution.

All seven steps are important, and they should be followed in sequence. Do not try to analyze the problem (Step 3) before you have defined the problem (Step 1).

To Gain Acceptability for an Idea, Program, or Decision

Suppose that your company has imposed a tough new security system requiring that all employees wear ID badges at all times regardless of their status or position. Anticipating resistance from many managers and other professionals in the company, you hold a series of meetings to explain, face to face, the rationale for the change in security procedures and to respond to questions and objections.

To Achieve a Training Objective

In one sense, all meetings have a training objective. Meetings offer younger executives an opportunity to observe and learn from more experienced executives. Some meetings, however, may be called for more explicit training objectives. For example, sales meetings may be called to provide sales representatives with information and techniques required to sell new or current products, or managers may meet to review performance evaluation procedures.

To Reconcile Conflicting Views

The smokers and nonsmokers in a department may sharply disagree over the issue of employee smoking. To ensure a sensible compromise that will allow both sides to work together peacefully, a meeting is called to air conflicting views. Such a meeting is most effective if it is chaired by an outside consultant specializing in conflict-resolution techniques.

To Communicate Essential Information to a Group

An example of such a meeting is a gathering of the officers of the trust department of a major bank to hear a briefing by a tax attorney on the implications for estate planning and management in the new federal tax bill. The presentation, supported by a variety of carefully prepared visual aids, is followed by a question-and-answer period.

To Relieve Tension or Insecurity by Providing Information and Management's Viewpoint

As an organization faces a crisis or a major change, employees hunger for authoritative information from management but often subsist on a diet of rumor and misinformation. A meeting with employees allows management to convey information personally, directly, and accurately. A meeting may also allow employees to ask questions and express their views.

To Ensure That Everyone Has the Same Understanding of Information

At times, an organization may choose to complement an important written message with face-to-face communication, especially if the message is highly controversial or complex. The major advantage of using a meeting for this purpose is the opportunity it provides for the source of the information to elicit feedback from the intended audience.

To Obtain Quick Reactions

Some managers occasionally call meetings to solicit comments about decisions or plans still being formulated. The comments may serve to alert management to possible reactions to the decision or plan, thus affecting implementation. Or input may actually be used to modify the final decision or plan.

To Reactivate a Stalled Project

When a project is stalled for lack of an administrative decision, a meeting may be called to force the decision. Such meetings can be highly political in nature.

To Demonstrate a Product or System

Meetings to demonstrate a product or service may be internal (a meeting to demonstrate the operation of the new corporate information center) or external (a meeting of automobile dealers held by the manufacturer to allow the dealers to observe and test-drive the new models). The external demonstration meeting, in particular, requires especially careful planning.

To Generate New Ideas or Concepts

Although a creative meeting called to generate new ideas or concepts is common at advertising and public relations firms, it is also employed by every type of organization from time to time. A common approach to this type of meeting, called brainstorming, is characterized by these guidelines:

1. Ideas are not evaluated positively or negatively as they are introduced; they are just recorded.
2. The emphasis is on the generation of as many ideas as possible.
3. Ideas may be combined or modified.
4. The final list of ideas is evaluated.

Brainstorming is often very productive, assuming, of course, that you have some good brains at work.

COMMON COMPLAINTS ABOUT MEETINGS

Complaints About Planning

When managers grumble about a meeting being poorly planned, the specific complaints are likely to be one or more of the following:

- An agenda was not prepared or sent out prior to the meeting; hence, the participants were unclear about the meeting's purpose.
- The wrong people were invited to attend (people who should have been there were not, while those who should not have been there were).
- The time for the meeting was inconvenient for most participants.
- The room was too small for the number of participants.
- Audiovisual equipment was not ordered.
- The meeting room was not set up correctly (wrong arrangement, too few chairs, etc.).

Complaints About Leadership

Meetings are often criticized for poor leadership. Common complaints about ineffective leadership include the following:

- The leader did not follow the agenda; the meeting went off track.
- The leader was domineering, monopolizing meeting discussion time and attempting to impose personal views on the group.

- The leader was weak, speaking infrequently and failing to control disruptive participants.
- The leader did not facilitate communication among all the participants of the meeting.

Complaints About Participation

A third source of dissatisfaction with meetings is the performance of participants other than the leader. Some common complaints are:

- Participants were unprepared for the meeting. (They were unfamiliar with the agenda, they had not read the background materials relevant to the issues to be addressed, or they had not prepared their own presentations carefully).
- Some participants contributed too much at the meeting. (This is especially a complaint about high-status participants.)
- Some participants contributed too little to a meeting. (This is often heard about participants who felt insecure psychologically or politically.)
- Some participants were disruptive or uncooperative, either intentionally or unintentionally.

Complaints About the Meeting's Outcomes

The most common complaint about meeting outcomes is, simply put, there "ain't" any. Other complaints include these:

- Decisions are not implemented.
- Assignments agreed to by participants are not done.
- Recommendations are not passed on.
- Findings are often ignored.

Given the cost of meetings, these are serious problems.

But successful executives do not dwell on what is wrong. They do what is right. Therefore, let's consider effective techniques for planning meetings, leading and conducting meetings, and participating in meetings, as well as ensuring desired outcomes after meetings.

PLANNING MEETINGS

Effective planning always increases the probability of a successful meeting. As you plan a meeting, consider these five questions.

What Is the Objective of This Meeting?

As earlier chapters have suggested, effective business communication requires a clear understanding of one's objective or objectives. An objective is more specific than a topic (e.g., "New Security Procedures at CONTECH"). An objective should describe what you expect the meeting to accomplish (e.g., "CONTECH managers will be thoroughly briefed on all aspects of the new Department of Defense security requirements").

Usually, meetings have more than one objective. Along with the first objective listed above, the following two objectives could also be linked with it: "Need for changes in the existing CONTECH security system will be assessed"; and "A timetable for the implementation of mandated changes in the security system will be prepared." As you will see in our discussion of agenda items later in this chapter, the objectives may serve as items for the agenda.

Who Should Attend This Meeting?

Avoid the two most obvious problems: inviting too many people and inviting too few. Consider the objective of the meeting as you consider whom to invite. If the objective is to brief managers on a new security system, then the subset of questions would include: Who should do the briefing? Who should be briefed? Does my boss need to be there? Do other corporate superiors or additional staff need to attend? Keep the number down as much as possible, since it costs money to meet.

When and Where Will the Meeting Be Held?

Be practical. The availability of key people and corporate superiors should be determined before choosing a meeting time and date, since you will have to accommodate them. In the absence of such considerations, preferences will vary among different corporate cultures. Some people will prefer a midmorning meeting on a Tuesday, Wednesday, or Thursday, with others preferring the impact of the Monday morning meeting or the sense of closure offered by a Friday afternoon meeting.

The where of a meeting should be determined by two basic considerations: convenience and suitability.

First, the convenience of the location for participants should be considered, with preference accorded to senior executives. Convenience, however, also refers to how close the meeting room is to telephones if someone needs to make a call, and how accessible people are if they need to be reached by their staff or boss. Some executives deliberately select locations that are inconvenient, hoping to minimize the interruptions of telephone calls. Having the meeting outside of the office at a conference center or hotel is one way to achieve this effect.

Second, assess the suitability of the meeting room, with the size of the room as the most important factor. Is the room large enough for the number of participants selected, along with the necessary tables, chairs, and audiovisual equipment required? Other factors affecting suitability are the noise level outside the room, physical appearance, and control over temperature (heat and air conditioning).

What Materials, Equipment, Refreshments, and Room Layout Will Be Required for the Meeting?

Be prepared with whatever materials are needed, including notepads and pencils for each participant, name/place cards, and handouts. Have such equipment as flip charts, an overhead projector, a slide projector, a VCR, or a lectern for speakers ready if necessary. Possible refreshments include water and glasses, coffee and danish, and soft drinks.

How should the room be laid out? Four popular meeting layouts are the table in the center of the room with all of the participants sitting around it, the U-shaped layout, the classroom layout, and the theatre layout. See Figure 11.2 for diagrams of the four types.

To serve as a checklist for the four issues we have just addressed, you may wish to use the meeting planning checklist from the 3M Meeting Management Team (see Figure 11.3).

What Should the Agenda Be?

An effective agenda should include the following information:

- Time of meeting
- Length of meeting
- Location of meeting
- List of participants
- Subject of meeting
- Background information
- Items to be covered
- Pre-meeting preparation

FIGURE 11.2   **Four Layouts for Meetings**

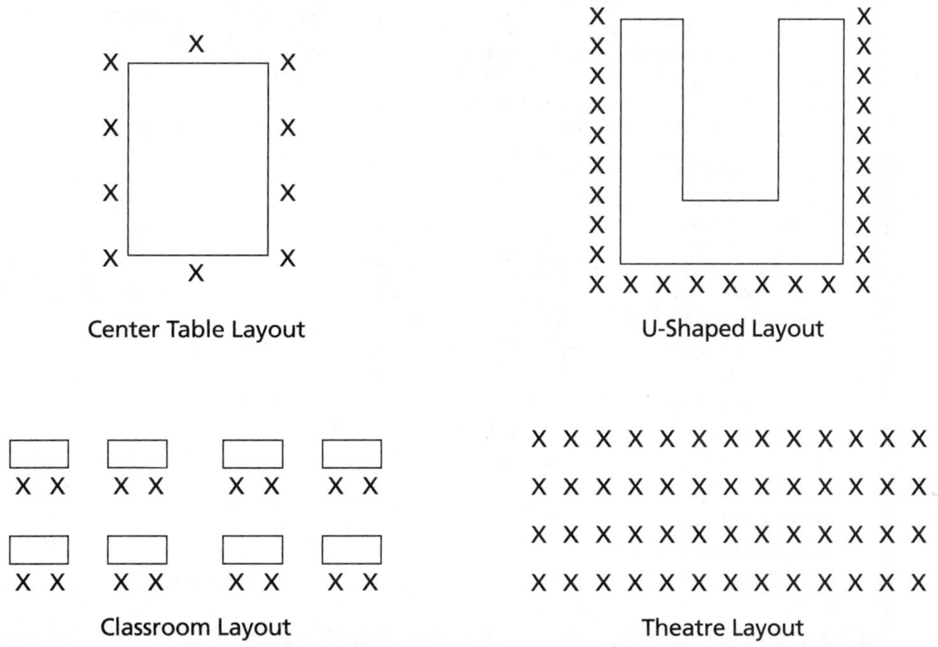

Center Table Layout

U-Shaped Layout

Classroom Layout

Theatre Layout

FIGURE 11.3   **Meeting Planning Checklist**

MEETING PLANNING CHECKLIST

Meeting objective: _____   Date _____
_____   Time _____ to _____ am/pm
Place _____
Participants _____   _____

_____ Room reserved
_____ Agenda (meeting notice)
_____ Prepared
_____ Sent
_____ Visuals prepared

Meeting Materials

_____ Note pads, pencils   _____ Name/place cards   _____ Name badges

_____ Handouts _____

Equipment

_____ LCD panel/PC
_____ Overhead projector   _____ Spare lamp
_____ Slide projec or . . . . .   _____ Spare lamp
_____ 16 mm . . . .   _____ Spare lamp
_____ Screen (Size) _____
_____ Charts   _____ Pointer
_____ Chalkboard   _____ Chalk
_____ Video tape/disc
_____ Marking pens
_____ Microphone
_____ Lectern
_____ Extension cord
_____ _____
_____ _____

Food, Beverage

_____ Coffee _____ Juice _____ Soft drinks
_____ Lunch _____

Post Meeting

_____ Action minutes
_____ Next meeting _____

Room Layout

Note: Designate No Smoking Area

Source: 3M Meeting Management Team, *How to Run Better Meetings: A Reference Guide for Managers,* McGraw-Hill, New York, 1987, p. 53. Used by permission.

The sample agenda in Figure 11.4 covers all this information.

The first five items in the list above were discussed earlier in this chapter. By background information we mean any information that will convey the reason for, or significance of, the meeting. In Figure 11.4, the background information consists of a reference to the new DOD security requirements and the need for a meeting to assess and plan modifications in CONTECH's current security system.

The items to be covered are really objectives of the meeting, and they should be specific and realistic. Some agendas specify the time that the item will be addressed or the amount of time to be devoted to each item during the meeting. These devices ensure that the group will not devote a wildly disproportionate amount of time to one item while neglecting others. Do not, however, view time limits as rigid requirements. Some items may require a little less time; some items may require a little more.

By including a section on pre-meeting preparation you inform participants about

FIGURE 11.4   Sample Agenda

CONTECH SYSTEMS

Dan Creange
Director of Security

AGENDA

TO: All Department Heads and Directors
FR: Dan Creange
RE: Meeting on New Department of Defense Security Requirements
BG: DOD has imposed a new set of security requirements for contractors engaged in classified work. We need to consider the new requirements, assess necessary changes for our present security system, and establish a timetable for implementation of the changes consistent with DOD requirements.

Time and Place
Wednesday, April 12, Room 319, 10:00 AM to 12:00 PM

Items
1. Briefing on new DOD security requirements
2. Assessment of security system changes required
3. Timetable for implementation of system changes

Meeting Prep
Attached are new security guidelines from DOD; please read. Please prepare a list of questions concerning implementation in your department.

your expectations regarding their level of preparation, as well as specific responsibilities for participation at the meeting. In our example (Figure 11.4), the agenda requests that all department heads and directors read the new DOD security guidelines and that they prepare a list of questions regarding the implementation of the new security system in their departments.

LEADING MEETINGS

The leader of a meeting has one basic goal: to accomplish the objectives of the meeting. The following guidelines will prove useful to you as you assume this role.

Starting Time

Start the meeting on time. Nothing says more about your philosophy of meeting management than starting a meeting promptly. It happens so infrequently that starting at the time specified in the agenda will serve as an excellent attention-getting device.

Opening Remarks

Once you have the group's attention, open the meeting with an appropriate set of remarks. Offer some remarks intended to achieve the following objectives:

1. Establish the right tone—usually serious and positive.
2. Be sure to identify any participants unknown to the group.
3. Offer any background comments that might prove useful to the group—for example, why the meeting was called.
4. Review the objectives of the meeting as expressed as items on the agenda.
5. Identify any time constraints not already expressed on the agenda—for example, when the meeting must end.

Getting to Business

After you finish your opening remarks, move to the first item on the agenda. Be careful not to let your opening remarks serve as a springboard for the group to get off track.

Participation

Facilitate balanced participation among meeting members. Some participants talk too much while others talk too little. Effective meeting leadership ensures that participation is balanced. If it is, a few members of the group will not dominate the discussion at the expense of less assertive colleagues. Rather than muzzle the more talkative participants, issue direct questions to the quiet ones, specifically soliciting their comments or advice.

Sometimes the group as a whole is quiet, and you may need to prime the pump.

If the group appears prepared but reticent, pose open questions to them. For example, you could say, "What problems should we anticipate as we implement the new security system?" If the group's silence is related to a general level of unpreparedness, then consider rescheduling the meeting or offering sufficient information (in the form of handouts or a briefing) to improve the level of preparation.

Deal assertively but patiently with disruptive members. A storyteller, for instance, can sidetrack a meeting with an irrelevant story, especially one that walks the group down memory lane. After the first story, inquire about the relevance of any later stories to the point under discussion. Do the same for humorists and digressors. But employ some strategic leniency at times, too. An occasional story or digression may prove a harmless diversion and even provide a useful release for group tension.

Agenda

Use your agenda to keep the discussion on track. If the discussion starts to drift from the item being considered, firmly steer the group back to the item. If a meeting member resists your request to change direction, ask for justification of the relevance of the comments to the agenda item under consideration. Remind participants of time constraints: "We'd better return to Item Two. We've got only an hour left to cover four more items!"

Again, remember to exercise some strategic flexibility when appropriate. If an agenda item elicits far more productive discussion than you anticipated while planning the agenda, do not attempt to limit discussion prematurely. Otherwise, attendees may feel muzzled. If it appears that an item may require substantially more time than the agenda allows, consider holding another meeting addressed to that item.

Closing

Close the meeting at the appropriate time. Once you have covered the items on the agenda, close the meeting. Meetings sometimes continue aimlessly after the items have been covered, and it is embarrassing to have someone inquire, "Is the meeting over?"

Before you close the meeting, signal the participants by asking for any final comments or questions. Offer a summary of what has been accomplished at the meeting, and explain what will occur next. For example, let people know that minutes will be sent to all participants; another meeting will be scheduled on this subject; etc. Finally, be sure to thank the group members for their time and contributions.

EFFECTIVE MEETING OUTCOMES

It is a shame to carefully plan and lead a meeting only to see poor results from your efforts. Assignments agreed to at the meeting are not completed, decisions are not implemented, or deadlines are missed. Follow-up is needed. To prevent these problems we recommend the development of a meeting action plan similar to the one developed by the 3M Meeting Management Team (see Figure 11.5).

FIGURE 11.5   **Meeting Action Plan**

_____ Meeting

Meeting date: _____ Recorder: _____

MEETING ACTION PLAN

Chair: _____

Action to be taken	Person responsible	Deadline	Completed

Key issues or discussion

_____

_____

_____

_____

_____

_____

_____

_____

_____

_____

_____

List of attendees attached

Time: End: _____

Start: _____

Next meeting: _____ **Length:** _____

Source: 3M Meeting Management Team, _How to Run Better Meetings: A Reference Guide for Managers,_ McGraw-Hill, New York, 1987, p. 53. Used by permission.

The meeting action plan replaces the traditional minutes of a meeting. First, it includes basic information about the meeting: subject, date, name of chair, and recorder. Second, it describes specific actions to be taken, the person responsible, the deadlines for the actions, and completion dates. Third, it lists the key issues discussed and the participants. Fourth, it records the meeting length. And fifth, it announces the next meeting.

A meeting action plan focuses on actions to be taken after the meeting rather than simply recording the minutes.

In sum, careful planning, effective leadership, and a meeting action plan will eliminate most of the complaints that were cited earlier in this chapter. Put meetings to work for your organizations.

SUMMARY

Meetings serve a large number of important organizational purposes. Common complaints about meetings fall into four categories: complaints about meeting planning, complaints about meeting leadership, complaints about participation, and complaints about meeting outcomes. Careful planning, skillful leadership, and ensuring meeting outcomes will eliminate most of these complaints.

DISCUSSION QUESTIONS

1. What types of meetings have you attended in the past six months?
2. Recall some recent meetings. How many of the common complaints described in this chapter apply to these meetings?
3. Recall some recent meetings. What was done well?
4. Would it be possible to eliminate some meetings in your organization? Which ones? Why?

NOTES

1. 3M Meeting Management Team, *How to Run Better Business Meetings: A Reference Guide for Managers*, McGraw-Hill, New York, 1987, pp. 8–12.

Applications

1. Next time you attend a meeting, evaluate the planning of the meeting.

    - Was the agenda adequate?
    - Were appropriate people invited to attend?
    - Were the room size and setup appropriate?

2. For the same meeting that you analyzed in Question 1, evaluate the leadership of the meeting.

    - Did the leader follow the agenda?
    - Was the leader's style appropriate?
    - Did the leader facilitate communication?

3. For the same meeting you analyzed in the previous questions, evaluate the quality of participation at the meeting.

    - Were participants prepared?
    - Was participation balanced?
    - Was participation disruptive or uncooperative?

4. For the same meeting already analyzed, evaluate the meeting outcomes.

    - Were decisions implemented?
    - Were recommendations passed on?
    - Were assignments agreed to by participants done?

'12'

Crisis Management

Employees of organizations spend large portions of their time in work-related activities that contribute to polishing the company's image. All of that work can be destroyed quickly when a crisis hits. Potential crises exist in every organization. Traditional businesses have prepared for the uncertainties. E-businesses have more recently learned that a few minutes of downtime can cause anger, and several hours of downtime can lose customers and cause the stock to plummet. The wise organizations search for the potential crises and develop processes that will either eliminate the threat or create opportunities to deal with the crisis immediately and successfully.

This chapter examines crises within the organization and methods of managing them. While we all know of large and small organizations that have been destroyed because a crisis developed, there are also many success stories of organizations that survive and do better in the future. We will examine many of the things that need to be done to ensure that your organization can weather the storms of crises and survive.

Many of us have Intel's Pentium or Celeron chips in our computers. Yet lots of us have forgotten how close Intel came to never getting the Pentium chip to the market. This chapter starts with a case study of Intel Corporation and the crisis it encountered in the fall of 1994. Intel survived, and you will read how it occurred. We then define and explain an organizational crisis. Next we describe a five-step crisis management process that each organization must develop. A major part of that process requires writing a crisis management plan. A portion of the chapter gives a detailed outline of what goes into such a plan. The process of developing a communication strategy is then examined. Finally, you will read how wise organizations guarantee that the media will treat them fairly by developing a media response, especially through press releases and press conferences.

INTEL'S BIG CRISIS

Intel's Hidden Crisis

Over a five-year period, starting in early 1990, Intel Corporation spent hundreds of millions of dollars on consumer advertising campaigns designed to establish its name and the first of its high-powered Pentium computer chips as household words. Between March and December of 1994, it spent $150 million on the *Intel Inside* campaign. The image-building process worked. Computer companies like IBM, Dell, Packard Bell, and Gateway shipped millions of computers to retail outlets in anticipation of successful holiday sales. But on Thursday, November 24, 1994, Thanksgiving Day, Intel's world almost fell apart.

The *New York Times* ran a business section front page with the headline, "Flaw Undermines Accuracy of Pentium Chips." The *Boston Globe* business page echoed a similar warning: "Sorry, Wrong Number." This was followed with the subtitle, "Results are in: Intel computer chip sometimes makes inaccurate math."[1] While this was the general public's first inkling that a problem existed with the Pentium chip, many computer users had already heard the message. For Intel, a crisis was brewing.

Intel's Pre-Crisis

The event that triggered Intel's crisis situation actually occurred on June 13, 1994. A college math professor had been running billions of calculations on his Pentium computer and couldn't get the numbers to divide right. For four months he continued to recalculate the formula and eventually figured out the error was being produced by the computer's microprocessor. The professor contacted Pentium and learned that he was the only one of two million users to report the problem. Believing that he had indeed discovered a problem, and seeking to find more data, he posted a message on the CompuServe on-line network. The issue spread across the Internet and was discussed for weeks by a network of scientists and engineers who need precise calculations and who were wondering if their work could be affected. So begin Intel's public relations quagmire.[2]

Eventually Intel announced it had discovered the bug in July 1994 but had determined there was no need for a recall. The company contacted technical and scientific users, big companies, and computer retailers. It issued press releases and held telephone conferences with Wall Street analysts. But it didn't run any mass-market print or TV ads explaining the situation or publicizing the toll-free phone number that it set up for concerned Pentium users. As one analyst stated, Intel's calculations showed a casual user might encounter a problem with the chip "once every 27,000 years."[3] The message seemed to be that "for the kind of computing most of us plain folks do, a defective Pentium is good enough."[4]

Intel's Full Crisis

Intel reached a new stage in its crisis management by mid-December. Walter Mossberg, who writes a popular weekly technology column in the *Wall Street Journal*, contacted

Intel about a replacement for his machine. Evidently someone unfamiliar with Mossberg's status responded grudgingly that Intel would replace computer chips for certain individuals. Before a replacement could be issued, the user had to prove to the company that the work being done on the computer was "mathematically complex enough to meet Intel's self-defined rules about who needed accuracy." In addition the user had to give Intel a credit card number and agree to a potential charge of $1,000 if the old Pentium chip was not returned within 29 days. The user also had to pay for having someone swap the chips. Word of Intel's actions caused the general public to become incensed. In Mossberg's weekly column, he found cause to describe the negative customer service he had experienced.[5]

On December 12, 1994, alerted to Mossberg's impending article, IBM announced that it was halting all shipments of its highest-power Intel PCs. It also stated that Intel Corporation had significantly underestimated the potential for errors to occur. This action caused Intel's stock to slide and forced a temporary halt to trading. Andrew Grove, Intel's president and chief executive officer, shot a verbal response to IBM. "You can always contrive situations that force this error. In other words, if you know where a meteor will land, you can go there and get hit."[6] The response by Intel's president seemed to typify its handling of the crisis events. At every turn they dismissed the flaw as a small problem even when customers complained. One crisis manager commented, "Whether it happens one in 10,000 times or one in a million, the reality becomes that the customer is concerned."[7] Crisis management expert Ian Mitroff responded, "Their [Intel's] technology may be in the Systems Age, but their management thinking is in the Stone Age." Mitroff believed the company should run high-profile ads to fully explain the issue and to commit to replace the chip for any consumer who asked. He compared the $250 million Intel had spent to build an image with how quickly its image could be tarnished for years.[8]

Intel continued to hold the line on its position until the events between December 16 and 19 occurred. A *Wall Street Journal* article described "at least 10 [law] suits in three states" that involved securities fraud, false advertising, and a violation of state consumer protection laws. Three days later the *New York Times* article on the lawsuits quoted Florida's deputy attorney general as saying, "They've [Intel] got to stop acting like a rinky-dink two-person operation in a garage and start acting like the major corporation they are." On the same day a *PC Week* cover article urged IS managers "to protect themselves against liability claims from use of flawed chips."[9]

Intel's Post-Crisis

On December 21, 1994, Intel came to its senses. Andrew Grove reversed his stand and announced Intel would give the owner of any Pentium-based computer a free replacement chip—no questions asked. Figure 12.1 shows a copy of the Intel press release announcing the replacement. A full-page, letter format advertisement appeared in most major newspapers. The letter read:

> To owners of Pentium™ processor-based computers and the PC community:
>   We at Intel wish to sincerely apologize for our handling of the recently publicized Pentium processor flaw.

The Intel Inside® symbol means that your computer has a microprocessor second to none in quality and performance. Thousands of Intel employees work very hard to ensure that this is true. But no microprocessor is ever perfect.

What Intel continues to believe is technically an extremely minor problem has taken on a life of its own. Although Intel firmly stands behind the quality of the current version of the Pentium processor, we recognize that many users have concerns.

We want to resolve these concerns.

Intel will exchange the current version of the Pentium processor for an updated version, in which this floating-point divide flaw is corrected, for any owner who requests it, free of charge anytime during the life of their computer. Just call 1-800-628-8686.

The letter was signed by Andrew S. Grove, president and chief executive officer; Craig R. Barrett, executive vice president and chief operating officer; and Gordon E. Moore, chairman of the board.[10]

Intel survived its crisis. Sales of Pentium processor-based systems set new sales records over the 1994 holidays. Intel's revenue for 1994 grew by 31 percent.[11] A few months later the average user gave little thought to an Intel machine's inability to perform. From a crisis management standpoint its major mistake was in waiting so long to arrive at an appropriate response. It approached the problem from an engineering rather than a consumer perspective. In fact, as one analyst stated, "Intel's stubbornness turned what could have been a minor problem, perhaps limited to a few scientists and engineers, into a costly fiasco."[12] The entire crisis episode cost Intel $475 million and was a pretax charge to fourth quarter 1994 earnings.

Ethically, Intel's pre-crisis decision was financially motivated. It knew that a total recall would take months and would cost millions. "Because chips take as long as 12 weeks to make . . . it would take months for Intel to start stamping out chips with revised circuitry. And because computer systems makers also take time to cycle through their inventories, as many as 5 million flawed chips would be sold before the new ones would hit the market, analysts [had] estimated."[13]

In the end the cost was financially the same, but the company's reputation was distorted in the minds of many users. Andrew Grove was right when he said in his public letter, "technically an extremely minor problem has taken on a life of its own." Years later we recognize that Intel managed the crisis well, for few people remember or care about the event. Intel and Pentium are synonymous and positive words.

DEFINING A CORPORATE CRISIS

The Intel case described a crisis situation that a large and successful organization encountered. While some damage was done to the Intel corporation, both financially and to its image, it survived. Many organizations that experience crises do not. We define a crisis as "a significant, unpredictable, disruptive event that has potentially negative results. The event stimulates news media coverage. The public scrutiny may impact the organization's normal operations, and its aftermath may significantly damage an organization and its employees, products, services, financial condition, and reputation."

FIGURE 12.1   **Intel Press Release**

INTEL ADOPTS UPON-REQUEST REPLACEMENT POLICY ON PENTIUM™ PROCESSORS WITH FLOATING POINT FLAW; WILL TAKE Q4 CHARGE AGAINST EARNINGS

SANTA CLARA, Calif., December 20, 1994—Intel today said it will exchange the processor for any owner of a Pentium™ processor-based system who is concerned about the subtle flaw in the floating point unit of the processor. The company has been criticized in recent weeks for replacing processors on the basis of need rather than on request. Intel will take a reserve against fourth quarter earnings to cover costs associated with the replacement program.

The flaw can produce reduced precision in floating point divide operations once every nine billion random number pairs. Intel said that while almost no one will ever encounter the flaw, the company will nevertheless replace the processor upon request with an updated version that does not have the flaw. This offer will be in effect for the lifetime of a user's PC, which means that users can conclude they do not currently want a replacement, but still have the option of replacing the chip in the future if they wish. Intel is making a rapid manufacturing transition to the updated version, and expects to be able to ship sufficient replacement parts to meet demand during the next few months.

"The past few weeks have been deeply troubling. What we view as an extremely minor technical problem has taken on a life of its own," said Dr. Andrew S. Grove, president and chief executive officer. "Our OEM customers and the retail channel have been very supportive during this difficult period, and we are very grateful," Dr. Grove said. "To support them and their customers, we are today announcing a no-questions-asked return policy on the current version of the Pentium processor.

"Our previous policy was to talk with users to determine whether their needs required replacement of the processor. To some people, this policy seemed arrogant and uncaring. We apologize. We were motivated by a belief that replacement is simply unnecessary for most people. We still feel that way, but we are changing our policy because we want there to be no doubt that we stand behind this product."

Intel will send a replacement processor to PC users who choose to do the replacement themselves, and will offer telephone technical assistance. Call 1-800-628-8686 for details. Intel also said it planned to contract with service providers to do replacements at no charge for PC owners who prefer to bring their PC's to a service location. Details will be provided in the next few weeks. Finally, Intel said it would work with its OEM customers to provide replacement for PC users who prefer to work with the manufacturer of their system.

The company said it would take an unspecified but material charge against fourth quarter earnings to cover costs associated with the replacement program announced today. Intel said it was unable to determine the amount of the reserve, but said an estimated total will be provided on or before January 17, the date of Intel's 1994 financial results announcement. Following this release is a copy of an advertisement that will appear starting on December 21 in major newspapers in North America.

Intel, the world's largest chip maker, is also a leading manufacturer of personal computer, networking and communications products.

Examples of Crisis Situations

According to the Institute for Crisis Management, the four basic causes of a business crisis are *acts of God* (storms, earthquakes, volcanic action, etc.), *mechanical problems* (ruptured pipes, metal fatigue, etc.), *human errors* (mistakes in making a product, etc.) and *management decisions/indecisions.*[14]

In the late 1990s, businesses had numerous crises. Those most frequently covered by the media were white collar crimes, labor disputes, general mismanagement, catastrophes (death, product tampering, etc.), labor disputes, environmental disputes, defects and recalls, and class action lawsuits. The crises that appear most frequently in news stories include sexual harassment allegations, hostile takeovers, and executive dismissals. According to Ian Davies, a professor of disaster management at Cranfield University in England, natural hazards have cost companies in the United States an average of $1 billion a week since 1989.[15] Businesses often avoid the word *crisis*, preferring to use words like *strike, layoff, accident, natural disaster, negative financial news, critical regulatory report, environmental problem*, or *legal issue*.[16]

The sample incidents listed in Figure 12.2 either resulted in significant damage or had the potential to cause significant damage to employees, consumers, the physical or financial operation of an organization, the organization's image, and even local communities or the general public. The organizational and individual victims of these unfortunate incidents ranged from large corporations to the federal government, from senior executives to common laborers. Every business organization should examine how many similar incidents have the potential of occurring within its boundaries and lines of operation. The organization should then create strategies for both preventing and dealing with the crises.

Basic Crisis Theses

Steven Fink, in his book *Crisis Management*, refers to the time of crisis as "an unstable time or state of affairs in which a decisive change is impending—either one with the distinct possibility of a highly undesirable outcome or one with the distinct possibility of a highly desirable and extremely positive outcome."[17] Fink's words are important for advanced business students to remember because each crisis has the potential for disastrous outcomes or quite positive outcomes. A crisis is like a disease. Consider the four crisis theses and how they apply to your organization.

A Crisis Can Be Anticipated Your organization should audit what it does and how it does it to determine every potential crisis. There are always tell-tale signs that, when observed, can clearly lead to crisis detection.

A Crisis Can Be Prevented Once the potential crisis is detected, your organization can take the proper measures to correct what is wrong and to ensure that a full-scale crisis does not develop.

FIGURE 12.2   Crisis Examples

ACTS OF GOD
- Oklahoma City tornado
- Florida hurricanes
- California earthquakes and forest fires

PUBLIC HEALTH AND SAFETY
- Jack in the Box hamburgers cause deaths
- Major airline crashes (Valujet, TWA, USAir, Egyptian Air)
- Mass killings of citizens and employees: McDonalds in San Diego; Luby's Cafeteria in Killeen, Texas; Columbine High School
- American Home Products: Fen-phen
- Texas A&M bonfire construction

LABOR RELATIONS
- Employee strikes at General Motors, American Airlines, and United Parcel Service

PRODUCT FAILURE
- Intel Pentium computer chip
- Dow Chemical silicone implants
- Ford Pinto gas tank placement

CORPORATE MISMANAGEMENT
- Sexual harassment (Mitsubishi, Ford, and Astra Pharmaceutical)
- Racial discrimination at Texaco and Denny's
- Bribery in the Salt Lake City 2002 Winter Olympic bids

TERRORISM
- Pan American Airlines explosion
- World Trade Center bombing
- Oklahoma City Federal Building bombing

FINANCIAL CALAMITIES
- ADM price-fixing
- New Era Foundation scam
- Daiwa Bank
- Orange County, California bankruptcy

INDIVIDUAL ACTIONS
- Falsification of individual résumés
- Office affairs
- Embezzlement by executives

CONVENTION EVENTS
- Hotel fire
- Phone system outage
- Keynote speaker collapse
- Death of attendee
- Protesters picketing meeting over industry issue

A Crisis Can Be Controlled Even if prevention is not possible, your organization can take steps to manage each stage of the crisis and to bring it to a complete end.

A Crisis Can Be Turned to an Advantage While the presence of a crisis almost always means that some type of negative outcome will occur, the overall impact does not have to remain negative. If your organization takes the right steps through the duration of the crisis, the end result can be more positive than negative. Remember, a crisis will run its course if it is untreated.

Intel referred to its crisis in its 1994 Annual Report as an event which brought the personal computer (PC) industry and consumers closer together. "This episode reflects a strategic turning point. Quite simply, the PC is now a standard consumer tool used by a wide range of people, from preschoolers to university researchers. Many of these PC customers have more demanding—and varied—expectations for product quality, performance and service than computer users have in the past. In many ways, Intel facilitated this transition."[18]

Management Mind-sets That Impede Crisis Management

The Intel case showed that top management during the pre-crisis period believed that it could get by without responding to the general public, issuing a recall, and answering many of the questions that had been generated. Intel's management held the first of several mind-sets, *there is only one correct approach to solving a problem.* They decided to stonewall the issue, pretending that only a few Pentium users could possibly be affected, and that all other users would eventually realize that their machines were not damaged. In doing this they fell prey to the second mind-set, *factual data is superior to subjective opinions when making a decision.* While it was true that errors were generated in answers that required extremely high calculations, they failed to take the beliefs of the ordinary user into account. By using the third mind-set, *it is possible to totally separate reason and emotion,* Intel disregarded the feelings of consumers and in essence called them "stupid" for not seeing that they would never be doing problems that could possibly generate errors. Finally, Intel believed that *severe change is only temporary . . . things will return to normal if one will just wait long enough.* Their problem with the waiting was that it gave those who were demanding Intel's response more time to generate additional support, especially through the Internet. What started as a small problem became a giant one.

Four Stages of a Crisis

Four stages can be identified in every example of an organizational crisis that has run its course. If management applies itself seriously to correcting problems as they develop in Stages One and Two, a full crisis can usually be averted. However, once the crisis hits Stage Three it is too late to avoid certain consequences. It is important that the organization at that point seek to resolve the crisis as quickly as possible and minimize the costs involved.

Stage One: The Hidden Crisis Just as when a disease invades a human body and the person is not yet aware of it, potential crises exist within every organization. They could be in the composition of a product, a particular response to a customer, a method of production, or a hundred other items. If management is wise and seeks to correct every problem and issue that develops, it may avoid a crisis. The organization will often not know the potential danger until the issue moves to Stage Two.

Stage Two: The Pre-Crisis If the hidden issue is recognized but not resolved, the organization will find itself in Stage Two. Managers here often believe that a problem will solve itself over time. For Intel this stage occurred in July 1994, when one of its engineers realized that the computer chip allowed errors to occur. The fatal mistake was that management believed that no one outside the organization would ever find the problem. Consequently it chose not to act. Even when the math professor notified Intel of his findings in September, the company led him to believe that he alone had made a mistake and that the chip was perfect.

Stage Three: The Crisis Here the problems can no longer be hidden from the public. Managers operate at a high degree of stress. Entire entities within the organization are in chaos. Rapid problem-solving attempts are made, but not enough time and resources are available to quickly bring the problem to an end. Input from people within the organization is narrowed to just a few. Outside help is not trusted or sought. Panic is the norm. If the crisis goes public, the media's agenda becomes the organization's agenda. Instead of giving attention to properly solving the problem, employees suddenly have to supply the media with information and strategy. Valuable time is wasted. Resources are improperly used.

Stage Four: The Post-Crisis Eventually a crisis will end. The organization hopes the outcome will be favorable. This stage is critical because the organization can now discover what went wrong, how it happened, and what should have been done about it in the first place. The wise organization uses this stage to reevaluate every potential crisis and to put in motion problem-solving groups that are empowered to correct whatever problem exists before a new crisis can occur.

THE CRISIS MANAGEMENT PROCESS

Every organization should recognize that crisis management is a process. The time and energy spent in investigating and planning will pay off should an actual crisis develop. The preparation steps allow management to ask hypothetical questions that are not thought of or that are too emotional to ask when a crisis develops. According to Barton, the organizations that actually take the time to prepare for a crisis recover an average of two and one-half times more quickly than those that do not prepare. In order to assure this favorable result, five steps need to be taken: determine the crisis potential, develop appropriate crisis teams and centers, write a crisis management plan, develop a communication strategy, and practice and revise the plan.

Step One: Determine the Crisis Potential

Each organization should determine how likely it is to suddenly encounter a crisis. To do this, ask "what if" questions. Examine your organization's internal and external environments. Start with the *personnel*. For instance, what would happen if your CEO or president suddenly died? Who would take charge? What immediate actions would be necessary? What could happen to people involved in a plant accident? How would your organization handle a libel or slander suit?

The next category deals with the organization's *facilities*. Companies that manufacture, transport, and store certain chemical and hazardous products are required by federal and state regulations to have available emergency response plans. Consequently, organizations in such industries have plans available to deal with emergencies at the incident site. Employees are usually trained in procedures to follow.[19]

Amazingly, many companies are not prepared to deal with catastrophic events or incidents. Ask questions like the following: What would happen if a fire, flood, or earthquake occurred? Where would my organization meet to conduct business? If a manufacturing plant was the target, how would the organization continue to make its products? Is there a backup source that you could have continue the production?

The Oklahoma City Chamber of Commerce experienced a disruption that affected both facilities and personnel on April 19, 1995, when the Murrah Federal Building was bombed. The chamber is a not-for-profit organization. It makes no product, but services dues-paying member organizations. The organization was housed in downtown Oklahoma City, a few blocks from the epicenter of the blast. At the time of the explosion, all personnel evacuated the building. No procedure was in place for where to go or where to meet. Because of the chaos in the downtown area, chamber personnel went in different directions. Some volunteered to help blast victims. Some became so distraught they went home and watched the happenings on television. Because of the telephone outages, it was several days before new office space was secured and all employees were notified and reassembled for work.

Another area of concern is with *products*. What will your organization do if a product is shown to be faulty, causes death or injury, or needs to be recalled? What plans are in place in case a product becomes obsolete? How will your organization respond to a patent infringement?

Competition should also be considered. What will your organization do if competition suddenly undercuts your price substantially? How will it respond to a major advertising campaign? What will happen if your company suddenly becomes a takeover target?

By asking many of the above questions, your organization can prepare to deal with uncertain and destructive events and can develop management strategies for the inevitable.

Figure 12.3 will give you some ideas regarding the potential risk for your organization. Barton found in a ten-year study of hundreds of organizations that certain types have a much higher degree of risk for crisis events than others do. Pinkerton's Inc. determined the specific security threats that cause many of the risks. Figure 12.4 lists the Top Ten Business Security Threats in the United States.

FIGURE 12.3   **Crisis Risk Categories**

CRISIS RISK CATEGORIES

HIGH-RISK CATEGORY
- Manufacturing organizations, especially chemical and nuclear
- All financial institutions: banks, credit unions
- Technological firms: chip and software makers, ammunition and weapons
- Public transportation: airlines, railroads, and subways
- Lodging properties: hotels and motels
- Food producers and distributors
- Nightclubs and casinos
- Federal and state buildings and agencies
- Amusement parks
- Public personalities: politicians, entertainers
- Craft renting: helicopter, excursion planes, hot-air balloons, water rafts
- Utilities and airports
- Builders, roofers, and structural engineering companies

MEDIUM-RISK CATEGORY
- Not-for-profit agencies, churches, colleges, hospitals
- Retail concerns
- Fast-food outlets and restaurants
- Telecommunications companies
- Household products manufacturers
- Computer manufacturers/distributors
- Physicians and related medical professionals
- Mall and shopping centers
- Health clubs, preschools
- Liquor, beer, and wine stores

LOW-RISK CATEGORY
- Radio and television broadcasters
- Certified Public Accountants
- Apparel manufacturers
- Neighborhood businesses: barber shops, pet stores, video rentals, dry cleaners
- Automobile repair shops
- Law firms
- Social organizations
- Car rental companies

Adapted from: Lawrence Barton, *Crisis in Organizations,* South-Western, Cincinnati, Ohio, 1993, pp. 65–66.

FIGURE 12.4   Top Ten Business Security Threats in the United States

TOP BUSINESS SECURITY THREATS
1. Workplace violence
2. Executive protection
3. Fraud/White-collar crime
4. Risk of hiring high-risk employees
5. Hardware/software theft
6. General employee theft
7. Internet/Intranet security
8. Drugs in the workplace
9. Unethical business conduct
10. Property crime (external theft/vandalism)

Adapted from: "What Worries Companies Most?" *Management Review*, July 1, 1999, p. 9.

Step Two: Develop Appropriate Crisis Teams and Centers

As potential crisis situations become evident, an organization should develop teams that take responsibility for previewing each crisis, developing a strategy to prevent occurrence, and then managing the event should it occur. *Senior executive* teams may include two or three key executives. *Support* teams may involve several department heads, key managers, and functional specialists. *Field* response management is developed based on the nature of each organization, its facilities, and operations. The important thing is that the team include multiple perspectives such as legal, marketing, operations, communications, security, and corporate, as well as an external communications counsel.[20]

Crisis centers are places where teams can assemble and carry out their activity. Activities like adding telephone lines to a conference room and predesignating computers, printers, and copy machines can help the support response operations and will save valuable time later.

As teams develop they should be carefully trained to make decisions and empowered to be able to carry them out. If a crisis occurs and the team is unsure of what to do, the staff will sense it and the media will notice it too. Conducting table top exercises or response drills exposes flaws in the support system and allows each member of the team to see how important his or her role is to the total endeavor.

Step Three: Write a Crisis Management Plan

Crisis management implies that to some degree each crisis situation can be managed. This management process takes place before, during, and after the crisis. For instance, the following things can be managed: anticipating a crisis, developing and training a crisis team, designing and equipping a crisis center, working through a plan for each potential crisis, developing the statements to be used in communication events, and handling media interviews. A smart organization develops all of these managerial processes into a Crisis Management Plan (CMP). Organizations put these plans into action if a crisis occurs. While the plan may not address "glass found in a company's product," it can address how the organization would respond to rumors or false media information, who would be responsible for talking to the media, and even things they would say.

The Crisis Management Plan Contents The best plan is one that is thought out and prepared thoroughly. Clarke Caywood, a crisis management specialist at Northwestern University, assembled what he considers to be "The Ultimate Crisis Plan." Caywood contends that a wise organization writes what is essentially an autobiography. This should be ready to pull from the shelf and use when a crisis hits. Usually the plan has already been reproduced and copies sent to key members of the management team. But, this is a document that will never be leaked to the outside world. In many ways it reveals an organization in its most vulnerable form.[21] Figure 12.5 gives an outline of a crisis management plan. In the completed plan, each item is fully documented and all requested information is listed.

Step Four: Develop a Communication Strategy

When a crisis hits, a company must communicate and do so quickly. History is full of organizations that did not respond, and their reputations suffered. NASA took five hours before commenting on the Challenger spacecraft explosion. Exxon took several days before it acknowledged its role in the Valdez incident. Intel, also, tried to avoid telling the truth. But in stories of crisis success, like that of Johnson & Johnson during the Tylenol tragedy, appropriate communication protected the organization's image.

In a study of 120 crisis cases over a 15-year period, three important communication problems were apparent.

- Managers spoke *without authority*. They often showed a lack of understanding of the organization's culture, procedures, or norms (43 percent).
- Managers *presented incorrect data or misspoke* based on faulty information presented to them by others in the organization (27 percent).
- Managers took *action that in turn complicated the crisis*. The steps taken were usually intended to help resolve the crisis but were perceived differently than anticipated (22 percent).[22]

The crisis management plan should designate who will take charge of the communication process. Usually the public relations department takes care of the mechan-

FIGURE 12.5   Crisis Management Plan Outline

I. Mission and related items

Mission. The organization's mission statement, goals, and objectives are briefly stated.

The organization's philosophy and behavior standards are listed.

Objectives. Objectives regarding what is important for your organization are then recorded. This describes what you hope your CMP will achieve and prevent. Prioritize the items listed so that if a crisis does occur, there will be no confusion as to what to do first.

Listed with the objectives are also the things that your organization wants to protect. This section can list items like an organization's image, customer and member safety, and product quality.

Rational for the CMP. This portion states explicitly the realization that crises could occur, how they would be handled by crisis teams, and vital information about the members.

II. History of Crises and Potential Crises

History of past crises. A review and critique of previous crises that have occurred within the organization are described, along with the way the situations were handled and changes that were made.

Listing of potential crises. This area lists the potential problems that were uncovered during the crisis audit.

Survey results. Here the results of any questionnaires used during the crisis audit are discussed.

Crisis stage development. For each potential crisis that is uncovered an outline of the stages of development should be constructed along with a timetable and the personnel assigned to handle it.

III. Preparing the Crisis Center

Crisis center furnishings. Each crisis center should be furnished with the items that will aid the crisis team and help bring an end to the crisis. A variety of items like those listed below should be considered:

- Sufficient electrical outlets
- Portable computers with modems that access company files; a laser printer
- Fax machines, blast fax, and fax cover sheets
- Preprogrammed cellular telephones and standard telephones equipped with a separate line for each member of the crisis team and voice mail with call interrupt
- Telephone directories for each organizational site along with updated organizational chairs and telephone trees
- Media, governmental, business, and professional directories
- Televisions with cable to receive CNN, C-Span, and multiple networks
- Radios equipped for shortwave
- Photocopier
- VCR and audio recorder with playback and copying ability and extra tapes
- Risk area maps in hard copy and software
- Body bags in the event of crisis-related deaths
- Legal pads, pens, pencils, paper clips, and staplers

FIGURE 12.5   Crisis Management Plan Outline (Continued)

- Organization stationery, envelopes, rapid-delivery containers
- Clocks
- Restroom and shower facilities nearby
- Lots of refreshments
- Corporate credit cards and cash

A media room. A media briefing room should also be established and equipped with the following items:

- General press kit: list of products, background of safety record and fact sheets
- Telephones
- Podium, microphone, and portable public address system
- Chairs, tables, and desks
- Computers, modems, and printers
- Photocopiers

IV. Directories of the Organization's Stakeholders

Directories of Stakeholders. Each directory should contain addresses and telephone numbers for some of the following groups:

- Emergency response personnel
- Board of directors
- Community and civic leaders
- Media
- Customers and/or members
- Shareholders
- Clients
- Neighbors
- Financial partners
- Government agencies
- Regulatory agencies
- Vendors
- Suppliers
- Certain competitors
- Family members
- Analysts
- Legal groups
- Media
- Subsidiary heads
- Employees
- Plant managers
- Union officials
- Retirees
- Pension holders
- Sales and marketing personnel
- Agencies

Appropriate channels of communication for each group. Mechanisms for reaching each of the above groups must be decided along with who in the organization will be responsible for reaching each stakeholder. Any prelimi-

FIGURE 12.5   Crisis Management Plan Outline (Continued)

nary steps that can be taken to have communication items ready should be taken. Typical mechanisms include:

- Press releases
- Letters
- Personal visits
- Telephone calls
- General meetings
- Video conferences
- Media advertising
- Video news releases (VNR)
- Internal publications
- News conferences
- Interoffice memos
- Faxes preprogrammed for multiple sending ability
- Telegrams and telexes
- Electronic mail
- Overnight mail

Government regulatory forms. All compliance forms that would be required by government regulatory organizations should be collected.

V. Media Awareness

Organization's media policy. This section should emphasize open, honest, and proactive actions with the media during the crisis.

Organization's spokespeople. The level and type of crisis will dictate the specific spokespeople. Identifying all the potential people at this point will allow the organization to do plenty of media interview training (see Chapter 13).

Organization gatekeeper and that person's function. This person will centralize and control the flow of information to ensure that it is accurate and valid and that it reaches the right people at the right time. The person will also monitor the flow of internal and external communication to ensure that the organization speaks with "one voice." He or she should always be accessible for both good and bad news.

Media databases and media contacts. A listing of each available media representative, prioritized in favor of those that have a positive relationship with the organization, should be drafted. List also media deadlines and policies. Be sure to keep this database current.

Third-party sources. Third-party sources should be developed and then updated continually. This lists friends of the organization and experts in the organization's field. The media can call these individuals for background information during a crisis. Make sure these contacts are credible, reliable, trusted sources who are often quoted in the media.

A process for handling media inquiries. This section should provide answers to questions like, "How will the calls be recorded?" "Who will the calls be forwarded to?" "How will they be prioritized when answered?" "How will they be answered (i.e., fax or phone)?"

Designate also who will check the validity and accuracy of the stories being printed and broadcast. This person should have access to the scene of the

FIGURE 12.5   **Crisis Management Plan Outline (Concluded)**

crisis and should monitor radio, television, and wire services, along with police, hospitals, and government agencies.

VI. Other Action to Take

Depending upon the specific industry, each organization will need to determine when and where to take appropriate action on a variety of issues like the following:

- Specify how security arrangements will be handled for facilities, possibly injured individuals, and the public.
- Cover items like what alarms will be activated, who will be responsible for first aid, and what evacuation routes to use.
- Determine how much crisis insurance to purchase. Policies normally cover types of events like securities confidence, hostile takeovers, and employment practices.
- Develop a list of professional counselors who can help "de-escalate" the crisis. Their help is often needed in the first few hours and days following an event. They can support, encourage, and listen in a caring way to traumatized employees.
- Consider establishing a reunification center, where dispersed individuals can be reunited. Make sure it can accommodate both vehicles and people. This necessity has become apparent with the major school crises.
- Create a cellular phone policy that can be put into effect for the first few hours of the situation. Often all members of a community are encouraged to avoid use to allow safety officials reliable service.

VII. Method of Evaluation

After a crisis is resolved, it is important that an organization review and analyze everything that occurred. This process should be started while the crisis is happening (the gathering of information) and completed immediately after it is resolved. Several things go into this process.

Interviews with both external and internal publics. The organization can interview, informally, people who are key to the system. They should be asked about their perception of how the company reacted and how the organization could have reacted better.

A content analysis of media clippings and tapes. Clippings collected by staff during the crisis should be analyzed for accuracy of reporting and fairness of treatment.

A cost-benefit analysis. After the crisis has ended and all data have been summarized, an organization should determine how much damage was done to the organization financially.

Modification of the crisis management plan. After all evaluations are completed the crisis management plan should be changed to allow the organization to better manage crises of the future.

Written case study. While the information is still fresh in the minds of all involved, a case study should be developed. This can be an excellent training tool to use in preparing future personnel for new crises. This also allows the organization to be more objective in its focus.

ics and a designated individual is selected to be the spokesperson. A good communication strategy has several parts.

Determine the Audience That Needs Information Figure 12.6 gives a list of potential stakeholders. Not every audience member will need to receive information in every crisis. As Whitesell states, "It is crucial to communicate only with the appropriate audiences. For instance, there is no need to alert the news media to a situation occurring internally that has no impact on the general public. A contingency plan should always be developed for secondary audiences, since crises can explode beyond their initial boundaries. For example, an angry customer or competitor may suddenly decide to call the news media as well. In that case, other audiences might be affected."[23]

Determine Who Will Be the Spokesperson for the Organization A single spokesperson is recommended, with a backup designated. In 99 percent of the cases the chief executive officer, or highest ranking official, takes charge. But some experts believe this is unwise. Larry Smitz, president of the Institute for Crisis Management, contends: "Your spokesperson should be someone high up who has credibility, but not the top person. It's better to reserve your CEO as a safety net. That way, if someone makes a statement that needs to be corrected, the CEO can step in. Deploy your top gun first and you've got no ammunition left."[24] Of course, severe crises involving

---

FIGURE 12.6   Organizational Stakeholders

Adversarial groups	Investors
Bankers	Law enforcement
Board members	Lawyers
Brokers	News media
Business groups	Politicians
Community leaders	Regulators
Competitors	Retirees
Customers/clients	Senior executives
Educators	Stockholders
Employees	Suppliers
Employee's families	Union officers
Franchisees	Vendors
International executives	

Source: Adapted from "Stakeholders in a Business Crisis," Institute for Crisis Management, Louisville, Kentucky, 1999, at www.crisisexperts.com/stakeholders_main.htm.

deaths or public health threats make the CEO a required spokesperson. The Coca-Cola case in Figure 12.7 shows the critical impact of a CEO's failure to appear at an appropriate time. Often the appearance itself shows strong organizational leadership.

For minor types of information sharing, a public relations member may be used. You may want to have a member of your board, a chief scientist, or the head of your board's audit committee. The real thing you should look for is, "Who has the credibility?" Usually a public relations person will be the designated receiver of all media requests, questions, and other sources of information. It is critical that each person in the organization be informed that only the designated spokesperson will comment to any outside source.

Determine the Appropriate Communication Style   Information should be communicated quickly, candidly, and in a positive way. It is critical that the organization tell the truth and never lie. This, of course, does not mean revealing confidential or competitive information. Since crisis situations are related to emotions, communication should recognize those areas and be developed and delivered with compassion. Finally, as in all written and spoken communication, the information should be clear, concise, and free of technical jargon and ambiguity.[25]

Determine the Appropriate Timing   Each communication device is affected by timely delivery. By drawing on the crisis management plan, some data can be accessed immediately and distributed to the necessary audiences. Policy statements must be developed. A question-and-answer sheet regarding the crisis should be prepared, especially for the media. Other written materials such as news releases, press kits, or letters must also be prepared and distributed when necessary. An organization will find that it will use various means of communicating during crisis situations: meetings, press conferences, memos, e-mail, telephone calls, letters, and personal interviews. Chapter 13 describes the appropriate methods of working with the news media.

In crisis situations the media are busy compiling the story. If you want your voice to be heard, use this opportunity to speak while the news is fresh. In a hurry, the media can sacrifice quality. Realize that when the media appear, you must have an organized statement that relays pertinent information. Make sure that this statement is prepared and delivered in a clear and concise manner.

Richard Brundage, at the Center for Advanced Media Studies, believes an organization should take control of a crisis situation within the first 6 hours—not 24 or 36 hours later. "Even if you have a press release already written for incidents like this, present it and then let them know when they will get more. Then, follow through. This is how to get the media off your back without making them mad." He describes the timing used by Waterworld USA when an accident occurred at its Concord, California, location in 1997. "It was obvious they had a well laid out plan well ahead of time. . . . Right from the outset, control was established. Not one media was allowed inside the park, . . . until all details, if not completed, were launched. The parties that needed to get in and do their work could. They had a clear-cut plan in place for an interim management team to come in and deal with the day-to-day communications with all the agencies and the media."[26]

Exxon misjudged its opportunity in the March 1989 oil spill off Alaska. As the public, environmentalists, government, and the media waited for the company to respond to and manage the spill, the situation grew worse. Most executives have learned to take immediate and visible action, and so a press conference seemed required. Other CEOs caught in similar crises have even jumped on a plane to head for the disaster scene. Lawrence Rawl, Exxon's CEO, did none of those things. In fact, he did not comment publicly for a week, and when he did make a statement he tended to blame others, including God.[27] It quickly became evident that neither Exxon nor the petroleum industry could find a reasonable solution. At that point, the media became their enemy. As one public relations expert put it:

> There was a window of opportunity with the news media. The reporting initially and for a period of time following the disaster was factual and pretty straightforward even though media representatives were undoubtedly as horrified as the rest of us at the scope of the disaster. But as Exxon stumbled, fumbled, stonewalled, denied, shifted the blame, ducked responsibility, and tried to manage the messages, the news media had no choice but to turn against them as well.[28]

Figure 12.7 describes a similar situation that Coca-Cola faced in Europe in the summer of 1999.

Since an organization should anticipate potential crises and have a crisis management plan in place, a prepared communication response plan is also needed. This will be the proactive communication approach.

American Airlines shocked many when it announced just eight days after its jet crashed into the mountains of Cali, Colombia, in late 1995, "that human error on the part of our people may have contributed to the accident." Most corporate lawyers fear that any concessions of that type may cost the company in court. Yet American, which had not had a crash in 16 years prior to that accident, had learned much from other airlines like Pan American and U.S. Air, and also from its two 1994 American Eagle affiliate accidents. Travelers will stop flying your airline if they do not trust your safety. A company is "better off admitting what they know, what went wrong and whether it was their fault."[29]

Determine Whether to Use the Proactive or Reactive Media Approach

An organization must decide whether it wants to take a proactive or reactive approach to the media. The proactive is by far the more successful, yet often the more threatening. With this approach a company is ready to start its crisis machinery whenever an unwanted situation occurs. In fact, proactive companies often contact the media before the media have a chance to call them.

Shell Oil found that the proactive style paid off in a 1971 disaster. A blowout in the Gulf of Mexico killed four people and threatened the safety of water, beaches, and wildlife. Shell chose not to stonewall the incident. It issued 150 press releases and arranged 50 interviews and six press conferences. It even took reporters to the site for personal inspection. This communication technique brought the media to Shell's side as it fought the fire and finally put it out.[30]

In using the proactive approach, it is important to make a clear distinction between what you know for certain, what you assume to be true, and what you really

FIGURE 12.7   Coca-Cola's Poor Crisis Response

The year 1999 was a bad one for Coca-Cola, the world's leading brand. In an average week, 70 million French and Belgian consumers drink 120 million servings of the beverage. Yet seven days is all it took "for the 113-year-old Atlanta-based [company] . . . to go from a much admired and trusted market leader in Europe, to a company scrambling to give away product in order to pick up the shreds of consumer confidence."[1]

In mid-May people in Belgium, many of them children, became sick after drinking Coke. Over 100 people were hospitalized with symptoms of headaches, nausea, and vomiting. Two days later the company withdrew 2.5 million bottles of Coca-Cola, Coca-Cola Light, Fanta, and Sprite. But then things took a strange turn. Coke was so sure of its product's innocence that it misread the consumer's level of concern and focused on denying that its product caused the illnesses. For seven days Coke failed to give an explanation or to even discuss the matter. Governments throughout Northern Europe banned and recalled Coke soft drinks, and in some countries, all Coke products (Nestea, Minute Maid, Aquarium, and bon Aqua).[2] A Belgian health minister described the scene: "People were angry and disturbed because there was a lack of communication. They did not say whether they knew what the problem was and if they did know they were keeping it to themselves. Coca-Cola has been seriously damaged in Belgium."[3]

That action got Coke's attention and it quickly responded. In Belgium, a "created in-house" newspaper ad offered an apology. Coke's CEO, M. Douglas Ivester, known for an extremely hands-on management style, finally got on a plane to Brussels to take charge. His first words were: "My apologies to the consumers of Belgium. I should have spoken to you earlier." Soon similar ads appeared in France and Poland with Ivester saying, "I want to reassure our consumers, customers and governments in Europe that the Coca-Cola company is taking all necessary steps."[4]

What caused the problem? Coke placed the blame on a batch of defective carbon dioxide in its Antwerp plant, as well as on a fungicide in Dunkirk, France, that may have rubbed off wooden pallets onto the soda cans. Others suspect that maybe errors were committed in the selection of plants or the dosage of extracts in the Coke concentrate. But months later the blame still is unsure . . . there is no evidence linking the illness to the product.[5]

FIGURE 12.7   Coca-Cola's Poor Crisis Response (Concluded)

What is sure is that Coca-Cola bungled its crisis management. It was slow to address the issue, insisting that no real problems existed. An apology was belated. Coke also failed to read the social fears. Belgium had just come off a devastating dioxin-contaminated food scare with pig farmers. European government agencies were cautiously trying to protect their reputations as watchdogs. Many fear Coke got caught in the middle. But one analyst also placed the blame on Ivester. "CEOs are still regarded as the ultimate face, voice and guardian of the enterprise. No other substitute can stand for the 'real thing'—the CEO."[6] Ball agrees with this: "The golden rules of crisis management are to get the message across that you are acting, to do it swiftly and to be seen to be transparent. Coca-Cola seems to have failed on almost all these points."[7] Perhaps the stock market and Coke's board of directors agreed. M. Douglas Ivester stunned employees and investors in early December 1999 by resigning.

1. Kathleen V. Schmidt, "Coke's Crisis," *Marketing News*, September 27, 1999, p. 1.
2. Ibid, p. 2.
3. Steve Ball, "Coke Pays the Price of a Mis-handled Crisis," *Marketing*, June 24, 1999, p. 15.
4. Ibid.
5. Branden Michener and Betsy McKay, "EU Criticizes Coke's Explanation of Contaminated-Drinks Scare." *Dow Jones Business News*, august 17, 1999.
6. Nikhil Deogun, "Coke's Public-Relations Fiasco in Europe Tests CEO," *Wall Street Journal Europe*, June 18, 1999, p. 5.
7. Leslie Gaines-Ross, "CEO Driving Lessons," *Advertising Age*, June 28, 1999, p. 34.

do not know at all. Help all members of the organization involved in the crisis know the kinds of information that fall into each category. Some of the members will be working with the press, some with the public, and others with the regulatory agencies that have a legitimate right to information.

In relation to the media, the designated company spokesperson should tell the press only as much as the firm wants the press to know, without being evasive or untruthful. How to fill white space or dead air is the media's problem, not the spokesperson's. Too many representatives keep talking well beyond the point at which they should quit, simply because they think it is their obligation to fill the airtime.

Opposite to the proactive approach is the reactive approach. Here, as Intel and Exxon did, the company takes a wait-and-see stance before making a statement. This often backfires because the lack of communication excites the already news-hungry media. In this age of media activism, a reactive approach combined with a defensive communication posture is seen as an indication of guilt. The proactive approach is more likely to be perceived as a sign of honesty.

Step Five: Practice and Revise the Plan

Practice the Plan Writing the CMP is not an easy task. Consequently, an organization that has a plan in place may be tempted to rest, wait, and hope the crisis never hits. But unless the plan is practiced it is like having a football team that has never trained.

On July 21, 1998, the town of Dearborn, Michigan, found out how important it is to practice for a disaster. In 1980 a severe storm left the town devastated for almost 15 days. But in the mid-1990s Dearborn city officials and private industry designed a disaster recovery process. After 18 months of preparation they conducted one of the largest mock disaster efforts ever held in the United States. More than 25,000 people participated in the two-day event. Providentially, the timing was perfect. When the 1998 storm hit, it killed three people and did more than $20 million in property damage. Afterward, community officials were quick to note that the training helped emergency personnel and public and private security respond in a coordinated and effective manner that minimized confusion and brought the crisis to a speedy end.[31]

Revise the Plan The useful life of a crisis plan is three or four years. Restructuring, new personnel (including spokespeople and organizational leaders), and new goals make updating necessary. Every three years the plan should be given a major revision, and human resources and operations departments should review it yearly.

James E. Lukaszewski, past chairman of the Public Relations Society of America, lists five most important crisis communication plan updating procedures. While all are useful and encourage a contingent thinking mentality, the first and last items should be continual.

- Ongoing preparation with annual simulations. An untested plan is an unworkable plan.
- Sharing critical crisis communication experience case studies.
- Useful right way/wrong way video-based, situation-specific refresher programs.
- Interpreting and packaging as case studies other organizations' crises in terms of how your organization might respond if faced with a similar difficulty.
- Crisis prevention/exposure management processes as an ongoing threat-reduction activity.[32]

SUMMARY

This chapter has examined a need that every organization has—managing crises. A crisis is any event or activity that can bring harm and danger to the organization and its people. Communication needs are at the heart of all organizational crises. This chapter started with the case of the Intel Corporation's big crisis in 1994. Intel successfully managed its crisis, although it was financially costly. The chapter then related the events from the Intel case to the typical organizational world.

As an advanced business communication student, you will likely be involved in an organizational crisis some day. By knowing what to expect and do, you can help your organization survive the crisis and maintain its image and strength.

Crises can be anticipated, prevented, controlled, and turned to an advantage. There are four stages that each crisis goes through: the hidden crisis, the pre-crisis, the actual crisis, and the post-crisis. An organization must attend to specific actions in each stage. All of these actions are tied into a crisis management process. This process has four steps: determining the crisis potential, developing appropriate crisis teams and centers, writing a crisis management plan, and developing a communication strategy. While each is important, developing the crisis management plan and a communication strategy are critical.

After you walk through the crisis management plan and communication strategy, we introduced a proactive process to follow in developing a working relationship with the media.

Applications

1. Brainstorm the possible crisis events that could occur at an organization where you are currently involved. This could be a company, school, church, or other organization. Choose one or two of the crisis events and try to determine the signs that will tell you when the crisis is in the hidden, pre-crisis, full, or post-crisis position.

2. Videotape an investigatory story from a news program like *20/20*, *60 Minutes*, or PBS's *Frontline*, that deals with an organizational crisis. With some of your classmates, analyze the program and discuss how successful or unsuccessful the organization was in managing its crisis.

3. Consider your job and your company in relation to potential crisis situations. Make a list of questions that you could be asked should that crisis occur.

4. Consider an organization that you have worked for or are familiar with. Work through a hypothetical crisis management plan that you think could apply to that company. This does not have to be detailed. After you have drafted it, present it to management for their consideration. In many instances you will be presenting information that they have never considered.

DISCUSSION QUESTIONS

1. Discuss the subtle differences that may exist with crises in the hidden, pre-crisis, or full state.
2. Discuss the full ramifications of the crisis definition given in this chapter as it relates to an organization to which you belong.
3. What additional "mind-sets" that impede crisis management can you come up with?
4. Think of a recent national or local organizational crisis that you observed through the media. Use the four-step crisis management process to describe how well the organization was prepared for and then managed the crisis.
5. Compare and contrast the many ways that organizations have managed crises in the past. What are some of the factors that contribute to both success and failure?

NOTES

1. John Markoff, "Flaw Undermines Accuracy of Pentium Chip," *New York Times*, November 24, 1994, p. D5; Aaron Zitner, "Sorry, Wrong Number," *Boston Globe,* November 24, 1994, p. 78.
2. Dean Takahashi, "Intel's Chip-on Shoulder Stance Draws Flames on Internet," *Dallas Morning News*, December 13, 1994, p. 4D.
3. Zitner, "Sorry, Wrong Number," p. 78.
4. Walter S. Mossberg, "Intel Isn't Serving Millions Who Bought Its Pentium Campaign," *Wall Street Journal*, December 15, 1994, p. B1.
5. Ibid.
6. Bart Ziegler and Don Clark, "Computer Giants' War Over Flaw in Pentium Jolts the PC Industry," *Wall Street Journal*, December 13, 1994, p. A8.
7. Ibid.
8. Bruce Horovitz, "Intel Needs Damage Control," *USA Today*, December 13, 1994, p. 3B.
9. Richard B. Schmitt, "Flurry of Lawsuits Filed Against Intel Over Pentium Flaw," *Wall Street Journal*, December 16, 1994, p. B8; Laurie Flynn, "A New York Banker Sees Pentium Problems," *New York Times*, December 19, 1994, p. D1–2.
10. Intel apology letter, *USA Today*, December 21, 1994, p. 9A.
11. Pentium's 1994 Annual Report to Stockholders, Internet: intel.com/intel/finance/annual/letter/index.html, p. 1.
12. James Kim, "Intel Puts Chips on the Table," *USA Today*, December 21, 1994, p. B1.
13. Takahashi, p. 4D.
14. "Crisis Definitions," Institute for Crisis Management, December 11, 1999, Internet: www.crisisexperts.com/crisisdef_main.htm.
15. Eva Sohlman, "Natural Catastrophes Spawn Surge in Disaster Studies," Reuters News Bureau, September 27, 1999. http://dailynews.yahoo.com/h/nm/19990927/sc/environment_disaster_1.html.
16. Roger Martin, "Small Business: Communications Plan Calms a Crisis," *Detroit News,* February 5, 1996, p 1.
17. Steven Fink, *Crisis Management,* Amacom—American Management Association, New York, 1986.
18. Intel's 1994 Annual Report to Stockholders, p. 1.
19. "Defining Crisis Management," Panact: Panaction Response International Guidelines, January 19, 1996, Internet: http://www.panact.com/crisis.html, p. 2.
20. Phil Mann, "Prepare for Crisis Before Crisis," *Plastic News,* August 23, 1999, p. 10.
21. Clarke L. Caywood and Kurt P. Stocker, "The Ultimate Crisis Plan," *Crisis Response*, Visible Ink Press, Detroit, 1993, pp. 413–427.
22. Lawrence Barton, *Crisis in Organizations*, South-Western, Cincinnati, 1993, p. 37.
23. Phil Whitesell, "Crisis Communications Guidelines," Barron & Whitesell, Public Relations/Marketing, Charlotte NC from Internet: http://web.sunbelt.net/pr/profile.htm, 1996. p. 5–1.
24. "Placing the Proper Figure Behind the Podium in Times of Crisis," *PR News*, August 30, 1999, p. 1.
25. Whitesell, p. 5–1.
26. Pam Sherborne, "Communication Critical in Crisis," *Amusement Business*, October 4, 1999, p. 30.
27. Chris Welles, "Exxon's Future: What Has Larry Rawl Wrought?" *Business Week*, April 2, 1990, p. 76.
28. James E. Lukaszewski, "Managing Bad News in America," *Vital Speeches of the Day*, July 1, 1990, pp. 568–573.
29. Terry Maxon, "Weighing the Financial Fallout of

Speaking Out," *Dallas Morning News*, January 14, 1996, p. 1H.

30. Thomas Petzinger, Jr., "When Disaster Comes, Public Relations Men Won't Be Far Behind," *Wall Street Journal*, August 23, 1979, p. 1.

31. Peter M. Locke, "Staying Calm Before the Storm," *Security Management*, October 1, 1999, p. 59.

32. James E. Lukaszewski, "Keeping Your Crisis Communication Management Plans Current," April–June 1994. Internet: www.e911.com/exacts/EAO14.html.

′13′

Media Management

While most of the communication skills of business executives are used within the business community, social issues and crises often require executives to communicate with the public through the media. Learning to work quickly and efficiently with the news media, whether the situation is positive or negative, is the mark of an effective organization's communication management program. Both the print and broadcast media have considerable power. However, a 1997 poll by the Center for Media and Public Affairs revealed that 86 percent of all Americans receive most of their information from local television news shows, 80 percent use national shows, and 77 percent use newspapers.[1]

Businesses have traditionally mistrusted the various media. But the dramatic increase in business reporting by the media and a continuing effort by business to initiate reports during the past two decades have forced many companies to improve their ability to use the media to their advantage. The relatively recent phenomenon of the major crisis, such as product tampering, has also emphasized the importance of a business/media relationship. Yet surprisingly, many upper-level executives still find themselves ill prepared to meet with and talk to the press under any condition.

We want you to feel comfortable with media representatives and to be ready when your call from a reporter arrives. This chapter is designed to get you ready by examining how organizations communicate with media personnel. The chapter is divided into two parts. First we will describe how companies use press releases to gain attention for their personnel, products, and business, and also to answer questions dealing with crises. Second, we will give you important steps that will help you prepare for face-to-face meetings with media representatives.

INVITING MEDIA RESPONSE: THE PRESS RELEASE

One of the best ways to attract the media is to understand the types of material that editors use in noncrisis times. Companies always want to obtain media coverage that promotes their personnel, products, policies, and programs. But the media seek only current and genuine *news* about executive changes, emergencies, litigation, and key issues. Editors are especially desirous of covering unfavorable issues or subjects embarrassing to a company. Given these two apparently different objectives, how does your company get its good news to the media and minimize the damage that bad news may represent? The answer is—the press release.

While the press release is a standard public relations tool, it is effective only when prepared, delivered, and used properly. Journalists can obtain news from around the world in an instant thanks to the Internet. This means that all large multinational companies need to have a global communications awareness.[2] While most press releases are handled by a company's public relations office, you as a manager should be familiar with the format and character of releases. You may be required to supply copy for such a release, prepare your own release, or respond to the media after they have received a release that someone else has mailed. Writing a good press release is the first step toward making your organization proactive in its media approach.

Rules to Follow in Preparing Press Releases

The eight rules that follow will give you an overview of what to include in a press release.

Present Sufficient News Andrea Brooks, real estate columnist for the *New York Times*, gives the following insider's view of press releases. While she tries to read every release that she receives, the reading is often only a scan. "I know within 30 seconds if it's worth reading in depth." The biggest problem that she finds in releases is the lack of sufficient information. "I think the more information you give the better off you are. Journalists like to write stories, and to do that they need information." The less work the editor has in making follow-up calls or in changing copy, the better your chance of getting your release published.[3]

The News Must Be Real News Reporters are interested in news, not in reading an advertisement for your business or products. What makes for real news? Generally news is something that is different or unusual. This is one reason why bad news always finds an open ear with the media. Commercial airplanes fly thousands of trips a day. That is not news. When an airplane crashes, that is truly news. According to Beard and Dalton, a manager has to work hard to find real news in ordinary information.

> . . . [you] have to search hard for a fresh angle that will give your story the proper appeal or "spin." This can be done by focusing on things like market share data, price comparisons, an outstanding statistic, or other numbers that play up the uniqueness, size, or quality of your company or product(s). . . . Any of these types

of things may be considered newsworthy, although it all really boils down to the timing and perceived value of such pronouncements.[4]

The News Must Have a Local Interest If there is no hometown angle or local discussion of a headquarters, plant, dealership, or other interest, the release will not be used. The media's need for local information is critical because international, national, and regional coverage is usually obtained by wire and syndicated services.[5] Of course, some of your company's news may affect the financial market both locally and internationally.

Use the Direct Message Approach As your high school English teacher told you, a good news article discusses the who, what, why, when, where, and how. A good press release answers those questions as briefly as possible in the body of the copy. Apply the same direct message approach that was discussed in Chapter 5. That approach called for leading with the most positive information and then following with the next most positive information and the next most positive, and so on, until the message is complete.

In Chapter 12 we described the crisis that Coca-Cola had in Belgium in the summer of 1999. Figure 13.1 shows the contents of the press release issued by Coke upon determination of the cause of contamination. This release uses the first five rules. Coke starts with a direct approach in the first paragraph, and supports that rational in the remainder of the release.

Other general rules are to use active, energetic verbs while avoiding adjectives. Never use words not used in everyday conversation. Avoid long, drawn out sentence structure. Sentences should be short and definite and have no more than one thought contained in each. The same rules also apply to paragraphs. They should not be longer than two or three sentences and, similar to the sentence, should carry the same idea or thought process. The point is to make it as easy as possible for the reader to understand and comprehend.

Avoid Buzz Words, Acronyms, and Jargon Bear in mind that reporters write about a variety of topics; they are usually generalists. Avoiding company or industry jargon and technical talk will help them understand your news quickly. For example, doctors addressing both patients and the media automatically use medical terms that are common to their trade, yet uncommon to a layperson. Putting those terms into plain language helps in communicating the real content. Examples are *angina* (chest pain or pressure); *glottis* (opening between the vocal cords); *hidrosis* (sweating); *migrainous cranial neuralgia* (a cluster headache or a variation of migraine headache); *otitis* (ear infection); and *septicemia* (blood poisoning).[6]

Include All Required Mechanical Elements Reporters look for several specific mechanical elements in a press release. To better ensure that your release will be used, include all these elements.

At the top of the press release, place the name and phone and fax number(s) of a

FIGURE 13.1   **Press Release by Coca-Cola Company**

**STATEMENT OF THE COCA-COLA COMPANY
REGARDING QUALITY ISSUES IN BELGIUM**

ATLANTA, June 15, 1999—The Coca-Cola Company has determined the cause of
two separate quality issues which have arisen in Belgium in the last week. These
issues caused health-related concerns, which prompted the Belgian health minister
to take precautionary measures. After thorough investigation, no health or safety
issues were found. Both issues are confined to the Belgian market, and these quality matters do not relate to products produced in other parts of the world.

The specifics on both issues:

The first issue affected the taste of bottles filled in the Antwerp bottling facility. The
bottling process includes filling bottles with the soft drink itself and combining with
carbon dioxide (which creates the bubbles in soft drinks). Independent laboratory
testing has shown that the cause of the off-taste in the bottled product was carbon
dioxide. That carbon dioxide was replaced and all bottles with off-taste have been
removed from the market. This issue affects the taste of the soft drinks only. The off-
taste bottled product from the Antwerp plant was in production for a limited period
of time and quickly replaced.

The second issue involves an external odor on some canned products. In the case
of the Belgian distribution system, a substance used in wood treatment has
caused an offensive odor on the outside bottom of the can. Independent analysis
determined the product is safe. The Company, in conjunction with its bottling
partner in Belgium, is taking all necessary steps to eliminate this offensive odor.

The Company continues to work closely with the Belgian Health Ministry in
addressing these issues to assure the safety and quality of our products for
Belgian consumers, in order to obtain final clearance for sales of the products in
the Belgian market.

# # #

contact person(s) in case more information is needed. The press release should also have the date of release and any restrictions on when the notice can be made public. If, for example, you are announcing a new product, but do not want that information to be made public until April 10, include the restriction, "for release after April 10." This type of restriction is called an *embargo*. If there are no date restrictions, mark the release "for immediate release."

Occasionally a publication will break an embargo. In that instance other publications may do the same. If your material is time sensitive, hold the release until the day that you want it released, and then fax it.

Headlines and subheads are technically optional. Editors prefer headlines—at least at the top of the page so that they can tell at a glance what the story is about. However, since most editors prefer to write their own headline, begin the press release about one-third of the way down the first page to give the editor room to create his or her own.

At the end of the press release, let the editor know you're finished by centering and typing "###," which signifies *the end*. If your release is more than one page in length, add the word *more* or *continued* at the bottom of each page that is not the last page. A *slug line,* which is a one- or two-word title that summarizes the subject, should be added to the top of each page after the first page.

Most editors like to see a press release typed and double-spaced on standard letter-size paper. It is preferable to use your company's letterhead to lend credibility and professionalism. Leave 1- to 1½-inch margins on the sides for the editor to use in placing notes or in editing.

The Appearance Must Be Flawless The appearance of the press release is critical. Editors and other readers rely on their first impression. If the appearance is not exactly as the editor prescribes, the first line will not be read. Just as with a résumé, if there is one spelling error, grammatical error, or untidy element, the chances of being successful are almost nothing. The document must be flawless.

Customize Your Release to Different Media Instead of sending a standard release to each media representative, consider customizing it to meet each representative's specific needs and format. A news magazine looks for an entirely different story than does the *Wall Street Journal* or a trade publication. Normally the major changes will occur in a rewriting of the first paragraph. Wayne Green—founder and publisher of some 27 magazines, including *Byte* and *CD Review*—indicates that he would have encouraged his employees to make three versions of the press release critiques in Figure 13.2, one each for the retail, music, and publishing industries.[7]

A Critique of a Press Release

The example in Figure 13.2 comes from a story in *Inc.* magazine. The release was issued by an employee of Green's company, an $8 million magazine and music distributorship in Hancock, New Hampshire. The critique is Green's view of the release.[8]

FIGURE 13.2   **Critique of a Press Release**

WGE PUBLISHING

Forest Road   Hancock, NH 03449-0278   603-525-4201   FAX: 603-525-4423

Contact Grace Cohen at:
1-800-722-7785

For Immediate Release:

<u>Publisher</u> <u>Introduces</u> <u>Custom</u> <u>Music</u> <u>Magazine</u> <u>Rack</u> <u>For</u> <u>Retailers</u>

CD REVIEW Magazine is introducing their new "Eight Pocket Rack Program" at SCES. The attractive, custom-designed spinner is a new way for the retailers to sell music and entertainment magazines. The rack creates maximum impact while using a minimal, 1½ square feet of floor space, and is free to retailers participating in the program. Retail outlets will be able to choose from a wide variety of magazines, customizing the mix of their particular demographics. Some of the titles available include, *CD REVIEW, Details, Option, Musician, Electronic Musician, Ear, Country Music, Spin,* and *Jazziz.*

Additional benefits, other than customizing product mix, include one-step billing, and an affidavit program to simplify credits. Billing for all eight publications will be handled with a single statement by *CD REVIEW's* parent company, WGE Publishing. Instead of returning unsold issues for credit, retailers will attest to the number of remaining copies by affidavit. Title allotment will be monitored to maintain highest possible sales for the retail outlet. This procedure will cut the time stores usually spend processing returns to almost nothing. Retailers will make a full 40% on each magazine sold, with an absolute minimum effort.

For additional information, please contact Retail Circulation Manager Phil Martus at 1-800-722-7785.

FIGURE 13.2   Critique of a Press Release (Concluded)

USE YOUR OWN LETTERHEAD
"If you use a public relations agency, supply it with your company's letterhead. If editors have to call an agency first, they might not bother calling at all."

FORMAT NOTES
"There's no date here. A press release should always be dated. You want to give editors a sense of timeliness and urgency and also let them know when to call to do a follow-up."

MAKE SURE YOUR CONTACT PEOPLE ARE INFORMED AND HELPFUL
"The name at the top of the release should be the person you want contacted. This should be someone who is fully informed about every aspect of your product or service and who will drop everything to get the editors what they need for their story angle. Names mentioned within the body of the copy, like Phil Martus's at the bottom, are those people you hope will be quoted or mentioned if your story gets into print—they are not intended to be primary contacts. However, editors may decide to dial them directly, so make sure whoever is named in the release has a file of information at his or her fingertips and is authorized to answer questions."

MAKE SURE IT'S NEWS
"Mistake! This headline simply trumpets the company's achievement. It should read like a news item and give the editor a story hook. I would rewrite the headline this way: New Concept in Magazine and Music Distribution Introduced. It never hurts to use the word *new*. This way the editor has to read on to find out about 'the concept'."

EMPHASIZE BENEFITS
"Don't tell me about the features of a product or service, tell me about the benefits. This is the most common mistake in public relations. You want the copy to get right into how easy the new product is to use or what problem it solves for the magazine's or newspaper's audience. That is what's newsworthy. It is also more difficult to write than simply listing a product's features."

KEEP TO THE POINT
"Don't try to cover the world in a press release. It's a coup for WGE that these magazines have signed on, but it's not critical to the story. I'd just say, 'eight other magazines.' If editors want to know which magazines, they can call. As a rule, try to keep product and company names to a minimum. Don't worry, if an article gets written, your company will get mentioned by virtue of the fact that it's the source of the news."

MAKE SURE IT'S ACCURATE
"This isn't even true. We aren't using affidavits, and WGE isn't doing the billing. We changed our strategy, but in the rush the writer wasn't informed. It sounds obvious, but never let a press release go out unless you're sure the facts are straight."

DON'T BURY THE LEAD
"These points are big news, but they're in the last few sentences. That's known in journalism as 'burying the lead.' This gets right to how easy the product is to use and how profitable it is. That's the kind of important, useful information you should deliver up front."

Use the Internet to Your Advantage

Today businesses post their press releases on the Internet as soon as they are written. Having that source as a place where reporters, stockholders, and the general public can learn about you has been tremendously cost-effective. Figures 13.3 and 13.4 are two examples of a business, Hewlett-Packard (HP), presenting exciting news to the public and the media. The election of Carly Fiorina as HP's new CEO demonstrated that the so-called glass ceiling for women was being shattered in a previously male dominated industry. Figure 13.3 was short and to the point. Issued at the time Fiorina accepted the post, July 19, it presented the most critical news. The announcement was of interest around the globe. The release quickly stated the essentials. Notice too that links to other information were available. Figure 13.4 was issued after the HP board of directors voted to approve Fiorina. While that release also stated the essentials of the appointment, it gave general financial news about the company . . . enough so that even a novice reporter could write a good story.

Video Press Releases

In the last few years the press release has taken on a new look. Today many corporations use videos to replace the paper releases that they once sent. Perhaps you and your organization will want to consider the possibility of using video. In the past, videos were used largely to provide information to employees about their company. Today they are also used for community relations, investor relations, crisis communication, environmental public relations, and other proactive types of communications.[9]

Corporations are increasing their use of video news releases (or VNRs) because they realize that their message can then be viewed by many who would never read it in a newspaper or magazine. There is also an advantage for the television stations. VNRs provide stations with video material that is produced like a news story and can be aired as part of a local newscast. On slow news days, a VNR is often used to fill the news gap. To accomplish this, however, it must be of the highest quality.

Companies that distribute VNRs regularly have learned that they must invest heavily in the process. A quality video must be produced, and it must be camouflaged to look like a television news feature. Its purpose is the same as that of all public relations and marketing communications. It must deliver a controlled client message to a targeted audience.

A question of ethics arises because many VNRs that are furnished to stations have more relevant information and are more professionally produced than any material that the station can produce locally. Consumer activist Ralph Nader decries the VNR: "It generates deception. . . . It generates homogeneity. It generates centralized manipulation. It pollutes the diversity and independent production of news." For this reason he and others demand that TV stations identify VNRs by superimposing a title saying "sponsored source."[10]

Your company might consider producing a VNR to announce a new product that is unlike any other on the market, to illuminate an issue or fact that is making news, or to counter negative publicity. The VNR can be prerecorded, or it can be a press conference or teleconference that is carried live and sent by satellite to a television station.

FIGURE 13.3   **Hewlett-Packard Press Release Announcing New CEO**

HP.com Home	HP Products	HP Services & Support	Buy HP

Feature Story

HP Names Carly Fiorina President and CEO

SEARCH

ASSISTANCE

Feature Story Archive

Feature Story Feedback

President of Lucent's $20+ Billion Global Service Provider Business is Dynamic Technology Leader with Proven Track Record of Growing Large Businesses

Hackborn, HP Veteran and Industry Innovator, to become Non-Executive Chairman at Year-End Upon Retirement of Platt

PALO ALTO, Calif., July 19, 1999 -- Hewlett-Packard Company (NYSE: HWP) today announced that Carleton (Carly) S. Fiorina has been named president and chief executive officer, succeeding Lewis E. Platt, who previously announced his intention to retire. Fiorina also will join the HP board of directors.

Fiorina was president of Lucent Technologies' Global Service Provider Business, Lucent's largest and fastest-growing division, with more than $20 billion in annual revenue.

Platt, 58, will remain chairman until year-end, by which time HP's computing and imaging businesses are expected to be independent of its measurement businesses. Upon Platt's retirement, Dec. 31, 1999, Richard (Dick) A. Hackborn, 60, a former HP executive and a current member of the board of directors, has agreed to become non-executive chairman.

➡ Go to *A Proven Track Record*

➡ Go to *A Seamless Transition*

➡ Go to *About Carly Fiorina*

➡ Go to *About Lew Platt*

➡ Go to *About Dick Hackborn*

➡ Go to *About HP*

Source: Reprinted by permission of Hewlett-Packard Company.

FIGURE 13.4   **Hewlett-Packard Dividend Press Release**

| HP.com Home | HP Products | HP Services & Support | Buy HP |

News Releases

SEARCH
ASSISTANCE
About HP HOME

Recent Releases
Financial Releases
News Release Archives

HP Declares Regular Dividend, Elects Fiorina to HP Board

Palo Alto, California. July 23, 1999

The board of directors of Hewlett-Packard Company (NYSE: HWP) today announced a regular dividend of 16 cents per share on the company's common stock. The dividend, the fourth in HP's 1999 fiscal year, is payable on Oct. 13, 1999, to shareholders of record as of Sept 22, 1999. As of April 30, 1999, the end of the second quarter of the fiscal year, HP had approximately 1.05 billion shares of common stock outstanding.

Fiorina Elected to Board

In a separate action, the board elected Carleton (Carly) S. Fiorina, HP's new president and chief executive officer, to the company's board of directors. (See announcement dated July 19.)

"The HP board was unanimous in its selection of Carly as HP's new president and CEO, and I am delighted to welcome her to the board," said Lewis E. Platt, HP chairman. "I look forward to partnering with Carly prior to Dick Hackborn's taking on the role of non-executive chairman next year. Doing so will ensure a smooth handoff of responsibilities at this turning point in HP's history."

HP previously announced that Platt, 58, will remain chairman until year-end, by which time HP's computing and imaging businesses are expected to be independent of its measurement businesses. Upon Platt's retirement, Dec. 31, 1999, Richard (Dick) A. Hackborn, 60, a former HP executive and a current member of the board of directors, has agreed to become non-executive chairman.

About HP

FIGURE 13.4   **Hewlett-Packard Dividend Press Release (Concluded)**

Hewlett-Packard Company -- a leading global provider of computing and imaging solutions and services for business and home -- is focused on capitalizing on the opportunities of the Internet and the proliferation of electronic services.

HP had computer-related revenue of $39.5 billion in its 1998 fiscal year. HP plans to launch a new company consisting of its industry-leading test-and-measurement, semiconductor products, chemical-analysis and medical businesses. These businesses represented $7.6 billion of HP's total revenue in fiscal 1998. With leading positions in multiple market segments, this technology-based company will focus on opportunities such as communications and life sciences.

HP has 123,000 employees worldwide and had total revenue of $47.1 billion in its 1998 fiscal year. Information about HP, its products and the company's Year 2000 program can be found on the World Wide Web at http://www.hp.com.

Current and historical financial information now is available at HP's Investor Information site at

Note: HP press releases are archived on this Web site for historical purposes. Information in the releases is accurate at the time of release. However, product specifications and availability, promotions, prices, relationships, contact numbers and other specific information may change over time. Some information about product pricing and availability may be limited to specific geographic areas and may differ in other areas. Information as stated in the release may or may not be in effect after the date on the release.

In addition, the press releases may contain statements that are forward-looking. These statements are based on current expectations as of the date of a particular release. Actual results may differ materially from those projected because of a number of risks and uncertainties, including those detailed from time to time in HP's reports filed with the Securities and Exchange Commission. Click here to review these   that could cause results to differ materially from those in any such forward-looking statements.

MAKE THE BEST USE OF A PRESS CONFERENCE

While it is apparent that press releases are a critical tool to use in an organization's relationship with the media, press conferences are also important. The crisis management plan described the attention that should go into equipping a room where a press conference will be held. The following ideas should be considered in making sure that the conference takes place at the right time and in the right way. Later in this chapter we will go into depth on the proper communication method that you should consider using if you are the designated spokesperson for the conference.

Determine Whether a Press Conference Is Necessary

News conferences are required when a disaster or crisis has occurred. This is a time when the media will ask questions and seek answers that they can use in getting stories to their audiences. If you are tempted to call a conference merely to make an announcement that can go into a press release, don't call the conference. If the media receive little worthwhile news they will likely hold a negative impression of your organization.

Pick the Right Location

Ideally, your organization will have the space for a conference room and it will be equipped with many of the items described in the crisis management plan. But the crisis may dictate that a conference be held in a local motel room or other off-site location. Avoid sites close to the disaster because scenes of the events can add negative impact to your positive words.

Choose the Right Time

As we have seen in previous examples, it is important that an organization communicate immediately when a crisis occurs. Often, a conference must be called just a short time after the event happens. While the sooner the better is the norm, make sure that you have ample time to get all the necessary information and also time to prepare for the conference questions.

Proper timing also refers to the time of day. Realize that each medium has story deadlines. One expert says that the 10 A.M. conference is such a popular time that all conferences often cannot be covered. He suggests 1 P.M. "It leaves plenty of time for the morning paper reporters, and you make evening drive (4 to 6 P.M.) on the radio."[11]

Be Prepared

Being interviewed by the media can be very intimidating, much more so than merely giving a speech. There is a great amount of preparation that must go into the typical press conference interview. Take the time to prepare. It will be to your advantage.

Some Final Thoughts

The following list offers some additional items that need to be considered. Attention to these can help make your conference a success.

- Provide a conducive atmosphere for the media. Consider having chairs, tables, pads, pencils, electrical outlets, telephone lines, typewriters, and microphones available.
- Prepare statements and handouts in advance—consider press releases, fact

sheets, photos, typical questions and answers, biographies, product samples, and a glossary of technical terms.

- Pay attention to who is invited. Typically all media should be notified.
- Arrange for supporting people, such as experts, to be available.
- Prepare supporting visual aids. Have backup equipment and supplies, such as bulbs, available.
- Keep the conference concise and short. Don't hold the press longer than necessary.
- Follow up by telephone with those media not in attendance. Get answers to those present who asked questions requiring research.

MEDIA INTERVIEWS

You may feel nervous and uncomfortable in delivering a planned business presentation. Imagine having a reporter arrive during an unexpected company emergency and, while holding a microphone in front of your face, say, "What does your company plan to do about this?" In many ways, today's manager has to expect the unexpected. While most graduates will not be expected to respond to interviews early in their careers, most will eventually participate in both print and broadcast interviews.

The first part of this section will explain how you should *preview the circumstances* of the interview before it begins. Second, we will lead you through the steps of *preparing* for the interview. Third, we will give reasons to *orally practice* for your interview. Fourth, we will address five *performance techniques to use* in the interview. Fifth, we will present 15 items that should be asked and answered as *post-interview evaluation questions*.

Preview the Circumstances

Before you ever agree to a media interview, assure yourself that you really want to be interviewed and that you will carry a positive mental attitude into the interview. This section prescribes five things that you should investigate prior to preparing for your interview.

Determine the Reason for the Interview Before you meet with the reporter, check out the reason for the meeting and decide whether you are the right person for the interview. Ego sometimes takes over when some executives receive a call from the press. While many would willingly dismiss the opportunity to give a speech, these same individuals often imagine themselves a star with their pictures on television or the front page of the paper. Be sure that the interview will be in your company's and your best interest. Do not let your ego damage your corporate career.

If you receive an unexpected call, make a quick excuse and do some checking before you respond. First, learn as much as you can about the reporter. What types of stories does he or she cover? What is the typical interviewing style? What are the potential reasons for the call? What are the expectations of the medium? It may not be possible to get answers to all these questions, given the usual short time frame, but try.

If the reason for the call is included in the invitation, then ask some additional questions. Is a response from you and your company necessary or appropriate? Are you the correct person to be involved? Do any company policies impinge on what you can say? An executive producer for CBS News said,

> If you cannot speak to the subject with interest and conviction, you ought not to. . . . Choose someone else in your organization who is articulate and knowledgeable.[12]

Anticipate Media Appearances If a crisis like those discussed in Chapter 12 has occurred, or if your company has a statement to make to the public, as shown in Figures 13.3 and 13.4, you may be the spokesperson selected. If you have anticipated a possible media appearance, you can respond quickly.[13]

Avoid a Negative Mind-Set Some managers seek any excuse to avoid talking to reporters. They are on the other extreme from the ego star; you should avoid this position, too. Your experience is indeed likely to be negative if you hold mental impressions such as "I've made it up the management ladder this far without going before a TV camera, so why should I risk my neck now?" or "I've never met a reporter who didn't try to crucify me with biased questions." Once you are "burned" by the media, the quick urge to respond disappears.

Jim Lehrer, host of the PBS's popular *The News Hour with Jim Lehrer,* cautions against taking the negative approach. He has said,

> the most serious thing that can hurt an interview is for the person who is being interviewed to think that, because a reporter asks a certain question, the reporter necessarily supports that position.[14]

While negative stories sometimes run, and inaccuracies do occur, most are the result of either a reporter's ignorance about the subject matter or time pressure in doing the interview and assembling the story. Build a positive mind-set that regards the reporter as a person who has a job to do with a deadline to meet and who wants to get all the facts. This gives you a wonderful opportunity to do your homework and supply the reporter with information that is clearly organized and presented in a polished and professional way.

Recognize Your Rights By recognizing your rights in relation to the media, you can avoid the negative mind-set and develop a positive media initiative. Gordon Andrew, a New York public relations consultant, lists several rights that a manager should remember.[15]

You have a right to check a reporter's credentials, to know the reasons for a requested interview, and to be told the nature of the questions you will be asked. You are not required to answer questions on the spot regardless of a tight time frame the reporter may have. In fact, delaying an answer until you can call back later often gives you the time needed to assemble your thoughts.

You have a right not to discuss certain information that might be sensitive to you or your company's interests. If the reporter asks a hypothetical question, you are not required to answer it. You also have the right "to reject a reporter's facts figures, and terminology." All of this must be done, however, calmly and with self-control.

You have a right to have your viewpoint fairly represented in an interview. This does not mean free advertising for you or your company. It merely means that you are protected from a reporter's verbal abuse.

You have a right to establish attribution rules with a reporter before the interview. Such an agreement needs to be made in advance because if you tell a reporter your comments are off the record *after* you have made them, he or she is not obligated to ignore them. Four standard agreements are normally used:

> *On the record* means that everything said may be used. *Not for attribution* means [your] statements will be attributed to a general source, such as "a company spokesperson." *Background* means that information will be used but not attributed. *Off the record* means that nothing said may be published; the interview is a means of briefing a reporter on a topic or situation.[16]

According to the public relations firm of Barron & Whitesell, an organization's crisis management plan should contain a media policy that spells out precisely the areas of a company that must be protected. Some companies by their very nature must protect proprietary information. Others need to restrict media access to certain parts of a plant or building because of dangerous working conditions or security requirements. Make sure that you and your employees understand company policy before critical events occur.

Develop a Media Initiative First, consult with the corporate communications or public relations department of your firm. Since these groups carefully develop media policies and strategies, they may give you some words of advice, help you prepare, and especially, help you parallel your statements with those of other company employees.

Second, develop a proactive attitude and prepare yourself to meet with the media. Familiarize yourself with the media facilities before you ever get in front of the camera: take guided tours of the press room or studio and join in live audience situations to get a feel for the way interviewers work in media situations.

Third, remember that you need not become buddies with the interviewers, but you should become more media conscious. Develop contacts with editors and reporters. Your public relations office can supply the names of contacts. In addition, you can develop your own list by telephoning or writing media offices. Building good relations with these individuals can help you for many years. Editorial directors will generally welcome your ideas for possible stories, and while they may not agree with your position, they will certainly benefit from your input. By having a media network in place, you can respond to both the positive and negative interviews. One reporter describes what occurs when the media initiative is missing.

> We find that most people who have something positive to say don't approach us at that point, but wait until something negative develops. Then when we reach them, they're in a position of defending themselves.[17]

With media contacts in place, you will find yourself less defensive and more eager to be interviewed.

Jim Lehrer comments on how a positive media relationship helped Goodyear bridge the gap between itself and the media when a potential health hazard in the manufacturing of a vinyl chloride monomer was detected in the company's Niagara Falls, New York, plant. "I think Goodyear set a tremendous precedent in its handling of this situation. Goodyear's public relations people were on the phone saying, 'This is what happened.' . . . And everytime we called Goodyear, they told us the good and the bad. . . . They answered every question we had. It was the first experience like that we've had in a long time."[18]

If you have gone from asking questions about the interviewer to developing a media initiative, you are now ready to enter the preparation phase.

Prepare for the Interview

Being anxious about an interview is normal, but there are positive ways to minimize the nervousness. Make a decision at the outset to be honest and to speak from your heart. Some interviewees ask a variety of questions about the reporter, develop their positive mind-set, and then go immediately into the interview performance. The majority of those interviews are disastrous. Instead, the wise interviewee will spend considerable time preparing for the interview. Good preparation always reaps good results.

There are five steps to good preparation: analyzing your audience, organizing your thoughts, anticipating topics and questions, developing your responses, and being aware of additional concerns. The five steps are, in essence, the same as those used for good preparation of both written materials and oral presentations, which were described in earlier chapters.

Analyze Your Dual Audience One of the first steps in preparing for a speech or business presentation is to analyze your audience. The same holds true for a media interview, but here you have a dual audience: the reporter and the public. Learn as much as you can about the person who will interview you. If you learn your reporter is not very pleasant, concentrate on how excited you are about the news you have to convey and how excited the reporter will be after you convey the information. Mary Munter, a communications professor at the Amos Tuck School at Dartmouth College, shares some sound words of advice for this preparation stage:

> Consider, first, reporters in general. Most of them are serious, hard-working professionals, just like you. Their job is to find newsworthy stories that will interest their audience. They are under time pressure to meet deadlines, commercial pressures to increase advertising revenues, and competitive pressures to scoop their rivals. They must compress what you say to fit space or airtime. They want to come up with something arousing and engaging.
>
> Consider also the individual reporters. What do they know about you? What do you represent to them? How do they perceive your expertise? What do you know about their age, their training, and background? What are their opinions and interests? What are they likely to agree with? To disagree with? Are they expert

business reporters or general reporters for whom you may have to simplify and define terms?

Next, consider your readers or listeners. Who are they? Middle America watching a general talk show or specialists reading a technical journal? What do they know about you, your topic, and your relationship to your topic? Once you have established their level of expertise, be sure to talk in terms they will understand.[19]

Realize an important difference between print and broadcast media. Newspaper and magazine reporters work on specific story lines and seek creditable sources for factual information. While they may have short-term deadlines (that evening for the next morning's newspaper edition), they often work on major stories for several days. In the latter situation, you often have more flexibility to get additional information to a reporter following the interview.

Broadcast media offer more immediate communication, where the public will first see and hear management talking about an event. Reporters who cover fast-breaking stories sometimes talk to whomever they can obtain for an interview. In emergency situations they arrive fast, cover as much territory as they can, and leave quickly to have their material on the next major newscast. While they may return for more material, you probably do not have much flexibility in establishing interviews at later times. If you, as an interviewee, are traveling to a radio or television station for an interview, you will probably find the personnel a little easier to work with, time frames more flexible, and the pressures not as great.

Organize Your Thoughts Lewis Young, former editor-in-chief of *Business Week*, believes that effective media responses are not the result of a well-spoken person, but of much preparation.

> Before the annual meeting, the CEO will spend days rehearsing, answering hypothetical questions that his key staff people put to him. On the day of the meeting he appears knowledgeable, in control, deft, and impressive. I am amazed at how many CEO's just show up for an important media interview, even though the interviewer is far more skilled at asking questions than anybody who will be at the annual meeting.[20]

Once you have organized your words, consider the style that you will employ in delivering them. Some critics believe that style is more important than substance because television is primarily a visual medium. Jack Hilton, in his book *On Television*, contends that executives should remember four things before going on camera:

> (1) very few viewers will remember their names; (2) virtually all will remember their affiliation; (3) few will remember a single point they make; (4) all viewers will decide promptly whether they like them or not.[21]

The key point to remember is that the person who is prepared and in control, not the one who tries to wing it, will leave the most positive impression.

Anticipate the Topics and Questions How do you prepare for an interview? After you have analyzed your audience, begin thinking of the possible topics of discussion and questions you might be asked. You can request a list of questions in advance from the reporter; however, you probably will not receive them. Many reporters work on such a tight time schedule that they prepare the questions while driving to your interview. Most reporters will tell you the general topics only, fearing that further disclosure might produce a dull, canned interview. You should be able to anticipate key questions, especially if the discussion is about an emergency situation. Brainstorm with your staff or colleagues. Let them play devil's advocate and help you decide on the most likely questions and the best responses. And keep in mind that any questions you are dreading will surely be asked. *Be prepared for the most difficult question and any others you can anticipate.*

As you prepare to develop your thoughts into responses, consider how you can get your most positive message across. The Canadian Psychological Association makes five recommendations to its members on preparation of media interviews:

Make the Story New   Your comments should add something new to the listener's knowledge base. Whether it is a new perspective on a familiar topic, or the results of a new study, your audience will be more interested if the material is new or stated in a new way.

Make the Information Interesting   Word your ideas in ways that will make your audience want to hear more. Deliver your words with excitement.

Make the Story Relevant   Word your material so that the listeners can relate to it. Develop it to fit their lives.

Make the Story Understandable   Avoid the jargon. Word your material so that an eight-year-old could comprehend the facts. Remember, the person on the street or at home watching the news is not your peer. The media love sound bites and good quotes. To help the potential listener clearly understand your message, list your points before you speak. "I would like to make three points before I take your questions." State the number as each point is spoken. Numbering the points also makes it hard for a reporter to interject other questions until you are finished. Editors also have a harder time cutting out important material.

Make the Story Memorable   Frame your ideas with a metaphor or story. Stick to one or two key points for ease of memory.[22]

Develop Your Responses   Starting with the toughest questions you can imagine, write down simple one-, two-, or three-point responses. Later, in private or with the aid of your colleagues, practice these responses orally.[23] For now, make sure the responses fit into a 30-second time frame. For the press or television this will consist of about 75 words. Radio newscasters love one-sentence statements. Television deals essentially in headline news. A business story that rates a column in a major newspaper may command only a single sentence on a national television network evening news program.

Brundage points out the danger of top management talking too long for a broadcast. "Top management is standing there talking and talking about the incident, and the reporter is standing there with the mike thinking about having to go back and stand in line at the editing booth to edit the interview. . . . That is where there is a possibility to be taken out of context. Top management should be taught ahead of time to talk in 10- or 15-second sound bites for radio and television."[24]

There are six important things to remember in developing the response you anticipate using.

Lead with the Most Important News Business people typically present ideas by leading up to the news. But the media require a different approach. Both the press and broadcast media reorganize what you say in order to meet their needs. You can help the reporter by stating your most important piece of news first. People will remember it better if you lead with the news and then support your statement. And if editors need to cut words because of time or space restrictions, your main ideas, which would have come at the end of your statement, will not be on the cutting room floor. Chester Burger, a media expert, believes that most businesspeople have an inability to get across what they want to say to the media:

> They fail to make the points they wanted to make, and then they blame the reporter. Usually, it is their own fault. They have been playing what is called the "ping-pong game." The reporter asks a question; they answer it. He asks another; they answer it. Back and forth the ball bounces but the executive does not know how to squeeze in what he regards as his important points.[25]

Follow the most important news with strong and substantial facts. Cite specific times and dates. Learn names and their correct pronunciation. While the use of statistics can be effective, they should be simple, easy to understand, and of interest to the listener. Remember, the message prepared for the eye of the reader will strike the ear of the listener in an entirely different way. To say, "70 percent of the public approves of our policy and 15 percent doesn't care," is much better than to say, "70 percent like the policy, and this consists of 80 percent metroplex dwellers and 20 percent rural residents. The 80 percent metroplex supporters are made up of 60 percent women and 40 percent men, with 30 percent being children." While the latter may be true, few readers or listeners will take the time to figure it out. You will also sound dull and disorganized.

Use the Public Position When developing answers, build in responses to the public's needs, desires, and wants. Tell them how they will benefit from a plan. Tell them also that they are free from danger. If plenty of time is available, you may even want to supply film footage of some specific examples.

Word Your Message with Care Aim your message at about a tenth-grade level for understandability. Avoid technical jargon and organizational acronyms and buzz words.

Use Positive Words During interviews, especially those involving an emergency or disaster, examine each word for its truth and for its implied meaning. Every company and industry has a list of positive and negative words. With your colleagues, decide which ones you should use and which you should avoid. For example:

Positive Words	Negative Words
Safety	Negligence
Care	Death
Concern	Accidents
Employment opportunities	Discrimination
Long record of service	Fired
Excellent relations	Catastrophe
Equal opportunities	Layoffs
Satisfactory	Probably could happen . . .

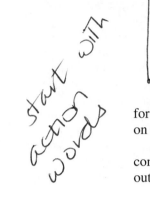

start with action words

The point is not to pick euphemisms, or words that substitute an inoffensive term for one considered offensively explicit, but to reword your thoughts by focusing first on the positive.

The usage becomes clearer when put into sentence form. Instead of saying, "The company does not consider this problem to be its fault. We have had four years without a serious accident," say:

> Our safety record is excellent. We constantly monitor the process and this has resulted in four years of accident-free work. Since we are concerned for safety, we were immediately on top of the situation when it occurred.

Build Strong Transitions and Bridges You can help media editors by flagging your most important points. This can be done with phrases like, "The main thing I would like the public to remember is . . ."

Bridging is also a way to move a reporter off a controversial question by reiterating key messages. Bridging is done when you briefly answer a question and then form a bridge to an idea you wish to make:

> Yes, I can see where that could be a possible way of chemical exposure. However, in the fifteen years that our company has produced this and other dangerous but necessary chemicals, I am happy to say that the EPA has praised our handling procedures.

Another example of bridging is:

> As your paper reported two weeks ago, in our Dallas facility 96 percent of our employees rated our safety procedures as either *excellent* or *superior*. In fact, we have received the national chemical makers' award for "Safety First" during the last five years.

Other bridge statements include "Let's consider the larger issue here . . ."; "Before I get to that, let me fill you in on . . ."; and even, "I don't know about that, but I do know . . ." But remember, states Karen Berg of CommCore Communication Strategies, "once you cross the bridge, blow it up. You don't go back over it or you will pay a toll."[26]

Develop a Plan for Handling the Tough and Tricky Questions Building a healthy respect for the media takes place as you recognize their power to influence.

While you should avoid developing an adversarial impression of journalists, recognize that their questions can sometimes be tough or tricky. This is all the more reason for you to practice with someone who asks you possible questions.

As you practice with your colleagues, have them throw you very difficult questions. There are six types of tough and tricky questions. Learn how to respond in a cool and professional manner, but not defensively. Responding to these questions is not easy, yet you can master the process with practice.

1. **False questions** are sometimes asked. Correct the false statement before you respond with an answer. Try to paraphrase the question a second time during the answer.

    Reporter: The XYZ Company has a track record for manufacturing faulty products. Does the recall of your product surprise you?

    Interviewee: XYZ Company's manufacturing record is the most solid in the industry. None of our products are faulty. We issued this recall to correct a potential problem that had been discovered and to assure our customers that they will continue to receive quality products.

2. **The loaded preface** is another problem encountered in questioning. If you miss the reporter's opening, you may find that in the final media presentation, you appear to agree with something you are completely against.

    Reporter: Mr. Jones, your company is under investigation for cost overruns and bribery in regard to one of your government contracts. Can you tell us, Mr. Jones, how are minority workers treated in your organization?

    The respondent in this example should fear that the reporter is really trying to do a story on cost overruns and bribery. The respondent should either dissect the question and handle both parts, or deny the loaded preface and then construct a bridge to the answer he wants to give.

3. **The "what if" question** asks about something that has not happened yet. For example, "I know it hasn't been announced officially yet, but what will you do if you are asked to serve as the next executive VP?" Unless you want this information public, refuse to answer the question, make the irrelevance clear, and bridge to your ideas.

4. **The irrelevant question** asks you about material totally unrelated to the subject of the interview. For example, you are being interviewed on several legal matters pertaining to your business, and you are asked about your views on legalizing marijuana. Again, refuse to answer the question, make the irrelevance clear, and bridge to your ideas.

5. **False relationship** is another unfair question which assumes that because an event precedes an outcome, it necessarily caused it. For example, "Metro's stock went down $3.65 as soon as you were appointed to the board. Would you care to comment on this?" Beware of the false causal relationship and don't let it go unchallenged.

6. **Popular prejudice** is shown when the reporter appeals to the popular idea, rather than to the specific situation. For example, "Don't you think it's un-American for Congress to agree to grain sales to the Soviets?" Interviewees should try to define or challenge words like *un-American* before moving on to their own points about the subject:

Interviewee: I challenge what you consider to be un-American in this bill, when it provides 2,500 jobs for American citizens who desperately need them. But the real point I want to make is . . .

Turn a Negative Question into a Positive Answer If an interviewer makes a statement or phrases a question in the negative, never answer it or repeat it. Many people have done so, only to watch themselves say the negative question on camera after it has been edited. Instead, rephrase the question into a positive statement and then add your answer.

Years ago, Carl A. Gerstacker, then chairman of Dow Chemical Company, went on the *Today* show to discuss an explosive, six-letter word: napalm. Gerstacker, using a carefully designed game plan, told Hugh Downs that yes, his company produced napalm for its country during a time of war but that it was now out of the napalm business. Gerstacker then artfully began to answer the questions by talking about the *life-saving* products his company manufactured, including measles vaccine. Michael Klepper, whose firm trains executives for encounters with the media, and who provided the game plan for Gerstacker, recalls: "He was able to turn the napalm issue around by concentrating on his company's lifesaving products, which he presented in a very favorable light. Downs finally told him: 'Gee, I didn't know chemical companies were also pharmaceutical companies.' "[27]

Techniques for turning negative questions into positive answers are displayed in the following examples.

Question: Isn't it true that your driver, Joe Firestone, who was involved in this fatal collision, was cited for driving while intoxicated in 1979, and at that time was in a very serious accident?

Answer: Joe Firestone came to work for us on February 15, 1982. He, like all our other drivers, was carefully checked and passed the Truckers' Safety Standards Test, administered by the County Vehicle Department, with a score of 89 out of 100. Since that date, he has worked steadily and up to today has had an accident-free record with our firm. Among our 65 steady drivers, he has been among the 90 percent with no reportable accident of record since June 1, 1983.

Question: Although your bank has some 35 vice presidents, how do you explain the fact that only 5 are women?

Answer: All appointments to vice president are made on the basis of board selection and an examination. Every opening is posted and any employee of the appropriate grade is eligible to apply. In the past three years, we have had nine openings for vice president. Ten women took the examination and two were appointed. In the same period 30 men took the examination and seven were appointed. Thus 20 percent of the women taking the exam were appointed and 23 percent of the men.

I would say that we had a similar level of treatment and equality in both cases, wouldn't you?[28]

Be Aware of Additional Concerns The final step in good interview preparation is to refresh your mind with some additional concerns.

Do Not Respond to Unchecked Statistics If an interviewer throws statistics at you that you do not know or have not checked out, do not answer the question. Answer instead, "I'm sorry, but I do not have those figures; they are presently being calculated. I will, however, obtain them and follow up with you this afternoon," or "I have not seen the figures."

Do Not Use a "No Comment" Comment At one time "no comment" meant simply that there was no news to share. Today when a company spokesperson uses the words it implies that there is something to hide. If you cannot answer, say why you can't answer. Saying "no comment" makes you sound evasive and secretive and it creates suspicion.[29] Say instead, "I am sorry, but we cannot make additional comments on the event until next of kin has been notified."

As the Intel case in Chapter 12 displayed, a crisis situation requires interaction with the media. You cannot hide behind a "no comment" statement and expect the media to go away. They will report the story with or without your help. If you have facts which they need, share them quickly and help resolve the issue quickly.[30]

Do Not Answer with a Simple "Yes" or "No" After uttering easy yes or no answers, you may be surprised to find them cut and pasted onto another question by an unscrupulous newsperson. Phrase your response in a yes or no context but expand it to at least a full sentence. For example, a reporter asks, "Will the merger be completed before the first of the month?" The answer may be yes, but you are better off saying, "Both sides are working hard to complete the merger by the month's end. I believe it will be accomplished by the first of next month."

Be Careful about Stating Your Personal Opinions In most instances, you are representing the company. Do not cross the line and state your position as the company's position unless you clearly know your positions are the same and you have been authorized to make that position public.

Tell Them If You Do Not Know the Answer If you are asked a question for which you have absolutely no answer, tell them, "I do not know the answer to that question at this time. I will, however, find the answer." If you know where the answer can be found, direct them to it.

Never Stonewall a Position Since the Watergate era of the 1970s, both the news industry and the public have become very suspicious of stonewalling tactics. Issues that are unequivocally denied, or statements such as, "I will be exonerated," seem to be offered by individuals who have not thought of good answers. The statements are often mere smoke screens.

Avoid Talking Off the Record In many cases, statements made off the record have a way of appearing in the middle of news stories. A good dictum is to say nothing that you do not wish to see in print, and follow this advice:

> The press will assume you are on the record: that is, that they have the right to quote and report what was said and done to attribute statements to you. A rule that some spokespersons learn the hard way is that you are not off the record just by saying so. If reporters agree to an off the record comment, they are saying they will not report it. If you go off the record in a press conference, all reporters must agree, not just the one asking questions.[31]

Record Your Own Interview You may want to take your own small tape recorder to your interview. Taping the session will not only be good for use in future practice sessions but also to check reporter's quotes against actual statements that you made. Be open with the reporter about wanting to make the recording. Most reporters will not care. If one does object, you should not only ask why but reconsider whether you want to go ahead with the interview.

Always Tell the Truth The press and public accept the fact that you may not tell the whole truth for many reasons, including competition. But if you resort to lying, even once, the press, the public, and your colleagues will never again trust your credibility.[32] The good news about bad news is that you can get it out of the way and prevent a continuing story. More often than not, lies lead to continuing probes and additional stories. A vice president of Hygrade Food Products, a meat processor that had to handle rumors that razor blades were in the company's hot dogs, makes this statement about lying: "One thing the experience taught me is that total candor can convert a reporter from a hard-nosed muckraker into a sympathetic company supporter. . . . Not only does honesty pay, it beats having to remember what you told the media yesterday."[33]

As we have seen in this section on preparation, wise interviewees spend a considerable amount of time preparing for the interview. They follow the steps of analyzing all audiences, organizing their thoughts, anticipating possible topics and questions, developing their responses, and being aware of various additional concerns.

Practice

There is a big difference between knowing the material and being able to talk about it. After you go through the preparation stages thoroughly, you may feel rather smug about the answers you have devised. Beware; crafty reporters have reduced many overconfident executives to bumbling, incoherent, embarrassed interviewees. Just watch *60 Minutes* or *20/20* to get the picture.

To protect yourself from disgrace and to turn in a magnificent performance requires practicing your material. Spend considerable time reading out loud the responses to all your anticipated questions. After you remember the material fairly well, turn your office into a mock studio and practice with your staff and colleagues. Have them ask you the questions in the style of a reporter, including their fast pace, vocal inflections, and nonverbal gestures. If you give the wrong answer, have them repeat the question. You should practice until you feel confident of your ability to meet and answer any question a reporter might ask, no matter how tough the question or abusive the reporter's style.

The practice process for interview questions and statements is almost identical to that described in the business presentation chapter.

Performance Techniques to Use

On the day of your interview the focus is on you—your statements, the issues you represent, and the image you create. You hope your preparation and practice time will pay off. If a print reporter interviews you, refer to the section on preparation earlier in this chapter. The following five ideas are primarily for television interviews.

Dress for the Occasion Pick comfortable clothing that reflects your profession. If you are warm blooded, choose cooler fabrics. Avoid dark colors: black and navy blue look black on television and they lose detail. Try grays, a lighter navy, and beiges. Avoid tweeds, large stripes, and bold patterns. Solid pastel colors are best for dresses. Whites can cause glare and make your face look dark. The best color shirts are off-white or light blue. Ties in muted colors are better than those with bright, large designs. According to Arnold Zenker, a media expert, "Your taste in clothing is your own business. But out-of-date, ill-fitting clothing creates an image that is out-of-date and unimpressive for an executive. Contemporary, professional clothing is a must for any television appearance."[34]

If you use makeup, be sure it has a powder base rather than oil, so your face will not be shiny. Keep jewelry to a minimum—wedding rings and watches are acceptable. Avoid any objects, such as rhinestones, that can reflect studio lights. Glasses can be another problem. Many people who wear them do not want their pictures taken with them on and will probably not want their television image to be one wearing glasses. But because the objects are so natural to the wearer, to be without them seems awkward, especially if the person cannot see properly. Glass lenses, on the other hand, can cause a reflection. If you appear regularly before the media, you may want to invest in a technique used by Preston Smith, a former governor of Texas. Smith felt uncomfortable without his glasses, but he grew tired of the glare they caused. He purchased a set of frames that matched his glasses and wore the frames, minus the glass, during his interviews.

Keep Your Cool As difficult as it may seem, you must maintain a totally calm appearance. Do a deep breathing exercise before meeting the reporter, or before the camera is turned on. This exercise requires that you exhale all the air out of your lungs and that you very slowly inhale through your nose. Doing this a couple of times helps to lower the anxiety and give you a greater sense of well being. If you are being interviewed during a live event, deep breathe again when there is a break for commercials. Look and act relaxed. Regardless of the turmoil in your stomach, never let the interviewer and audience suspect that you are not in control. Knowing your material and having practiced your comments is the first step in making this a reality. Second, work on maintaining the positive image of a professional executive that you have viewed so many times on television. If a reporter tries to provoke you or get you off balance, do not take it personally. Maintain your calm and unemotional manner. As Jim Lehrer says, "An executive who cannot hold his cool and who takes everything personally is a setup in an interview. I mean you're going to get to him."[35]

The classic example is when Bill Gates, in 1994, got mad and walked out of a network-televised interview with newscaster Connie Chung. For watchers, that established a negative image of Mr. Gates as a rich and arrogant person. The image, in fact, was hard to overcome as Gates testified in the 1998–1999 Microsoft antitrust case. Years later it was evident as Gates was interviewed by Barbara Walters that Gates had undergone extensive media training.[36]

Jack Hilton offers this tip for those who easily perspire. "Ideally, you should discipline yourself not to perspire. Practically, if you need to wipe your brow, do it with a forefinger, and discreetly wipe your forefinger with your handkerchief. The finger will make you look thoughtful."[37]

Be Ready for the Spontaneous Questions If you have done your preparation you will be ready to answer all the questions a reporter might have. But here is a trick to use for a spontaneous question that you were not expecting. Quickly bridge the question to a previous question or answer, or to a response that you wanted to make but were not given the opportunity. With your thought in mind, develop two or three quick statements that support or clarify your thought. Now state your ideas in a quick 30-second or one-minute response.

Let Your Body Talk A large percentage of our information about the world comes from nonverbal cues. In interviews, the nonverbal image is extremely important. Avoid defensive-looking body language. This can take the form of clenched fists, tightened facial expressions, crossed arms, or poor eye contact. Learn to relax your body, sit in a comfortable and professional manner, and wear a warm facial expression. Here are some nonverbal expressions that are important to remember:

- Use natural hand gestures to highlight your points.
- Maintain good eye contact with the interviewer.
- Stay alert physically, even when you are not talking.
- Lean forward slightly in your chair. Do not swivel about.
- Rest your hands naturally in your lap.[38]

Try to Ignore the Cameras The technicians and director will take the shots they want, and you should keep your attention focused on the interviewer. The exception to this guideline is when you want to directly address the television audience. At that point, look and talk directly into the camera lens that has the red light. Even when the light is off, continue to stay alert because another camera may be on you. Don't try to see yourself on the monitor. Often there is a time delay between the picture and your voice. This asynchrony can be very distracting and can cause you to lose your train of thought.[39] Have someone videotape your performance for your later viewing.

If you are delivering a prepared statement to the press, avoid reading your material. You can look at the notes from time to time, but leave the impression that you know precisely what you want to say. Likewise, if you are to use a TelePrompTer, distribute your eye contact from side to side or from one TelePrompter to another. Keep a light pleasant look on your face and a natural smile that you would give to an ordinary speech audience. While you are seeing words through the glass prompters, your audience is seeing only your image. Your facial expression should convey a very professional look.

Display Confidence in Your Voice Develop a professional sound. Ordinary conversational tones are the best. Keep a consistent volume and rate. Avoid letting your voice drop at the end of sentences. Also avoid displaying anger or high emotion. Maintaining an erect posture and good breath control while talking can help you through the rough spots. Remember, you are the expert.

If you are to use a microphone, ask for a microphone check before you start talking. This will help you determine how loud to talk. If you use a lavalier microphone (one attached to the lapel or tie), avoid coughing, crossing your arms, or slapping your chest. While you do not hear it, your audience will receive a big bang each time such actions occur. Assume that your microphone is always "live," even during cut-aways to commercials.

Post-Interview Evaluation Questions

Following each press or media interview, you should evaluate your performance. The information gathered will prove valuable as you prepare for future interviews. Talk through the following questions alone and with your staff and colleagues. Take careful notes; they will be helpful during the next preparation stage.

1. Prior to the interview, did you take the reporter for granted? If so, what was the result?
2. Did you assume that the reporter understood the issue? Did he or she? If not, what was the impact?
3. Did you anticipate that the reporter might oppose or support your position? Which position did he actually take?
4. Before the interview, were you prepared to defend your position through a fair and accurate rebuttal?
5. Did you start the interview by presenting your most important news?
6. Did you answer the questions directly and briefly, or did you occasionally get off track and get into too much depth?
7. Did you allow the reporter to get away from the point of the interview?
8. Did you find yourself answering questions that you knew nothing about?
9. Did you use positive instead of negative words?
10. Were you able to build bridges to your desired answers?
11. Was the reporter overt or covert in nature?
12. Were you familiar with your material?
13. Before the interview, did you feel reluctant, enthusiastic, or neutral about meeting the press?
14. Were you bothered by the studio lights, the use of the microphone, the clothing you wore, the heat, or your posture?
15. What specific things do you want to change before your next interview?

SUMMARY

Today every business manager needs to perfect his or her media management skills. These new and important skills complement what we have described in earlier chapters where we noted the importance of writing letters and reports, and making regular business presentations and public speeches. Increasingly, managers are drawn into writing press releases and in having to clearly and convincingly give press and media interviews. The first part of this chapter introduced you to a proactive process that you can follow in developing a working relationship with the media. This process involves constant communication, sending press releases, and holding press conferences. By using all of this material, the wise organization can avoid many crises and successfully work through those that are encountered.

The second part of the chapter focused on media interviews. At the moment you give an interview, you are the company. Both your individual credibility and the company image are on the line. With the proper work you can be a star.

Your success depends on five important steps: previewing, preparing, practicing, performing, and evaluating the interview. Before you can prepare for the interview you must know why an interview is needed and who will be interviewing you. Check the record and style of the reporter before you respond to an unsolicited call. If a crisis is involved, make sure you are the person who should really address the issue. If there is someone with more authority on or knowledge of the subject, let that individual give the interview. Once you agree to the interview, avoid developing a negative mind-set. Maintain a positive picture of how you will convey exciting and useful information. From that moment through the preparation stages you should have a "media initiative" that will help you discover the correct steps to take.

The preparation stage is more important than the actual interview. First, you should clearly understand both of your audiences: the interviewer and the public. Next, organize the thoughts and ideas you want to convey. With the help of your staff or colleagues, anticipate the topics and questions you might be asked, starting with the most difficult. From those questions, develop complete answers. Decide upon the most important news based on your organization's aims and your perception of the public's needs, desires, and wants, then lead with it. Word your message with care, avoiding jargon and employing positive words. Learn to build bridges from the questions asked by the interviewer to the statements that you wish to make. Develop a style for handling the tough questions. More important, learn how to turn negative questions into positive answers.

Before interviews, as before business presentations or public speeches, practice is extremely important. Knowing what you are going to say and saying it are two different things. Media interviews often require that you talk in 30-second statements and respond to tricky questions. This is foreign to the way we usually interact or speak. Spend ample time practicing it with your staff, colleagues, or friends. The results will be well worth it.

After successful preparation and practice, the real performance is less threatening. Dress appropriately for the occasion. Learn to keep your cool during the interview regardless of the circumstances or interviewer's style. Convince your interviewer and the audience of your credibility with a confident voice and effective body language.

After you read this chapter and before your press or media interview occurs, learn to observe the hundreds of people who are interviewed each day in the paper and on television. Be aware of what they do right and wrong. Learn from the worst and copy the best.

DISCUSSION QUESTIONS

1. Look at the examples of the press releases in this chapter. Now look at the material that describes what should go into a good press release. How do they compare?
2. Use an Internet search engine server and do a search for "Press Releases." Look at the different ways that an organization presents information about itself. Analyze the approaches in relation to the textbook.
3. Go to the library and obtain back issues of business periodicals. Look up two or three business leaders who have recently been in the headlines. Determine the factors that lead you to believe that they possessed either a negative or positive mind-set about the media. How did they perform in their media appearances?
4. Watch a televised news report after you read this chapter. Observe the segments where reporters are questioning an interviewee. Were the questions tough and tricky, or fair? How would you have planned for the interview if you had been the interviewee?
5. Compare television interviews on different channels (ABC, NBC, CBS, CNN, C-SPAN). How do the interviews compare and contrast?

Applications

1. Comb the business section of your local paper and find two or three articles about local companies. Construct a one-page press release for each company based on the material in the article. Be sure to follow the direct message approach.

2. Watch C-SPAN during the evening press conference broadcasts. Analyze a press conference by referring to the material in this chapter.

3. Compare and contrast the different ways a manager would prepare for a media interview as opposed to a standard business presentation.

4. Select someone who is being interviewed nationally on radio or television news. Make notes on the person's comments . . . especially direct quotes. In the days that follow look at print sources like newspapers (*New York Times*, *Wall Street Journal*, *USA Today*) and magazines (*Time*, *Newsweek*, *U.S. News & World Report*). How do the print articles compare in accuracy to what you saw and heard on radio or television?

5. Videotape your local nightly news. Examine it for segments that display reporters questioning individuals. Write down the questions that were asked and then write answers that you would have given had you been the interviewee. Afterward, replay the tape and compare your answers to those the interviewee gave.

6. Videotape an investigatory news program like *20/20*, *60 Minutes*, or *Dateline*. Select a segment where the reporter is playing an antagonistic role. Compare the reporter's questions and the interviewee's answers to those on pages 318–321. What do you find? How would you have answered the same questions differently? Be very specific.

NOTES

1. "What the People Want from the Press," *Center for Media and Public Affairs,* September 1977, p. 1, Internet: www.cmpa.com/archive/wdtpwftp.htm.

2. Sophie McKenzie, "Public Relations: Panic Situations," *Marketing Week*, November 19, 1998. p. 39.

3. Frank DiCostanzo, "What the Press Thinks of Press Releases," *Public Relations Quarterly*, Winter 1986, pp. 22–23.

4. Christel K. Beard and H. J. Dalton Jr., "The Power of Positive Press," *Sales & Marketing Management, January 1991,* p. 38.

5. Dick Elfenbein, "Business Journalists Say If It's Not Local, It's Trashed," *Public Relations Quarterly*, Summer 1986, p. 17.

6. "Helping Physicians Master the 'De-Jargonizing' Process," *Healthcare PR & Marketing News*, July 9, 1998, p.3.

7. Teri Lammers, "The Press-Release Primer," *Inc.,* August 1991, p. 36.

8. Ibid., pp. 34–36.

9. Adam Shell, "Reaching Out to the TV Generation," *Public Relations Journal,* November 1990, pp. 28–32.

10. Randell Rothenberg, "Promotional News: Videos Gain Support," *New York Times,* September 11, 1989.

11. James Harris, "Get the Most Out of a News Conference," *Public Relations Journal*, September 1986, p. 33.

12. William Hoffer, "You're on the Air," *Association Management*, September 1983, p. 93.

13. R. L. Dilensschneider and Richard C. Hyde, "Crisis Communication: Planning for the Unplanned," *Business Horizons,* January/February 1985, p. 36.

14. Lane Talburt, "How to Be Effective in a TV Interview," *Association Management*, April 1975, p. 31.

15. Gordon G. Andrew, "When a Reporter Calls," *Business Marketing*, April 1990, p. 71.

16. Beard and Dalton, "The Power of Positive Press," p. 40.

17. Talburt, "How to Be Effective," p. 34.

18. Ibid.

19. Mary Munter, "Managing Public Affairs: How to Conduct a Successful Media Interview," *California Management Review*, Summer 1983, p. 145.

20. Lewis Young, "What Business Media Expect from Corporations and Public Relations People," speech to National Conference of the Public Relations Society of America in Atlanta, Georgia, November 19, 1981.

21. Randall Poe, "Showtime for the CEO," *Across the Board,* December 1981, p. 47.

22. Joseph M. Byrne, Juanita M. Mureika, and James H. Newton, "Working with the Media: A Guide for Psychologists," Canadian Psychological Association, January 31, 1996, Internet: http://www.cycor.ca/psych/media.htm, pp. 2–3, 1996.

23. Diane Gage, "Media Interviews: Follow the Scout's Motto and Be Prepared," *San Diego Business Journal*, October 19, 1992, p. 16.

24. Pam Sherborne, "Communication in Crisis," *Amusement Business*, October 4, 1999, p. 33.

25. C. Burger, "How to Meet the Press," *Harvard Business Review*, July–August 1975, pp. 62–70.

26. "'Demystifying' the Interview: Media, Training Teaches Control Tactics," *PR News*, January 4, 1999, p. 3.

27. Poe, "Showtime for the CEO," p. 39.

28. Norman B. Sigband, "Coping Successfully with the Media," *Advanced Management Journal*, Winter 1985.

29. David Migdal, "Managing the Media," *Meetings and Conventions*, September 1991, p. 49.

30. Sandi Sonnenfeld, "Media Policy: What Media Policy?" *Harvard Business Review*, July–August 1994, p. 28.

31. John M. Penrose, Jr., "The Manager as Spokesperson for the Corporation: Handling the Press," in Louis DiGaetani (ed.), *The Handbook of Executive Communication,* Homewood, Illinois: Dow Jones–Irwin, 1986, p. 69.

32. Deidre Peterson, "No Comment? No Way! Tips for Successful Press Interviews," *Bank Marketing*, October 1990, p. 69.

33. Robert Levy, "Crisis Public Relations," *Duns Business Month,* August 1983, p. 50.

34. Talburt, "How to Be Effective," p. 33.

35. Ibid., p. 30.

36. Geoffrey James, "Stupid CEO Tricks," *MC Technology Marketing Intelligence*, December 1, 1999, p. 54.

37. Poe, "Showtime for the CEO," p. 47.

38. Byrne, Mureika, and Newton, "Working with the Media, p. 6.

39. Ibid.

P A R T   F O U R

Reporting
Case Analyses

′14′

Analyzing a Case and
Writing a Case Report

The first 13 chapters of this book have presented information designed to help you survive and succeed in your professional life once you leave the graduate program. The last two chapters of the book, Chapters 16 and 17, are designed to help you survive in the job market and obtain a job with your "dream" organization. This chapter and the next, Chapters 14 and 15, will help you survive a very important part of your graduate program: the case course.

The case method of teaching is popular in graduate business programs throughout the United States. Although schools of law have long used it and the Harvard Graduate School of Business made it a central instrument of its program in the 1920s, many MBAs find the case method to be a new and anxiety-producing experience.

In this chapter, you will learn the proper way to analyze and write a case report for any of the three different types of cases: the formal case, the case story, and the critical incident. To fully understand the case you are assigned, and to effectively analyze it, requires mastering a different learning style, overcoming the fear of writing and speaking, and developing your own personal system of analysis.

There is a proper four-step way to read a case. First, preview by looking at the basic outline of the case. Second, skim to identify the key issues. Third, read and reread the case to develop strategic notes. Fourth, scan the case again prior to the class discussion.

As you read a case, you should consider the four approaches to case analysis. Should your case be examined from an organization as-a-system approach? Would a behavioral perspective, which examines people within the organization, work better? Could a decision-making approach be employed? Would you be better off to use a strategy approach?

As you start your case analysis, you should use the six-step problem-solving model: (1) define the problem, (2) consider all relevant information and any underlying assumptions, (3) list all possible solutions to the problem, (4) select a solution and prepare to defend it, (5) determine the correct way to implement the solution, and (6) decide how you will communicate your decisions in your analysis.

This chapter will show you how to communicate your findings by way of a written report. Three organizational formats for the written report are examined: the suspense mode, the news-first mode, and the strategic issues format.

UNDERSTANDING THE CASE METHOD OF LEARNING

What Is the Case Method?

The case method applies the ancient Socratic technique of teaching people how to think and how to ask questions. It develops skills in diagnosing situations, defining problems, analyzing the sources and constraints of problems, developing alternative courses of action, and deciding on particular courses of action. The premise of the case method is that you are more likely to retain and use concepts learned through a guided discovery than you would through lectures and note taking.

Skill development distinguishes the case method from other teaching styles. Case courses pull together a broad array of the latest theories, concepts, or techniques of finance, accounting, management, or marketing, and present a general and useful way of thinking about, analyzing, and solving actual business problems. Along the way, you will discover your strengths and weaknesses in thinking and decision making, and you will refine your ability to take risks when faced with unknown outcomes. The case method helps you develop the skills necessary for becoming an effective manager.

Different Types of Cases

You will probably find at least three types of cases being used in your classes: the formal case, the case story, and the critical incident.

The Formal Case A formal case describes a simulated or real-life situation faced by management. It may deal with a specific problem experienced by one company or by an industry as a whole. Problems and events in the simulated situation are not identified as good and bad; the cases often involve complex financial data and can cover 15 or 20 pages. A single best solution may or may not exist, although you may apply some theories you have learned and arrive at what you consider to be the best answer.

The case might focus on issues such as: Should a franchise fast-food chain add a new food product? Should a company move from one location to another? Should a company diversify, merge, or acquire a competitor? What marketing strategy should a real estate firm use when the sales are down?

The Case Story The second type of case presentation, the case story, differs from the formal case in several ways. It is usually written, much like a news story, as a chronological history of a decision made by management. The outcome and an analysis of the decision is presented and little excess information is given. In this form of case presentation, management's answer may not be the best answer.

This type of case can be two or three pages long and usually follows the form of a good magazine or newspaper article that has a one- or two-point thesis and lots of narrative to describe actions taken by individuals or the company.

The Critical Incident The third type of case gives little background information and usually presents a situation where the impact is greater on the interpersonal relationships than on the organization itself. While the formal case often involves long-term, strategic decisions, the critical incident asks, "What should we do now?" and involves more immediate issues.

The opening paragraph of this type of case often throws you into the middle of a dilemma. For instance, a critical incident case might begin by saying, "A chemical manufacturing company has had an explosion at a local plant." The case, while short (two or three pages), gives many of the possible solutions that can be developed.

Overcoming the Difficulties of the Case Method

While the case method is often used in business schools, some people experience difficulties in learning a new style of both studying and responding. The following ideas should help you overcome any anxieties you may experience in learning by the case method.

Conquering a Different Learning Style The case method is well suited for individuals who like to deal with real-life situations. It is not as well suited for people who find it difficult to operate in an environment of ambiguity and uncertainty or who must have a final or correct solution to a problem.

If you find the case method uncomfortable, strive to transfer from the traditional learning process of teacher-to-student to a student-to-student mode. As your colleagues share their ideas and analyses, listen to them carefully and add up their thoughts in order to develop your own critical analytical abilities.

The case approach demands that you do extensive preparation outside the classroom. This preparation includes reading, note taking, conducting library research on data not given in the case or textbook, and organizing your thoughts into writing.

Overcoming the Fear of Writing and Speaking If you are timid about your ability to present your problem statements or solutions either on paper or orally, take heart. The remainder of this chapter will help you develop a method for reading and analyzing a case and then writing a case analysis. Chapter 15 will present ideas on how to effectively present an oral case analysis. Chapters 2 through 9 should be reviewed for ideas on writing improvement.

Developing Your Personal System of Case Analysis As you read the following pages and begin the process of case analysis, work on developing your personal system of thinking and decision making. Instead of merely getting by in the classroom, you will soon be enjoying the new method of learning. You will also find that learning how to think and analyze information will carry over into an effective personal analytical process that will help you long after you leave school.

READING A CASE PROPERLY

Every manager desires solutions to his or her business problems; but solutions can be found only through properly analyzing the problem. With the case method, a proper analysis can be conducted only after careful reading. Your main objectives in reading should be, as efficiently as possible, to cover the material thoroughly and glean the most significant points. Proper analysis generally requires at least two readings of each case. If you are unfamiliar with the case study method and anxious about how to properly analyze a case, you should probably count on several additional readings. Always assume that your instructor is an expert on each case and can respond to any questions or statements you may have.

There are four basic steps to properly reading a case: previewing, skimming, reading, and scanning. The first three should be done prior to writing your analysis or making an oral presentation in class. The last, scanning, should be done as you prepare to discuss the case in class. The early preparation pays off in allowing you to better remember the information and to feel confident of being able to discuss it.

Previewing

Previewing a case serves the same purpose as previewing a magazine article or a book. Your goal is to learn as much about the case as possible before actually reading it. Look at the title and subtitle. Does this information tell you anything about the focus you should have as you read the case? Examine the title and name of the author. Has your professor, another academician, or a practitioner in the business community authored the case? Size up the case by looking at each page and familiarizing yourself with the main headings and subheadings. Review the organizational pattern around which the information has been developed.

Most cases are divided into two parts: text and supporting exhibits. As you look through the text, highlight key names of individuals and businesses and any proper nouns that will give you valuable information needed to understand the case. As you look at the illustrations and exhibits, carefully note their context and the relevance of their information. In the previewing stage, resist the temptation to mark any items on the case. At this stage you are merely sizing up the case to determine how you are going to read and dissect it.

Skimming

Skimming involves previewing in greater detail. Avoid the desire to read each word and especially to underline or mark items in the text. As you skim, look for major ideas, issues, problems, and potential solutions—anything that will help you analyze the case. Your chief objective in the skimming phase is to determine the thesis or key problems or issues in the case. Often, this information is found at the beginning of the case. If it is not, search until you find it.

Reading

Now you are ready for your first reading of the case. Read at a comfortable pace and look for answers to questions, specific facts, or details that you will need in deciding on solutions. Resist underlining on the first reading, since it is time consuming and generally indicates you do not understand the information. You can save underlining for a second reading. In this way, you are less likely to highlight unimportant information. If absolutely necessary, make brief penciled notations to yourself. Later, erase the notes or make them bolder with ink. Some find the use of self-stick notes effective in marking observations made during the reading.

During your second reading, dissect and analyze the case from the standpoint of problems, major issues, and potential solutions. A case story or critical incident usually gives you only facts. Formal cases, on the other hand, contain extensive background material, but much of it provides no real clues to the solutions. While you may find the background information interesting, look for the key information that will benefit you in your analysis.

Scanning

After you have absorbed the main points in the case, scanning the highlights and your attached notes should be sufficient to refresh the information in your mind. Scanning allows you to review names and facts that are pertinent to the case.

As you read the case, look for the common elements that everyone examines, but also look for unexpected items that might give you an edge on cracking the case. These items might be actions of individuals, methods of recording financial data, or ways inventories are ordered or recorded. If you make a habit of looking for the unexpected, you may find the most significant elements that will improve your analysis of the case. Work on understanding the flow of information from beginning to end, the technical nature of elements as they are described, what characters say and do, and any discrepancies in their actions. Constantly ask yourself, "What is not being said here?"

Be sure to look for issues your instructor may have mentioned when assigning the case. How does the case fit into the flow of the subject matter of any other cases discussed thus far in the class? What comments or inferences did your instructor make about the company or major characters? Was his or her attitude critical or favorable? You may have to make inferences about your instructor at first, but as you work through cases during the semester, you will pick up on his or her philosophy. Finally, look at all aspects of the case; do not attempt to separate marketing considerations from accounting, finance, or management issues unless you have been instructed to do so. If you have done an adequate job of reading, the task of analyzing the case will be much simpler.

CASE ANALYSIS APPROACHES

Before you begin your analysis, determine the specific approach you will take toward the case. Four different approaches are often used and are discussed below.[1] An effective case analysis may focus on one of these approaches; most will involve two or more.

The Systems Approach

In the systems approach, organizations are viewed as systems engaged in the process of converting inputs into outputs. In this view you can often better see problems, opportunities, and actions if you can understand the components of a system and the ways in which those components relate to each other. In a manufacturing organization, for example, raw goods are purchased and converted into products that are sold to distributors and, ultimately, to consumers. Manufacturing, as a process, makes more sense from this systems view than from a view that sees it as merely an assembly-line procedure.

The Behavioral Approach

The behavioral approach focuses on the people within an organization and their behavior. The way individuals are managed within an organizational setting is often the best approach for an analysis. Ronstadt, however, encourages going beyond the ordinary elements:

> In addition, we should analyze how case protagonists relate to environments [that] are external to the organization. You should ask: what values, norms, and social structures do protagonists embody and bring to their organizations? How do these values relate to relevant organizational and technological factors that constitute internal or organizational environments?[2]

The Decision Approach

In using the decision approach, one or more decision-making theories or models are employed. The trick to using this approach is to apply the appropriate theory in the appropriate instance by making sure that you are answering the problem you have stated. Do not analyze numbers just for the sake of crunching numbers; make sure your analysis is relevant. Table 14.1 lists many tools that you will cover and employ in your advanced business program. Consider how each may help you examine your case; if any apply, use them in your analysis.

The Strategy Approach

The strategy approach is most often used with longer, formal cases and typically in business school policy courses. The learning objective of such courses is to help man-

TABLE 14.1	Decision-Making Tools

Financial Analysis

Financial Measures
Liquidity tests
Current ratio
Working capital

Turnover Ratios
Accounts payable turnover
Accounts receivable turnover
Inventory turnover
Cash turnover

Profitability Measures
Return on investment
Payback
Net present value
Internal rate of return

Other Ratios
Debt-equity ratio
Assets to sales ratio

Projection of Financial Statements
Profit and loss pro formas
Balance sheet pro formas
Cash flow pro formas

Cost–Revenue Analysis

Contribution analysis
Break-even analysis
Operating leverage
Relevant costs and benefits

Alternate Analysis

Process flow diagramming and capacity analysis
Decision tree diagramming and probability assessment

Industry and Market Analysis

Industry definition related to specific organizations:
    Organizations compared to other companies in the industry
    Characteristics and attitudes of buyers
    Market size projections
    Economic changes or markets
    Industry and business success criteria

agers develop strategic thinking abilities. Using the strategy approach, a manager would attempt to find a strategic fit between the goals and objectives of an organization, the external environment, the structure of the organization, and the resources needed to carry out the described strategy.

Such an environmental approach is a good place to ask, "What do we know about this organization?" and "What don't we know?" From the questions come answers regarding the organization's "present" *internal and external strengths and weaknesses*, and "future" *internal and external strengths and weaknesses*. The acronym SWOT is used to refer to this form of analysis.

To identify internal strengths and weaknesses you can assess "resources" (inputs), "present strategy" (process), and "performance" (outputs). Usually your case will have information on inputs such as salaries, supplier, the physical plant, and full-time equivalent personnel. Unfortunately, the cases usually do not give a clear idea of the organization's philosophy, core values, distinctive competencies, and culture.

Conduct the SWOT process by addressing each of the parts. **Strengths** are advantages like resources, market position, new products, professional staff, unique and creative aspects, and leadership expertise, upon which the organization can capitalize. Organizations always desire to build upon their strengths. **Weaknesses** are disadvantages that can hinder performance and goal achievement. For an organization it is often difficult to honestly identify weaknesses. At the same time, strengths are often exaggerated. In reality strengths and weaknesses are often similar and can mirror one another. An organization's greatest strength can also be its greatest weakness. **Opportunities** focus on the future. They are advantages that the organization should use wisely. Items that often surface here are technology, experienced personnel, or quality manufacturing. **Threats** are future events or happenings that can prevent success and cause difficulty. A good list here will allow you to minimize danger. Sometimes threats appear to be current weaknesses projected into the future.

Now that you have a better understanding of the case method, realize the importance of a proper reading process, and recognize several case analysis approaches, the job of analyzing a case will be easier.

ANALYZING THE CASE

Before you can write a case report, you must first analyze the case. Proper case analysis requires good decision-making skills, which usually follow a six-step process. Most of the cases in your management, marketing, finance, policy, and accounting courses will follow this six-step process:

Step 1 Define the case problem.
Step 2 Consider the relevant information and underlying assumptions.
Step 3 List the possible solutions to the problem.
Step 4 Select a solution and prepare to defend it.
Step 5 Decide how to implement the solution.
Step 6 Decide how to communicate your analysis.

Before you attempt an analysis of a "formal" case, like those that you will find in many of your classes, we encourage you to use the following primer. The EK&G case is a short, fictitious, even humorous case. But it will allow you to easily generate answers to the six steps above. Read it and write your own answers to each step. When you have finished, check your answers with those listed at the end of this chapter in Figure 14.1.

EK&G Case[3]

Founded in 1980 as a medical technology firm, EK&G Products spent its early years searching for "the right product" to manufacture. The two owners, Fred Eghart and

Irving Kleptow, were engineers from the medical technology field who believed that starting up their own firm could eventually fill the voids in the market left by the larger manufacturers.

In early 1982 the Pulsomatic was developed and tested on a limited basis. The Pulsomatic was a small box affixed to a stand, much like a gumball machine. After inserting a quarter in the machine, a customer would place his thumb in a small hole in the front of the unit. In 45 seconds, a small slip of paper would come out indicating the customer's pulse rate and also a fortune.

Eghart and Kleptow believed that a large market existed for this product. Supermarkets, restaurants, bars, and nursing homes would be ideal spots for the Pulsomatic. A marketing manager could be used to help distribute the product.

As production began, the costs of the Pulsomatic began to rise. Initial cost estimates had been around $175 per unit. But the fortune-telling logic unit (FTLU) was a specialty item that soon began to rise in price. Since the only manufacturers of FTLUs were in China, there was no way to insulate against price rises or currency fluctuations.

As the manufacturing costs exceeded $250 per unit, Eghart and Kleptow began to wonder if sufficient quantities of the unit could be produced in order to achieve economies in production. Production estimates showed that average costs per unit could be reduced to $200 if more than 1,000 units were produced each year. Since orders of the product totaled 1,000 after three months of marketing, it became apparent that the idea of hiring a marketing manager was well founded.

After screening a number of qualified MBA graduates, Eghart and Kleptow hired Hal Sigoin. Mr. Sigoin promptly increased the number of orders to 2,500 and production resumed.

Delivery began in June 1985, with ten units going out. The revenues from sales of the machine were split as follows: 25 percent to the business where each machine was located, and 75 percent to EK&G. Original estimates showed that revenues would average $150 per machine per month. This would mean that EK&G would recoup its costs in about two and one-half to three months. Over that same time, the host business would receive revenues of more than $100.

On the evening of August 1, 1985, Eghart and Kleptow poured champagne at their victory celebration. It looked as if the product would be a success, and they wanted to share this success with their staff of five dedicated employees.

When you finish reading this case, develop answers to analysis steps 1–5. After that, check your answers to the ones found in Figure 14.1, at the end of the chapter.

Now we will look at a more "formal" case. This case typifies many "formal" cases that you will find in your classes.

The New GM Assembly Plant [4]

In early 1980, General Motors (GM) was the largest industrial corporation in the United States. Their sales from the previous year were $66 billion and they had over 850,000 employees. But GM, along with the other auto makers, faced trouble. Trends toward tighter government regulations and foreign auto competition had produced low sales, production cutbacks, and widespread layoffs. GM's change strategy for staying competitive involved a $40 billion five-year capital investment program that would begin in that same year.

One phase of the program required that two existing Detroit manufacturing facilities, Cadillac Assembly and Fisher Body Fleetwood Plant, would be demolished and one state-of-the-art facility be constructed. GM did not care where the new plant was built (they were examining sites in both Detroit and in Midwestern states within the Sun Belt). The new plant had several needs, however. It must be close to suppliers to utilize the new just-in-time inventory methods, it required about 500 acres to allow for a new robotics system, and it had to be completed by mid-1981. GM estimated the cost of constructing the facility would be $500 million.

Immediately Detroit mayor Coleman Young started applying pressure for GM to remain in the greater Detroit area. Detroit had experienced many years of economic difficulties. Large firms had moved many to the suburbs and others out of the state. Unemployment at the time was 18 percent. The closing of the two plants would create a loss of 6,000 auto assembly jobs and thousands of other jobs in design, manufacturing, and sales. Because of business closings the structures in the inner city were decaying. The tax burden was high and the base was low. The inner city was 63 percent minority and high in elderly, disadvantaged, and poor.

As GM examined the Detroit area, only one site became a possibility. There were 300 acres in "Poletown" and an adjoining 165 acres in Hamtramck. The latter property presented no acquisition problems. Poletown was another story. The resident base consisted of first- and second-generation Polish descendants, mostly elderly and retired. They considered their homes to be their most valued asset.

General Motors agreed to the site in concept but threw the resident problem back to the city of Detroit, since officials were applying pressure on GM to remain in the area. The Detroit City Council, without consulting the Poletown residents, learned of the plot and formed the Poletown Neighborhood Council that immediately brought a lawsuit against the city of Detroit. They asserted that the eminent domain legislation was designed for public usage. They argued that the new plant constituted "private use" and not public. Further, the use of the law in such a way violated the Michigan Constitution and destroyed both the cultural and social environment of a community. The court voted 5–2 against Poletown.

While the suit cleared the way for General Motors, it left other problems. Poletown had 3,438 persons who would be displaced and 1,176 homes that would be demolished. GM estimated the following costs: $62 million to the Poletown residents for their property, $28 million for their relocation, $35 million for the home demolition, and $82 million for site preparation. The total cost would be $207 million.

Knowing that the Sun Belt states had offered large tax incentives, the city of Detroit made its proposal. It would find a way to cover the $207 million and would give a 50 percent tax abatement for 12 years, or $13.35 million per year. When capitalized at 12 percent interest, that would amount to $83 million.

Assume that you are in a decision-making position at General Motors. What would you encourage the company to do, and why?

The GM case is a short financial case story. The case analysis approaches used as examples for this case story combine the decision and strategy approaches. We will now work through the case by using the six-step analysis process.

Step 1: Define the Case Problem and Write a Problem Statement The philosopher John Dewey once stated that a problem well defined is half solved. Defining a problem is not simple, but once done, the definition logically leads the person doing an analysis toward the possible solutions. Is the company making a wise decision? Or are there options that will allow the company to be more efficient?

Start the GM case by listing the different problems or issues that you observe. Next, narrow the issues into a written problem statement. If you find that the statement is too vague as you proceed with the analysis, rewrite it.

Four significant problems are apparent in the GM case:

1. There is pressure from Detroit and the GM stakeholders (union, employees) to remain in the area.
2. Rebuilding in the Detroit area will be more costly than going to the Sun Belt, although the city and other groups will cover most of those costs.
3. There will be a high toll in human pain and the loss of ethnic identity associated with having to use the eminent domain law to remove the Poletown residents.
4. GM and Detroit may sustain a tarnished image due to treatment of Poletown residents.

After narrowing these issues, we recognize that the most significant problems in the GM case are pressure from Detroit and the local stakeholders to build on the Poletown site, and the pain and harm to be dealt on the Poletown residents. In fact, a dilemma is present because GM is being pressured from both sides. Whatever its decision, one side will be unhappy.

Step 2: Consider Relevant Information and Underlying Assumptions After defining the case problem, and before you list the possible solutions, consider the relevant information in the case and any underlying assumptions that can be made.

According to Rowe et al., there are several areas to consider in looking for relevant information:

- **Environmental and industry analysis.** An organization must determine what effect marketing dynamics, competitive factors, foreign competition, government regulations, product portfolio, and so forth will have on it. These factors should be stated in terms that affect the strategic options available to the firm.
- **Organizational analysis.** Organizational factors are crucial in determining an organization's ability to carry out proposed strategies and achieve effective performance. Approaches to alternative organization structures and functional integration are often key determinants of success. The effect of mergers on the culture and leadership of an organization are also important considerations.
- **Internal operations.** Operations form the basis for carrying out strategies that have been formulated. Greater emphasis is placed on the organization's ability to achieve high quality, high performance, and strategic control. Issues such as robotics, just-in-time manufacturing, computer applications,

motivation, culture, and human resource management increasingly determine the competitive advantage of an organization.

- **Resources.** Resources are the lifeblood of an organization. Investments, capacity, facilities, cash flow, return-on-investments (ROI), and the budgeting of strategic funds are considered by many to be the bottom line of strategy formulation. Financial analysis, revenue forecasts, and resource allocation, especially for R&D, are important aspects of analyzing cases to determine feasible strategies.[5]

Scan the case again to determine the significant facts and events. List these as statements. After you finish, review your list and outline the facts and events. In the GM case, several significant items can be listed.

1. GM was the largest industrial corporation in the United States, and was profitable.
2. GM, like the other auto manufacturers, faced pressures from increased government regulations and foreign competition.
3. A capital campaign called for two existing plants in the Detroit area to be demolished and a new plant built either in Detroit or another location.
4. The new plant would be designed around state-of-the-art techniques.
5. The city of Detroit was in economic difficulty, it did not want to lose the GM plant, and it applied pressure to GM to rebuild in the city.
6. One site in the greater Detroit area suited GM. Part of the site consisted of mostly retired and elderly Polish residents.
7. While the residents did not want to move, Detroit gave GM the power to receive the Poletown land through eminent domain.
8. While the cost of purchasing and preparing the Poletown property was more expensive than purchasing property in a Sun Belt location, the city of Detroit offered to cover the cost, and through tax incentives would even contribute more to GM than other communities.

With a good feel for the case and a listing of significant facts and events, you are ready to follow the systematic decision-making process.

Now consider the underlying assumptions in the case. Are your assumptions reasonable and realistic? Do your assumptions relate to decisions the company or key decision makers in the case are making as a result of their control? Or are the decisions related to uncertainty factors—factors that the company or managers do not control? Can you support the assumptions with information and facts found in the case? Make sure you distinguish between facts, inferences, and opinions.

In searching for assumptions, also distinguish between causes and effects, which are often related. For example, a retail organization is losing money (effect). One reason (cause) is that customers are no longer buying the company's product (effect). Careful examination shows that the product is of poor quality (cause). Yet the poor quality of the product (effect) is a direct result of management not spending research development dollars on updating the product (cause). Further searching shows that top management made a decision several months earlier to cut the R&D budget (effect) because of cost-cutting measures (cause).

In examining the GM case we can pull out several assumptions.

1. GM assumes no other site is available around Detroit.
2. Detroit assumes that keeping GM is critical to its economic well being.
3. Detroit assumes the tax dollars it will lose from the tax incentive package will be recouped from GM personnel and their spending.
4. GM and Detroit assume from the start that the Poletown residents are against selling their homes. In reality they may be for the idea if they are allowed to participate in the decision-making process.
5. Detroit and GM assume that the best problem-solving method in this case is the cost-benefit analysis.

It is evident that the list of assumptions is by no means exhaustive. Instead, it points to a seemingly endless string of questions that can be developed from a simple case. If other subject matters were considered (for example, accounting, finance, and management), the list would grow even longer. Remember as you are analyzing material to list it in a readily accessible form. Availability facilitates your writing of an analysis.

At this point you can also do a SWOT analysis of the case. Such an approach might give you the information found in Table 14.2.

TABLE 14.2   **SWOT Analysis**

Internal Assessment	External Assessment
Major Strengths - employee layoffs - market position - employee comfort	*Major Strengths* - largest U.S. corporation - market position - popular image
Major Weaknesses - too many employees - low sales - production cutbacks	*Major Weaknesses* -outdated facilities - distance from suppliers
Major Opportunitiess - state-of-art plant - just-in-time inventory - reduce jobs - tax incentive	*Major Opportunities* - move closer to suppliers - Poletown site
Major Threats - loss of creative employees - difficulty in learning new tasks - strikes - poor relationship with unions	*Major Threats* - government regulations - foreign competition - pressure from Detroit - increased unemployment - tarnished image - displacement of residents - public paying for tax incentives

Step 3: List Possible Solutions to the Problem There are at least three solutions to every problem, one of which is to do nothing. What are the possible solutions to the major problem you have identified? Alternative solutions for GM are:

1. It can agree to build its new plant on the Poletown site.
2. It can conduct a more extensive survey of the Detroit area to see if a comparable or more suitable site exists.
3. It can allow the Poletown residents to have an active voice in the decision-making process.
4. It can put its human and social responsibilities ahead of its profit maximization responsibilities.

As you identify solutions, consider the criteria that must be met in order to accomplish each solution. You should also list advantages and disadvantages to each. Do not predetermine the best solution at this point; it may cause you to ignore important contradictory information and will detract from your analysis. Also consider the pros and cons of each alternative solution. Weighing these against each other often logically guides you to the best solution.

Step 4: Select a Solution and Prepare to Defend It After analyzing the case in depth, you should be able to select the best solution. If you have analyzed the case carefully, you should know the likelihood of being able to achieve the selected option and what will be needed for implementation. "For example, it would be unrealistic to recommend expansion of a product line without a thorough knowledge of competitor strength, the resources required for the project, and the capability and willingness of the organization to pursue the project."[6]

In stating your solution, also include recommendations for correcting the problem. The points and recommendations should be made in short and concise form. Use the logic and reasoning from the case analysis to defend your recommendation. You may desire to list advantages and disadvantages of your recommendation.

As you examined the GM case, you probably arrived at your preferred solution. You may have felt the best solution was to agree to build the new plant on the Poletown site. An alternative could have employed a stepping-stone approach:

> I recommend that GM follow its human and social responsibility and invite the Poletown Neighborhood Council to participate in the problem-solving process, while at the same time examining greater Detroit more closely to see if a comparable site is available.

Step 5: Decide How to Implement the Solution A plan of action is now needed. Your plan should identify the specific actions required, the time element, the needed resources, the people involved, the impact on the organizational structure, and a way to measure the expected results.

A recommendation for the implementation of a solution to the GM case could be: "Since the plant needs to be built by mid-1981, GM should move as quickly as possible to contact the Poletown Neighborhood Council, get them involved in the problem-solving process, and at the same time start an extensive search of the greater Detroit area to see if a comparable site is available."

Step 6: Decide How to Communicate Your Analysis After completing the first five steps of case analysis, you are ready to communicate your findings. In most advanced business programs, three settings exist: written case analysis, class discussion, and group presentation. We will examine only the first setting in this chapter; Chapter 15 covers the latter two. In almost every instance, your instructor will determine which method you and your classmates will follow.

THE WRITTEN REPORT

While there is no one correct way to prepare a written case analysis, most include certain specific items and follow one of a few generally accepted formats. The majority of your study time will probably be devoted to analyzing the case, but leave sufficient time to prepare the written report. When you are under time constraint, it is tempting to consider the completion of your analysis as the end of your assignment. However, your grade is based on the written report, so you should devote ample time to writing and developing your ideas. This section presents four different formats for a written case analysis. (At this point you may find it helpful to review Chapters 8 and 9 on proposal and report writing, especially the material on the inductive and deductive styles. Many of the ideas and techniques discussed there can apply here.)

Even though you will have spent many hours analyzing the case, your instructor will usually spend only 20 to 30 minutes grading each written report. It is therefore important that you write clearly enough so that he or she can understand the main points that you want to communicate. You may be tempted to write your report in the same six-step process that you used for analysis. However, your instructor already knows the case and does not wish to read a restatement of the facts, although he or she may want to see your logic. Organize your material in a very succinct and direct manner. There are three schools of thought on the written analysis format: the suspense format, the news-first format, and the strategic issues format. Ask your instructor which he or she prefers.

The Suspense Format

The suspense format report follows a three-step progression: (1) identify the strategic issues and problems, (2) analyze and evaluate the possible solutions to these issues, and (3) make recommendations. Kerin and Peterson encourage this approach. They believe that

> The first heading should contain a focused paragraph that defines the problem and specifies the constraints and options available to the organization. Material under the second heading should provide a carefully developed assessment of the industry, market and buyer behavior, the organization, and the alternative courses of action. *Analysis and evaluation should represent the bulk of the written report.* This section should not contain a restatement of case information. It should

contain an assessment of the facts, quantitative data, and management views. The last heading should contain a set of recommendations. These recommendations should be documented from the previous section and should be *operational* given the case situation. By all means, commit to a decision![7]

The News-First Format

In the news-first format, you (1) present your recommended solution first, (2) support your recommendation, (3) list the other alternatives and why you did not select them, and (4) provide evidence supporting your observation and recommendations.

The Strategic Issues Format

Use the strategic issues format in writing reports on strategy cases. The length of such a report is short, normally one to two pages. To produce such a report in an adequate manner requires careful and thorough analysis. In this written format, you cite (1) the crucial strategic issues, (2) the assumptions you made about those issues, (3) the strategies you recommend for dealing with the issues, (4) the justification for your recommendations, (5) the plan of action for implementation, and (6) the expected results.[8]

Exhibits and Typing

Many written reports use case exhibits. Remember that the data in any exhibit should help to support the positions you have taken in your text. If your exhibits are short, place them strategically in your text to help explain your conclusions. Otherwise, present long exhibits in an appendix at the end of your report. Designate each exhibit by a clear title that describes its purpose; the reader should be able to understand the material contained in the exhibit without referring to the text. Whenever you refer to an exhibit in the case, make sure that you give an explanation for the exhibit.

Your final typed report should follow the rules of good writing that are discussed in this text. To give you an idea of what a sample written report looks like, we include a case, "Accounting Procedures at Champion Marketing," and a student's written report of the case in Appendices A and B, respectively, on pages 429–432 and 433–436 at the end of the book. The case is a critical incident, and the analysis follows the suspense format. You should read and analyze the case in Appendix A, following the guidelines provided in this chapter, before reading the student analysis in Appendix B.

SOME DO'S AND DON'TS FOR CASE PREPARATION

Do's of Case Analysis

1. Accept the fact that much of the material in the case is useless to your investigation. This is a valuable lesson. As a future manager, you must learn to slice through the fluff and make decisions based on relevant information.

2. Realize that different professors, in different classes and disciplines, want you to conduct different types of analyses. Just as there is no one managerial style that is perfect for all, there is no one case analysis style. Learn early in the class to identify personality and behavioral characteristics of your professors that will indicate how they want the cases analyzed. Often, the professor gives his or her pet analysis outline at the introduction to the course. Be looking for it.

3. Follow a logical, clear, and consistent path through the case analysis. The conclusion should always flow out of your recommendations, and your recommendations should clearly be supported by your analysis. If this does not occur, your problem statement may be faulty.

4. Recognize the difference between facts and inferences or suppositions. Much case material is clearly presented, but you are often required to make subjective interpretations. Learn to distinguish clearly between the two and refer to inferences as such in your analysis. The more suppositions you make, the weaker your analysis becomes; strive to base your analysis on facts whenever possible.

5. Take a stand in your analysis and support it. Many students try to hedge and take a "let's wait and see what others will say" approach. Instructors recognize this and your peers see it. Learn to trust your judgment, take a stand, and build the necessary support for it. Recognize also that your peers will constantly take shots at your stance. The stronger and better supported your stand, the better you will look.

Don'ts of Case Analysis

1. Don't expect a right conclusion to be available following the study of a case. Many case instructors will not give the correct answer even if they know it. Case information is often based on a specific event or a short period of time. Often, the actual businesses or individuals within the case never know what would have really happened if an alternative decision had been made and followed. Your job is to learn to analyze problems and arrive at good solutions.

2. Don't tell the instructor that you need more information before arriving at a decision. Lack of information is common to all cases. Working with incomplete information is good practice because, as a manager, you often will not have all the needed information. Since gathering all the information takes time, and managers must make quick decisions, learn to make proper assumptions based on the information that is available.

3. Don't expect cases to cover a single discipline or to lend themselves to a solution by a given theory or concept. Situations are complicated and, even though you may be in a marketing position, the financial, managerial, and strategic planning areas of the business can affect your work. The broad view is especially true in policy courses, where an objective is to relate material you have covered to a variety of courses.

4. Don't expect your instructor to give you clear instructions on what he or she expects from your analysis. One professor at a major university tells his

students on the first assigned analysis, "I cannot tell you what an excellent analysis will look like, but I will know it when I see it." Although everyone has the same case, the professor expects a multitude of different methods from students as they seek a solution. Most instructors will encourage you to develop your best analysis by not telling you precisely what they want.

5. Don't be so short-sighted that you decide on a conclusion early in the analysis and become locked into that conclusion. The person who develops several solutions will have the advantage and will learn more. This person wisely selects a hypothesis and works through to the conclusion.

6. Don't feel that you have to solve all the problems in the case. This is impossible in case studies. Instead, confront only the major problems. Develop alternative solutions to one problem at a time and then move on to other problems. Businesses have hundreds of minor problems; it is the major ones that are life threatening. Practice quickly identifying the major problems and finding solutions for them.

SUMMARY

The case method is a common style of teaching in advanced business programs. The learning potential of this approach has been demonstrated numerous times. If you learn an effective procedure for analyzing a case and writing an effective report, you will be rewarded both in the classroom and later in your career.

In this chapter, we examined the correct way to analyze a case and write a case report. There are three different types of cases: the formal case, the case story, and the critical incident. There is a proper way to read a case too. The first step is to preview by looking at the basic outline of the case. The second stage is skimming, where you identify the key issues. The third stage is to read and reread the case, making strategic notes to yourself. The fourth stage is scanning prior to class discussion. Proper reading of a case helps you in the case analysis process.

There are four case analysis approaches. First, consider the organization as a system. Second, look at people within the organization and approach the analysis from a behavioral perspective. Third, use a decision-making approach by employing theories or models to help you arrive at decisions about the information in the case. Fourth, use the strategy approach.

As you analyze the case, follow six important steps: (1) define the case problem, (2) consider relevant information and underlying assumptions, (3) list possible solutions to the problem, (4) select a solution and prepare to defend it, (5) decide how to implement the solution, and (6) decide how to communicate your analysis.

Communicate your analysis in one of three ways: through a written report, class discussion, or group presentation. In this chapter, we concentrated on the written report. While there is no one correct way to prepare a report, three specific organizational formats were given. The first style is the suspense mode, which identifies the problem first, analyzes and evaluates possible solutions, and makes the recommendation. The second style is the news-first mode. Here you present your recommendation first, support why you chose one solution over another, list the alternatives you did not select and the reasons for not choosing them, and, finally, give evidence that supports your observation and recommendations. The third style is the strategic issues format, which summarizes the key points in a one- or two-page memo format.

Applications

1. For your next case analysis try to employ the steps that have been described in this chapter. First, open the chapter to page 330 and look at how you should approach the reading of the case. Preview, skim, and then read the entire case. Second, make a decision regarding which of the four analysis approaches you will use: systems, behavior, decision, or strategy. Third analyze the case on paper by using the six-step process on pages 340–344. As you work through each step, you should find that the analysis is greatly improved. Compare the results from the use of this process to the results you obtained using your previous process.

2. When your next written analysis is due, turn back to this chapter and reread the pages that explain the analysis. On paper outline your possible analysis with each of the three different formats: suspense, news first, and strategic issues. Now decide which format best fits the case, the class objectives, and your instructor's desired style. Write your analysis.

DISCUSSION QUESTIONS

1. How is the case method different from other forms of learning?
2. What is the difference between a formal case, a case story, and a critical incident?
3. What is the four-step sequence for reading cases effectively? Describe each of the four steps.
4. How do the four different case analysis approaches really differ?
5. What are the six steps described for analyzing cases? List and explain each of the steps.
6. How does a writer determine which of the four case formats to use for a written analysis?

NOTES

1. Robert Ronstadt, *The Art of Case Analysis*, 2nd ed., Lord, Dover, Massachusetts, 1980, pp. 18–20.
2. Ibid., p. 19.
3. Robert W. Rasberry, "EK&G Products," A Cox School of Business Case, Southern Methodist University, Dallas, Texas, 1984. Prepared with the aid of David Rudman.
4. Material for this case was adapted from Joseph Auerbach, "The Poletown Dilemma," *Harvard Business Review*, May–June 1985, pp. 93–99; "The Poletown Dilemma," *Harvard Business School Case*, 1988, 14 pages.
5. Alan J. Rowe, Richard O. Mason, and Karl E. Dickel, *Cases in Strategic Management*, Addison-Wesley, Boston, 1986, pp. vii–viii.
6. Ibid., p. viii.
7. Roger A. Kerin and Robert A. Peterson, *Strategic Marketing Problems: Cases and Comments*, 4th ed., Allyn & Bacon, Boston, 1987, p. 51.
8. Rowe, Mason, and Dickel, *Cases in Strategic Management*, p. vii.

Appendix:
Sample Case Analysis

T his chapter concludes with a sample student analysis of the EK&G Products case. As you read the analysis compare the notes that you made earlier to those presented here.

FIGURE 14.1   Sample Case Analysis

EK&G CASE ANALYSIS

Step 1: Define the Case Problem and Write a Problem Statement

First, list the different problems or issues that you observe. Second, narrow the issues into a written problem statement.

Four significant problems are apparent in the EK&G Products case:
1. a lack of proper market research or market "feel"
2. a lack of a substantial number of orders
3. very high overhead and fixed costs
4. no firm marketing plans or distribution system

The most significant problems in the EK&G Products case are low sales and high per-unit costs, resulting in low profits.

Step 2: Consider Relevant Information and Underlying Assumptions

In the EK&G Products case, several significant items can be listed. In this particular case, a chronological listing works well.
1. EK&G was formed in 1980 as a medical technology firm.
2. Pulsomatic was developed and tested in 1981.
3. The company believed that a large market existed and geared up for production of the Pulsomatic.
4. Early estimates of production costs were around $175.
5. Only 1,000 units were first ordered.
6. With a small number of sales the unit cost soared to over $250.
7. Hal Sigoin was hired as marketing manager.
8. Delivery began in June 1984.
9. Between June and August 1984, 2,500 units were ordered.
10. The owners celebrated their "success" on August 1, 1984.

In looking at the EK&G Products case, we can pull out several assumptions:
1. A target market is not clearly defined.
2. Sufficient demand does not currently exist. (Can it be created?)
3. The break-even quantity is not determined.
4. In order to sell the Pulsomatic, a marketing representative may need to be hired in addition to Hal Sigoin. (How will this hiring affect break-even costs?)
5. The actual costs of each unit must be determined, including whether or not the unit cost will increase or decrease.
6. Eghart and Kleptow seem to assume that no similar product currently exists. They must discover if this is indeed the case.
7. The partners are assuming that the product and the revenue proposition are attractive to merchants.

FIGURE 14.1 **Sample Case Analysis (Concluded)**

Step 3: List Possible Solutions to the Problem

What are the possible solutions to the major problem you have identified? Alternative solutions for EK&G are:

1. Close down the business.
2. Examine the viability of the entire Pulsomatic venture to determine the likelihood of success. If it is deemed worthwhile,
    a. find a way to market the Pulsomatic broadly to many stores and public locations, or
    b. find a small segment of retail stores or food service locations that are customer intensive and market to that segment.

Step 4: Select a Solution and Prepare to Defend It

A possible solution to this case might be:

"I recommend that EK&G Products examine the viability of the entire Pulsomatic venture to determine the likelihood of success. If the Pulsomatic is determined to be a feasible product, a strategic business plan must then be developed. The plan should include considerations of how to achieve increased sales in one or two markets."

Step 5: Decide How to Implement the Solution

A recommendation for implementation of a solution to EK&G could be:

"Restaurants and bars throughout the state and adjoining states are places of customer intensiveness. Mr. Sigoin should aggressively pursue sales to these businesses either by himself or with the help of commissioned salesmen. This or some other measure should be taken in order to stimulate sales, and therefore increase production, in order to reduce the per-unit cost."

Source: Robert W. Rasberry, "EK&G Products," A Cox School of Business Case, Southern Methodist University, Dallas, Texas, 1984. Prepared with the aid of David Rudman.

'15'

Discussing and Presenting a Case Study

Chapter 14 described how most advanced business programs employ some form of case study. Often the teaching methodology of an entire school revolves around the case approach; such is true of the Harvard Business School. You will use the case analysis process in a general way to analyze real-life business problems. For these reasons, it is academically important that all business students learn to adapt to the case method. Your process of analyzing cases—and how you discuss and present your analyses—will affect your grade in the course and will determine your success in your business life.

There is rationale for individuals making oral case presentations and discussing cases in class. More information can be exchanged quickly as a result of a large group discussion; thus, knowledge can be gained more readily. Because class discussion is democratic, everyone has a fair chance to learn and grow. Finally, a positive result of the discussion is the immediate feedback received by individuals as their peers evaluate their ideas and make additional suggestions. Better solutions are selected this way, and individual confidence and professionalism is gained.

While Chapter 14 described a process of written analysis, Chapter 15 takes the analysis process one step further and shows how to prepare and present case analyses orally. The overall objective of Chapters 14 and 15 is to help you analyze cases. Our specific emphasis in this chapter will be on class discussions. But since this method is also important for practical business situations, some techniques for group and individual presentations will also be given. To gain additional information about oral presentations in business, refer to Chapters 10 and 11. A review of Chapter 3, on visual devices, will also be useful.

Assuming that you have mastered the case analysis process presented in Chapter 14, you should now learn to prepare, present, and review the oral case analysis.

PREPARATION STEPS FOR THE ORAL CASE PRESENTATION

You should ask yourself the questions in the following sections as you prepare for your oral case presentation, regardless of whether it is during a class discussion, group presentation, or individual presentation.

What Type of Discussion Strategy Should You Adopt?

The strategy that you pick for presenting a case should depend on several factors. First, consider your knowledge about different parts of the particular discipline (e.g., finance, accounting, marketing). Work experience that you may have from previous jobs or your exposure to an industry or profession will add to your knowledge. Your skills at both analyzing a problem and communicating your ideas will also influence your strategy choice. Finally, consider your confidence level for the particular discipline; that is, how you see yourself and how you desire to appear and communicate within the classroom.

How Visible Do You Desire to Be?

Visibility relates to how active you want to be in the classroom. If your desire is to be conspicuous, you probably will take a very active role in discussing the material. If you desire to have a major impact and perhaps be an authority type, you may desire a more moderately visible seat, since you plan to talk anyway. If, however, you are fearful and desire not to talk at all, you will probably find yourself seeking a hideout position. While nervousness may drive you to such a place, your grade will probably reflect your passiveness and lack of participation.

What Role Do You Want to Play?

The strategy you take in class generally relates to the discussion role that you desire to play. Ronstadt describes eight possible discussion roles that we normally see in case courses:

1. *Expert Witness.* The individual who has insider information or in-depth knowledge about the case or the case's relationship to other cases plays this role.
2. *Bail 'em Out.* This individual usually has a very clear understanding of the case and generally understands an appropriate solution. He or she often waits until the class gets stuck and then comes to its aid.
3. *Assume a Personality.* The strategy here requires assuming the particular role of an individual within the organization being discussed. During a discus-

sion, questions often are directed to the person who likes to assume a particular personality.

4. *Get the Facts.* The student using this strategy desires a minimum amount of participation. He or she usually throws out facts, which can be easily drawn from the case, in a quick and unimportant manner. Such a person, despite talking, has low visibility because others quickly add further information, and the discussion moves on rapidly. If you choose this strategy, avoid one-line statements. Construct your statements with clarity and substance so that it is evident to the instructor that you fully understand the facts of the case.

5. *Industry Expert.* This person is an authority because he or she has analyzed the industry in question and can offer trends and clarification on the case.

6. *I've Got Experience.* This role is generally played by someone who has had work experience in business and who desires that others know he or she has been in situations of the type under discussion. Often the impact of their information sharing is minimal. If the information is good, however, this person probably becomes the expert witness and is sought out for specific reasons.

7. *Questioner.* The questioner is not someone who merely speaks in class in order to make a statement. Instead, this person generally directs crucial questions toward participants who have made statements regarding analysis, purpose, solutions, and so forth. This role is an important one because it shows an overall understanding of the case and it helps control the direction of the discussion. It also helps to clarify questions that more silent participants may have but are afraid to ask.

8. *Wrap-It-Up.* The person who plays this role has listened carefully throughout the discussion and is capable of taking all the major issues and boiling them together into a coherent line of thought. This individual goes beyond merely repeating what has been said and helps to leave participants with a clearer understanding of the entire case and discussion.[1]

During your first case course, you may find that you adopt a particular case strategy in the middle of the semester and will either stay with it or change it periodically. Learn from that first experience and adopt a strategy prior to the first class meeting in later semesters. Besides developing a professional approach to problem solving, you may improve your grade considerably.

One of your objectives during the discussion is to be seen by the instructor as a major contributor to the problem-solving process. Instructors determine contributions in a variety of ways:

1. Significant information that leads toward a solution
2. A statement encouraging movement from one part of the case to another
3. A new alternative
4. A statement about key assumptions
5. An insightful generalization ·
6. Input from use of a key analytical tool
7. A suggested plan of action
8. Clarification of financial statements or quantitative data

9. A quality summary
10. The ability to relate one case to another

Who Is Your Competition?

The case methodology requires a give-and-take movement, flowing from an analysis of problems to a discussion of solutions, in order that a natural collaboration will develop among participants. Even though a grade is given for participation, try not to think of in-class competition as a win-lose situation. Instead, seek to establish the win-win position where you and your fellow classmates will be cooperating. You will be competing in a puzzle process, trying to arrive quickly and accurately at workable solutions.

During the first few classes, observe which classmates talk the most. Determine whether their comments are accurate. Who plays which of the roles outlined above? How can you work with these different individuals and their strategies so that true collaboration occurs? Likewise, who is less visible? How can you help draw out these individuals so that they, too, will be contributors?

What Is the Instructor's Style?

In order to prepare adequately, you must also understand your instructor's teaching style. If you have never had the instructor for a previous course, ask questions of your colleagues and try to find out as much as possible about his or her style prior to the first class. During the first class, listen carefully to what the instructor says. Watch, too, for how the instructor communicates and is attracted to communicators. Does the instructor prime participants for discussion? Is he or she attracted to the most vocal participant? Is the instructor active (energetically following an agenda), or passive (letting the group determine the direction and flow of the discussion)? Does the instructor often digress and add personal comments about the case? If digression does occur, are the comments important or distracting?

Ronstadt cites five instructor discussion styles most often used in the case classroom. Some instructors adopt one style and stick with it, whereas others shift styles from case to case or even within a single case. Learn your instructor's style and prepare for the type of discussion that will take place in the classroom:

1. *The Cross-Examiner.* The cross-examiner thoroughly questions each statement made by a student. The goal is to pull out additional information and to develop the logic of a student's position. While the tone may sound adversarial, the instructor is not using the process to harass the individual but merely to advance the discussion.
2. *Devil's Advocate.* The devil's advocate questions students in relation to positions taken. Often, the instructor's line of questioning assumes an opposing position or role; through the discussion process, the instructor has the class either support or refute the opposing position. The point of such a discussion is to see if other possibilities are indeed tenable.

3. *The Hypothetical Position.* Instead of questioning a position or statement, the instructor may pose a hypothetical situation that is an extreme example of the position. He or she then pushes the student to consider the example in terms of the student's previous recommendations. This style is used to uncover and display the strength of a discussion's logic.

4. *Role Playing.* The instructor may divide the class into various personalities represented within the case. Each student will assume a personality and the discussion will revolve around how each would make decisions if he or she were the actual person.

5. *The Silent Style.* Often in the course of discussion, the instructor will adopt a silent stance. When this happens, the instructor makes little or no input and allows the discussion to continue so that someone in the class will exert leadership and offer suggestions that will move the class forward or that will turn the course of the discussion. It is important during this time to realize that big points can be gained if you are the one who offers carefully constructed comments that move the class forward.[2]

As you read the case you should get a sense of the exciting problems and personalities involved. The instructor will then peel back layers of the case to reveal its depth to students. If you saw "X" in your reading of the case, the instructor will help you see "2X" through the discussion. Listening is a key to making this happen. Your instructor will listen carefully and will guide you to a successful end.[3]

How Will You Handle the Instructor's Questions?

After previewing possible instructor styles, it is important to consider how you will handle questions posed in the classroom. Because the class operates within a time restraint, coordination between instructor and students is important. Good case teachers use several questioning techniques. First, they ask directive questions that do not invite memorized statements—"What do you project the sales to be for the next quarter, and why?" By asking such a question they are looking for ideas on controversial issues and on how the case material relates to the course theories.

While certain questions may be directed to particular students, the instructor really desires that the entire class answer the question in their own minds. The instructor is interested in the entire class participating in the orchestration process of the discussion. For this reason, instructors usually do not repeat their questions; they expect you to listen carefully and to realize that a question, and its answer, must be incorporated into the orchestrated process. Likewise, instructors do not repeat participant's answers unless they incorporate the answer into part of the next question or summarize what has been said.

Your ability to handle a lead-off question is particularly important. The lead-off question is crucial because it stimulates further discussion. Answers often reflect who is best prepared to discuss the case. If for some reason you are not ready to discuss the case or participate in class, tell the instructor. While this may create a negative image in the instructor's mind about your participation, it will save you the embarrassment of being called on and being unable to answer the question in class. Usually, however, you can use this out only one time. If you are perpetually unprepared, your grade will be adversely affected. If you beg out one class period, you should give an excellent performance during the following class.

A good instructor will ask you what information you need and how you will use it. If you are asked a question that you do not understand, try to direct the question and your answer into an area of the case where you feel confident. Also, do not use the excuse "there's not enough information"; too much information will tell you the complete story of the case and therefore will make discussion unimportant.

Remember that your instructor, in asking questions, realizes that each class member has a different opinion. Such a difference is healthy and students are encouraged not only to have their own opinions but to learn to support their opinions carefully. The freedom of expression of different ideas is key to the decision-making process of the case approach. In asking questions, the instructor will take generalizations and will try to help students channel these into constructive facts that are related to the course. The discussion is most productive when the theories of the course are highlighted and facts from the case are used to further develop the theory.

How Will You Ask Questions?

As part of a case discussion, you will find yourself both answering and asking questions. Several ideas can guide you to ask effective questions. First, minimize the direct questions you pose to the instructor during class discussion that do not relate specifically to the case discussion statement—avoid such questions as "Isn't this just another example of a poorly managed organization?" Instructors are busy working the class through the case and are interested in your input, not your questions. The exceptions to this rule are when you ask clarifying questions or move the discussion with a question that is really addressed to the entire class—such as saying "This situation reminds me of the McGuire case that we examined two weeks ago. Isn't the main problem here the weakness of the manager and consequently a poorly managed organization?" Such questions should relate to the logical sequence of the discussion. Avoid a question that asks for premature information; for example, if the class is discussing the analysis of facts, you should not pose a question about a solution to the case.

Second, when you ask a question, make sure it is logical and self-explanatory. A case discussion is not the place for many of the normal questions of why, how, when, and so forth, that passive listeners and talkers insert into normal interpersonal conversations. During class discussion, each participant should strive to make statements and questions simple, clear, and meaningful.

How Should You Prepare Your Discussion Notes?

Before you can prepare your notes, you must adequately analyze the case. In Chapter 14, we discussed a six-step analysis process:

1. Define the case problem.
2. Consider the relevant information and underlying assumptions.
3. List the possible solutions to the problem.
4. Select a solution and prepare to defend it.

5. Decide how to implement the solution.
6. Decide how to communicate your analysis.

Many students do excellent, time-consuming analyses, only to be unable to discuss their analyses and findings in class. It is important that you combine the analytical and communicative process into your presentation.

Rescripting Your Notes Rescripting your original analysis notes, or revising them so that they will better serve you in the discussion, is important. During your analysis, remember that certain information and analytical tools will always be a part of class discussion. As you analyze the overall case, remember the various financial statements found in the exhibits. Although you may be tempted to breeze over them quickly, ask yourself instead, "What is the financial stability of the organization?" In your rescripting, make notations regarding questions you can ask or responses you can make about the financial statements. If you learn to do this task well in the classroom, you will find it an invaluable tool in future business world meetings.

Refer to the Analytical Tools As you further analyze the case, you will undoubtedly use many of the analytical tools listed in Table 14.1 (page 336). Whether these tools are profitability measures, projections of financial statements, or cost-revenue analysis formulas, you should be prepared to discuss the case using the tools that will provide the most information. Be careful to make sure your solution encompasses both qualitative reasons and quantitative facts; avoid the tendency to focus on just one or the other.

Make Keyword Notes After you have analyzed the case, make notes that can be used as quick references in class discussion or as you deliver your presentation. Such notes generally require larger lettering, keywords instead of complete sentences, and facts or statistics organized in a readily usable manner. The key is to design material so it is easily accessible to prevent you from shuffling through piles of paper.

Use the Instructor's Note Pattern One excellent method of note organization is to design your notes in the same pattern that your instructor uses on the chalkboard. Watch as your instructor diagrams cases. Does he or she use an ordering process? Does the instructor list facts chronologically, list alternatives with their pros and cons, put problems with solutions, or arrange a sequence of ideas and information? Is the analysis on the left and the recommendations on the right? Some instructors even use different colors of chalk or markers. By ordering your ideas into the patterns your instructor uses, you can easily follow the class discussion and contribute your own ideas.

Should You Prepare for Class Discussion by Joining a Study Group?

Some instructors require that class members participate in study groups prior to class discussion. If your instructor does not have such a requirement, you should still consider developing a study group for the following reasons. First, study groups improve case learning, since they require you to practice the development and support of logical positions. They are useful as well because they employ creative brainstorming, which is a by-product of class discussion. Also, small groups are much easier to talk in than large classes of 60 to 80 participants. By practicing in a study group, your confidence for speaking in the classroom should be increased. Finally, while they may not be called *study groups*, you will find that your time will be spent in numerous work groups of one sort or another once you are in the business world. The learning from your case study group will carry over into that environment.

There are several things to consider in organizing a study group. First, you should be acquainted with the other members of the group. Know how they perform in class. Are they shy or assertive? Are they outspoken or knowledgeable? Are they motivated to work? A group should pick individuals who contribute equally to the overall effort. This means that all members agree to meet at the same time, to be fully prepared to discuss each case, and to be committed to helping the entire group effort. Do not join a group if you feel intimidated by any other group participant.

Just as in business, it is often helpful to combine different types of participant knowledge. For example, a study group can use persons with backgrounds in accounting, finance, marketing, and communication. When your group first meets, establish ground rules by which you will operate. Ground rules might include what style of leadership the group will follow, time limits, who will take the notes, how you will handle digressions in discussion, and, finally, how you will ensure that each member is fully prepared for each session. Preparation should include a thorough reading and understanding of the case and a full analysis of the case by each individual.

PRESENTATION OF THE ORAL CASE ANALYSIS

In making an oral case presentation, three methods can be used: class discussion, group presentation, and individual presentation. The material that follows on class discussion and group presentations relates to the material on meeting management found in Chapter 11. The material for individual presentations is related to Chapter 10.

Class Discussions

As you participate in class discussion, remember that such a discussion process usually follows an abbreviated form of case analysis: identifying and analyzing the case situation, analyzing key solutions, and choosing a particular solution with recommendations for specific action. While the discussion generally revolves around these three areas, you should be aware that the process is often altered depending on the nature of the case and the opening statements made by both the instructor and the students.

When Should You Talk? Your first decision is whether you will talk immediately or sit quietly. The strategy you selected during your preparation has prepared you for the discussion. If you talk first, you make yourself vulnerable, but you also set the pace for the remaining class discussion. Such an assertive position takes courage—you may be wrong, but at least you have started talking.

If you decide to be quiet at the outset, however, you can determine the direction of the class discussion and you can contribute to the direction and flow of the process. Here you run the risk, if you are nervous, of eventually not talking at all. For this reason, you must develop your strategy during the preparatory stages and follow that strategy once the class discussion has started. If everyone starts talking at first, tailor your comments to those made by your colleagues.

While class discussions of cases require risk on your part, they are akin to business decisions in management situations, which also involve risk. Through proper analysis you try to minimize the risk. While speaking out in class is often one of the most risky aspects, it is far worse to sit day after day and never say a word. Your boss on the job would never allow this to happen, and neither will a good case instructor. Because most case-oriented classes include participation as a major portion of the grade, it is important that you talk. The instructor often takes little responsibility for getting you involved or for limiting the input of class members who monopolize discussion. The instructor usually feels this is part of the group participation problem that must be handled by the group itself. Ronstadt summarizes this process of talking versus not talking.

> . . . if you are an active participant, you cannot realistically expect to be right all the time. After all, good learning comes partly from making mistakes. And you can expect to make errors of analysis or reasoning. If your classmates or your professor reveal an error, do not defend it to the death. Defending a defenseless position is foolhardy and the mark of a poor manager who cannot recognize plain facts because of an emotional need to always be right. Remember, people do not do poorly in case courses for being honestly wrong. They do poorly for not doing.[4]

Actively Listen One of the most important skills to practice during class discussion, and one that will have terrific payoffs in the business world, is listening. It is crucial that you listen to the person who leads the discussion. Avoid the temptation to shuffle your papers and order your thoughts. Listen instead, and allow your mind to follow the discussion flow. Be ready to go wherever the discussion goes. As the discussion is taking place, try to keep in mind which phase of the analysis process the participants are talking about. Watch and listen carefully. Keep in mind a mental outline of the overall analysis, the points made thus far, and the key ideas expressed under each point. Mentally extend your own analysis by building on comments made by your colleagues. You can even offer these ideas orally, which may help the instructor stay within the prepared format.

Keep in mind that listening is not the end result of the exercise. As Harvard professor Charles Gragg states, "It can be said flatly that the mere act of listening to wise statements and sound advice does little for anyone. In the process of learning, the learner's dynamic cooperation is required." If you are listening with the overall idea in mind, you can help the class minimize digressions and wandering. Digressions usually occur because of confusion regarding the process of decision making. Help direct the discussion back toward the key unresolved issues with your comments. The solution will then be easier to see. "The desired result of student participation is achieved by the opening of free channels of communication between students and students, and between students and teachers."[5]

Follow the Instructor's Pace Within the Discussion The role of the instructor during class discussion is to keep the process moving in an orderly and productive manner. He or she will ask questions that invite responses. The strategy you choose should determine the role that you will play in responding. Observe the instructor's verbal and nonverbal communication. How does he or she signal the class to shift gears and focus on new and different material? By observing the instructor's style, you will be better able to participate in the discussion, to move the class toward an excellent solution, and to improve your own grades. A sample class plan is listed in Table 15.1. Refer to this for a general idea of how a case class could be conducted. Realize, however, that individual instructors design and carry out class discussion in their own unique ways.

TABLE 15.1 **A Sample Class Plan Outline**

Time (minutes)	Sequence	Activity
	1.	People to call on during this class if they do not volunteer (six or eight names).
0–10	2.	General class announcements.
	3.	Comments about the next class and its assignment.
10–15	4.	Review of the theory readings assigned: a. Any questions or comments? b. Specific questions to be raised if students do not discuss on their own initiative.
15–25	5.	Case introduction. An anecdote about the industry. A tie-back to previous class discussions, etc.
	6.	Who will start? Will I ask or will I wait for a volunteer?
	7.	Key questions I may want to ask.
25–40	8.	Important points to cover: a. *Diagnosis:* What is the problem and why is it occurring? b. *Alternatives:* What are they? How to evaluate them? c. *Action:* What is the decision? What are short-term actions? What are long-term actions?
5–15	9.	Conclusion if any: a. Questions to ask: Is this problem similar to one in other courses? How different/similar was this case from previous cases? b. Variations that might exist, relevant current news items, relative importance with course content, and further related readings.

Source: Adapted from James A. Erskine, Michiel R. Leenders, and Louise A. Mauffeette-Leenders, *Teaching with Cases,* Research and Publications Division, School of Business Administration, University of Western Ontario, London, Ontario, 1981, p. 126.

Look for a Place to Insert Good Qualitative Statements Regardless of whether or not you are a whiz at numbers, many of the most useful statements in a case discussion are phrased from a qualitative, not a quantitative, standpoint. To the financial expert, the bottom line may say it all. If numbers are not your strong suit, however, do not spend all your time looking for answers as you run the numbers. Instead, consider the more difficult questions. For example, a manufacturing firm may have to choose between two parts. By purchasing one, the ROI (return on investment) may be higher than by using the more costly part, but the difficult questions that you should ask may revolve around the implications for product quality.

Give Effective Summaries Many students expect the instructor to summarize the discussion that has taken place within the classroom. Most instructors prefer that a member of the class not only summarize what has taken place but also relate the case and discussion to the overall context of the theories being studied within the course. At the same time, they realize that this is a difficult thing to ask of most students. If you really want to impress your instructor, giving effective summaries is one way you can probably do it.

Do Not Expect a Correct Answer to the Case Problem Few instructors provide their solutions to the case or describe what the organization actually did. Most prefer that the alternatives developed by the class be the ones used in relating the course theory. They believe that disclosing what actually happened is risky and discourages students from carefully providing their own alternatives to cases. They know that in the business world there will always be several available alternatives for solving problems.

Group Presentation

If the instructor assigns a group presentation, start by forming your group if the group composition has not already been assigned. If you have a choice in picking your colleagues, remember that groups are best formed on the basis of complementary skills, not friendships. Skills should represent the analysis process, expertise in the fields of discipline, and so forth. Form the group, like the study group, with members who are committed and dependable and who will work hard to deliver a professional presentation.

Before your group meets, each member should analyze the case and arrive at a solution. Make extensive notes and arrange the notes in a manner that will make it easy to discuss what you have found. Meet together to discuss the analysis and arrive at your group's solution to the problem. After your discussion, divide the parts of the presentation for ease of preparation and presentation. Division may be made by expertise, knowledge, or communicative skills. One method of dividing the group calls for one member to make the introduction and conclusion, another member to provide background information, a third member to present the problem analysis, a fourth member to cover possible solutions, and the final member to give the group's selected solution.

Decide how your group needs to use visual aids. Review Chapter 3 at this point and consider the use of a software graphics package. Various packages exist and are probably available at your school on the local network. Some of the easiest to use are Microsoft "PowerPoint," Lotus "Freelance Graphics," and "Harvard Graphics."

After the aids are assembled, your group should meet for a practice session. As you practice, look over all handouts and aids to make sure that they are error free, will be easy to use, and will facilitate retention.

Arrive early on the day of the presentation. Dress appropriately. If you and your group are to be in front of the class, consider wearing appropriate business attire. Arrange the seats in a way that will create a professional image and will aid you in making your presentation. Stick to the time limit. Speak in a professional manner and bridge together the individual contributions through well-thought-out and rehearsed transitions. As each person speaks before the class, support each other with both words and actions (eye contact and facial expressions). Let the class see that the project is a unified effort, not the work of one or two individuals. Talk to the class and not to the overhead machine or the screen. Never disagree with members of your group in front of the class, unless you have previously decided to do so in order to make a point during the case.

When you are finished with the presentation, be prepared to answer any questions from the audience. You can follow the format given in the chapter on individual presentations.

The Individual Case Presentation

If you are given the assignment to make an individual case presentation in class, take the assignment seriously. This presentation is your opportunity to shine and score points for yourself. Be aware of the three areas that must adequately cover: preparation, practice, and presentation. This is also a good place to reread Chapter 10 on business presentations.

Preparation Start your preparation just as you would for a class discussion. Analyze the case carefully and make notes of your analysis. After the analysis is finished, rescript these notes in a manner that will allow you to follow them when you are making your presentation.

As you organize your thoughts, be careful not to repeat a lot of the preliminary information and facts that everyone in the class already knows. If there are major analytical tools that you have employed in the analysis, mention them and outline the information gleaned from them. The outline that you will use is crucial. Reduce your notes to just a few pages. Work from key categories, columns, and breakdowns that trigger in your mind the information that is on your page. The more easily you can interpret your notes, the more easily you will be able to communicate to your audience.

While rescripting your notes, consider whether you will use visual aids. (Refer to Chapter 3 on graphics at this point.) Three aids that are easy for students to use in individual case presentations are the chalkboard, transparencies, and handouts. If your classroom is equipped with a personal computer and projection system, there are several graphics packages that you might consider using.

Practice After you have organized and prepared your presentation, go through several practice sessions. First, look over your notes mentally at least once. Second, read through your notes out loud and emphasize the major points you want your audience to remember. Third, talk out loud about your notes and refer to them only occasionally. Practice in this manner at least three or four times. If you do not have time for numerous out-loud sessions, at least practice major blocks of the presentation. Remember, practicing the delivery of the analysis makes for an excellent presentation.

It is to your advantage to memorize two parts: the introduction and the conclusion. If these are clear in your mind, you will have no problem getting into and out of your presentation, and the rest of the material will make more sense to the listeners. Do not try to memorize the entire analysis. Such a task is not time effective, and if you lose your place you will probably freeze. Also, an entirely memorized presentation looks passive and canned, not professional. Rely on your notes during practice and, after several run-throughs, you will have little difficulty getting through the talk.

If you are going to use visual aids, such as the chalkboard or overhead projector with transparencies, make sure you practice with these aids until your presentation is smooth.

Presentation On the day of your presentation, arrive early to set up the room. If possible, stand during your presentation, but avoid standing locked behind a podium. Look at your audience. Speak to them. Try to establish a dialogue whereby you seem to be carrying on a conversation together. Do not talk to the screen if you are using the overhead projector. Be sure to observe the time limit and save room for questions and answers at the end.

Some rules to follow in the question-and-answer session are:

1. Repeat all questions before answering them.
2. Recognize the questions in the order given.
3. Relate the questions to the logic of your presentation.
4. Avoid digressing and getting into individual conversations with classmates.
5. Make your answers brief.
6. Be courteous.
7. Do not be afraid to say, "I don't know," if you do not have an answer. Do not use the phrase as a cop-out, however.

REVIEWING THE ORAL CASE ANALYSIS

During class discussion, you should be listening, watching, and talking instead of writing. But as soon as class is over, the wise student summarizes what happened in class. A format such as questions/issues/specific facts/comments is helpful. Within your summary, list the key ideas and any overall generalizations. Be sure to note how this case related to cases previously covered in the course. Compare and contrast the issues and cases. Also list any analytical tools that were employed to explain the case. A thorough review, written out immediately after the discussion, will help you in your overall understanding of the course theories and will save you time in studying for the final test. An example of just such a review list is found in Table 15.2. Ronstadt uses the acronym *FIG* to guide the summarization notes. The letters stand for *facts*, *ideas*, and *generalizations*.

TABLE 15.2	A FIG Review List

Session No. 1

Fact 1: More than half of all retail businesses fail within the first two years of operation.

Fact 2: The average business life span is six years.

Fact 3: You cannot buy time when running a business operation, and there is no such thing as a sure deal.

Fact 4: There are 2,575,000 dry cleaning businesses in the United States.

Fact 5: There are 4,150,000 grocery stores in the United States.

Idea 1: The concept of "interstice theory" applies to large corporations that are too small for large companies to get involved with and too large for small business ventures. An example would be producing wooden spools for large cable and wire manufacturers.

Generalization 1: You need three primary resources to start a business: people, capital, and an idea.

Generalization 2: A marginal business will return a lower profit than the salary realized if one had decided to work for someone else.

Generalization 3: The entrepreneur's basic goal is to maintain a level of survival.

Source: Adapted from Robert Ronstadt, *The Art of Case Analysis: A Guide to the Diagnosis of Business Situations,* 2nd ed., Lord, Dover, Massachusetts, 1980, p. 38.

SUMMARY

While Chapter 14 helped you develop the tools for analyzing a case and writing a case report, this chapter gave you an understanding of how to discuss and present a case analysis in the classroom.

As you prepare for the oral case presentation, there are nine important questions that you should ask. First, what type of discussion strategy should you adopt? The answer to this question depends on how conspicuous and vulnerable you wish to become. Second, how visible do you desire to be? If you desire to take an active role in the discussion, you will have a highly visible profile in the class. Third, what role do you want to play? The strategy you take in class relates to one of eight possible roles: expert witness, bail'em out, assume a personality, get the facts out, industry expert, I've got experience, questioner, or wrap-it-up. The fourth question to ask is, who is your competition? Knowing something about your class-mates' styles will help you in planning your role. Fifth, what is your instructor's style? This is a vital question; the answer determines how you will strategically prepare for the discussion. Instructors have one of five styles: the cross-examiner, the devil's advocate, the hypothetical position, the role player, or the silent style. Sixth, how will you handle the instructor's questions? This determines not only the strategy you will take in the discussion but also how you will prepare for the process. Seventh, how will you ask questions? As a student your role is generally one of providing answers, but there are important ways to ask questions. Eighth, how should you prepare your discussion notes? Proper note preparation requires rescripting your notes, making references to the analytical tools, making keyword notes, and using the instructor's note pattern. Finally, should you prepare for class discussion by joining a study group?

Preparation pays off during the final presentation that generally takes the form of class discussions, group presentations, or individual presentations. There are several points that are important for the class discussion. They are knowing when to talk, learning to actively listen, following the pace the instructor sets within the discussion, looking for a place to insert good qualitative statements within the discussion, learning to give effective summaries, and learning not to expect a correct answer for the overall case. Group presentations closely follow Chapter 11 on meeting management. An effective group presentation requires a great deal of coordination between members before, during, and after the actual presentation. Individual presentations follow the points made in Chapter 10 on business presentations. Preparation is vital and so is learning the correct visual aids to use.

Finally, the wise student reviews the case analysis immediately following a class. A useful analysis summary focuses on three aspects: facts, ideas, and generalizations.

DISCUSSION QUESTIONS

1. One determinant of the discussion role that you will use in the classroom is your instructor's discussion style. What are the five different instructor styles for discussion? Which one does your instructor follow the most?

2. Handling the instructor's questions requires knowing something about his or her questioning techniques. How would you handle each of the different techniques? Discuss this with others in your class.

3. Proper preparation of your discussion notes can be an art. What are the four steps of preparation and what must you do in each step?

4. Describe how class discussions, group presentations, and individual presentations of cases differ. How should you prepare and present each type?

Applications

1. After reading this chapter you should be able to identify and better understand any instructor who uses the case study method. Establish a meeting time with the instructor and discuss any questions that you have regarding the case study approach in his or her class. Try to leave the meeting with a better understanding of how you can best employ the case analysis process both in and out of class.

2. As you prepare for your next case discussion in the classroom, decide which role to play. Take a sheet of paper and write down the eight possible roles described in this chapter. List under each role type the pros and cons of playing each role, given the composition of your class. Next, list several techniques that you could use in employing each technique. Finally, take your list with you to class and try to use at least two or three of the techniques during the next case analysis.

NOTES

1. Robert Ronstadt, *The Art of Case Analysis: A Guide to the Diagnosis of Business Situations*, 2nd ed., Lord, Dover, Massachusetts, 1980, pp. 33–35.
2. Ibid., pp. 30–32.
3. "Talking with Professor John Quelch," *Teaching Materials*, Harvard Business School Press, Boston, Massachusetts, Fall 1998, p. 2.
4. Robert Ronstadt, *Art of Case Analysis*, p. 36.
5. "Leading Classroom Discussion: Learning vs. Listening," *Teaching Materials*, Harvard Business School Press, Boston, Massachusetts, Spring 1998, p. 1.

Job Search Strategies

‘16‘

Résumés and Employment Letters

The past three sections have presented several chapters with the main objective of survival through communication: how to survive your academic course work and how to survive in the world of work. These survival chapters have focused on the importance of communication skills as both a writer and speaker. In these final two chapters, we offer you some important information on an additional form of survival: the job search.

As an advanced business student, you and your peers—at school or at work—have many qualities in common. Each of you is well educated and able to apply course work to your career. If you are not presently employed in a career-path job, you probably also share a desire to find that special job where you will be rewarded with top pay and praise for your contribution to the team. But do not be fooled into thinking that this special job will be easy to acquire. For the majority of students, obtaining the first major job takes a lot of hard work. Likewise, for those who are currently employed and working on a graduate degree, a new job, one that will allow you to use your newly acquired skills, is sometimes difficult to acquire.

Traditionally the job search process requires conducting a personal assessment, researching an organization, preparing a personal résumé, writing letters of application, interviewing with several prospective employers both on and off campus, and sometimes applying for jobs through employment agencies. Today the process has been enhanced enormously by taking your job search on-line. Electronic job searching and on-line career discussion groups that were once used by only a few are now considered important job-finding alternatives. In fact, employers are more frequently bypassing the campus recruiting process and are going straight to potential employees through on-line job advertising.

We want you to be prepared for whatever trials your job search may present. In this chapter and the next, we will help you equip yourself for the last step before leaving the campus for the working world. We will take you through the steps of learning who you are and what you want to do, deciding how to market yourself through the preparation of a résumé and different types of employment letters, and selling yourself in the job interview.

This chapter focuses on the first two steps of this process: clarifying who you are and what you want to do, and preparing your résumé and employment correspondence. As a part of your job search, you communicate to others what you would like to do, how you are prepared to do it, and other important details that you want a future employer to know. We will show you how to describe yourself in four types of résumés (traditional, functional, skills, and electronic) and several different letters. The next chapter will give you some tips to follow in interviewing for the job.

PLANNING YOUR CAREER PATH

Anyone can find a job; finding the *right* job is more difficult. As an advanced business candidate, you are faced with tremendous pressures. School administrators and placement center personnel push you early in the program to complete a résumé, make a decision on your major area of emphasis, and start the interviewing process. All too often, candidates do not consider what they want out of a job until, with résumés completed, they find themselves in the middle of the interviewing season. Presumably, you will have made that decision before developing your résumé; but if you have not, realize that you are competing with other fast-moving candidates who know what they want in the job market. Take some time to assess who you are and what you want to do.

Consider Your Skills

Begin by assessing your skills and interests and clarifying what is most important to you in your career. One method of doing this is to think back over your life and to identify several successful accomplishments. Describe each accomplishment in detail and list specific skills that you utilized in the different successes. Generally you will be able to list three or four skills for each accomplishment.

Another method is to compile an inventory of all the major activities that you have been involved in during your life. Use the following list as a starting point:

- *Educational/Vocational programs* that you enrolled in and completed, and which contributed significantly to your overall education.
- *Course work accomplishments* that were challenging and beneficial.
- *Employment and jobs* that you were paid to perform and in which you learned specific skills.
- *Volunteer, community, and extracurricular activities* which added to your skills, knowledge, and leadership abilities.
- *Personal hobbies* that you have enjoyed.

- *Military experiences* and jobs to which you were assigned.
- *Recreational activities* which you found enjoyable.
- *Travel experiences* to different countries and the learnings you acquired.

Go back over the inventory and identify specific skills that you have learned and enjoyed using in the different activities and experiences.

As you review the accomplishment list and longer inventory, circle the specific skills that are apparent. Cluster the skills that are listed repeatedly. Finally, review Table 16.1 and circle the functional skills that are the same as those that you identified as your own. If there are others on the list that you believe you possess, circle them as well. In most instances the circled skills represent those that you would enjoy using in your career.[1]

Table 16.1   **Functional Skills Needed for Professional Employment**

Functional Skills Needed for Professional Employment

Communication & Persuasion	**Research & Investigation**
writing	analyzing
listening	researching
training	reading
selling ability	data gathering
interviewing ability	critical thinking
making presentations	data analysis
negotiating	observing
thinking on one's feet	outlining
conversational ability	
public speaking	**Human Service**
teaching	interpersonal skills
	group process skills
Organization Management	sensitivity to needs
problem solving	empathizing ability
time management	counseling skills
decision making	
leadership	**Information Management**
meeting deadlines	math skills
supervision	ability to organize information
motivation ability	information management
organization	recordkeeping
coordination	attention to detail
administration	logical ability
ability to put theory into practice	
ability to delegate	**Design & Planning**
applying policies	anticipating problems
giving directions	planning
assuming responsibility	conceptualizing
discriminating tasks	designing programs
interpreting policies	anticipating consequences of action
setting priorities	seeking new ideas
	visual thinking

Source: Adapted from *Stanford University Career Planning Guide*, 1995–1996, p. 14.

Consider Your Interests and Values

Richard Bolles, in his best-seller *What Color Is Your Parachute?*, stresses the three major wants of a job candidate who is more interested in developing a career than in just getting a job, and the three questions that should be answered.[2] First, where do you want to live? Since the major portion of your life will be spent working, consider the geographical location where you want to spend the remainder of your time. This may be the place where you live now or an entirely different place. The location should include the kinds of people and surroundings you enjoy.

Second, what do you want to do in life? Consider your personal and professional goals. You undoubtedly want work that supports growth and fulfillment as well as professional development. How can you find satisfaction and reward in the broadest sense? Review Table 16.2 and consider work values that are an important source of your satisfaction. Write a brief description of your personal wants, dreams, career interests, and job values.

TABLE 16.2   Values that Affect Career Choice

Values That Affect Career Choice

Some wise person said, "Work without value is just mere labor." Work values are the aspects of our work that we regard as important sources of satisfaction. Values can generally be categorized as those that affect:

- work enjoyment
- work condition
- work of importance to others

Work Enjoyment values might include:
- **Excitement, Change, Variety**—experiencing a high degree of any of these in the course of one's work
- **Creativity**—creating new ideas, programs, organizational structures, etc., or not following a format previously developed by others
- **Knowledge**—engaging oneself in the pursuit of knowledge, truth, and understanding
- **Profit, Gain**—having a strong likelihood of accumulating large amounts of money or other material gain
- **Recognition**—being recognized for the quality of one's work in some visible or public way

Work Condition values might include:
- **Work Alone/Work with Others**—doing work which emphasizes either of these conditions
- **Independence**—being able to determine the nature of one's work without significant direction from others
- **Time Freedom**—having work responsibilities which allow for flexible time schedules or working on one's own time schedule
- **Stability**—having a work routine that is largely predictable and not likely to change over a given period of time
- **Adventure**—having work duties which involve frequent risk taking

Work of Importance to Others might include values of:
- Moral fulfillment
- Helping society and contributing to the betterment of the world
- Helping others, usually in a direct way, individually or in small groups
- Friendship and community

Source: Adapted from Howard Figler, *The Complete Job Search Handbook,* 1979, and *Stanford University Career Planning Guide,* 1995–1996, p. 15.

Now that you have completed the self-assessment, you are ready to consider the third question that Bolles poses for a job candidate: who do you want to work for? With the help of the summary of the goals, interests, and values you want your skills to serve, evaluate the types of jobs that can help you more fully develop your total personality, potential, and lifestyle.

Consider the Kind of Work You Want to Do and With Whom You Want to Work

The difficulty with this part of the planning process is that you must conduct extensive research on the organizations that interest you. If you do your research long before you write your résumé and try to establish interview dates, you will come closer to knowing precisely which companies you do and do not want to work for. You will also prepare a better résumé and will be better able to ask and answer questions during your interviews.

As you proceed, the kind of work you want to do and who you want to work for should begin to emerge. As you learn about different companies, consider how each one will allow you to be truly fulfilled. For example, a study conducted by *Inc.* magazine showed the characteristics that employees most want from their jobs. The list, which is ranked in order of most importance, was tallied from employees working in a wide variety of jobs and industries.[3]

1. Health insurance and other benefits
2. Interesting work
3. Job security
4. Opportunity to learn new skills
5. Vacation time
6. Working independently
7. Recognition from team members
8. Regular hours
9. A job in which I can help others
10. Little job stress
11. High income
12. Working close to home
13. Work important to society
14. Chances for promotion
15. Contact with people

Do you identify with these motivators? Develop your own list, then question whether the organizations that you are considering will allow you to meet your objectives.

If you are able to answer "yes, the companies I have chosen to pursue for employment offer these motivators," then ask yourself five additional questions about each organization. These are considered classic questions, first posed by career specialist Edgar H. Schein:

1. Will this company give me the opportunity to stretch and really discover what I am capable of doing?

2. Will I really matter inside this organization? Will they see me as a person of worth? Will they give me real responsibility and a chance to show what I can really do?

3. Will I be able to maintain my integrity? Will this company help me achieve a balance in my life, to have a family, and to pursue my individual interests?

4. Will this job give me a real chance to grow? Will I be able to learn new things and develop new talents?

5. Will this company meet the ideals of the sound and ethical businesses that I have studied about? Will my self-image be enhanced by working for this organization?[4]

If you have answered these questions affirmatively about a particular company and you are still interested in pursuing employment with that company, start your résumé preparation and interview planning.

PREPARING YOUR RÉSUMÉ

Is the résumé important? Yes! It is the vital first step of your marketing program. As an applicant, you may have excellent qualifications; however, if you cannot communicate your qualifications clearly in a résumé, you may never reach the interview stage. Even if you are well qualified, you may never have the chance to discuss those strengths with an interviewer if your résumé is weak. A good résumé is a marketing tool. It should portray you in the most favorable manner possible. The résumé is typically used by employers to determine whether they will interview you.

The résumé is often your first contact with an employer. **Résumé** comes from the French verb meaning *to summarize*; a résumé is a summary of pertinent facts about the candidate. The typical résumé consists of one to three typed pages about the candidate and includes job objectives, past employment, education, and personal data.

Writing a résumé is an easy task—at first glance. Almost anyone can sit down for 30 minutes and produce a mediocre employment summary. No wonder one corporate personnel officer said, "We get up to a hundred résumés a day; they all look pretty much the same. They lack what we really need to know; they are dull and boring. Guess where most of them end up?" Developing a strategic plan that focuses on what you want to do now and several years down the road will help ensure both that your résumé does not end up with the others and that you get a fair shot at the job of your choice.

What Should Be in Your Résumé?

As a marketing tool, the purpose of the résumé is to sell yourself. Your résumé should include the most important information about you: your education and your work experience. From this, your prospective employer will make a preliminary determination about whether you qualify for the job. Résumés contain lots of different information. The categories listed below, while including the generally desired information, may not be appropriate to all people.

- Personal/data (name, address, telephone, fax number, and e-mail address)
- Career/job objective
- Educational background
- Work experience (both full and part-time/summer)
- Military service
- Special qualifications, awards, honors, and publications
- Community activities
- Personal interests, special skills, and hobbies
- Statement about references

Although most people agree on the general information, there is some debate when it comes to the specifics. In fact, the Harvard University Graduate School of Business *Student Handbook On Résumé Writing* makes the following statement:

> Authorities differ as to exactly what should be included in a résumé. A sound and proven fundamental approach is to consider your résumé as a truthful sales presentation which you have prepared for potential employers. Since its purpose is to help you sell your services, it should include the facts about yourself which will give consistency and strength to your stated job and career objective.
>
> Don't write an autobiography or an obituary; the résumé is not an all-inclusive life history! In it you work mostly with the "plus factors" that will help you sell yourself, so emphasize your most important assets. Above all, it must be factual. Each statement needs to be accurate and not blown up beyond its value; on the other hand, it need not be underplayed. Executives are seeking capabilities, so write up your achievements with the employer's needs in mind.[5]

You share many things with your colleagues in your degree program or in the business world; perhaps, at this moment, you share the need to write a résumé. Each of you is different. You have different educations, experiences, and jobs. Should the résumé for each of you take the same form? No! By drawing from your individual strategic plans, each of you will be able to construct a balance between the needs of your employer and your needs as a job candidate.

A good way to picture the balance of employer needs versus what you offer is:

Employer Needs	**Your Résumé Description**
Who are you?	Identification section
What do you want to do?	Job objective section
What do you have to offer?	Education and work history
What can you do?	Personal skills

Your résumé can accomplish the needed match between you and a company. The following material describes four kinds of résumés. The first three are standard. The fourth represents the new electronic résumé. By examining a variety of different résumés, both traditional and on-line, you will see how each meets a specific need and describes individual accomplishments.

Three Kinds of Standard Résumés

A Traditional Résumé A traditional résumé lists your educational background and your work experience in reverse chronological order. It highlights job titles, company and school names, dates of enrollment and employment, and other pertinent information needed by the employer. A traditional résumé is best if you have steady career growth, if you intend to remain with your current employer, or if your intended profession calls for it. Certain professions, such as education, law, and accounting, require a traditional résumé. A traditional format would also benefit you in the consulting, finance, and information technology fields.

If you can answer the following questions "yes," you should consider constructing a traditional résumé:

1. Can you show continuity in your work history?
2. Are you looking for a job related to your past experience?
3. Are you unconcerned about employers seeing gaps in your past?
4. Do you want to emphasize nonprofessional jobs that you have held?

As you may have gathered from these questions, there are dangers in using the traditional form. Less impressive jobs and titles are easily seen, frequent job changes are apparent, gaps between jobs are evident, and less professional jobs (for example, summer and part-time work, or work as a clerk, waitress, construction worker, or secretary) receive as much emphasis as professional ones. These problems are especially disconcerting for people reentering the job market, for a graduate student with no work experience, and for the college student whose only work experience has been part-time and summer jobs in fast-food restaurants, at local supermarkets, as a life guard, or as a clerk in the family business. If you fall within one of these categories, read on, but also consider using a functional or skills emphasis résumé, which will be described later. In addition, a traditional résumé places little value on nonpaid work, such as community programs, campus activities, and volunteer associations. Table 16.3 highlights the parts of a traditional résumé in the order in which those parts should appear.

If you are currently in school, you may want to replace the headings following *Educational Background*. Possible changes include *Employment Background, Work Experience, Financial/Banking Experience, Business Experience, Other Experience, Skills Areas, Honors and Activities,* or *Languages*. The résumé in Figure 16.1 represents the traditional format.

A Functional Résumé The functional résumé is preferable to a traditional résumé if there are gaps you do not want to emphasize or if your background does not include the normal things that go into the traditional format (for example, work experience).

The functional résumé does list your education and jobs, but it organizes this material in a more concise way and allows your experiences to be described by function instead of by employment history, job titles, company names, and dates of

TABLE 16.3   **Parts of a Traditional Résumé**

Identification	Includes your name, address with zip code (permanent and local address if applicable), your telephone and fax numbers with an area code, and your e-mail address.
Job Objective	Relatively short-term in nature, expresses your job goal and implies what you are capable of doing for an employer. In this part, describe a specific job, functional field, or type of industry, but do not list two unrelated fields, such as real estate and banking, because it will make you appear indecisive. Similar to the thesis of a report, your job objective should set the focus for the rest of your résumé. There is a negative to consider in listing a job objective. Such a listing takes up valuable space and could limit you to only a particular job.
Educational Background	Lists each of your degrees in order of importance, beginning with the highest level. If you have had no work experience, your education is most likely to be your best asset, so place this section immediately following the job objective. Your description should include the names of both your graduate and undergraduate schools, the specific title of your degrees, the dates received, the area of academic concentration, and any significant research papers or reports. List grade point average and class standing only if they are exceptional.
Work Experience	Describes your jobs in reverse chronological order. Be factual, but emphasize the more important positions, and minimize the less important. State the number of people supervised, amount of budget controlled, and special projects. If you have limited work experience, include summer and part-time employment. Do not mention salary.
Volunteer or Community Activities	Describes jobs you have done, significant responsibilities you held, and the learning that you obtained.
Military Service	Lists the branch, dates of service, rank, and present obligation. If your military work assignments relate to your present job objective, describe them here. If your discharge was honorable, mention that.
Personal Background	Highlights interests, hobbies, languages, computer competency, publications, certifications, professional associations, special honors, and accomplishments. Be careful here. This section works well if you have done something unusual or have had little work experience. Nothing is gained, however, if you simply list tennis and skiing.
References	Identifies people who are in a position to describe you and your ability or characteristics and perhaps your previous work record. Do not use names unless the people listed have agreed to write a recommendation for you. In most instances it is probably best to have potential employers ask you to have references sent to them.

employment. You can describe what functions you have found most satisfying, what research you have done, and how you have handled problems or managed people. A functional résumé allows you to relate your material in an exciting and personal way. You can even include travel, community activities, and sports. The functional résumé is preferred to the traditional if you are

1. Changing careers
2. Entering the job market with no work history, but have other relevant experience to offer
3. Returning to the job market after an absence

FIGURE 16.1   A Traditional Résumé

Kyle Woo
123 Baseline
Boulder, CO 23920
(310) 555-7321
kwoo@mail.eoc.edu

Career Focus: International Business

Education

University of Colorado

B.S., Business Administration (2001)
Emphasis: **International Business**

Representative Coursework

Introduction to International Business	International Finance
Management of Multinational Enterprises	International Marketing
World Commerce and Development	International Management

Related Experiences

– **Pacific Rim Trip:** Visited Hong Kong, Bangkok, Seoul, and Singapore in connection with CU coursework. Opportunity gave exposure to conducting business in the Pacific Rim.

– **International Business Internship:** Under direction of CU Small Business Center, worked with entrepreneurs from Ireland in researching, identifying, and contacting companies offering potential for import/export business.

– **Import Experience:** Presently employed with Far East Trade Company which specializes in importing fine jewelry from Hong Kong, Malaysia, and India; recommend product purchase, maintain inventory, and organize shows for sales in five western states.

Computer Usage

Extensive computer coursework (60+ hours) with knowledge of various desktop hardware and software applications, including Lotus 1-2-3, Microsoft Office, and dBase III+ and IV. Extensive application of World Wide Web.

Employment Summary

Personally financed 100% of education through the following employment:

Import/Sales: Far East Trade Company	1999–Present
Assistant Manager/Driver: Boulder Cab	1998–1999
Convention Coordinator: Broker Hotel	1997–1998
Waiter: Bouldrado Hotel	1996–1997

Affiliations

International Business Association
Pacific Rim Trade Association
Toastmasters International

Desire to Relocate—References Upon Request

4. Seeking a position unrelated to your previous employment
5. Moving from one professional realm into another (for example, office assistant to manager)

Some activities that provide relevant experience include course work, internships, student government, volunteer work, extracurricular involvement, and military experience.

In Figure 16.2, John Espinoza's résumé highlights his experience in casework, group work, and administration in a way that the traditional résumé would not allow. Note that he illustrates each function with good examples. Be creative. Describe how, as a residence hall advisor, you reacted to disruptive behavior on your hall floor; how you tied together the material learned in two or three classes to produce a significant research project; how your professor incorporated your research in a paper; how you established and managed a house-painting company in the summers of your college years and sold it upon graduation; how your quick reaction saved a drowning child at the swimming pool.

If you have been working for several years, you are probably leery of using the functional style. Yes, some personnel officers and employment agencies frown on its use. Yes, 99 percent of the résumés in the marketplace seem to be of the traditional variety. But remember, your résumé works as it is intended as a marketing tool if it gets people to see you—and believe in you—in a way they otherwise would not. If your résumé looks like 200 other résumés, all traditional, how is an employer going to pull your sheet from the pile in order to grant the interview? You have to choose what puts you in the best light. Do not discard the functional résumé just because it is not as commonly used as the traditional.

A Skills Emphasis Résumé A skills emphasis résumé resembles a functional résumé in format. It always leads off with an identification section (see parts of a traditional résumé), followed by an objective or desired position. The objective should highlight some of the skills that the applicant describes in the résumé. For example, "Desired: A SALES POSITION leading to a career in staff marketing and management that calls for skills in leadership, communication, financial analysis, and creativity." Next, include a short background narrative, then a description of how that background has helped develop various skills, such as leadership, communication, analysis, or creativity. Possible skill headings include:

- Supervisory and Management Experience
- Computational and Analytical Skills
- Writing and Editing Experience
- Administrative and Leadership Experience
- Creativity and Physical Dexterity
- Teaching and Communication Skills
- Retailing and Sales Experience
- Interpersonal Communication Skills
- Market Research and Writing Skills
- Financial Development and Planning Skills
- Sales and Fund Raising Experience.

Figure 16.3 shows the skills emphasis résumé of Sarah Dunn. Figures 16.4 and 16.5 show how Debbie Moore turned her traditional résumé into one that emphasizes skills.

FIGURE 16.2   A Functional Résumé

John T. Espinoza
1125 Bennet Way   (408) 555-4360 (home)
San Jose, California   (408) 555-0157 (work)
                         espinoza@aol.org

OBJECTIVE: Seek directorship of community-based social organization.

EDUCATION: Master of Business Administration, May 2001
                   University of California, Berkeley, California

                   Master of Social Work, May 1999
                   San Jose State University, San Jose, California

                   Thesis: "Effective Design of Community-Based Programs for Juveniles in Santa Clara County."
                   A comprehensive survey of junior and senior high students and community program administra-
                   tors to determine effectiveness of community-based adolescent programs.

                   Bachelor of Arts in Social Services, May 1993
                   University of the Pacific, Stockton, California

                   Able to read, write, and speak Spanish fluently.

EXPERIENCE: Coordinator and Counselor for community-based agencies, experienced in assessing immediate
Casework   and long-range needs of families in a variety of stress areas including marital discord, delin-
                   quency, drug abuse, and unemployment. Interacted with clients both individually and in groups,
                   making referrals to service agencies as needed. Initiated individual follow-up and reevaluation
                   procedures.

Group Work   Created, organized, and supervised after-school and weekend recreational programs for adoles-
                   cents. Designed and implemented local ongoing basketball competition program as a major
                   group fund-raising event. Cofacilitated parent group counseling sessions on teenage drug abuse.

Administration   Organized, trained, and supervised group of volunteers for operation of stress hotline program;
                   wrote and was awarded grant for development of a social service handbook. Coordinated the
                   research and publishing of *Directory of Community Services* currently in use by American Red
                   Cross, YMCA, and Santa Clara County Department of Social Services.

AFFILIATIONS: Member of National Association of Social Workers, 1993–Present.
                   President of Undergraduate School of Social Work Organization at University of Pacific,
                   1992–1993. Publicity Chairperson of Cinco de Mayo Festival, City of Stockton, 1994.

EMPLOYMENT: *GROUP COUNSELOR MANAGER/COORDINATOR*
                   (field work practicum), 1999–2001
                   Salvation Army–San Jose Community Center
                   San Jose, California

                   COUNSELOR, 1997–1999
                   Family Service Association of the Mid-Peninsula
                   1103 Carmel Avenue
                   Palo Alto, California

                   COORDINATOR, 1994–1996
                   Big Brothers Agency of San Joaquin County
                   Stockton, California

FIGURE 16.3   A Skills Emphasis Résumé

SARAH DUNN
1234 Harvest Avenue
Atlanta, Georgia 49532

Work (422)555-3567
Home (422)555-7654
sdunn@mail.master.edu

CAREER OBJECTIVE

MARKETING SUPPORT REPRESENTATIVE where skills in administration and management, program development, public relations, and writing can be used.

PROFESSIONAL ACCOMPLISHMENTS

Administrative/Management
- Selected and trained sales and volunteer staffs of up to twenty individuals.
- Managed and authorized expenditures of budgets exceeding $600,000.
- Received "State Award for High Achievement in Health Field."

Program Development
- Created innovative public health education and patient services programs for three counties.
- Raised over $150,000 for American Heart Association through "Run-for-Life" program.

Public Relations
- Engineered sales achievement campaigns netting increased revenues of $75,000 in two months.
- Designed marketing-oriented brochures, posters, and fliers for numerous organizations.

Writing/Editing
- Served as editor of community health newsletter with a circulation of 20,000.
- Authored *Training Manual for Volunteer Health Educators.*
- Researched and was awarded grants totaling over $50,000.

EXPERIENCE SUMMARY

Assistant Director, American Heart Association, Atlanta. Initiated and developed tri-county programs for community education. Developed and implemented budgets. Wrote several grants for additional funding of programs. Administered extensive community education projects. (May 2000–present)

Advisor, Academic Advisement Center, University of Georgia, Athens, Georgia. Counseled and advised diverse populations on academic concerns. Set up peer counseling program. Developed ongoing training program for volunteer staff. (Sept. 1998–May 2000)

Sales Supervisor, Nemann Marcus Department Store, Sunnyvale, California. Supervised four departments, twenty full- and part-time salespersons. Trained all new personnel. Completed weekly sales progress reports. (June 1997–May 1998)

EDUCATION

Master of Business Administration (May 2000)
University of Georgia, Athens, Georgia

Bachelor of Arts Degree in Psychology (May 1997)
Tulane University, New Orleans, Louisiana

FIGURE 16.4 **The Traditional Résumé of Deborah Moore**

Deborah Moore
129 Main Oak #27
Plano, Texas 75243
214-555-3125
dmoore@mail.smu.edu

EDUCATION:

1998–2001 *Southern Methodist University, Dallas, Texas*
MBA – Finance emphasis, August, 2001

1985–1989 *Miami University, Oxford, Ohio*
BBA – Marketing/Psychology, June 1989

WORK EXPERIENCE:

1997–Present *Frito-Lay, Inc. – Plano, Texas*
Senior Buyer – Capital Equipment
Negotiated, prepared, and administered major domestic and international capital equipment contracts for new plant construction and companywide production innovations. Procurement project coordinator for Engineering and Research divisions. Total budget: $100 million.

1993–1997 *Quality Chemical Corporation – Dallas, Texas and Cleveland, Ohio*
Senior Buyer – Chemicals
Responsible for procurement of bulk commodities and specialty chemicals for Electrochemical, Soda Products, and Plastics divisions. Transportation interface included truck, rail, barge, and ocean vessel movements. Total budget: $40 million.
Buyer – Chemicals
Procurement of bulk commodities and minor metals for Electrochemical and Soda Products divisions. Total budget: $15 million.

1991–1993 *Arthur G. McKee Corporation – Cleveland, Ohio*
Purchasing Agent
Responsible for total instrumentation and control panel procurement for petrochemical contracts.
Administrative Assistant to Project Purchasing Manager
Assisted in the coordination of total procurement for domestic iron and steel and petrochemical projects.
Assistant Chief Expeditor
Supervised fourteen Assistant Buyers and In-Plant Expeditors.
Assistant Buyer
Expedited U.S. capital equipment for the construction of a Brazilian steel mill.

1985–1987 *Procter & Gamble, Health & Beauty Aids Division – New Orleans, Louisiana*
Sales Representative for wholesale grocery, drug, variety, and mass merchandise outlets in Louisiana and Mississippi with responsibility for complete merchandising and advertising programs. Winner of three first place awards for direct shipment contests.

ADDITIONAL EDUCATION AND ACTIVITIES

ISO 9000 Compliance Seminar, Karass Negotiating Seminar, Kepner-Tregoe Problem Solving/Decision Analysis, Total Quality Management Training, Phases I and II, Juran Institute, Purchasing Management Association, Career-Track Seminar: "High Impact Communication Skills," "Personal Power For Unlimited Success," with Tony Robbins, "Completeness: Managing For The 21st Century" with Phillip Crosby

FIGURE 16.5   **Deborah Moore's Résumé Revised for Skills Emphasis**

Deborah Moore
129 Main Oak #27
Dallas, Texas 75243
214-555-3125
dmoore@mail.smu.edu

DESIRE

A PROCUREMENT MANAGEMENT POSITION, leading to the Vice Presidency, that requires skills in negotiation, communication, financial analysis, planning and budgeting, and leadership.

Background includes: negotiating major domestic and international capital equipment contracts; individual and group presentation training and experience; contract financial background supplemented by MBA finance emphasis; contract renewal, inventory, and standard cost planning and budgeting skills; direct supervisory experience; knowledge of various skill seminar training techniques.

RELATED EXPERIENCE AND ACCOMPLISHMENTS

NEGOTIATION As a chemical and equipment senior buyer, led many successful individual and team negotiations for multimillion dollar contracts, resulting in outstanding cost savings.
When buying feedstock chemicals, completed purchasing negotiation seminar led by leading consultant in field.

COMMUNICATION As a sales representative, have had professional training and experience in making presentations. While working as a chemical buyer, further developed skills through quarterly presentations to upper management.
Past performance reviews have favorably rated oral and written communication abilities.

FINANCIAL ANALYSIS All previous purchasing positions strengthened skills in numerical analysis.
As a graduate student, MBA courses were taken in Advanced Finance, International Finance, and financial intermediaries.
Through employment as a senior capital equipment buyer, gained experience in the use of a personal computer and various financial software packages.

PLANNING AND BUDGETING After attaining the position of senior buyer, administered $40–$100 million dollar per year procurement budgets; successfully managed time, money, and human resource constraints.

LEADERSHIP As a sales representative, won three volume sales contests.
Throughout career have shown rapid progression from associate to senior buyer.
With all employers, developed direct supervisory experience over buyers and expeditors.
While working as a graduate assistant, wrote portions of a management text teaching manual.

WORK HISTORY

Senior Buyer, Frito-Lay, Inc., Dallas, TX. Contracted capital equipment for new plant construction from 1997 to present.
Senior Buyer/Buyer, Quality Chemical Corp., Dallas, TX and Cleveland, OH. Purchased commodity chemical feedstocks, 1993–1997.
Purchasing Agent/Assistant Chief Expeditor/Assistant Buyer, Arthur G. McKee Corporation, Cleveland, OH. International capital equipment procurement experience in petrochemical and iron and steel industries, 1991–1993.
Sales Representative, Procter & Gamble Distributing Co., New Orleans, LA, 1989–1991.

EDUCATION

MBA, Southern Methodist University, Dallas, TX, August 2001. Emphasis in Finance.
BBA, Miami University, Oxford, OH, June 1989. Business studies in Psychology and Marketing.

Do's and Don'ts for Standard Résumés

As an advanced business student, you will have more education and in many instances more work experience than undergraduates. Use this to your advantage in writing your résumé. Instead of having a résumé like those produced by many under-graduates—listing the basics in general terms—focus your résumé on the specific company you desire to work for and on the specific job you desire to do. With the help of a word processor, you can even tailor a separate résumé to the requirements of each job you apply for. Before you write your résumé, read the following list of do's and don'ts.

Do's for Résumés

1. Strive for a balance between what you say you have done on the job and what you have actually done. Do not worry about listing a multitude of titles and meaningless accomplishments. Instead, selectively relate the major activities that have made you the person your future employer needs.

2. Present yourself in several ways, to different employers, with different résumés. For an interview, the *traditional* format may facilitate the question-and-answer process. For showing that your abilities are exactly what a company needs for a specific job, the *skills emphasis* résumé may be the best. For the employer who wants to know more about you than your previous work experience listing might show, the *functional* approach may be in order.

3. State your job objective in terms of the type of employment needs at the organization you are approaching. If you are simultaneously applying for an administrative position with a health organization and for a management training program with a corporate bank, your objective will differ significantly. Write two résumés, each with a different objective. Make your objective in each very specific; it will give the impression that you have a clear understanding of the job you are seeking and that you desire to do that work.

4. Organize and focus your résumé. You can use the journalistic approach for this. Reporters always start their story with a headline and a leading paragraph that not only captures the reader's attention but gives the reader the basic information needed to understand the story that follows. Each major division and subdivision of your résumé should lead with a headline, contain an excellently worded and focused lead paragraph, and complete the unit of thought with the remaining words.

5. Save a few important items about yourself that are not placed in your résumé. Since few people are hired from the reading of a résumé, you should say what needs to be said and no more. Be honest, but never volunteer information that could preclude a face-to-face interview.

6. Update your résumé every six months. This will make you more eligible for available promotions, allow you to list pertinent material while it is still fresh in your mind, and purge information as it becomes obsolete. For instance, by the time you are completing advanced work, you should no longer be listing the high school or prep school you attended. As you become established in your profession, limit college activities and substitute activities related to

your job and postcollege years. Keep a file of résumé information handy; put a reminder in the file each time you begin an activity or write something that is résumé material. The accumulated notes will help you update your résumé on short notice and remember all items of importance. Periodically this material can then be added to the résumé file in your word processor. It is a good idea to have an up-to-date résumé available at all times.

7. Follow the rules of good writing as you prepare your résumé. Avoid using personal pronouns and other egotistical references. Avoid jargon, cliches, and technical terms that others will not understand. Try for originality in wording and never borrow phrases from other people's résumés. Use Table 16.4 to translate earlier identified skills, interests, and values into expressive action verbs. The résumé should contain no typos or crossed out information. Use a high-quality printer to ensure that the final copy is clean and reproduces well.

8. Avoid the canned look. Your résumé should look polished but not like you have received assistance with it. Résumés prepared by professional services often start with a general statement of objective. They are easy to pick out and boring to read. Avoid this by making your objective personal and specific.

TABLE 16.4   **Action Verb List**

Abstracted	Corresponded	Founded	Observed	Reduced
Accomplished	Counseled	Generated	Obtained	Referred
Administered	Created	Hired	Operated	Represented
Advised	Decided	Identified	Ordered	Reported
Analyzed	Delegated	Improved	Organized	Researched
Appraised	Delivered	Implemented	Originated	Responsible
Arbitrated	Demonstrated	Increased	Oversaw	for
Arranged	Designed	Initiated	Participated	Resolved
Assembled	Detected	Innovated	Performed	Restored
Assessed	Determined	Installed	Persuaded	Reviewed
Assisted	Developed	Instituted	Photographed	Routed
Attended	Devised	Interacted	Planned	Scheduled
Audited	Diagnosed	Interpreted	Predicted	Scored
Built	Directed	Instructed	Prepared	Selected
Calculated	Discovered	Interviewed	Presented	Served
Campaigned	Dispensed	Invented	Processed	Sold
Charted	Disproved	Investigated	Produced	Solved
Classified	Distributed	Judged	Programmed	Spoke
Coached	Drafted	Learned	Promoted	Streamlined
Collected	Drew up	Lectured	Protected	Studied
Completed	Edited	Led	Provided	Supervised
Compiled	Elected	Listened	Published	Supplied
Composed	Eliminated	Logged	Purchased	Synthesized
Computed	Evaluated	Maintained	Questioned	Systematized
Conducted	Examined	Managed	Raised	Taught
Consulted	Expanded	Mediated	Realized	Tested
Consolidated	Expedited	Monitored	Received	Trained
Constructed	Facilitated	Motivated	Recommended	Translated
Contributed	Financed	Navigated	Recorded	Updated
Coordinated	Formulated	Negotiated	Recruited	Wrote

9. Be careful when listing community activities. Always make sure the items support the job you are seeking. Some employers may not see your church activities or Rotary Club office as valuable to them or as evidence of leadership, especially if the overall focus of your extracurricular activities is narrow.

Don'ts for Résumés

1. Don't follow the free-flowing form of writing and put everything about yourself onto paper in a helter-skelter manner. Organize your message into a simple, complete, and concise outline. Always ask, "How will this document sell me?" A few years ago the *Wall Street Journal* assembled a group of recruiters who reviewed an executive résumé and indicated how the wording either added or subtracted from the applicant's value to a company. The results can be viewed in Figure 16.6.[6]

2. Don't assume that a prospective employer will carefully read through your résumé. Most authorities agree that your résumé has less than 30 seconds to make an impression on the reader, an impression that is either good or bad. Since many personnel professionals use résumés to try to eliminate applicants, they read them with a negative bias. Avoid listing anything that will immediately disqualify you.

3. Don't let college placement officers persuade you to limit your résumé to only one page if you truly need more space. While the majority of placement experts agree that one page is best, the consensus is that two pages or even three are acceptable, *if your information is pertinent and necessary*. The key is to make sure everything you include is necessary. The Harvard Graduate School of Business Administration several years ago laid down a general guideline for its graduates and alumni:

   1 or 2 pages—for business school students with business experience
   2 pages—for business school alumni up to ten years out
   3 pages—for business school alumni more than ten years out.[7]

   Often advanced students submit to the placement officer the requested one-page résumé, only later to expand the one page into two or three pages. This is generally referred to as the **expanded data sheet**. The applicant carries the expanded form into the interview and can highlight new items for the interviewer.

4. Don't let the basic questions go unanswered. List your strengths, what you have done in the past, and what you want to do for the company.

5. Don't mention salary in your résumé. This may scare off some employers, limit your negotiation potential, and lock you into an undesirable salary range. Salaries should be discussed only during an interview, preferably the second one.

6. Don't list references in your résumé. They are seldom called until you are asked about them, the list consumes valuable space, and the individuals may resent the intrusion into their privacy if they are called repeatedly.

7. Don't list information that might violate fair employment practice laws.

FIGURE 16.6   The Value of Résumé Wording

Pricing the Past

More than you may realize, your past is a price tag. What you've done, where you've lived and worked, the schools you've attended, even your hobbies—any and all of it can play into your pay. And those doing the playing and paying—recruiters and employers— are rarely more brutal than in tough times like these.

Here's how one professional might fare in the pricing game, based on suggestions from recruiters with an eye for detail—and a sharp pencil.

—Gilbert Fuchsberg

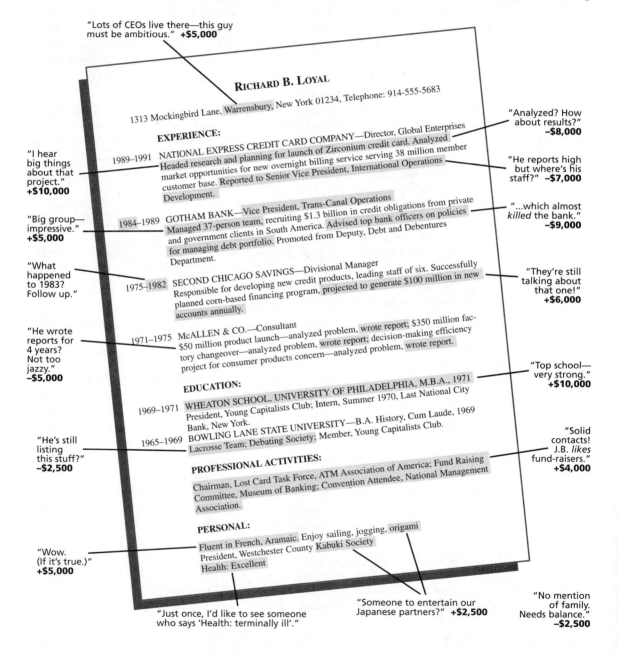

"Lots of CEOs live there—this guy must be ambitious." **+$5,000**

RICHARD B. LOYAL

1313 Mockingbird Lane, Warrensbury, New York 01234, Telephone: 914-555-5683

"Analyzed? How about results?" **–$8,000**

EXPERIENCE:

"I hear big things about that project." **+$10,000**

1989–1991   NATIONAL EXPRESS CREDIT CARD COMPANY—Director, Global Enterprises Headed research and planning for launch of Zirconium credit card. Analyzed market opportunities for new overnight billing service serving 38 million member customer base. Reported to Senior Vice President, International Operations Development.

"He reports high but where's his staff?" **–$7,000**

"Big group—impressive." **+$5,000**

1984–1989   GOTHAM BANK—Vice President, Trans-Canal Operations Managed 37-person team, recruiting $1.3 billion in credit obligations from private and government clients in South America. Advised top bank officers on policies for managing debt portfolio. Promoted from Deputy, Debt and Debentures Department.

"...which almost *killed* the bank." **–$9,000**

"What happened to 1983? Follow up."

1975–1982   SECOND CHICAGO SAVINGS—Divisional Manager Responsible for developing new credit products, leading staff of six. Successfully planned corn-based financing program, projected to generate $100 million in new accounts annually.

"They're still talking about that one!" **+$6,000**

"He wrote reports for 4 years? Not too jazzy." **–$5,000**

1971–1975   McALLEN & CO.—Consultant $50 million product launch—analyzed problem, wrote report; $350 million factory changeover—analyzed problem, wrote report; decision-making efficiency project for consumer products concern—analyzed problem, wrote report.

EDUCATION:

"Top school—very strong." **+$10,000**

1969–1971   WHEATON SCHOOL, UNIVERSITY OF PHILADELPHIA, M.B.A., 1971 President, Young Capitalists Club; Intern, Summer 1970, Last National City Bank, New York.

1965–1969   BOWLING LANE STATE UNIVERSITY—B.A. History, Cum Laude, 1969 Lacrosse Team; Debating Society; Member, Young Capitalists Club.

"He's still listing this stuff?" **–$2,500**

PROFESSIONAL ACTIVITIES:

"Solid contacts! J.B. *likes* fund-raisers." **+$4,000**

Chairman, Lost Card Task Force, ATM Association of America; Fund Raising Committee, Museum of Banking; Convention Attendee, National Management Association.

PERSONAL:

"Wow. (If it's true.)" **+$5,000**

Fluent in French, Aramaic. Enjoy sailing, jogging, origami President, Westchester County Kabuki Society Health: Excellent

"Just once, I'd like to see someone who says 'Health: terminally ill'."

"Someone to entertain our Japanese partners?" **+$2,500**

"No mention of family. Needs balance." **–$2,500**

(These laws will be discussed in Chapter 17.) Listing information such as your age, marital status, and number of children is permissible, but be aware that some companies and government agencies cannot consider résumés that might allow them to discriminate through age, ancestry, gender, color, national origin, marital status, children, health (including any handicap or disability), military status or service (if applicable or recent), race, or religious preference. Usually, photographs should not be included with résumés.

8. Don't lie on your résumé. While you may never be caught, the use of small puffed-up facts can grow into the habit of falsifying more important data. Once you are caught, your job will surely end, and with damaged credibility your professional life will probably be finished. How should you avoid lying?

- Don't list more titles than you have had.
- Don't list degrees that you have never earned.
- Don't call yourself a supervisor if you have never supervised.
- Don't state that you have had more job responsibility than you have actually had.
- Don't list jobs you have never had.
- Don't stretch facts in order to outsmart the interviewer. (A person making $50,000 says he is making $55,000 in hopes of pushing his new salary to $60,000.)

9. Don't list reasons for leaving previous employers. Such statements are open to misinterpretation and assumptions. This information is best discussed during the interview.

Consider an Electronic Approach to Job Searching

We have talked about the design and writing of standard résumés. Library research, parents, friends, and on-campus recruiting will probably remain the main networking tool used by most college job seekers for some time. However, technological changes have forced organizations to rethink the data collection process. Employers now scan, download, upload, keyword-search, and then bank thousands of résumés that they receive. All of this can be done in a matter of minutes, saved on a small disc as compared to several file drawers, and never be read by an individual. Consequently full text-searchable on-line job and résumé databases have grown quickly. Realizing this change, an increasing number of college students now use the growing web of computer networks to enhance their chances of getting the best job.

Consider the following statistics at the end of 1999.

- 2.5 million . . . Estimated number of résumés posted on the Internet
- 28 million . . . Estimated number of Web sites that offer job-posting services
- 65% . . . Percentage of on-line job seekers who are not engineers or computer professionals
- $105 million . . . Amount employers spent on on-line recruiting in 1998
- $1.7 billion . . . Amount employers will spend on on-line recruiting by 2003
- 45% . . . Percentage of Fortune Global 500 companies actively recruiting on Internet in January 1999.[8]

When you bring it down to an individual company basis, the remarkable movement makes sense. At Cisco Systems, 81 percent of the résumés received come via the Web, 66 percent of new hires come from on-line recruiting, and 68 days are shaved off the company's hiring cycle by using this method. Another employer said the change makes great economic sense. The hiring cost of an employee goes from $12,000 for a classified newspaper ad to $1,650 via the Web.[9]

The traditional job search process and on-line searching are similar in that both require networking, preparing and sending résumés, preparing for interviews, and sending correspondence. But, according to job expert Richard Bolles, there are five primary uses of on-line services for job hunting or career planning:

1. They are a place to post your *résumé*;
2. They are a place for you to search for *vacancies* listed by employers;
3. They are a place to get some job-hunting help or *career counseling*;
4. They are a place to find out *information* about companies or organizations;
5. They are a place to make *contacts* who may help you find information or may help you get in for an interview at a particular place.[10]

Dixon and Tiersten add four other advantages to Bolles's list:

1. *Global Availability*. For just a few dollars a month you can make contact with thousands of employers throughout the world and save thousands of dollars in travel expenses.
2. *Low Cost*. For just a few dollars you can reach thousands of potential employers at a fraction of the cost of printing and mailing résumés.
3. *Quick Access*. The real-time availability of discussion groups and referrals, and the ability to send your résumé instantly and to answer employers' questions in turn, cuts your job search time from days to minutes. You can be one of the first to apply for a job.
4. *Personality Tailoring*. With the exception of your creative writing style, the traditional job search approach requires you to wait until the interview to demonstrate your real personality. By going on-line, you increase your potential. This is especially true if you use the World Wide Web, where you can add photos of yourself, audio snippets of your voice, and even video segments of your work and projects.[11]

Three Electronic Résumés

As we have seen, the wise job hunter has two versions of a résumé available: one for actual interviews, the other for the Internet. Within the electronic category three possible résumé types exist: scannable, plain paper, and Web.[12] After you read about these, spend some time reviewing information about electronic résumés by referring to Tables 16.5 and 16.6.

Scannable Résumé This is a standard paper résumé that has been redesigned for potential employers to scan into a computer database. Be careful here. The smart job hunter doesn't settle on producing the scannable version, but makes one for the computer to read and one for people to read that includes more sophisticated formatting.

Most employer systems use an "electronic applicant tracking" (EAT) system. After the text is scanned, the system "reads" the text and looks for specific criteria like work history, titles, years of experience, education, and skills. If your résumé is unscannable it is rejected. Here are several tips that will make a scannable résumé more effective.

1. **Use Keywords** When people read résumés they like to see action verbs. When computers read résumés they look for keywords—nouns or short phrases. These words describe the knowledge, skills, abilities, and experiences that a candidate possesses. In essence the words describe what you have done in the past, and thus, what qualifies you for the present job. When there is a match between what the company wants and what you have, you score a "hit." It is important to get as many "hits" as possible. The scannable résumé must be rewritten to use keywords and not verbs. The examples below show the necessary conversion.

Functional Résumé
"I am a corporate safety analyst with a bachelor's degree in a related field. I have four years of experience in the field."

Scannable Résumé
"I am a corporate safety analyst. I have a bachelor's degree in Chemical Engineering from the University of Michigan. I have four years of experience with OSHA regulations."

Functional Résumé
"I assisted the marketing director in creating a new marketing strategy for e-commerce."

Scannable Résumé
"Assistant creator of new e-commerce marketing strategy."

Employer databases today use around 25 keywords as they scan résumés. The keywords are some of the most common words used in the marketplace. In the examples above the keywords are "safety analyst," "chemical engineering," and "OSHA," "assistant," "creator," "marketing strategy," and "e-commerce." In an on-line search, individual words are important, and the correct placement of the words is just as critical for effectiveness and description. The computer doesn't care if you are "empowered," "directed," or "accomplished." It looks for the words it has been programmed to find.

2. **Keep Your Language Current** Industry-specific language changes constantly. In order to use keywords that will be noticed, you have to familiarize yourself with the words pertinent to your field. This requires constantly browsing publications, newspapers ads, and other on-line résumés.

While jargon should be avoided in standard résumés, you should make use of it if employers use it to describe job requirements. The same is true for acronyms and detailed technical terms.

3. **Avoid Overusing Important Words** In most searches, each keyword counts only once, regardless of how many times it is used. In the previous example, "OSHA" will give only one point . . . even if it is used 25 times. Therefore, your chances of having more matchable words is increased with the variety of words that you use.

4. **Career Objectives Must Be Tightly Focused** You can get by with, "I want to be a computer systems engineer," in a traditional résumé. In an electronic résumé, the more specific the better, e.g., "I want to manage system and network configurations for UNIX 4.1.2, SOLARIS 1.2, and SYBASE Relational Database 4.9.2."[13]

5. **Format Your Electronic Résumé for Scanning** Your standard résumés need lots of white space, bold type, and different fonts for eye appeal. The opposite is true for an electronic résumé. Efficiency, not elegance, is the rule. Scanners often mistranslate serif, underline, boldface, and italic type styles. Colored and textured papers, borders, bold lines, pictures, and graphics also prove hard to read.[14]

The most appropriate layout for a scannable résumé follows some basic rules:

- Left justify everything.
- Place your name, in caps, alone on the first line and on the first line of all other pages.
- Use 8½ × 11-inch white paper with black ink.
- Use a serif font—Times New Roman, Palatino, New Century Schoolbook, and Courier.
- Use a font size of 10–14.
- Capitalize and set off major section titles with boldface lettering.
- Start the résumé with a concise, comprehensive keyword summary of your credentials.
- Don't condense spacing between letters.
- Avoid fancy treatment like italics, underline, and shadows.
- Make sure letters don't touch.
- Use white space to separate sections.
- If you are presently working, follow the keyword summary with an "experience" section that details your occupational background. If you are presently a student, list your "education" qualifications after the summary.
- Normally the last sections of the résumé describe your education, professional affiliations, and any awards. Personal data and reference statements should be omitted.

Figure 16.7 gives an example of an electronic résumé.

Plain Text Résumé After you have developed a scannable résumé you will want to convert it to ensure that it can be read by everyone. To do this, save it in ASCII or DOS format. This can easily be sent by e-mail. Such a file contains just plain words. The characteristics removed are the same as those of the scannable résumé: no pic-

FIGURE 16.7   An Electronic Résumé

PAUL M. GREELEY
P.O. Box 818
Oklahoma City, OK 73150
405-555-8765
greeley@aol.org

OBJECTIVE
Desire senior management human resource director position

PROFILE
Human Resources Specialist with over 10 years experience in personnel functions including management development, training, employee relations, benefits compensation, recruitment and outplacement. Certificate in ADA, Coaching, Negotiating, Myers-Briggs Type Assessment, and TQM Training. Specific training skills include Computer-Based, Interactive Video, Workplace Attitude, Diversity, Adult Learning, Needs Analysis, Teams, and Group Facilitation.

PROFESSIONAL BACKGROUND
03/98 to Present   General Motors Assembly, Oklahoma City, OK
Personnel Manager — report to Plant Manager of a manufacturing facility with over 1,500 employees. Involved in all corporate Human Resource related functions.
- Coordinate all recruiting, hiring, compensation management, employee benefits packages, and pension and insurance administration.
- Oversee labor/management/employee relations.
- Negotiated a four year labor contract that met corporate objectives.
- Reduced annual cost of Worker's Compensation Insurance and Group Health Plan by over 25%.
- Designed and implemented policies for Family & Medical Leave, Americans with Disabilities Act, Drug & Alcohol Abuse, and Sexual Harassment.

12/94 to 2/98   Dell Computers, Austin, TX
Training Director—reported to Vice President of Human Resources for computer manufacturing plant of 1,500 employees.
- Designed, developed and delivered customized training which was determined by needs assessment.
- Coordinated all employee training, including vendor contracting for on-site programs.
- Reduced in-house cost of personal computer (PC) training by 27%.
- Designed database system for recording employee training records as part of ISO 9000 compliance.
- Provided company's highly popular diversity training program to 20 corporate clients.

FIGURE 16.7 **An Electronic Résumé (Concluded)**

6/93 to 11/94   Hallmark Corporation, Kansas City, MO

Human Resource Generalist—reported to Human Resource Director for greeting card company with 2,000 employees.

- Successfully recruited artists, designers, programmers, and managers for corporate office.
- Wrote interviewing manual for supervisors and managers.
- Designed campus interview process for recruiters.

6/91 to 5/93   Fred Pryor Training, Kansas City, KS

Trainer—reported to owner of pre-packaged seminar company.

- Initiated start-up functions for needs analysis and development of 25 client training programs.
- Created and developed 12 in-house training courses.
- Instructed five "public seminars" at sites across the nation and in Canada.
- Gained overview of training field through temporary assignments for several clients.
- Wrote copy for bi-monthly newsletter.

EDUCATION

- Executive MBA from University of Oklahoma
- BBA from University of Kansas
- Additional training in human resources at Harvard Business School. Certificate in human relations from the University of Oklahoma, Attended numerous management seminars conducted by various employers.

PROFESSIONAL ORGANIZATIONS

- American Society for Training & Development
- Human Resource Exchange
- Society for Human Resource Management
- Toastmaster's International

---

tures, special fonts, graphics, page numbers, or even boldface or italic highlighting. On this résumé make sure you include your e-mail and personal Web site addresses. Be sure to print it out and check it for errors before you send it to an employer.

In sending the plain text résumé by e-mail it is better to cut and paste it than to "attach" it as a file to your message. This will allow for immediate reading without having to download the file and exit to a word processor. One word of warning: don't e-mail your résumé from work. "A recent survey by the American Management

Association found that 27 percent of employers monitor their employees' e-mail. Some even set up alerts when words such as *résumé* appear."[15]

Web Résumé If you want to show your technological abilities, placing the résumé on a database website or on your personal Web site is a good move. If you post it on your personal Web page, you will want to save your scannable document as an HTML document and then open it in your HTML editor. The advantage of this form of résumé is that you can add pictures, audio clips, video clips, and links to created projects. If you send it to Internet employment services you will find that each Web site will have its own rules and procedures for posting your résumé. Remember that once you post it, you lose some control over who will see it.

Top Job Databases on the Web

Hundreds of employment sites list thousands of job advertisements. According to a recent Fortune list, the sites in Table 16.5 are among the best sources to use in finding jobs.[16]

EMPLOYMENT CORRESPONDENCE

After you have completed both your standard and electronic résumés, you should begin considering the types of employment correspondence that you may need to write. This section addresses three primary letter types (application, cold call, and thank-you for the interview), and then suggests ideas for five secondary letter types (oversubscribed interviews, acknowledging an offer, accepting an offer, declining an offer, and inquiring about the status of your application). All of these letters use the formats described earlier in the chapters on writing letters (Chapters 4 through 7) and include the necessary letter parts: correct address, return address, date, signature, and enclosure statement.

The Applicant Letter

The majority of applicants receive job offers as a result of an interview, not in direct response to sending or posting a résumé and application letter. Yet a situation may arise where distance and timing prohibit you from talking to the employer in person. On those rare occasions, a good application letter may win you a key interview or a job.

Before you actually write the letter, gather as many facts as you can about the job and the company. Address your letter to a specific person. Verify the person's correct title and the proper spelling of the name. Even if you must gather this information through a long-distance call to the company, it could save you embarrassment and a rejection based on spelling errors.

TABLE 16.5   **On-line Job Hunter Service**

Top Job Databases on the Web

Hundreds of employment sites list thousands of job advertisements. According to a recent *Fortune* list the following Web sites would be good places to look when searching for jobs.

1. Monster Board (www.monster.com)
Designed for a "younger" crowd, those below 35 years of age and still in the first ten years of their careers. Over a million résumés are posted with password-protection. Excellent set of references and career tools. Attracts over five million hits a month.

2. Career Path (www.careerpath.com/)
Listings of want ads from over 80 U.S. and English newspapers makes this site useful for recent college graduates or relocation needs. The half-million résumé database is private.

3. Career Mosaic (www.careermosaic.com)
A popular employer site for executive-level candidates in high-tech engineering and financial areas. This open résumé database can be searched by job title, description, keyword, or location. It receives more than 300,000 queries daily. Links to sites are geared to certain professions.

4. America's Job Bank (www.jobsearch.org)
A predominately government site that gets its listings from state public employment agencies. Excellent selection of diverse jobs available. You can search by geographic location, education, salary, and or experience.

5. Head Hunter (www.headhunter.net)
Designed like a classified ad, you can post a résumé for free and get enhanced display for a fee. Can be searched by job category, location, education required, pay and employee or contract work. Over 100,000 daily users with 125,000 résumés. New résumés are held in a select pool for a week before public posting.

6. Nation Job Network (www.nationjob.com)
This general job search engine lets you seek jobs or it will even e-mail you job possibilities. Searches can be done by career field, geographic region, education, or salary. A highlight is the special job databases.

7. Hot Jobs (www.hotjobs.com)
You can search by city, region, keywords, job type, and even international opportunities. Employers who use this site can create a "test manager" for specific openings. A "candidate manager" even sifts through résumés for organizations.

8. Net-Temps (www.net-temps.com)
This site is known as a giant for high-quality full- and part-time jobs. It has over 75,000 positions posted by over 1,500 firms. The listings are never more than 30 days old. Company personnel offices never get to review the résumés, only net-temp members who are third-party recruiters.

9. Dice.Com (www.dice.com)
A prime location for computer information technology professionals like programmers and system analysts. The problem with this site is that a searcher must go through a third-party recruiter.

10. Career Builder (www.careerbuilder.com/)
In addition to job listings this site provides helpful tools like a salary survey, salary calculator, and career advice.

Source: Jerry Useem, "For Sale Online: You," *Fortune,* July 5, 1999, pp. 67–78.

TABLE 16.6   **Other General Databases**

www.americanjobs.com	www.itjobsonline.com
www.bestjobsusa.com	www.jobbankusa.com
www.black-collegian.com	www.jobdirect.com
www.careerbuilder.com	www.jobfind.com
www.careercast.com	www.job-hunt.org
www.careercentral.com	www.job-listings.com
www.careercity.com	www.thejobmarket.com
www.careerexchange.com	www.job-searcher.com
www.careerindex.com	www.joboptions.com
www.careermart.com	www.jobtrak.com
www.careersite.com	www.LAIcompass.com
www.careers.wsj.com	www.occ.com
www.cweb.com	www.topjobsusa.com
www.cooljobs.com	www.searchbase.com
www.futurestep.com	www.net-temps.com
www.globecareers.com	www.topjobsusa.com

Four key topics should be discussed in the letter. These items generally constitute complete paragraphs. Figure 16.8 lists them in the preferred order. Figure 16.9 gives an example of an application letter.

Cold Call Letter

In their eagerness to find work, some applicants gather numerous names of organizations and send out résumés en masse. The likelihood of receiving an interview from this approach is low. Nevertheless, because many try this approach, Figure 16.10 gives you the areas to include in your cover letter.

The letter should be brief and should not restate the information contained in your résumé. Be sure to address the letter to a specific person; otherwise it will be sent to the personnel department, which is an immediate dead-end. It is vital that you personalize your message to avoid the look of a form letter.

Thank-You for the Interview Letter

Immediately following a job interview with a company, rush home and prepare a thank-you letter to the key people you talked with. Mail it the same day, if possible. Interviewers are mixed on whether the "thank-you" should be formal (typed) or informal (handwritten). The culture of the organization should give you an indication. If in doubt, type it.

The "thank-you" should be warm, personally focused, and professional in tone. Never fax the thank-you. If it is a note, preferably put it on a heavy vellum stationery, and never on an employer's letterhead. Normally you should not e-mail a thank-you. This is especially true if the interviewer is a "traditionalist," or if you want the e-mail

FIGURE 16.8   **Content of an Application Letter**

Your full address with zip code
Date

Person's name
Title
Company name
Full address with zip code

Dear _____:

(Paragraph 1) Identify the specific position you are applying for, explain how you learned of it, and state your desire to be an applicant.

(Paragraph 2) Describe your understanding of the job requirements and your interest in the company or field of work.

(Paragraph 3) State why you are applying for the job and refer the reader to your résumé. This is a good place to clarify your job or career objective, especially if you have not included it in your résumé. Briefly describe your main qualifications (education and work experience). Stress your strongest offering that relates to the job or field.

(Paragraph 4) Request an interview or an answer to your letter. Display positive eagerness here. While you should give your phone number, with area code, you will find it more advantageous to call the employer after a few days.

Complimentary closing
(Sincerely or Truly yours,)

Your handwritten signature

Your full name typed

Enclosure: (résumé)

FIGURE 16.9   Sample Application Letter

2433 Cox Street
Chicago, IL 73549
February 5, 2001

Mr. Stephen Watts
Vice-President of Training
Macy's Department Store
2500 Park Avenue
New York, NY 20062

Dear Mr. Watts:

I am excited that Macy's Department Store has recently opened a new store in the Chicago suburb. I am interested in joining your energetic team as a member of the buyer training program.

Macy's has stood for quality in the Chicago area, and I have long had a desire to be a part of your quality organization. I especially like your method of having buyers serve as department managers. This is consistent with my objectives in buying and retail management.

In May 2001, I will graduate from the University of Chicago with a degree in Business Administration, with a concentration in marketing. Throughout my academic program, I have taken courses to complement my business degree. Specific courses that I believe have helped prepare me for a career in retailing are advanced psychology, fashion design, layout, organizational behavior, management, interpersonal communications, accounting, and computer science. As you will note on my enclosed résumé, I have supplemented my formal course work with cooperative education work experience at Dillards Department Store. I believe that this work experience, coupled with my academic background, makes me an excellent choice for your buyer training program.

May I meet and talk with you, at your earliest convenience, regarding my interest in Macy's? I will call your office in a few days to arrange an appointment.

Sincerely,

Harry Duncan

Harry Duncan

Enclosure: Résumé

FIGURE 16.10   **Content of a Blind Search Letter**

Your full address with zip code
Date

Name of person
Title of person
Company name
Full address with zip code

Dear _____:

(Paragraph 1) State your desire, as an upcoming graduate, to work for this company. Mention any training programs or work areas for which you would like to be considered.

(Paragraph 2) Refer the reader to your résumé and briefly highlight the areas that relate to the company's field.

(Paragraph 3) Request an interview or consideration for the job.

Complimentary closing
(Sincerely or Truly yours,)

Your handwritten signature

Your full name typed

Enclosure (résumé)

placed in your file. Do use e-mail when quick action matters, if that was the way you sent your résumé, if you are dealing with a high-tech firm, and if your instinct tells you it's the right conduct.[16]

While you may never hear from the company, this letter indicates your maturity and understanding of good business etiquette. Such responses will impress the right person. The initial letter may only state a thank-you and your desire to be considered a real applicant and to have an additional interview. If the additional interviews materialize, your letter could respond to the following situations if they apply:

1. Your out-of-town transportation charges and hotel expenses were paid by the company.
2. You met with future colleagues and discussed the job and the company.
3. You were allowed to observe the work in a department where you would be working, or you were able to observe the work in several departments through which you would rotate during a training program.
4. You were shown various parts of the city, including potential areas where you might want to live.
5. You may have been offered the job and now:
   • Wish to consider it
   • Wish to discuss it with your spouse
   • Wish to accept or reject it
6. If no offer was made, but you want to remain an applicant, express continued interest and a desire to either furnish additional information or participate in additional interviews.

A sample thank-you letter is found in Figure 16.11.

Additional Employment Letters

You may need to write a variety of additional employment letters. Use the following checklist to organize these letters if the occasion arises:

Oversubscribed Placement Center Interviews
1. State your desire to interview on campus, yet your inability to secure a slot on the sign-up sheet.
2. Ask for an interview at the employer's convenience.
3. State your willingness to cover any expenses involved.
4. Refer the employer to your enclosed résumé.

Acknowledging an Offer
1. Acknowledge the company's offer.
2. Express thanks and happiness for having received the offer.
3. If you have decided to accept the offer, state your acceptance.
4. If you are still considering the offer, state the date you will notify them of your decision.

FIGURE 16.11   Sample Thank-You Letter

6115 Dolby Avenue
Colorado Springs, CO 94321
March 13, 2001

Ms. Sharla Barber, President
Barber/Fox Advertising Agency
P.O. Box 1452
Colorado Springs, CO 94325

Dear Ms. Barber:

Thank you for your time and courtesy in meeting with me on Monday, regarding
your position for an account executive at Barber/Fox. The tour of your advertising
facility and the conversations with your staff gave me a clear picture of the accounts
that I would be supervising. I was especially impressed with your creative talent
and your computerized accounting process.

My visit to the Barber/Fox Agency has reaffirmed my desire to be a part of your
organization. I believe my previous account experience with Tracy-Locke, in Dallas,
and my sales work with IBM, in Denver, qualify me for your position.

Thank you once again for interviewing me and allowing me to meet your people. I
would welcome the opportunity to work for Barber/Fox. I look forward to hearing
from you soon.

Sincerely,

Ann Foley

Ann Foley

Accepting an Offer

1. Refer to the date of the letter or telephone call whereby the offer was made.
   (A sample letter accepting an offer is found in Figure 16.12.)
2. Give any information regarding your starting date and necessary moving
   plans.
3. State your warm appreciation of the offer and your pleasure in becoming a
   member of the company.

FIGURE 16.12   Sample Acceptance Letter

P.O. Box SMU 152
Dallas, TX 75275
May 10, 2001

Mr. Gene Burns
Training Director
West-Tex Corporation
1200 W. Commerce
Dallas, TX 75205

Dear Mr. Burns:

I was excited to open my mail today and see your letter of May 5, offering me a position in the training program at West-Tex. I accept!

As I told you during our interview and in my correspondence, West-Tex has been the organization I have dreamed of working for.

The starting date of July 5, 2001, will work perfectly. I am sure we will talk several times prior to my arrival on that date, so any information that you need from me I will be happy to furnish.

I look forward to seeing you, and joining my colleagues in the training program at West-Tex on July 5.

Sincerely,

Herb Finch

Herb Finch

Declining an Offer

1. Thank the employer for the offer.
2. Decline the offer and give a good reason.
3. Express your appreciation for the company's interest in you. (A sample letter which declines an offer is found in Figure 16.13.)

FIGURE 16.13   **Sample Letter Declining an Offer**

12 Lions Way
Memphis, TN 30301
May 10, 2001

Mr. George Clark, President
Valley Savings and Loan
P.O. Box 1421
St. Paul, MN 80522

Dear Mr. Clark:

Thank you for your letter of May 7, 2001, offering me the position of finanical analyst with Valley Savings.

I must decline your offer because I accepted a position last week with First Republic Bank in Nashville.

While I was waiting for the last six weeks to hear from you, I was contacted by the people at First Republic. While the job and salary are comparable, the First Republic position allows me to stay in Tennessee and be closer to my aging parents.

I appreciate your interest in me and I wish you and your staff at Valley Savings the best.

Sincerely,

Mary Lewis Ryan

Mary Lewis-Ryan

Inquiring About Your Application Status

1. Request information regarding the status of your application.
2. State the reason you need this information (especially if you have an offer from another company and must respond to them).
3. Restate your desire to work for the company.
4. Thank the employer for his or her cooperation.

SUMMARY

In your job search, the résumé is often your first contact with an employer. Your résumé should portray you in the most favorable manner possible. Three standard résumé formats are available. The one you decide to use should depend on your educational background and your work experience.

The traditional résumé format lists your educational background and work experience in reverse chronological order. Information about community activities and personal interests can also be included. This résumé style is preferred by people in such fields as education, law, accounting, finance, consulting, and computers.

The functional résumé format is preferred if you have a gap in your work experience or if you prefer to describe your experiences by functions rather than by job titles and company names. This format style is especially preferred by those who want to give a detailed description of specific work or educational projects.

A skills emphasis résumé format resembles the functional résumé because it tends to use paragraphs instead of a traditional outline form. In this résumé, you state your job objective and the skills necessary to do the job. The body of the résumé is then divided into headings of the various skills you listed, followed by a description of how you have mastered and used these skills in your educational and work life.

In addition to the traditional job application process, job seekers should also prepare an electronic résumé. The job search for employ-

ees has been greatly enhanced by on-line employment services. More employers and potential employees are using these services. The chapter described three types: scannable, plain paper, and Web résumés. Résumés created for electronic scanning and review must be prepared differently than standard résumés. Active verbs are replaced with nouns that characterize your skills accurately and which potential employers use and look for. Once entered electronically, a résumé must be constantly maintained and necessary changes quickly made.

After you have written your résumé and you start your job search, there are three different letters you will probably write. The application letter is sent to a specific person in regard to a specific position. The cold call letter is one that is sent out to unknown people in hopes of finding a possible opening. The response on this form of letter is minimal. The thank-you letter is sent immediately following each interview that you have. Additional types of employment letters that you may use are a letter accepting an offer, a letter declining an offer, and a letter inquiring about the status of your application.

The time and effort that you put into producing a high-quality résumé and high-quality employment letters will pay off in helping you get high-quality interviews and, we hope, the job that you desire. In the next chapter, we will walk you through the correct things to do during an interview.

Applications

1. Before starting the interview process, get together with a group of your friends and discuss the three points that Bolles makes in his book: where do you want to live, what do you want to do, and with what company do you want to work? Try to be honest in your discussion and accept the feedback of your friends for real consideration.

2. After you have considered your skills, interests, and values, draft a résumé in each of the three standard formats (traditional, functional, and skills emphasis). Make copies of each and distribute them to friends for review. Ask them to judge which one presents the best verbal picture of you. Find several businesspeople who would also be interested in giving you feedback. Tell them the type of job that you are seeking and ask them which résumé presents the best verbal picture of you in light of that job. After you have done this, decide which standard format you need to use.

3. Using the information provided in the chapter, create an electronic résumé. Next, using the list of Internet Web sites, look at several of the different databases. Consider how they can help you in your job search.

4. To practice for your future job search, take a local paper and turn to the help-wanted section. Pick a job for which you are qualified. Write a letter asking for an interview. Then, assuming that you have had the interview, write a thank-you letter to the company representative. Take both to your instructor and ask for feedback.

DISCUSSION QUESTIONS

1. As a marketing tool, the résumé should include what different categories of information?

2. How does a résumé balance the information needed by an employer and what you want to present?

3. Each of the three standard résumés described in this chapter (traditional, functional, and skills emphasis) serves a different purpose. Describe the types of standard résumés. How do they differ from each other? Under what conditions should you consider using each type?

4. Describe the importance of the electronic résumé. How does it differ from the standard résumé types? In what ways are the electronic résumés similar and different?

5. What five do's and five don'ts for preparing your résumé have helped you as you consider your own résumé?

6. What are some of the items that you should remember as you plan to write and send various types of employment correspondence?

NOTES

1. If you are interested in a more comprehensive examination of your skills, there are a variety of good career books which will probably be housed in your campus career office, or which you can find at a quality bookstore. Richard N. Bolles continues to be a wonderful source. His *The 2000 What Color Is Your Parachute?* devotes more than a hundred pages to the topic. This book has been the premiere source for career planning for over 30 years.

2. Ibid.

3. C. Caggiano, "What Do Workers Want?" *Inc.*, November 1992, p. 101.

4. Edgar H. Schein, "How to Break in the College Graduate," *Harvard Business Review,* November–December 1964, pp. 68–76.

5. *Student Handbook On Résumé Writing*, Harvard Graduate School of Business and Administration, Boston, Massachusetts, p. 2.

6. Gilbert Fuchsberg, "Pricing the Past," *Wall Street Journal*, April 17, 1991, p. R3.

7. *Student Handbook on Résumé Writing*, p. 7.

8. Jerry Useem, "For Sale Online: You," *Fortune*, July 5, 1999, pp. 67–78.

9. Thomas York, "Net Matches Up Employers, Job Seekers," *Investor Business Daily*, May 3, 1999, p. A7.

10. Richard N. Bolles, *The 1995 What Color Is Your Parachute?* Ten Speed Press, Berkeley, California, 1995.

11. Pam Dixon and Sylvia Tiersten, *Be Your Own Headhunter Online*, Random House, New York, 1995, pp. 4–5.

12. The following are two excellent discussions of electronic résumés that were useful for preparing this chapter. *Web's Best Job Sites*, Vol. 5, Issue 6, Sandhills Publishing, Lincoln, Nebraska, 1999; Pam Dixon, *Job Searching Online for Dummies,* IDG Books Worldwide, Chicago, Illinois, 1998.

13. Peter D. Weddle, "Write a High-Powered Electronic Résumé," *National Business Employment Weekly,* August 6–12, 1995, p. 22.

14. Lisa Kalis, "From Click to Corner Office," *Smart Money*, October 1999, pp. 106–120.

15 Ibid. p. 115.

16. Useem, "For Sale Online: You," pp. 67–78.

The Job Interview

In Chapter 16, you read about the importance of having a thoroughly developed, well-written résumé. You also learned the formulas for several employment-related letters. While résumés and employment letters are crucial, you should remember that they are marketing tools and that their primary objective is to help you obtain an interview. The interview is important for both the company and you. Your potential employer measures the value of your talents against the needs of the company and tries to determine whether you will be satisfied with the position and willing to make a true commitment to the organization. The interview offers your best opportunity to sell yourself to your prospective employer. You should leave the interview with a better understanding of the company, whether or not there is good chemistry between you and the company, and whether or not you truly want the job. If there is a match, and if you want the job, then you need to convince the employer that you are qualified for the position and that you will be a positive asset to the company.

Interviewers approach interviews with graduate and undergraduate students differently. If you are an advanced business student, they assume that your continued focus on education and your possible work experience give you a higher maturity level. They also assume that you have given more thought to your career and have spent considerable time researching the company with which you want to work. Finally, since the advanced degree places you in a higher pay range, interviewers expect more from you.

This chapter provides you with an understanding of what to expect during interviews and how to prepare. First, we describe some ways you can learn information about the company you will interview with. Second, we offer you some tips on preparing for the interview by examining different types of interviews and questioning approaches, and by encouraging you to develop answers to the questions in preparation for the interview. Third, we stress that practicing for an interview is just as important as practicing for a business presentation or media interview. Finally, we suggest some ideas for mental preparation regarding the interview location and the necessity of creating an excellent first impression, ending with some do's and don'ts that can guide you.

PREPARING FOR THE INTERVIEW

Once you have narrowed the focus of your career search to a potential employer, there are several things that you should consider about the interviewing process. This section is designed to help you prepare better for the interview. You will review some important areas that you should research about the organization, and you will become familiar with the types of interviews you can expect, types of questioning approaches, frequently asked questions, and illegal or unfair questions. The section concludes with comments on employment tests.

According to a Chicago magazine marketing director, many university graduates today are woefully unprepared for interviews. When she was recently hiring a marketing assistant for her magazine, she found the following. "Only two of the dozen candidates I met with bothered to locate a copy of our magazine in advance. . . . One young man . . . arrived completely unprepared, sans notebook, pen or pencil. Several other candidates asked, 'What's the magazine about and who reads it?' Another [asked], 'Do you really think there's a future in the marketing track?'"[1]

Do Your Interview Homework

As you approach the interview process, it is important that you learn as much as possible about the organization that you will interview with. In particular, research the following aspects of the organization.

The Organization's Industry
- Is the organization in a stable or a cyclical industry?
- What is the current and potential growth of the industry?
- What is the future outlook for the industry?

The Company
- What is the dollar volume of the organization's annual business?
- How many employees work for the organization?
- What products or services does the organization manufacture or provide?
- Are the products or services diversified?
- Is the scope of the organization international, national, or regional?
- What is the overall growth potential of the organization?
- What is the history of the organization's culture?

- Is the organization stable?
- Is there a threat of merger or possible buyout by others?
- What are the names of the top executives in the organization?
- How would you describe the organization's management?
- What are the personnel policies that can affect you?
- What are the organization's social and economic goals?
- Has the organization had any ethical violations?

In addition to the answers to these questions, you should know the general content of the organization's most recent annual report and whether the company is public and the report is published, as well as information published in major newspaper and magazine articles. You can learn such details on the Internet, through your campus library, by talking to personal contacts and alumni, or by reading company literature. If possible, you should also study some of the pertinent technology the company is using.

The Company's Values Besides knowing about the company's industry, products, and economic success, it is also critical to determine if your personal core values are the same as those espoused by the company. Information regarding this area is found in the company's mission statement, value statement, and code of ethics, and in the types of lawsuits that it currently is facing. Organizations want to make sure that your core values also equate with theirs. Savio Chan, president and CEO of Technology Training Solutions, contends that most people regard technical competence as the No. 1 requirement of potential new hires. "I beg to differ . . . technical competence is No. 2 when hiring, the most important thing to look for is if the interviewee understands where the company is going and agrees with its core values."[2]

According to Taunee Besson, president of Dallas, Texas–based Career Dimensions, answers to the following questions will tell you about an employer's environment before you accept an offer.

- Does the employer have clear goals and live by them?
- Is the employer's strategic plan understood and embraced by all levels?
- How effective are the company's communications?
- Are employees a part of a team?
- Is the company open to change?
- Do employees have fun?
- Do individual employees have the chance to make contributions?
- What training is available?
- How does the firm reward employees?
- Does the company have a development plan for each employee?
- Do employees share in company profits?
- What's the firm's customer focus?[3]

With these preliminary items completed, you will need to decide whether or not the company is a good "fit." You will also be ready to start your interview preparation. Be sure to note gaps in the information about the company that you found. Prepare questions that you can ask the employer about this information during the interview.

According to Austin, it is critical that you know about the company that you are interviewing to work for—that you have adequately done your homework. She lists seven things that make a good impression on the interviewer:

- Research my organization
- Prepare good questions for me
- Tell me what you can do for me, not how the job might further your personal growth
- Be tenacious
- Follow up
- Beware of shortcuts
- Remember the golden rule[4]

Types of Interviews

There are several types of employment interviews. Consider the type that you will be participating in and follow the appropriate guidelines for preparation suggested below.

The Screening Interview The purpose of the screening interview is to conduct a "first cut" brief evaluation of a candidate. Typically it is conducted in college or university placement centers. Usually someone other than the person you would be working for conducts the interview. While a company's personnel department employees often screen undergraduates, a division manager or someone with ties to the university, such as one of the alumni, usually screens MBA candidates.

The typical breakdown for a 30-minute screening interview is

Interviewer's objectives	2 minutes
You talk	10–15 minutes
Interviewer gives you company data	5 minutes
You can ask questions—interviewer answers	5 minutes
Interviewer tells how the decision will be made	2 minutes
Interviewer concludes the interview	1 minute
Total time	25–30 minutes

Your objectives in the screening interview are to make a good impression and to allow sufficient information to be passed between you and the interviewer to determine whether a compatible relationship exists. If you succeed, the interviewer may plan a second interview where you can meet appropriate members of the management team and participate in a more detailed analysis of your suitability for the job.

The Follow-up Interview Typically, you will receive a letter inviting you to a second interview at the employer's facilities. Receiving this invitation means that the company desires to further investigate your qualifications, abilities, and potential. The follow-up interview covers more in-depth topics. You can expect to meet and talk with key executives and potential peers at this meeting.

Listen carefully to all the questions. Learn to quickly assimilate what you are seeing and hearing with what you already know about the organization. Try to ask some well-thought-out questions (more guidance on asking questions appears below). Be polite and friendly, and try to look relaxed.

While your overriding objectives in the screening interview are to make a good impression and survive the cut, your objectives in the second interview are to be extremely familiar with the company and to effectively answer all questions. At this stage, you should also be concerned with the various thank-you letters and other forms of correspondence that you must write.

The Social Interview The social interview often occurs at the MBA level prior to or in place of the screening interview. Here several interviewees are invited to a cocktail reception or dinner. The event can be held on neutral territory (a downtown club) or at the company's facility. Since the reception is usually unstructured, it may not feel like an interview. You will probably be encouraged to talk about yourself and pose any questions to company representatives. Be careful! You may not know which of several people are the important ones to impress. The important people may be the quiet ones who are listening to your questions and answers. The best rules are to drink little, circulate, remain calm, ask well-thought-out questions, and respond with confidence but not cockiness.

The Behavioral Interview Often your personality and a few good answers can get you through the screening interview and maybe even the second interview. But when you undergo a behavioral interview you can't bluff your way through the answers. "Behavioral interviews are the in-thing for human resource experts and personnel consultants from coast to coast who now stress finding out what a person is going to do on the job, not just verifying that he or she has the credentials to do it."[5]

Organizations that use the behavioral approach first develop clear job descriptions. They then identify and prioritize the quality dimensions necessary for achieving success in the position (e.g., planning, decision making, selling, or organizational skills). Finally, they design open-ended questions that will allow each interviewer to determine if an applicant possesses the dimensions.

While behavioral interviews are tough, they are also fair. Since the questions are based on specific job requirements, illegal and irrelevant issues are avoided. Further, every applicant for a specific job is asked the same set of questions. The detailed job description is not offered until the interview is over, and interviewers "are trained to avoid reacting to your replies or asking leading questions that betray their preferences."[6]

Behavioral interviewers go beyond the general questions about your job performance and training. Instead they center on *how* and *what* you did in very concrete terms. In the selection interview you may score points by telling the interviewer about a team project that you worked on. In the behavioral interview the interviewer will want to know whether the information is accurate or misleading. Did you help or hinder the team? To what extent did you contribute? Did the team meet the original objectives? Was the project finished on time, under or over budget? According to Eyler, "Each problem is designed to draw you out and make you demonstrate your ability to deal with problems, show your strengths and weaknesses, and help interviewers judge whether you have the skills and personal characteristics that will make you a successful part of the organization."[7]

To arrive at accurate answers, skilled behavioral interviewers use the "**STAR**" method. This stands for:

The **S**ituation or **T**ask that the candidate experienced;
The **A**ction taken by the candidate; and
The **R**esult of the action.[8]

Here is one example of how a behavioral question was handled by an applicant who was told, "Give me an example of a job-related situation where you felt you were in over your head. What made you feel that way? What did you do to handle the situation?" Your response might be:

Situation or Task "The first job that I had after college was to work with my boss in producing an annual conference for over 1,000 attendees. I was highly excited about the opportunity and plans were running smoothly. But after three weeks on the job my boss took sick and was out of the office for over four weeks. He returned one week before the event."

Action "I kept in constant touch by phone and e-mail. Still, I had to make major decisions in his absence, and often felt very uncomfortable in doing so.

I made four trips to the conference site, which was in Chicago. I learned to bargain with the property management, figured out how to create backup plans in case speakers and vendors fell through, even handled a minor crisis regarding meals for an off-site event."

Result "The result was a highly successful meeting. The final attendance was 100 participants more than anticipated. I found them lodging and worked out all the logistics. I brought the conference in under budget. The evaluations were the highest of any conference to date. My colleagues were highly complimentary. My boss wrote a wonderful letter of praise for my file. I even received a $1,500 raise at my six-month evaluation."

Since behavioral interviews often last for two hours or more, it becomes difficult to continually be specific in your answers. To be successful stay focused, continue to think, and avoid vague, canned, or hypothetical answers. Remember to practice the STAR method and answer each question seriously, constructively, and specifically.[9]

The Assignment Interview Assignment interviews serve as job-related test situations. Here the interviewer really wants to see how you would perform in simulated job events. You might be asked to prepare and deliver a sales presentation, analyze a financial problem, recommend a solution to a problem, or facilitate a mock meeting. "One applicant for a systems analyst post was handed a calendar, a box full of memos, messages and a list of scheduled meetings and projects. He was then given 45 minutes to prepare a schedule and priority list."[10]

The best way to perform well on assignment interviews is to take your time, do your best, and work on being cooperative with all the other participants who might also be interviewing.

The Video Conferencing Interview A few firms are making use of technology in the interviewing stage. At Heidrick & Struggles, one of the nation's leading CEO headhunters uses video conferencing to interview potential candidates. For the firm the advantages are reduced travel and accommodation costs and the ability to interview a wider range of recruits. But video conference interviews are often difficult on the recruit. Many are uncomfortable with the technology and have trouble smiling, making eye contact, and using the new process to their advantage. Added to this is the necessity to travel to a site that is equipped with video conferencing equipment.[11] While many in the business world see an advantage in using this technology to hire at lower levels of the organization, others believe the practice can be an offensive, demeaning, and impersonal approach to recruiting a company's senior officials.[12]

As technology advances, Internet job interviews will be the next step. ViewCast.com, a Dallas, Texas–based firm, has software available that will allow almost anyone with a computer to interview for that job in the comfort of home.[13]

Types of Questioning Approaches

Open Questions Open questions are broad and unstructured and allow you to develop the answer you want the interviewer to receive. If you have prepared answers to a variety of questions, you can really score well with your answers. Usually these questions will have a leadoff such as, "Tell me about . . ." or "What do you think about . . . ?"

If interviewers are effective at the open approach, you will find them listening with interest and courtesy. They use silence to reflect on or clarify what you are saying and ask "why" and "how" questions to encourage you to elaborate on certain points. Effective interviewers also avoid comments that reflect their personal values, criticism, or approval.

Yes-No Questions Yes-no questions allow you little flexibility in your answers. Questions that check on specific dates, degrees, or schools attended might call for a yes or no response. The interviewer who continues to use this type of questioning is inexperienced, however. You should use the opportunity to expand your answers and even try posing questions to the interviewer.

Direct Questions Expect direct questions like "Tell me about your major area of study" or "What were the specific tasks of your job at the XYZ Company?" These questions usually relate to work/education/skills that you possess, or specific experiences that you have had in the past. This type of question calls for simple, clearly thought out, and intelligent answers. In answering these questions, as in all others, avoid contradicting yourself and answer each question truthfully.

While you should supply answers to the questions, look for the right opportunity to include some important thoughts that you have prepared in your research on the company. Do this carefully, however, and do not upstage the interviewer.

Probing Questions Probing questions may follow either the direct or indirect approach. These questions generally are unplanned and are used to clarify previous answers or to discover your attitudes and feelings on issues. An interviewer often uses probing questions to follow up on partial or superficial responses by directly indicating the kind of information he or she is seeking. Such probes might include, "That's interesting. I would like to know more about your thoughts on that" or "Why do you feel that way?" or "Give me a specific example of what you mean."

Expect a good interviewer to probe, especially on the second interview. Do not become defensive, but answer the questions by bridging them to the flow of your comments. At times an interviewer may ask a probing question while you are in the middle of a statement. If you answer it immediately, make a mental note to return to your original comments.

Stress-Related Questions Stress questions are designed to challenge you and make you think and respond quickly. They allow the interviewer to see if you can handle a tough environment. Some interviewers use the approach simply to change the beat of ordinary interviews.

True stress interviews are appropriate only when the job you are seeking poses regular stress and pressures. Otherwise, the approach is not useful. Dr. Sandra Davis, a psychologist for the MDA Consulting Group, contends:

> Deliberate stress in interviews is only appropriate when the job requires one to deal day-to-day with interpersonal stress and challenge. If a job is stressful because of time pressures, then creating interpersonal pressure in an interview situation reveals nothing to me about the person's capacity to cope with pressure on the job. The information is useless, and I run the risk of alienating an otherwise outstanding candidate.[14]

The overall objective of an interviewer who uses stress questioning is to prevent you from using rehearsed answers. Your objective is to maintain your poise, respond in a calm and intelligent manner, and outlast the interviewer.

You may receive questions like, "We don't have an opening at the present time, but if we did, tell me why I should hire you" or "I have checked your grades and they are not that good. How can I know you can really perform?" These questions are obvious put-downs. Other questions might force you to leap from your mental position to a more creative mode. "See that chair you are sitting on? Sell it to me!" or "Evaluate this interview."

Interviewers who use stress questioning are more concerned with your method of handling the questions than with the answers themselves. Sometimes the interviewer uses nonverbal cues, rather than actual questions, to try to induce stress. An interviewer may look at you critically or establish no eye contact with you, looking out the window instead. Or he or she may sit in absolute silence while you walk in, waiting for you to start the discussion. Davis cites such an approach: "A common technique used by some is to ask a vague, open-ended question and then not respond in any way [to your answer], creating an awkward silence. You are left not knowing whether you answered the question, let alone whether you said something wrong."[15]

How can you prepare for possible stress questions? Do not concern yourself with what the interviewer wants to hear. Instead, mentally arrive at one or two answers and respond with those. Also, use pauses to your advantage. Five seconds may seem like an eternity, but it gives you valuable time to come up with an answer. When you see distracting nonverbal tactics, accept them for what they are and continue your discussion as if the interviewer were being polite. If you are greeted with silence, start with a line like, "I would like to tell you some things about my work experience." Your best device for handling a stress question is to be direct and respond with certainty.

Frequently Asked Questions

According to Marcia Fox, a consultant, 99 out of 100 college students put on their best dress for success outfits and polish their credentials, but they never make the effort to develop answers for such typical interview questions as:

- How did you happen to select your career choices?
- What are the qualities necessary for success in your field?
- What are your chief strengths?
- Why do you think you would like to work for our company?

As she states, "There's no way you can answer these questions without revealing whether or not you have done your homework about yourself, your career decisions, and the company."[16] Be ready for unexpected and seemingly irrelevant questions. In fact, anticipate at least one surprise question. You would be wise to spend considerable time developing answers to questions in the following four categories: ice-breaking, education-oriented, company-oriented, and you-oriented. Work on being spontaneous. Your answers should show your uniqueness and individuality.

Ice-Breaking Questions
- Tell me about yourself
- How would you describe yourself?
- How would a close friend describe you?
- What did you do over the weekend?
- What are your hobbies?
- How do you like to spend your free time?

Education-Oriented Questions
- Why did you seek an advanced degree?
- Why did you choose your college or university?
- What did you learn in the advanced program that you did not learn as an undergraduate?
- What led you to choose your major area of study?
- Are your grades a good indication of your academic achievement?
- Do you have thoughts about seeking an additional degree?
- How has your advanced program prepared you for a business career?
- Describe your most rewarding college experience.
- What did you learn from participation in extracurricular activities?

Company-Oriented Questions

- Why did you decide to seek a position with this company?
- What do you know about us?
- Are you seeking employment in a company of a certain size? Why?
- What criteria are you using to evaluate the company for which you hope to work?
- In what ways do you think you can make a contribution to our company?
- If you were hiring someone with an advanced degree for this position, what qualities would you look for?
- Why should I hire you?

You-Oriented Questions

- What are your long-range and short-range goals and objectives? When and why did you establish these goals, and how are you preparing yourself to achieve them?
- What specific goals, other than those related to your occupation, have you established for yourself for the next ten years?
- What do you see yourself doing five years from now?
- What do you *really* want to do in life?
- What are your long-range career objectives?
- How do you plan to achieve your career goals?
- What are the most important rewards you expect in your business career?
- What do you expect to be earning in five years?
- Why did you choose the career for which you are preparing?
- Which is more important to you, the money or the opportunity?
- What do you consider to be your greatest strengths and weaknesses?
- What motivates you to put forth your best effort?
- What qualifications do you have that make you think you will be successful in business?
- How do you determine or evaluate success?
- What two or three accomplishments have given you the most satisfaction? Why?
- Do you do any charity or community work?
- What major problem have you encountered and how did you deal with it?
- What have you learned from your mistakes?
- Do you like people? Do you believe people like you?
- Do you prefer working with people or alone?
- Do you have a geographical preference? Why?
- Will you relocate? Does relocation bother you?
- Are you willing to travel?
- Are you willing to spend at least six months as a trainee?
- Why do you think you might like to live in the community in which our company is located?
- Can you accept constructive criticism?
- Can you laugh at yourself?
- How do you work under pressure? Give me an example!

Illegal or Unfair Questions

Illegal or unfair questions are occasionally raised during interviews, so be prepared to respond to such questions. In most of these instances, the interviewer is probably just being careless, but discrimination can arise. Since state and local antidiscrimination laws vary, you should check with the appropriate labor and human rights agencies in your area to find out how local laws compare to the federal versions. Contrary to popular belief, there is no list of questions that employers are forbidden by federal law to ask. However, court cases have held that certain questions have violated specific federal laws in specific instances.

Questions about race, color, age, gender, religion, national origin, marital status, childbearing plans, past arrests, alcohol and drug abuse, and credit history become illegal if answers are used to discriminate. When it comes to enforcement, the parameters of discrimination are wide.

If you are asked illegal or unfair questions, first consider the context of the questions and the interviewer. If you feel the interviewer was not aware of how the question sounded and is not being discriminatory, simply pass it off. Should the flow of the conversation continue to offend you, tactfully tell the interviewer that the question is not appropriate to ask and has no bearing on the job description.

If you feel, however, that you are the subject of discrimination by a company, you have two options: you can overlook the discrimination issue and hope that once you are hired you will have no additional problems; or you can call local enforcement agencies to push for your rights. The agencies would need substantial proof of discrimination to initiate a case against the company.

Table 17.1 presents fair and unfair preemployment questions. You can use this information to determine when an interviewer is asking questions that may be biasing his or her views toward you.

Potential Employment Tests

More employers are beginning to request that interviewees submit to employment tests prior to their making those candidates a job offer. Such a request usually is made during an interview. As an interviewee you need to realize that an employer may make such a request. You should understand the reason the tests are being used, which tests are commonly used, and the risks you face when taking such tests. The following section describes three types of employment tests: lie detector, drug, and psychological.

Lie Detector Tests For years lie detector testing was used to screen job applicants and to check employee honesty. But in 1988 the passage of the Employee Polygraph Protection Act (EPPA) banned the use of lie detectors, except polygraphs, in most private-sector settings. Under limited circumstances, and with procedural safeguards, banks and other private-sector employers may still give polygraph tests to their employees. These must be limited to specific internal investigations and post-termination decisions to prosecute an employee for dishonest acts, however.[17]

TABLE 17.1   **Antidiscrimination Questions That Can and Cannot Be Asked**

Subject	Fair Preemployment Questions (What they can ask you)	Unfair Preemployment Questions (What they cannot ask you)
Name	Have you ever worked for this company under a different name? Is any additional information relative to change of name or nickname necessary to enable a check on your work record? If yes, explain.	Original name of an applicant whose name has been changed by court order or otherwise. Maiden name of a married woman. If you have ever worked under another name, state name and date.
Address or duration of residence	Applicant's place of residence. How long a resident of this state or city?	
Birthplace		Birthplace of applicant. Birthplace of applicant's parents, spouse, or other close relatives.
Race or color		Complexion or color of skin. Coloring.
Age	Are you between 18 and 65 years of age? If not, state your age.	How old are you? What is your date of birth?
Gender		A preemployment inquiry as to gender on an application form is unlawful.
Marital status		Are you married? Where does your spouse work? What are the ages of your children, if any?
Religion	Under special circumstances an applicant may be advised of normal hours and days of week required by the job to avoid possible conflict with religious or other personal convictions.	Inquiry into an applicant's religious denomination, religious affiliations, church, parish, pastor, or religious holidays observed. An applicant may not be told: "This is a (Catholic, Protestant, or Jewish) organization."
National origin		Inquiry into applicant's lineage, ancestry, national origin, descent, parentage, or nationality. Nationality of applicant's parents or spouse. What is applicant's mother tongue?
Citizenship	Are you a citizen of the United States? If not a citizen of the United States, do you intend to become a citizen of the United States? If you are not a United States citizen, have you the legal right to remain permanently in the United States? Requirement that applicants state whether they have ever been interned or arrested as an enemy alien.	Of what country are you a citizen? Whether an applicant is a naturalized or a native-born citizen. The date when the applicant acquired citizenship. Requirement that applicant produce naturalization papers or first papers. Whether applicant's parents or spouse are naturalized or native-born citizens of the United States. The date when such parents or spouse acquired citizenship.
Language	Inquiry into languages applicant speaks and writes fluently. What foreign languages do you read fluently? Write fluently? Speak fluently?	Inquiry into how applicant acquired ability to read, write, or speak a foreign language.

TABLE 17.1   **Antidiscrimination Questions That Can and Cannot Be Asked (Concluded)**

Subject	Fair Preemployment Questions (What they can ask you)	Unfair Preemployment Questions (What they cannot ask you)
Education	Inquiry into the academic, vocational, or professional education of an applicant and the public and private schools he or she has attended.	
Experience	Inquiry into work experience. Inquiry into countries applicant has visited.	
Character	Have you ever been convicted of any crime? If so, when and where, and what was the disposition of offense?	Have you ever been arrested? (An employer's use of individual's arrest record to deny employment would, in the absence of business necessity, constitute a violation of the human rights law.)
Relatives	Names of applicant's relatives already employed by this company.	Names, addresses, ages, number, or other information concerning applicant's children or other relatives not employed by the company.
Disability	Do you have any impairments, physical or mental, which would interfere with your ability to perform the job for which you have applied? If there are any positions or types of positions for which you should not be considered or job duties you cannot perform because of a physical handicap, please explain.	Do you have a disability? Have you ever been treated for any of the following diseases? (List diseases.) Has any member of your family ever had any of the following diseases? (List diseases.)
Notice in case of emergency	Name and address of person to be notified in case of an accident or emergency.	
Military experience	Have you ever been a member of the armed services of the United States or in a state militia? If so, did your military experience have any relationship to the position for which you applied?	
Organizations	Are you a member of any clubs, organizations, etc. (exclude organizations, the name or character of which indicates the race, creed, color, or national origin of its members).	List all clubs, societies, and lodges to which you belong.
References	Who suggested that you apply for a position here?	
Photograph	May be requested after hiring for identification purposes.	Requirement that an applicant affix a photograph to the employment form at any time before hiring, or at his or her option.

Drug Tests The American Management Association (AMA) runs a yearly survey on workplace testing. When the survey was first conducted in 1987, only 21 percent of the responding companies tested for drug usage. By 1995 over 77 percent had drug tests in place and used them as a component of their policy. The increase was due to five factors:

- Department of Transportation (DOT) and Department of Defense (DOD) regulations which, with local and state legislation, mandated testing in certain job categories;
- The practical effects of the Drug Free Workplace Act of 1988;
- Court decisions that recognize an employer's right to test both employees and job applicants in the private sector;
- Action by insurance carriers to reduce accident liability and control health care costs; and
- Corporate requirements that vendors and contractors certify that they have a drug-free workplace.[18]

Work categories determine the frequency of corporate drug testing.

Manufacturers (89%) lead the service sector (67%). Within the service sector, 88% of transportation firms test; they are most affected by DOT regulations. Elsewhere, testing is performed by 71% of wholesalers and retailers, 55% of business service providers, 47% of financial service providers, and 69% of general service providers. In the public sector, 83% of respondent organizations test, compared with 77% of private sector firms.[19]

If you select work in the above areas you can expect random drug test notification.

Personality and Psychological Tests Employers increasingly realize that productivity, teamwork, and workplace harmony are the result of employees who easily fit into the organization's culture and climate. As a result the use of psychological tests has risen, albeit slowly. The 1999 AMA survey found that 40 percent of employers require some form of psychological measurements. For job applicants, 39 percent use tests, and to evaluate current employees, 31 percent make use of such tests. The AMA survey listed five specific categories of measurement: cognitive ability, interest inventories, managerial assessments, personality measurements, and physical stimulation of job tasks.[20]

Certain industries are more prone than others to use such measurements. According to one source, "more than 25% of companies filling IT positions assess candidates' personalities before making a job offer. Assessments range from multiple-choice questions for junior positions to an evaluation that could last up to four hours and include an interview with a behavioral psychologist for the most senior positions."[21]

The employee psychological test is a paper-and-pencil questionnaire designed to identify the right employee for the right job. The organizations using such tests believe that the resulting profile describes the candidate's values and beliefs, which in turn can objectively be compared to the company's profile of the ideal candidate for the position.

There are definite advantages of testing. A test can provide information on an individual's overall intellectual ability, basic skills, interests and inclinations, and personality characteristics. Tests can be very economical, especially if they result in hiring an employee who is committed, has improved performance, and is matched to the job. Some of the more popular tests are Cattell 16 Personality Factor Questionnaire (16-PF); Gordon Personal Profile (GPP); Gordon Personal Inventory (GPI); Kostick Perception and Preference Inventory (PAPI); Myers-Briggs Type Indicator; California Psychological Inventory; Personal Profile Analysis (PPA); PAL Personality Profile System (PPS); Performax Personal Profile System Personality; Poppleton-Allen Sales Aptitude Test; and several forms of the Occupational Personality Questionnaire. All of these tests are self-appraisal inventories that are reported to be useful in selection and training.[22]

To avoid being embarrassed if a future employer asks you to submit to one of these tests, there are two things you should do prior to the interview. First, know whether testing is the norm for new hires or promotions in the industry in which you are applying for employment. Second, understand the consequences of refusing to take a test. While refusing may guarantee your privacy, it may also cause you not to get the job.[23]

PRACTICING FOR THE INTERVIEW

With your preparation complete, you are now ready to practice for your interview. Rehearsing is really the last stage in preparation. If you have been previously employed or if you have already gone through several interviews, you will be tempted to skip this part. Keep in mind, however, that every interview is a new performance and you must be ready for the task. True professionals in every walk of life, from music to sports to speaking, prepare and practice for the big event.

In the chapters on business presentations, meeting management, broadcast interviews, and case presentations, you saw numerous ideas for practicing. Use those ideas to ensure that you handle your anxiety well, communicate positive nonverbal messages, and remember what you want to say to the interviewer.

Practice includes both mental and oral rehearsals. Mentally picture yourself walking into an interview, sitting in front of the interviewer, successfully answering each question, projecting a positive image, and smoothly leaving the room. Play and replay that positive mental tape many times prior to the interview. Act out each imagined behavior characteristic during the actual interview.

MAKING THE INTERVIEW COUNT

When the big day arrives, you want the effort you have put into the preparation and practice segments of your interview to pay off. In this section, you will see how the location, the first five minutes of the interview, and the do's and don'ts will help you present the right image and with luck obtain the job you desire.

The Interview Location

The majority of interviews occur either at job placement centers on college campuses or at the company offices. You will be able to preview the placement center interview rooms prior to your campus interviews. If you are invited to the company location, you can discern important information about the company and its culture by observing the physical layout. Remember that the majority of information received in any message is nonverbal. Look, listen, and be aware of the features listed below; then let the information you learn guide you in the asking and answering of your interview questions.

The Grounds Is the office in a downtown high-rise building, an industrial park, or a country club setting? Each communicates a different message to you and to the employees.

The Aesthetics Are the rooms airy and bright or dull and dingy? Is the color scheme of the walls and carpet pleasing? Do windows offer pleasant views and sunlight? Are plants and artwork apparent? Do you feel comfortable here?

Noise Level Do you detect a quiet hum or a loud clatter? Do phones ring constantly, or do office workers carry on loud conversations? Is this a place where you would like to work?

Floor Plan How are the offices and departments arranged? Is there an open office system with partitions or permanent walls? Can you picture yourself in this type of environment?

The First Five Minutes: Forming a Positive Impression

The job interview has two critical segments. If you create the wrong impression in the first part, your chances of getting the job are slim, regardless of how well you perform in the second. Research indicates that most interviewers make up their minds about a job applicant in the first 30 seconds. Psychologists call this 30-second decision the "halo effect." It refers to the first impression an applicant makes upon an interviewer.[24] One study showed that if an interviewer had a negative impression about an applicant after the first five minutes, that person was not hired 90 percent of the time. If, however, the impression was positive, the applicant was hired 75 percent of the time.[25]

How can you create that positive impression? Work on developing an engaging smile and a firm handshake. Give the interviewer the feeling that you are absolutely delighted to meet him, not only because you want the job but because you like people. Walk and talk with authority, not cockiness but an air that vibrates the sense that you feel good about yourself. When you start talking to the interviewer, establish a dialogue—a real conversation.

Your appearance, your nonverbal behavior, and your words all help to build the first impression. If you have seriously prepared for your interview, the following list of do's and don'ts will help you make a positive first impression.

The Do's of Interviewing

1. Arrive on time for the interview. Lateness creates a poor impression that is almost impossible to overcome. Be courteous, enthusiastic, confident, poised, and prepared. Have an extra copy of your résumé and literature about the company, especially if you wish to refer to them in a question. Have a pen and paper handy in case you want to make notes.

2. Dress appropriately for the interview and the profession. In the past most professional jobs required a suit, sport coat, and tie. Today, many industries have virtually abandoned the "corporate uniform." A 1999 survey of 3,700 executives found 40 percent saying suits and ties may disappear entirely in a few years.[26] So what should you wear? Ask your interviewer what is apropos. "The purpose of the interview is to get to know you better. You and your accomplishments—not your clothes—should leave the lasting impression. When in doubt, your best bet is to stick with a suit or appropriate business attire."[27]

3. Be aware of your body language. Walk erectly and professionally, sit straight but at ease in your chair, smile warmly, and maintain eye contact with the interviewer. In fact, treat everyone you meet with courtesy. You never know when the interviewer might ask the receptionist for an impression of you as a person. Avoid indicating nervousness by wringing your hands or tapping your pen. Speak clearly. Constantly be aware of the image you are projecting.

4. Do your homework about the company. Reading the annual report is only a start. Read articles in *Fortune, Business Week*, and the *Wall Street Journal* that will allow you to talk about the company's strengths and weaknesses. Many interviewers state that too many MBA students fail to adequately research the companies with which they interview. As one professional recruiter put it, "The biggest problem with MBAs is that they don't do their homework."[28]

5. Display a courteous and active interest in the interviewer, the job, and the company, even if you sense a few minutes into the interview that your match-up with the company is wrong. Remain flexible and open-minded. At the end of the interview, express your interest, or lack of interest, in the job. If you want the job, *ask for it*. If you do not like the company but you are offered the job, turn it down—it is a pleasant experience.

6. Help the interviewer during the discussion by avoiding a yes-and-no answer pattern. Avoid talking too much and keep your answers to short (30-second to one-minute) responses unless you are asked to elaborate. Even then, constantly be aware of the length of your responses. Be prepared to ask pertinent questions about the company or job that cannot be answered by looking in the company brochures.

7. Answer all questions with a positive tone and in a professional manner. Never let yourself be drawn into a detailed discussion about your past employers or other companies. Do not be critical or complain of working conditions you have experienced. Always leave the impression that you are a positive thinker and a pleasant and professional person.

8. Be prepared for the most frequently asked questions. Rehearse the questions in the preparation section. Some interviewing experts even advise carrying a list of questions about the company into the interview. At some point, you may want to ask the interviewer some of the questions. Asking good questions implies that you have done your homework. While the earlier list is a "must" review for this occasion, the short list in Table 17.2 brings in some personal questions you can pose to the interviewer.

9. Avoid the routine of note taking during the interview, unless the interviewer wishes you to remember the name of a person, a book, dates, or other items. If you feel the need to write down information, do it quickly and with a professional look, or do it immediately after you finish the interview and exit the room. Always convey the impression of confidence and control.

10. Watch for verbal and nonverbal signals that the interview is over. Do not continue to talk, but rather work with the interviewer on controlling the time frame, especially if you are in a placement center.

The Don'ts Of Interviewing

1. Don't forget the interviewer's name. State it several times and be sure to pronounce it correctly. Consider asking for a business card to which you can refer if you have difficulty with the interviewer's name.

2. Don't chew gum in an interview. It is also best not to smoke, even if the interviewer gives you permission. If the interview is held in a reception format, drink very little alcohol. In fact, it is probably best to stick with a soft drink, juice, or club soda and a twist of lime.

TABLE 17.2   **Immediate Interview Questions**

What is a typical day like here?
What will my typical day be like?
How and how often will I be evaluated?
What are your dress and meal policies?
What is the turnover rate of people in this position?
What is the last person who held this position doing now?
What is the atmosphere of the company?
What is the company's philosophy toward [line of business]?
When was my predecessor promoted?
What kind of training, if any, can I expect?
What skills/experiences would help someone do well in this position?
What skills/experiences do you think I lack for this position?
Do most managers have advanced degrees? Which ones? What degrees?
To whom would I report?
Will I have a chance to meet him/her?
Will I have a chance to meet my coworkers?
Will I be assigned to a specific department or rotated throughout the company?
Does the company anticipate a change in structure soon?
What do you like about working here?
What do you dislike about working here?
What are the characteristics of a successful [position]?
What is the company's philosophy of management?

---

3. Don't become lethargic. As soon as you walk in the door, push your energy button and strive to be constantly up and active as you listen to and talk with the interviewer. Avoid eating a heavy meal before an interview, and if you have a tendency to get the jitters after drinking much coffee, limit your intake before the interview.

4. Don't be conceited, arrogant, overbearing, or overly aggressive in your attitude and responses. While confidence is contagious and most interviewers are impressed by it, arrogance and brashness are immediate turnoffs. Avoid overusing "I." Many interviewees will say, "I did this, I did that, I accomplished." Overuse of "I" can cause an interviewer to be cautious. Try using the "we" and "you" approach also.

5. Don't become defensive or hostile if the interviewer puts you under fire. Remain courteous, endure the stress, and finish the interview on as positive a note as possible. However, you should always preserve your dignity. If you feel the interviewer is belligerent and is placing you in a degrading position, get up and walk out.

6. Don't make statements that imply you are merely seeking the best dollar offer.

7. Don't make excuses or be evasive when discussing unfavorable facts that are listed on your résumé. Practice your responses to such questions.

8. Don't communicate an unwillingness to start at the bottom of a job classification (unless the position is listed as higher) if you are seeking your first job. Also, avoid stating your desire for a guaranteed future.

9. Don't discuss salary during the first interview. Most companies have a salary range that the interviewer will describe. If you mention salary, it may be too much or too little and can reduce your chances of being offered the job. When it is established that the company wants you, and you know that you want to work with the company, negotiation is much easier.

10. Don't lie. Your nonverbal expressions give you away, but even if they do not, it is not worth the risk. Most companies fire a person immediately when a lie or misrepresentation is discovered.

SUMMARY

The job interview is important for both you and the company. Because you can assume the company representative will be prepared, your task is to be equally prepared and to make an excellent impression.

As you plan your career path, decide where you want to live, what you want to do, and for which companies you would like to work. Next, do your interview homework on the company you have chosen. Start by asking some basic questions about your job desires. Go on to gather basic information about the company and its industry. This information is vital to asking and answering questions during the interview.

As you prepare for the interview, consider the various types of interviews that you may encounter with the company (screening, follow-up, social, behavioral, and assignment). Consider and prepare for the different types of questioning approaches that interviewers may use (open, yes-no, direct, probing, and stress).

Next, develop answers to the most-asked interview questions. Finally, to protect yourself, become familiar with possible illegal or unfair questions. Be prepared for the possibility of taking some kind of preemployment test.

Practice for every presentation is important for a skill-building professional. Since you are seeking to develop your interview skills, practice asking and answering questions for your interview with both mental and oral rehearsals.

Obtaining the job is the result of an effective presentation. If you have gone through the planning, preparation, and practice phases properly, you will then be ready for the presentation. Observe and learn from the interview location. Consider the importance of forming a positive impression during the first five minutes. Know the different immediate questions that you can ask. Finally, master the do's and don'ts of successful interviewing. They will help you present the proper image, learn specifics about the interviewer and the company, and accomplish the best interview possible.

DISCUSSION QUESTIONS

1. As you do your interview homework, what are some important points that you should find out about the company you are considering?
2. This chapter listed six major types of employment interviews: the screening interview, the follow-up interview, the social interview, the behavioral interview, the assignment interview, and the video conferencing interview. Which types of questioning approaches might you expect in each of these interviews?
3. What are some of the general subject areas where illegal or unfair questions may be asked?
4. What are five specific do's and five specific don'ts that you should remember while interviewing?

Applications

1. Before your next interview, go to the library and do a periodical search of your company. Try to assemble as many articles as possible. Make copies of the material and take it home for review. When you have the interview, try to mention at least one of the articles, or ask the interviewer some pertinent questions that you gleaned from the material. After the interview, assess the value of the library search.

2. Take the list of most-asked questions found on pages 416–417. Develop answers for these questions based on the information that you have about the company that you will interview with next. Use your responses in the interview, and ask the interviewer some questions based on the answers you developed.

NOTES

1. Vickie Axford Austin, "The View from the Other Side of the Desk," *Managing Your Career,* Spring/Summer 1999, p. 19.
2. David Myron, "Job Interviewing—Keeping Employees All in the Family." *Varbusiness,* May 24, 1999, p. 40.
3. Taunee Besson, "Corporate Culture—A Candidate's Checklist," *National Business Employment Weekly*, July 31, 1999, pp. 15–16.
4. Vickie Axford Austin, "Clueless About Interviewing," *National Business Employment Weekly*, July 31, 1999, p. 30.
5. John Byrne, "All the Right Moves for Interviews," *Business Week*, September 17, 1990, p. 156.
6. Paula Apynys, "How to Survive a Nontraditional Interview," *National Business Employment Weekly*, August 6, 1995, p. 15.
7. David R. Eyler, *Job Interviews That Mean Business,"* Random House, New York, 1992, p. 91.
8. Apynys, "How to Survive a Nontraditional Interview," p. 15.
9. Ibid.
10. Ibid.
11. Tim Ouellette and Barb Cole-Gomolski, "Hiring Managers Turn to Video," *Computer World*, April 1998, p. 29.
12. Joann S. Lublin, "Hunting CEOs on a 32-Inch Screen," *Wall Street Journal*, April 27, 1999, p. B1.
13. Vikas Bajaj, "Face-to-Face Job Interviews Get Clicking Online," *Dallas Morning News,* November 25, 1999, pp. D1–2.
14. Sandra L. Davis, "How to Handle the Stress Interview," *Business Week's Guide to Careers*, Spring 1986, p. 28.
15. Ibid.
16. Marcia Fox, "Interview Do's and Don'ts," *Business Week's Guide to Careers,* Spring 1985, p. 54.
17. Durwood Ruegger, "When Polygraph Testing Is Allowed: Limited Exceptions Under the EPPA," *Banking Law Journal,* November–December 1991, pp. 555–564.
18. Eric Greenberg, ed., "1995 AMA Survey: Workplace Drug Testing and Drug Abuse Policies," a research report by the American Management Association, 1995.
19. Ibid.
20. Eric Greenberg, ed., "1999 AMA Survey: Psychological Measurement," a research report by the American Management Association, 1999, Internet: www.amanet.org/research/skilpsyc/measure.htm.
21. Diane Sierpina, "Personality Plays Bigger Role in IT Recruitment," *Information Week,* April 19, 1999, p. 152.
22. Robert J. Sahl, "Probing How People Think," *Personnel Journal*, December 1990, pp. 48–56.
23. Ibid.
24. Joyce Brothers, "How to Get The Job You Want." *Parade*, November 16, 1986, p. 4.
25. Mary Bakeman et al., "Job Seeking Skills Reference Manual," 3rd ed., Minnesota Rehabilitation Center, Minneapolis, November 1991, p. 57.
26. Cassandra Hayes, "Casual for an Interview," *Black Enterprise,* February 1999, p. 73.
27. Bill Leonard, "Apparel in Peril: Suits and Ties Are Wearing Thin," *HR Magazine*, January 1999, p. 20.
28. Fox, "Interview Do's and Don'ts," p. 54.

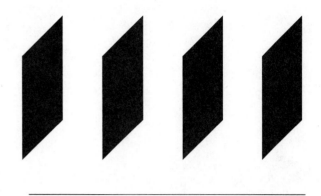

Appendices

Appendix A
A Formal Case

The following case, and the evaluation of it in Appendix B, serve as an example of an effectively written analysis. The case describes an ethical quandary being faced by a managerial accountant at Venture Sports, a division of Champion Marketing, Inc.

Work through the case using the steps presented in the chapter on case studies. Take the time to list the significant events and facts, the major problems, the possible solutions, and your recommendations. Do all of this before reading the student analysis of the case in Appendix B.

CASE: ACCOUNTING PROCEDURES AT CHAMPION MARKETING, INC.

Introduction

In the late afternoon of Friday, May 9, 2000, Cathy Rodgers walked slowly to her car. As she climbed inside, the warmth from the afternoon sun suddenly felt soothing. She had just completed a two-day continuing education program for CPAs. Throughout the sessions, she had been troubled about a recurring problem at work. It all started as the seminar leader led the participants through a discussion of the ethical behavior of accountants. The objective was to raise the sensitivity of the men and women attending, and to help them see clearly the many ethical pitfalls they could possibly encounter as CPAs. But for Rodgers, the message was more immediate. For the past six months Rodgers had bounced between solutions regarding an ethical problem at her company—Champion Marketing. As she put the key into the ignition of her car, she knew that she had to resolve the problem and that she had to do it quickly.

Champion Marketing, Inc.

Champion Marketing, Inc., is headquartered in Lansing, Michigan, with four sales offices located in different regions. It is a large specialty marketing firm that has traditionally sold promotional items to sales representatives. Their products include mainstream items like calendars, pens, pencils, coffee mugs, and watches, and a variety of other items that carry a company logo or salesperson's name, address, and telephone number. For the last five years, Champion has been the most profitable company among the four major specialty marketing firms in the United States.

Venture Sports Products

In January 2000 Champion began an acquisition program. One of the first companies that it purchased was Venture Sports Products. Venture was a financially successful operation responsible for selling most of the giveaway items distributed to fans at collegiate and professional sports events across the nation. The items are purchased by large corporate sponsors who advertise regularly at sporting events. These sponsors are firms who make and sell alcoholic beverages, soft drinks, sporting goods, fast-food items, and automotive products. A typical giveaway item might be a full-color poster of the team's players or a T-shirt with the team's name embossed across the front. The sponsoring firm would place its name in a significant location such as the back of the T-shirt.

Mike McMann founded Venture Sports Products in 1990 in Detroit. Mike had played college football at Michigan State University in Lansing and graduated in 1984. For four years he was a linebacker for the New Orleans Saints, before a serious injury ended his professional career in 1989. Drawing upon his numerous contacts in the collegiate and professional ranks, McMann formed Venture so he could return to his hometown, create a firm with real growth potential, and remain close to the sports world he loved.

From the beginning Venture was successful. As sales grew, McMann added more employees. Soon he found himself constantly on the road servicing old customers, discussing promotional items with manufacturers in Japan and Hong Kong, and selling new people on the merits of specialty advertising.

In late 1999 Cecil Osburn, president of Champion Marketing, approached Mike about the possibility of selling his company. He was willing to pay a premium for the company, and he asked McMann to remain as an employee of Champion. When McMann agreed to the sale, he became vice president of Champion Marketing, heading the Venture Sports Product Division.

Cathy Rodgers

Cathy joined the accounting staff at Champion in 1997, following her graduation from Michigan State University. At MSU she had majored in accounting and was a member of the Beta Alpha Psi Accounting Fraternity. In the summer she worked as a relief teller in a hometown bank. During tax season she worked at a Lansing branch of Quick Tax. The faculty sponsor of the fraternity helped Rodgers land the job in the accounting department at Champion. Rodgers seemed to fit in from the very start. She started in general accounting and was quickly promoted to the managerial accounting level.

In early January 1999, Cecil Osburn called Rodgers into his office. For the next hour he told her about the board of directors' plans to expand the company. A few days later that expansion started with the acquisition of Venture Sports Products. Venture Sports became a new division of Champion, and Rodgers became the management accountant responsible for the new area, reporting to Mike McMann. She was elated. She received a promotion, a sizable pay increase, and the promise that she would become a regional office assistant vice president within three to five years.

THE ETHICAL QUANDARY

For the first two months Rodgers was exuberant, but the feeling soon faded when Mike McMann arrived on the scene. After just a few weeks she became concerned about McMann's honesty.

The first event occurred when McMann turned in an expense account for a ten-day sales trip to California. Included were the customary receipts for travel, lodging, meals with drinks at expensive restaurants, and sporting events. But Rodgers became troubled when she saw that receipts for a weekend stay for two at a resort in Phoenix were attached to those of the sales trip.

After reviewing the expense report, Rodgers asked McMann about the charges. He became defensive and told her he had worked so hard while in California that he needed the down time with his wife before starting the sales calls the following week. When pressed further he told her, "The California trip was very productive, as was the trip to the Midwest the following week. The time in Phoenix was my 'charge-up' for the days to follow. It was part of the expense of doing business." Rodgers did not argue further with him because the expense form had the signature of Cecil Osburn, to whom McMann directly reported.

From mid-March until the seminar, McMann seemed to stretch his spending past the limit. He purchased a camera, a car phone, a VCR, cases of wine, and a variety of other items that clearly seemed not to be a part of ordinary sales expenses. Cecil Osburn had signed each of the expense reports that Rodgers reviewed. In April she again confronted him. This time she was told, "Cecil brought me on board to make this division financially successful. I am doing that and our sales are higher than ever. Besides, he signs off on all my expenses. Seems to me that you would realize I know what is right and wrong, and I'm not about to turn in an expenditure that does not qualify for reimbursement. I'm going to make this division the most profitable in the entire company. I like you, Cathy, and I hope you are on my team, and not against me." Rodgers left that meeting shaken. As the division accountant, she had to enforce the policies and procedures regarding expense reports, review the expense reports, record the expenses, and, in case of discrepancies, check all questionable expenditures to make sure that policies were accurately enforced.

Rodgers's Deliberation

As Rodgers tried to resolve the quandary, she considered several possible factors. Was Cecil Osburn testing her, or did he just not look at the types of expenses on McMann's forms when he approved them? Did McMann really have a special deal established with Osburn? Could he be entering the items after Osburn signed off on the reports? Rodgers felt the real bind of not only having to post the expenses but also approving them—but she questioned whether they should be approved.

She was hesitant to share her problem with others. Whom should she tell? Jerry Parr, vice president of accounting, chaired a review board of which she and the other divisional accountants were members. This board customarily heard discrepancy issues of this nature. If she talked to one or more of her colleagues she could jeopardize her case if she had to eventually send the issue to the board of review. She knew she could go directly to Osburn and find out if McMann had a special deal or if Osburn was merely overlooking the items listed on the reports.

The Seminar's Impact

The seminar that Rodgers attended was sponsored by the American Institute of Certified Public Accountants (AICPA), of which she was a member. During a session on ethical behavior, the facilitator talked about how an AICPA member had to assume an obligation of self-discipline above and beyond the requirements of laws and regulations. According to the AICPA Principles of the Code of Professional Conduct, Rodgers has a responsibility to her employer and her colleagues to display ethical behavior, even at the sacrifice of personal advantage. There are lots of risks for her. She knows that she could lose not only her future promotion but also her job. Monday morning will arrive too soon. Rodgers has the weekend to decide what she will do.

A Written Analysis
of a Formal Case

The following sample represents an effective case analysis. The suspense format is used to determine the actions that Cathy Rodgers should take regarding expense report discrepancies. Before you read this analysis, you should read the case in Appendix A.

CASE: ACCOUNTING PROCEDURES AT CHAMPION MARKETING, INC.

Strategic Issues and Problems

Cathy Rodgers faces a perplexing moral quandary. As the accountant for Venture Sports Division, she is in a position to review expense reports submitted by her boss, Mike McMann. McMann has repeatedly presented expense reports with unreasonable expenses. In addition he has requested reimbursement for items that are clearly against company policy. Rodgers confronted him on the policy discrepancies and left with the impression that her job could be in jeopardy if she pursued the issue further. To make matters more difficult, she believes that McMann's boss, Cecil Osburn, automatically approves the expense reports and expects her to check them. She is not absolutely sure that McMann does not have some kind of special arrangement with Osburn. Since Venture is a new acquisition of Champion and the transition between cultures is still under way, his actions may be anticipated by the president.

It is evident that management has not made it clear to Rodgers how she should proceed when faced with apparent violations of company policy within this new division. She has been left to decide for herself what procedures to follow. Rodgers has to decide her true role. Is it to adjust the accounting practices of a division in order to accommodate the individual wishes of employees, or is it to serve as a professional expert who interprets the activities of the division in an unbiased manner? As a managerial accountant she cannot afford to become the middle person, caught between presenting facts accurately and honestly and pleasing a superior who wants data presented in the most favorable light. Her duty as a professional is to uphold the standards of accounting, and this should help her make decisions concerning her actions.

As a result of attending the seminar, Rodgers is motivated to resolve the quandary. She wishes to maintain her integrity, fulfill her responsibility to the company, and not damage her career.

Analysis and Evaluation

Typically in a corporate environment the board of directors and the CEO endorse a philosophy related to various business practices. The philosophy is then supported with policy statements, which are distributed throughout the organization for all employees to know and follow. These policy statements include what reimbursable expenses are approved. As an accountant Rodgers obviously knows these policies and has applied them in her work. It seems safe to assume that McMann is also familiar with the policies, especially since she has discussed them with him. It is logical that, if McMann had received special approval from Osburn regarding particular expenditures, Osburn would have told Rodgers.

Is McMann wrong to request reimbursement on the expenses? After all, he is an executive with Champion and is helping the company make a profit. The answer to this question is determined at the level at which particular policy is made. If McMann is given authority to establish policy, he is also given authority to change it. The policies in question would be within his authority to change. In this case, however, he is claiming authority not given to him. To the extent that this results in personal gain for McMann, he is, in every legal sense, stealing from Champion, Inc.

Osburn's role in this situation is critical. He must sign McMann's expense report. This indicates that the company requires a higher-level approval for cash reimbursements. The reason for this policy is to ensure that cash is reimbursed strictly for authorized company expenses. By rubber stamping McMann's reports, Osburn is an unknowing participant to the deception.

Rodgers has been placed in a delicate situation. Generally it is not the accounting department's responsibility to make judgment calls concerning reimbursement expenses. But because Osburn has not stopped reimbursables that violate corporate policy, she believes she has to double-check the items. Because she is emotionally stressed over this issue, we can assume that she wants to act in an ethical way and to continue working at Champion.

Rodgers's Alternatives

Rodgers has four alternative courses of action for resolving the problem. First, she can do nothing. This will mean going along with McMann and making no issue of the policy violations. This will avoid further confrontations with him that could end her career. She will, however, allow a double standard to exist for enforcement of company policy. She will also be ignoring her obligation to the company and to Osburn regarding the safeguarding of company assets. If McMann continues to purchase more disallowed items, she could even be labeled an accomplice. Rodgers also runs a risk that the expense discrepancies would be discovered later by someone else in the organization. At a minimum her reputation for integrity would be tarnished; at a maximum her job could be in jeopardy. There is even an outside possibility that McMann is getting Osburn to sign the reports and then adding the expensive items to it before submitting it to accounting, thus leaving Osburn unaware of the fraud.

The second alternative is to approach the audit review board and let it hear the case. Taking this action will result not only in identifying McMann's violations of company policy, but also in focusing attention on Osburn for approving expenses contrary to the company policy. While this step would allow Rodgers to fulfill her obligation to the company and maintain her integrity, it could also be very detrimental to her career at Champion. This procedure does not follow the organizational chain of command; it bypasses Osburn, who will probably become upset when his managerial actions are questioned. It is also possible that McMann does have some special arrangement regarding expenses or that Osburn has other reasons for approving Mike's reports. Going around Osburn would result in embarrassment for everyone involved and would not win Rodgers the future support and confidence of him or of those on the review board. Rodgers simply does not have enough information to follow this alternative, and she would be foolish to escalate the matter into a board audit before learning the facts.

The third alternative is to go directly to Osburn and, using McMann's expense report as an example, ask for clarification of company policy. At least three possibilities could result. Osburn could clarify that McMann does have special arrangements for expense claims; he could realize that McMann is using company assets for his personal benefit and that changes are in order; or he could become aware that McMann is following habits from his old company and that new guidelines need to be issued. While this alternative does follow the chain of command, it still places Rodgers in a precarious position if McMann, in fact, does have a special arrangement with Osburn.

The last alternative focuses on policy instead of personality. Without mentioning McMann, Rodgers can ask Osburn if he expects her to rubber stamp all expense reports that he approves or whether he is relying upon her to surface irregularities. If Osburn desires that she approve all reports, she can then request that he send a memo to that effect to everyone in the division. This step would enhance her position without making her denounce McMann to Osburn. If he expects automatic acceptance of his approvals, she could ask Jerry Parr, vice president of accounting at headquarters, if there are printed guidelines for the proper way to handle a questionable expense that has been approved by management. If guidelines do exist, she should then ask that they be distributed to every division in the company. If guidelines do not exist, she should request that they be established and then distributed to all divisions.

Plan of Action

Rodgers's best alternative is to take the policy approach. This allows her to avoid personalities and to focus on the policy regarding reimbursable expenses. If guidelines do exist, she should ask Parr to distribute those to every division as quickly as possible, along with a memo encouraging employees to refamiliarize themselves with the policy. If guidelines are not available, she could be the catalyst for clarifying necessary policy at Champion. She could even volunteer to serve on a committee to draft the policy statement.

This alternative addresses the policy of reimbursable expenses and will allow all employees in the future to know what is and is not allowed. It will give management and accounting the sufficient data to be able to make conclusions and recommendations that will allow them to uphold accounting principles and resolve future issues correctly. Employees will see that top management has set the tone for the company regarding approved expenditures and the rules of accounting. Sent from top management, this helps establish the attitude of cooperation and professionalism throughout the organization. It should tell all parties that accounting serves an integral role at Champion Marketing, and it is not there to constantly question each expense and raise unnecessary flags.

This procedure will also help Rodgers in future communication with McMann. While he will not appreciate the distribution of the policy, he will have the written statement to refer to when submitting future reports. She can use the statement to justify nonpayment of any items from the recent past. If McMann questions the policy, he should be directed to Parr in the headquarters office for further clarification. Parr, in turn, can direct Rodgers to Osburn for answers to additional questions. With this plan of action, Rodgers's integrity is intact and her job security is maintained.

Index